BUS

ALLEN COUNTY PUBLIC LIBRARY

ACPL ITEM

DISCARDE

D0173912

Praise for *Blue Frontier*

"The most comprehensive account available of the state of our nation's oceans, and the best reporting about how they got that way."
—Bill McKibben

"Helvarg writes with humor, compassion, concern, and a keen eye for fascinating detail. Pick up *Blue Frontier* and you won't be able to put it down."
—Paul R. Ehrlich

"An infuriating portrayal of mankind's most breathtaking crime, the destruction of the oceans that birthed our species."
—Robert F. Kennedy Jr.

"[Helvarg] takes us on the ultimate wave, cresting and carrying us at breakneck speed. It's a fast, watery ride, and you're going to get wet before it's over."
—*Los Angeles Times,* Best Books of 2001

"The author connects the dots among the various threats to America's oceans surpassingly well."
—*Washington Post Book World*

"A vivid tapestry of an America interwoven with the sea."
—*San Jose Mercury News*

"Reads like a scientific detective novel."
—*Sacramento Bee*

"An illuminating, insightful and sobering look at our imperiled oceans—and the challenges we must overcome if we are to save our 'blue frontier.'"
—Ted Danson, actor,
Oceana board member

"This whirlwind tour highlights the intertwining challenges facing America's coasts and oceans. Helvarg's on-site and at-sea narrative puts you where the action is."

—Carl Safina, author of *Song for the Blue Ocean* and *Eye of the Albatross*

"*Blue Frontier* transports readers on a fascinating and sobering field trip—back through key historic events, around the nation's shorelines and beyond."

—Jane Lubchenco, Ph.D., president, International Council for Science

Blue Frontier

BOOKS BY DAVID HELVARG

The War against the Greens
Trouble in Paradise (foreword)
Feeling the Heat (coauthored)
Ocean and Coastal Conservation Guide
50 Ways to Save the Ocean

Blue Frontier

Dispatches from America's Ocean Wilderness

Second Edition

David Helvarg

SIERRA CLUB BOOKS
San Francisco

The Sierra Club, founded in 1892 by John Muir, has devoted itself to the study and protection of the earth's scenic and ecological resources—mountains, wetlands, woodlands, wild shores and rivers, deserts and plains. The publishing program of the Sierra Club offers books to the public as a nonprofit educational service in the hope that they may enlarge the public's understanding of the Club's basic concerns. The point of view expressed in each book, however, does not necessarily represent that of the Club. The Sierra Club has some sixty chapters throughout the United States. For information about how you may participate in its programs to preserve wilderness and the quality of life, please address inquiries to Sierra Club, 85 Second Street, San Francisco, California 94105, or visit our website at www.sierraclub.org.

Copyright © 2006, 2001 by David Helvarg

All rights reserved under International and Pan-American Copyright Conventions. No part of this book may be reproduced in any form or by any electronic or mechanical means, including information storage and retrieval systems, without permission in writing from the publisher.

Second Edition

Published by Sierra Club Books
85 Second Street, San Francisco, CA 94105
www.sierraclub.org/books

Produced and distributed by
University of California Press
Berkeley and Los Angeles, California
University of California Press, Ltd.
London, England
www.ucpress.edu

Sierra Club, Sierra Club Books, and the Sierra Club design logos are registered trademarks of the Sierra Club.

The previous edition of this book was published in hardcover in 2001 by W. H. Freeman and Company and in paperback in 2002 by Owl Books.

Library of Congress Cataloging-in-Publication Data

Helvarg, David, 1951 –
    Blue frontier : dispatches from America's ocean wilderness / David Helvarg. — 2nd ed.
        p.   cm.
    Includes bibliographical references.
    ISBN: 1–57805–157–6 (alk. paper)
    1. Marine resources conservation — United States.   I. Title.
GC1020.H45   2006
333.91'64160973 — dc22   2005056339

Cover design by Lynne O'Neil

Printed in the United States of America on New Leaf Ecobook 50 acid-free paper, which contains a minimum of 50 percent post-consumer waste, processed chlorine free. Of the balance, 25 percent is Forest Stewardship Council certified to contain no old-growth trees and to be pulped totally chlorine free.

10   09   08   07   06
10   9   8   7   6   5   4   3   2   1

To Ed Ricketts
for making it fun

To Rachel Carson
for celebrating the life

To Roger Revelle
for having some regrets

And to Rell Sunn
for surfing through the pain

Contents

Acknowledgments

When the first edition of this book was allowed to go out of print after three years, I knew who to talk to about re-spawning it. Editor-in-chief Danny Moses and the folks at Sierra Club Books recognize that, like the ocean, the public's interest in the marine environment is dynamic and ever-changing. He was more than willing to test these waters, provided I was willing to take a fresh plunge into the issues and subjects addressed within. With the help of a dynamic and engaged editor, Diana Landau, and the support of staff and friends at the Blue Frontier Campaign, the Center for the Study of Responsive Law, and other supporters, I've been able to dedicate the time needed to update the story of America's ocean frontier. The extensive revisions to this edition cover new discoveries in marine science and exploration, impacts from 9/11 and major hurricane seasons in 2004 and 2005, the findings of two major U.S. ocean commissions, the dead-zone politics of Washington, D.C., and my own transition from journalism to ocean advocacy. I was also greatly helped by the advice, information, and inspiration offered by many "seaweed rebels," marine grassroots activists I've come to know and admire.

I really don't know why it is that all of us are so committed
to the sea, except I think it's because in addition to the fact
that the sea changes, and the light changes, and ships change,
it's because we all came from the sea.

— *President John F. Kennedy, 1962*

Thrashed

And I have loved thee, Ocean! and my joy
Of youthful sports was on thy breast to be
Borne, like thy bubbles, onward; from a boy
I wantoned with thy breakers. They to me
Were a delight; and if the freshening sea
Made them a terror, 'twas a pleasing fear.
— *Lord Byron, 1818*

Catch a wave, and you're sitting on top of
the world.
— *The Beach Boys, 1963*

I turn around and catch Tim's longboard straight across my throat. I go under and come back up and look down Stinson Beach and it's all red; the people, the pine-covered hills that were green a moment ago, the sand and breaking waves are all crimson to my eye. I cough a dry hacking cough because it feels as though a large twig has just snapped inside my windpipe. Tim asks if I'm okay. "Everything's red," I croak, but even as I do so, the blood begins to recede from behind my eyeballs. He grabs the ten-foot surfboard I'd been trying to master before it got loose in the waves and offers me his free arm, but I wave it off, staggering ashore. We strip off our wetsuits back at his car. I've gone hoarse and raspy, but the karate-chop pain has now receded to a constant scratchy constriction of my throat. We drive back to my place in Sausalito, and later I go to the hospital where I get CAT scanned. The doctor tells me my larynx is bruised but not broken and sends me home with some codeine and steroids. I can't eat for several days and sound like Marge Simpson for two weeks, but other than that I'm fine.

Not really fine. I'm about to leave the ocean and the shore that I love for the first time in more than 20 years, heading to Washington, D.C., for work and other reasons. My East Coast cousin, after hearing of my accident, asks, "Aren't you a little old to be surfing?" and it makes me even edgier about the move. A man in his forties, splinting his shins jogging around the Central Park Reservoir in Manhattan or through Washington's Rock Creek Park, is considered sensible, taking care of his health, even if he gets shredded by a Doberman. But find your pleasure in the ocean off Northern California where a few big sharks feed, and you're suspected of being an arrested adolescent, of taking needless risks. Even those I've come to know who earn their living from the sea— sailors, fishermen, oil platform roughnecks, commercial divers, charter boat operators, and lifeguards—are often accused by the mainstream culture of "running away from life," of not facing up to the responsibilities that come with low-risk, highly regimented work far from the siren song of the everlasting sea.

I grew up on Long Island Sound, spending as much time as I could in the swamps and the water. When I was eight I wanted to be a navy frogman and fight for dolphins and America. By the age of 12 I was thinking I would become an oceanographer. The son of Jewish refugees from Nazi Germany and the Ukraine, I also knew that life was not predictable, that history could sweep you away at any time. At 13 I went to my first civil rights demonstration and got swept away by the social movements and moments of my youth. At 17 I was in Chicago at the Democratic National Convention where the police rioted, and I got my first taste of mace, gas, and blunt-force trauma. At 18 I was busted for fighting back at another demonstration. I turned 21 organizing antiwar protests against President Nixon and the Republican National Convention planned for San Diego, while being targeted by heavily armed right-wing vigilantes.

By the time I was 22 it was pretty clear there wasn't going to be urban guerrilla warfare in America, so I went to Belfast as a reporter to see what it looked like. It looked pretty mean, but it was also personally challenging and made me realize I had a vocation for writing and reporting. After five months in Ulster, I returned to my flat from the scene of a car bombing to the news that my mother had contracted lung cancer (she was a pack-and-a-half-a-day woman). I flew home and helped care for her in the few months before she died. I then moved back to the beach in San Diego, where I built a career as a freelance journalist while also finding time to bodysurf.

The ocean took me back to the salty dreams of my childhood. I started writing stories about U.S. Navy dolphins, sharks, offshore oil, and sea-floor mining—whatever could keep me connected to the sea. Later some colleagues would warn me that I was sidetracking my career by staying on in San Diego, a "happy news beach town." They joked that I'd lost touch with reality. This is the same accusation faced by an earlier generation of greenhorn adventurers who left the farms and towns of the eastern seaboard to settle the arid open spaces of our nineteenth-century frontier. As I've discovered in visits to places like coastal Alaska and maritime Antarctica, frontiers tend to attract fools and visionaries. And like those earlier frontier settlers who clashed with the native inhabitants and slaughtered the indigenous wildlife, today's ocean settlers—be they beachfront home owners on exposed barrier islands, drag trawl fishermen tearing up benthic communities of bottom-dwelling life, or recreational divers drifting with turtles and sharks—are facing many of the same problems and perils seen on America's last great wilderness range.

But the oceans are a rougher and more difficult wilderness for humans to function in than any encountered by terrestrial or space explorers. The sea pummels researchers and adventurers with an unbreathable and corrosive liquid medium, altered visual and acoustic characteristics, changing temperature and depth and pressure, upwellings, tides, rips and currents, sudden storms, undersea subsidence, invisible obstructions, and giant waves, not to mention unpredictable creatures and their strange habitats. No other place on this or any nearby planet is both so alien and yet so alluring.

If there is much we still don't know about this, our final physical frontier, we know that it is our lifeblood. The seas cover 71 percent of the earth's surface, giving our ocean planet its blue marble appearance. Although the tropical rain forests have been called the lungs of the world, the oceans actually absorb far greater amounts of carbon dioxide. Microscopic phytoplankton in the top layer of the sea act as a biological pump, extracting some 2.5 billion tons of organic carbon out of the atmosphere annually (replacing it with 70 percent of the life-giving oxygen we need to survive). The top two feet of seawater contain as much heat as the entire atmosphere. Scientists recently have come to recognize ocean currents as key to the creation of climate, clouds, and weather, but they still don't know enough about the internal workings of the sea (or have the historical records) to fully incorporate the ocean's thermodynamics into computer models of global warming. More is known about the dark side of the moon than is known about the depths of the oceans.

Photosynthesis of carbon dioxide by plankton and terrestrial plants was thought to be the basis of all organic life until nearly 30 years ago when, in 1977, scientists aboard a deep-diving submarine off the Galápagos Islands discovered sulfurous hot water vents 8,000 feet below the surface of the sea. The area was colonized by giant tube worms, clams, white crabs, and other animals that contain sulfur-burning bacteria, which provide an alternative basis for sustaining life. NASA scientists now believe that similar "chemosynthetic" life forms might exist around volcanic deep-ocean vents beneath the icy crust of the Jupiter moon Europa.

If the possibility of extraterrestrials in the solar system is not enough to excite our media-driven culture, let's consider the ocean's connection to cable news. Deep-sea vents, chimneys, and black smokers are also home to a number of recently discovered microbes and whole new classifications of microbial species such as *Archaea,* or the "ancient ones" — chemosynthetic life forms thought to be the first living creatures on Earth. Among these is *Pyrococcus,* which acts as the key to the polymerase chain reaction (PCR), the replication engine that drives the DNA "fingerprinting" process, which can match DNA strands to individuals with odds of an error of one in a billion. As a result, PCR has played a prominent role in the growing number of high-profile domestic murder and celebrity trials seen on cable.

Photosynthesizing phytoplankton, aside from cleansing our atmosphere, also compose the big pasture at the bottom of the marine food web. For millions of years the ocean has maintained a fecundity of life unmatched on land, an enthralling variety of creatures and an unimaginable wealth of protein. Humans have always relied on this wild-caught source of protein as part of their omnivorous diet. I've even heard it argued (by fishermen) that *Homo sapiens* had an evolutionary edge over Neanderthals because they colonized coastal regions and rivers and consumed large amounts of cold-water fish and therefore developed better brains. Recent studies have confirmed that DHA, a component of omega-3 fatty acid found in certain marine fish, may in fact improve brain function. Whether large, complex brains provide a long-term evolutionary advantage for our species or the many other species we affect remains an unresolved question.

Along with its practical role in maintaining the tides of life, our ocean planet also holds a spiritual resonance for our species, calling us back to a common waterborne birth state we all have experienced on both an individual and evolutionary basis. Our bodies, like the planet, are 71 percent salt water; our blood exactly as salty as the sea was when our ancestors first emerged from it. This may explain why it's easier to fall asleep to the sound of the ocean. The rhythm of the waves is like our mother's heartbeat.

During my last seven years in San Diego I lived with two roommates in a brown clapboard house 60 feet above the pounding Pacific on an ice-plant-covered cliff. I never slept better in my life. From our back porch I could watch gray whales migrating by in winter; I'd keep an eye out across the slate-colored waters for the spray clouds of their breath. Sometimes they would breach, leaping full-bodied toward the sky. Sometimes out sailing with friends we'd see them pass within yards of us, their arching backs slick or else crusty with barnacles. In the spring and summer, when hollowed-out aquamarine waves left rooster tails of spray in the diamond-dappled sea, I'd clamber down the sandstone cliff with Charlie or Manny, bodysurfing flippers in hand, and dive off the rocks to catch the breaking wave off Crab Island, a small outcrop of rock just to our north. On more than one occasion, on our short amble to the water, we'd encounter a hauled-up sea lion or tide pool octopus trying to blend in with the rocks.

But even as we took our pleasure in the sea, we never forgot that we were also living on the edge of a vast and threatening wilderness. Once I had to throw one of Charlie's longboards down to a pair of lifeguards trying to rescue a young girl who had fallen off the narrow sandstone path that ran below our deck. She died on the way to the hospital. Another time we saw a cabin cruiser breaking up in the surf. Charlie, a shooter for the local CBS affiliate, grabbed his video camera while I took hold of the sound deck. By the time we joined the paramedics at the beach below Pescadero Street it was getting dark. We provided illumination from the camera's portable light as they applied their shock paddles to the chest of the victim, a heavyset man who had just washed up in swimming trunks and a white T-shirt. Again it was too late. Three of the six people on that boat drowned.

It's like Ken Kelton, a kayaker I interviewed who'd been attacked by a great white shark, explained: "The ocean is a dangerous place, but it's also a place you can still go and have to yourself, a place that's clean, and, yes, wild. If you go in the ocean, you're making a choice. You need to know you can drown, you can get lost, or you can be eaten by great beasts."

Thanks to the late Jacques Cousteau, Emile Gagnan, and the self-contained underwater breathing apparatus (scuba) they invented, you can spend quality time with the beasts and the beauties: whale sharks;

makos; squid; humpbacks; parrotfish; squirrelfish; frogfish; stonefish; moray eels; turtles; Steller's sea lions; hammerheads; barracudas; starfish; strawberry anemones; sea hares; spiny lobsters; groupers; dolphins; brain, whip, leaf, and staghorn corals; barrel sponges; sea dragons; and rainbow-colored nudibranchs. Advances in face-mask design, self-purging snorkels, and flexible fins offer millions more the opportunity to go snorkeling with the colorful denizens of shallow reefs, kelp forests, and rocky shorelines. In addition, some 600,000 U.S. households maintain saltwater aquariums, seeking to recreate on a small scale the wonders of the ocean environment.

Of course, I number myself among the tens of millions of Americans who have found their way back to the sea at least in part through visual media, including film and television. From *Gidget* and *The Endless Summer* to *Step into Liquid, Sponge Bob,* and *Blue Crush,* from Jacques Cousteau, *Sea Hunt, Flipper,* and *Jaws* to *Baywatch, Riding Giants,* and *Finding Nemo,* from the sublime to the ridiculous, the ocean remains a popular theme for popular culture.

Today, with improved underwater film techniques and lighting, dive technology, and communications, the chances to appreciate the blue frontier's wild beauty without actually getting wet have expanded exponentially. *National Geographic* and other television documentaries have begun to include point-of-view wildlife images shot with "critter cams" temporarily attached to the backs of dolphins, seals, white sharks, and blue whales. Real-time images from the underwater sea lab Aquarius, the deep ocean, and other frontier realms are being brought to the classroom and online via educational projects like the JASON Foundation (founded by deep-sea explorer Robert Ballard) and collaborative efforts between broadcasters and scientists. Giant IMAX screens offer large-as-life ocean images, including 3-D panoramas of marine wonders, some produced by Hollywood figures such as James Cameron, the director of *The Abyss* and *Titanic.*

In music, art, and literature—tragic, wild, or inspirational—the blue frontier ripples through the American soul. From sea chanteys to Hawaiian hula to the music of the singer-songwriters Jimmy Buffett, Brian Wilson, and Jack Johnson (also a surfer), the oceans offer their syncopated inspiration to American musicians of every age, race, and disposition.

In painting, Winslow Homer was perhaps America's greatest marine artist. He showed the blue frontier in its fathomless indifference to those who seek to live and work upon its waters or, conversely, its hypnotic attraction for those who have survived the ravages of civilization (such as the American Civil War he illustrated). From the sail-happy youth of *Breezing Up* (1876) to the edgy wonder of a fisherman in his dory in *Fog Warning* (1885), to the simple interface of land and sea in *West Point, Prout's Neck* (1900), Homer offered the public a vision of redemption through saltwater immersion, while rejecting the gauzy romanticism of the Hudson River school and other self-conscious stylists.

Much of today's marine art, by contrast, tends toward the kitschy—smiling dolphins, leaping whales, and come-hither mermaids swimming through reefs of clownfish. The California artist Wyland has opted instead for the monumental, his building-sized whale murals gracing cities across America and inspiring many a reflective thought among commuters stuck in traffic from Boston to San Diego, Orlando to Seattle.

The Alaskan illustrator Ray Troll combines humor and subtle anger in his depictions of the blue frontier's sea life under siege. Faced with a "bass ackwards" world, he forces us to confront our genetic connections in images like *Spawn Till You Die,* showing a human skull above crossed salmon, with naked people and fish floating about the perimeter. A gentler prod to our conscience comes in the daily comics section of more than 250 newspapers in the form of *Sherman's Lagoon.* Jim Toomey's Sherman is a shark, sharper of tooth than of mind. Along with his shark-wife, Megan, Fillmore the sea turtle, Hawthorne the hermit crab, and other characters, Sherman reminds us that we're not the only critters on this blue planet and that the food chain can nibble up as well as down. And of course, almost every marine scientist pines for the day Gary Larson might return to draw more *Far Side* panels with their anthropomorphic reversals of life and nature—including the one in which biologists wonder what the dolphins' vocalizations might mean as a captive cetacean asks, "¿Habla español?"

There is also the utilitarian art of surfboard shapers like Skip Frye, boat designers like Hobart "Hobie Cat" Alter, and the underwater photographers David Doubilet, Flip Nicklin, Wolcott Henry, Wayne Levin, and Victoria McCormick. Perhaps some of the finest ocean expressionism I've seen has been in children's murals, drawings, and artworks in classrooms and at aquariums, day-care centers, marine fairs, and science centers. I particularly enjoyed the thank-you notes featuring surfing penguins, diving whales, and a hand-cut crab I received after speaking to my nephew Ethan's sixth-grade class. Of course, kids have an advantage, being closer to the source. Fear of water, it turns out, is an acquired rather than a natural state of being.

Richard Henry Dana's *Two Years before the Mast* and Herman Melville's *Moby-Dick* gave nineteenth-century America a realistic sense of the sea, as did the writings of Jack London, John Steinbeck, Rachel Carson, and others in the twentieth century. Many poets have also found inspiration in the living sea, from "She sells sea shells by the seashore," to T. S. Eliot's "The Dry Salvages": "The sea has many voices. Many gods, and many voices." Among contemporary writers, John McPhee, Daniel Duane, Susan Casey, and Sebastian Junger impress me as having the stoke (awesome spirit), although this kind of listing can be as idiosyncratic as whoever chooses to compose it.

For years I wanted to write a book on the oceans, an opportunity I finally landed in 1999 when I signed a contract for the first edition of this work. The following year was an adventure in learning, during which I got to interview several hundred knowledgeable watermen and -women; visit research centers, fishing boats, marine sanctuaries, oil platforms, an aircraft carrier, and an underwater laboratory; and begin to organize my notes at a writer's retreat outside Point Reyes National Seashore in Northern California. The book came out in 2001, and a lightly updated paperback was issued in 2002.

That was also the year in which a loved one died from cancer, and my emotional moorings seemed to come undone. One result was that I moved from reporting on the cascading crisis of the oceans to trying to do something about them. This shift from journalism to advocacy led to the establishment of the Blue Frontier Campaign in 2003. Since then I've been able to recruit a number of impressive volunteers, board members, and interns, and together we've worked to build the "seaweed rebellion" discussed in chapter 12.

As I tracked the convergence of two major U.S. ocean commissions, the Bush administration's response to them, the evolving science of the ocean environment, and the popular response to changing ocean conditions—including a number of solution-oriented initiatives now under way—I was inspired to undertake a major revision of this work. About a third of what you will read is information new to these pages, much of which has emerged only in the last three to five years. This rewriting and reordering also gave me a chance to update the lives of certain characters and introduce some new and salty ones who give me hope that it's still not too late to turn the tide. All it will take is popular will, political organizing, luck, perseverance, and faith. And more readers, of course.

I've often found that literature, art, and popular culture tend to splash over into our daily lives. For example, when a poorly maintained Mexican patrol boat came to rescue four of us where we had shipwrecked on the Sea of Cortez, I couldn't help but think: *McHale's Navy* meets *Gilligan's Island*. A few years later I celebrated my birthday with friends at an overnight anchorage in the Coronado Islands, 13 miles off San Diego. After a morning dive with a curious seal, we were headed back to the bay. My friend Jon Christensen was at the wheel of the 37-foot sloop. Crosby, Stills & Nash were on the sound system, and Pacific white-sided dolphins rode our bow wave. I was leaning back against the bulkhead with a Corona beer in one hand while another friend, Scott Fielder, packed away his dive gear. The song "To the Last Whale" began playing, an arrangement that includes a recorded humpback song.

"All we need now is a whale," I grinned at Scott. He nodded casually: "There's one." Just off to our starboard side rolled the crusty back, followed by the broad paddle tail of a California gray whale. Just another frontier moment.

I recently motored out of Marina del Rey Harbor in Los Angeles on board the patrol boat of the Santa Monica Baykeeper, a marine activist group. Two miles off America's most urbanized landscape we stopped to watch leaping dolphins, sea lions, and diving pelicans feeding on a live bait ball. I imagined the national media frenzy that would occur if bears, mountain lions, and condors were spotted feasting on swarms of prairie dogs in LA's Griffith Park. Yet just this sort of thing happens every day within sight of shore.

The blue frontier offers a greater biodiversity of life than the richest terrestrial habitats on earth, including rain forests. Disrupting any part of this oceanic ecosystem—the humble spiny urchin or the magnificent bluefin tuna—can affect the whole in ways we still don't fully understand. Our actions on land—overfertilizing cornfields in Iowa or golf courses in St. Louis, running factory farms in Maryland and Alabama, dripping hydraulic fluid on LA freeways—can, by way of watersheds, rivers, and storm drains, create massive nutrient-fed algal blooms and anoxic (oxygen-depleted) dead zones in our coastal waters. This has already occurred in the Gulf of Mexico.

Now we're industrializing our offshore waters to the point where we can take marine life out of the seas at a faster rate than the animals can reproduce. In the last half century, the annual harvest of marine life for human consumption has jumped from 20 million to 90 million metric tons. This living biomass being dredged up from the world's oceans every year is equal in weight to more than 900 fully armed aircraft carriers.

With technologies developed by the military—including radar, sonar, improved navigation and communications systems, spotter planes, satellite surveillance, stronger marine engines, nylon for netting, and strengthened steel and fiberglass hulls—the world's fishing fleets have been waging a highly efficient, market-driven war of extermination on a growing list of fish species and marine creatures. As a result, the 1990s saw a precipitous decline in the world's catch so that by early in the twenty-first century some 75 percent of commercial fisheries were fully exploited, overexploited, or in a state of collapse, according to the United Nations Food and Agriculture Organization.

Despite the warnings of scientific pioneers such as Dr. Ransom Myers, who published a study showing that 90 percent of the ocean's large predators—sharks, swordfish, and the like—have been eliminated since 1950, the pace of exploitation of marine resources has not slowed. It's a process of chaotic and rapacious frontier development similar to what took place in the Wild West. Instead of buffalo hunters and cattlemen killing off native animals and replacing them with cows that overgrazed the range and trampled the rivers, we now have giant factory trawlers and draggers overharvesting our seas and destroying bottom habitat even as dams, development, and polluting fish farms threaten the water quality, genetic diversity, and complex ecosystems necessary for wild fish to thrive.

In place of army forts and anti-Indian campaigns we have a post–Cold War navy moving from blue water to brown, looking at the continental shallows and beachfront littoral—the areas where our living resources are most at risk—as their next staging area for antiterrorism operations and warfare, extended combat exercises, and coastal bombing practice.

Just as the Seventh Cavalry gave protection to profit-hungry white gold miners, opening up Dakota's Black Hills to mineral extraction, today's coastal real-estate developers are being given special dispensations by the Army Corps of Engineers to fill in wetlands and mangrove swamps that act as the storm barriers, nurseries, and filters of the sea, undermining laws such as the Clean Water Act in their rush to accommodate more high-priced "gold coasts."

The silting up and poisoning of salmon and trout rivers near nineteenth-century frontier mining towns are magnified ten thousand-fold in the agricultural, urban, and industrial runoff—some 32 billion gallons a day of oil, pesticides, manure, and more—that suffocates our coastal bays and estuaries, poisons marine mammals, and feeds outbreaks

3 1833 04998 5960

of Pfiesteria and harmful algal blooms. These in turn threaten human health and safety, resulting in more than 20,000 beach closures per year.

And where once a corrupt Congress sold off public lands to the railroad trusts for pennies on the dollar, today's Mineral Management Service grants fire-sale leases of offshore oil and gas, while Congress declares royalty holidays and tax breaks for its friends in the energy industry. Clearly the "take it while you can get it" gold rush mentality didn't end in the 1880s.

In the 1980s, when it was still believed that vast fortunes would be made by mining the deep-sea floor, a number of nations began fencing off their coastal oceans. In 1983 President Ronald Reagan, in one of the most momentous yet least noted actions of his administration, proclaimed that all ocean waters within 200 miles of the U.S. coastline were henceforth to be an Exclusive Economic Zone (EEZ). In so doing he virtually annexed 3.4 million square nautical miles of new territory, extending U.S. sovereignty over a wet frontier six times the size of the Louisiana Purchase, and larger than all the lands of the United States. It's an oceanic domain that stretches from New England's Georges Bank to St. Croix, Virgin Islands, and from Dutch Harbor, Alaska, to beyond the outer reefs of Guam.

Unlike our western frontier, however, the creation of this new blue one has failed to spark the public imagination, to inspire grand plans and visions, or even to resolve the ongoing competition and struggle over our nation's maritime resources. That conflict could lead either to the protection and sustainable use of America's greatest natural treasure or condemn our oceans to a final industrial onslaught of destruction, leaving them fit only for the sulfur-eating seaworms and giant bacterial clams of Oregon's deep-ocean geothermal vents and chimneys—assuming these mineral-rich areas are not themselves strip-mined by high-tech dredges and robots.

This is why there is a desperate need to develop and expand not only our biological knowledge of the seas, but also an active and educated political constituency to protect the ocean's living resources and coastal communities at risk. Unfortunately, with a few honorable exceptions, our politicians and national leaders seem either oblivious or intentionally blind to the value of our living blue frontier.

More than a decade ago, in 1995, the self-styled right-wing "revolutionaries" of the 104th Congress abolished the House Merchant Marine and Fisheries Committee, which had operated for 107 years. The committee was noted for its bipartisan commitment to marine issues. Some of its oceanic responsibilities were shunted off to a subcommittee of the House Resources Committee (formerly the Natural Resources Committee). Under the chairmanship of Congressman Don Young of Alaska, this committee was packed with western Republicans from places like Nevada, Utah, Wyoming, and Idaho, who spent more time railing against the reintroduction of wolves into Yellowstone than considering the plight of America's great seas. Young was followed in the chairmanship by Dick Pombo of California, a real-estate agent and self-styled rancher who considers gutting the Endangered Species Act a higher legislative priority than protecting the public seas.

The 104th Congress also attempted to abolish the Department of Commerce, apparently without realizing that some 8,000 people in its largest division worked for the National Oceanic and Atmospheric Administration (NOAA), America's lead agency on the blue frontier. Only after the U.S. Chamber of Commerce and other business interests pointed out the commercial importance of the National Weather Service, the National Hurricane Center, and other NOAA operations did the congressional firebrands retreat.

Three years later, in 1998, the Clinton administration, looking for some way to respond to the United Nations–declared International Year of the Ocean, sponsored a national ocean conference by the shoreline in Monterey, California. But this turned out to be little more than a scenic photo op for the upcoming presidential campaign of Al Gore, with few if any new initiatives taken. Still, the conference's title, "Oceans of Commerce, Oceans of Life," at least identified the government's policy priorities. It's not particularly surprising that business should trump life on America's blue frontier since, from its creation in 1970, NOAA has been anchored deep within the trade-driven Department of Commerce.

The years 1997–1999 were also marked by Congress's refusal to pass an "American Oceans Act" that would establish a national blue-ribbon commission to consider the plight of America's blue frontier. The American Petroleum Institute, not wanting to jeopardize its position of power in Washington, lobbied hard against the measure on Capitol Hill. Navy officials, worried about new environmental players interfering in their national security projects, also let the administration know that they didn't much like the idea of establishing a commission. Finally, in 2000, the establishment of an independent oceans commission funded by the Pew Charitable Trusts helped inspire Congress to pass the Oceans Act. (Then–Senate majority leader Trent Lott of Mississippi feared the Pew Commission report would be "too green.")

The 18-member Pew Oceans Commission was made up primarily of scientists, fishermen, environmentalists, and elected officials and made its prime focus the status of America's living marine resources.

In June 2000 President George W. Bush named a 16-member U.S. Commission on Ocean Policy with a broader mandate to look at all aspects of America's seas, including commerce and defense. It was front-loaded with industry reps from the offshore oil and shipping industries and from ports, as well as Navy admirals and academics.

The Pew commission's final report came out in June 2003, and that of the U.S. commission in September 2004. Given their very different make-ups, their conclusions proved remarkably similar. Following several years of public hearings around the country, and each having taken a fair and dispassionate approach to their work, they reported that America's coasts and oceans are in serious enough trouble to threaten America's environment, economy, and security. This trouble stems from overfishing for the global seafood market, coastal sprawl, urban and agricultural pollution of coastal waters, government mismanagement of our public seas, and fossil-fuel-driven climate change (though neither commission dealt with climate in any depth).

Neither commission actively pursued the blue frontier analogy. Yet both recognized that fencing off the American seas has failed to slow the pillaging of our last great wilderness range. And both offered hundreds of practical solutions: ways we can begin to turn the tide and start prac-ticing what they call "ecosystems-based management" to restore our public waters and prevent natural events like Hurricane Katrina from turning into human catastrophes.

Despite the continuing wide-open frontier activity, the declaration of an EEZ has given Americans an opportunity for a new approach to ocean governance. We need to recognize that when we claim sovereign rights over large parts of the ocean, we are also taking on a higher level of responsibility for its protection, exploration, and restoration. The marine realm is our greatest public trust and natural treasure. Its wise stewardship is a mission that growing numbers of coastal citizens, local governments, and waterfront communities are no longer waiting pa-tiently for Washington politicians to assume.

They have begun the watery equivalent of a grassroots campaign: a seaweed rebellion. Like the giant kelp plant once it has found its holdfast, this movement has the potential to grow at a terrific rate. It's a rebellion that can be seen from the Web pages of surfer activists ("No way, dude! We don't want your crude!") to the cleanup, rediscovery, and celebration of historic waterfronts in Portsmouth, Boston, Baltimore, Jacksonville, Galveston, San Diego, Monterey, Seattle, Seward, Hilo, and hundreds of other maritime communities large and small. It's annual volunteer beach cleanups and divers taking fish counts and the establishment of citizen advisory panels for marine sanctuaries; it's sailing trips for youth at risk and marine education efforts like the Los Marinaros program for grade-schoolers in Salinas, California, the high school Mast Academy in Miami, Florida, and the Discovery Hall Program for 30,000 students per year at Alabama's Dauphin Island Sea Lab.

It's sometimes angry environmental protests at public hearings on coastal development and offshore oil and gas drilling. It's fun but messy restoration projects that can aid the ocean's healing on a muddy duck pond in Rhode Island, a coastal river in Oregon, or the Everglades of south Florida. It's coalitions of fishermen and conservationists, marine scientists, and urban planners in the Northwest, fighting to restore the iconic wild salmon and protect its damaged habitat from rural Idaho to urban Seattle, whose mayor argues, "By saving the salmon we may very well be saving ourselves." It's a little girl sleeping snuggled up against her stuffed dolphin or squealing with delight when her father holds her in a wave. It's the future.

For now it's an uncertain future based on a largely inchoate rebellion, not effectively organized to take the fight to every coastal statehouse, the halls of Congress, or beyond. Still, like green phosphorescence sparkling in a wine-dark sea, it's more than an illusion. It's more like a reconciliation of the soul among tens of millions of Americans, both young and young in spirit, who have come to recognize the limitless possibilities that a living sea has to offer. It's a damp and salty uprising aimed at nothing less than the recovery of our maritime culture and heritage, nothing less than the renewal of our journey home to the American sea.

CHAPTER I

Fool's Gold

If you found this deposit on dry land, you'd call these
bonanza figures.

> — *Australian scientist describing a deep-sea*
> *mineral find,* New York Times, 2003

The sea is not a bargain basement.

> — *Jacques Cousteau, 1963*

On a dark summer night in June 1977, I watched the *Deep Sea Miner Two,* a 560-foot, 20,000-ton converted Liberian ore carrier, slip out of San Diego harbor. The dock area around the Tenth Avenue Terminal had been sealed off to curious onlookers hours before the ship's unpublicized departure. I stood alone outside the barbed wire–topped hurricane fence, taking notes as a pair of uniformed guards on the pier watched me, speaking nervously into their walkie-talkies.

The crew members who had tipped me off to the ship's departure were warned not to discuss their destination or the nature of the tests to be conducted. For several of them who had served in the Navy, it was not unlike going on a WestPac (Western Pacific) deployment, except that this ship, with its strange radarlike white geodesic dome covering the derrick at midship and its pipe storage racks and air compressors crowding the topside and superstructure from bow to stern, looked far more peculiar than any of the warships tied up at the Thirty-second Street Naval Station.

The ship, I discovered, was owned by Ocean Mining Associates of Gloucester Point, Virginia, a joint venture of U.S. Steel, the Sun Company (formerly Sun Oil), and Union Minière of Belgium. This consortium was one of several formed in the early 1970s in response to news that Howard Hughes's Summa Corporation was committing hundreds of millions of dollars to an unprecedented deep-sea venture.

The *Deep Sea Miner* would be working 1,000 to 1,500 miles southwest of San Diego. There, in waters up to 20,000 feet deep, using dynamic positioning props to keep the ship steady, crewmen would sink dredges attached to several miles of pipeline. Compressed air would then be fed into each pipe to create a suction that would pull manganese nodules off the bottom of the sea. It was dangerous work, comparable to dropping a long, potentially explosive siphon from a blimp that was trying to remain stationary in gusting winds and clouds four miles above the Earth. If the pipe string ruptured, the pressure could turn sections of broken pipe into steel spears, impaling both ship and crew. Still, like many dangerous shipboard operations that take place every day on America's blue frontier, the *Deep Sea Miner* managed to get the job done without incident, recovering several tons of nodules during its few months at sea.

A manganese nodule itself is fairly unimpressive. You can probably see one at your local oceanographic center or university marine lab. Up to eight inches across, it lacks the speckled shine of a good mineralized throwing rock, looking more like a lump of soft coal. This may be because its growth pattern is less that of the hardened spawn of the Earth's upthrusting mantle than that of an oyster pearl. It precipitates minerals out of the surrounding sea around a small nucleus such as a shell shard or shark's tooth. These accreted nodules are said to cobble parts of the deep ocean floor like the fabled streets of El Dorado and are invariably described in news reports as potato-sized, although you would have to be talking about those little gourmet numbers, not an Idaho spud. Their mineral content includes manganese, copper, nickel, and cobalt. And while most assays tend to be low, their total volume is truly staggering.

Samples of manganese nodules have been found and analyzed for their mineral content as far back as the cruise of the HMS *Challenger* in 1872–1876. Carrying out the first modern oceanographic expedition, *Challenger* used rope dredges to retrieve the slime-covered lumps from 5,000-meter depths in the mid-Pacific.

By the 1960s the Scripps Institution of Oceanography and other research stations were involved in the Moho and Deep Sea Drilling Projects, attempts to drill through the ocean floor to the Earth's mantle— big science projects conceived as a way to match the drama and attention space exploration was then receiving. Using converted oil-drilling ships with multiscrew dynamic positioning, they developed many of the techniques that are today used for deep-sea oil exploration in the Gulf of Mexico. A number of marine geologists also saw these techniques as having potential uses in manganese mineral mining.

Meanwhile, some smaller nations were growing concerned about the potential domination of marine-based resources by the great powers. On September 21, 1967, the Maltese ambassador to the United Nations, Dr. Arvid Pardo, fearing that the United States and the Soviet Union might place nuclear weapons on the bottom of the sea, gave a three-hour speech to the UN General Assembly suggesting that the deep ocean floor, with its vast mineral wealth, be seen as "the common heritage of mankind," an idea adopted by the UN in 1970.

Then, in November 1972, Howard Hughes's newly formed Summa Corporation announced the launch of a massive 619-foot ship, the Hughes *Glomar Explorer*, to begin commercial recovery of deep-sea nodules. Dozens of enthusiastic articles on the project began appearing in major mainstream and scientific journals around the world. Few doubted that although the economic risks were enormous, the reclusive billionaire was just the type of man to make a daring investment in order to corner a new market.

While the voyage of the *Glomar Explorer* would indeed launch a race to mine the oceans and redraw the world's marine frontiers—a global competition I would report on from San Diego five years later—its real aim was the recovery not of accreted nodules but of an object far more deadly than sharks' teeth.

For Russian and American submariners during the Cold War, the seas were a cold, dark, claustrophobic place in which to hunt and hide, where submariners were as blind as whales in black water but with far less sophisticated propulsion and sonar systems.

In March 1968 a diesel-powered, nuclear-armed Golf II Soviet submarine, the *Red Star*, sank in the North Pacific about 750 miles northwest of Hawaii. A venting problem during recharging of its storage batteries probably caused the powerful explosion that tore open its stern plates, sending seawater surging into the tail section of the craft, pulling it backward and downward in a deadly fast spiral. Within moments the *Red Star* had reached crush depth before plowing into the soft bottom more than three miles down, traveling close to 200 miles per hour on impact. Her entire crew, some 100 men, perished. They were among many submariners from both sides who would be crushed, drowned, burned to death, or irradiated during the Cold War, including, only two months later, 99 men aboard the USS *Scorpion*, lost in the depths of the Atlantic.

While Moscow had no idea where or why its submarine had disappeared, the U.S. Navy—using intercepted satellite transmissions and its top-secret $16 billion sound surveillance system (SOSUS) of undersea hydrophones—was able to key in on the area where the Soviet sub had gone down.

In their definitive book on Cold War spy submarines, *Blind Man's Bluff,* reporters Sherry Sontag and Christopher Drew describe how the Navy, in a major intelligence coup, had the spy submarine USS *Halibut* pinpoint and photograph the sunken *Red Star* using cable-winched sonar and cameras (which also showed the skeleton of a sailor in a sheepskin coat lying outside the wreck). The Russian sub contained code books and encryption gear and three nuclear missiles and their guidance systems, all valuable booty if they could be recovered. Leaders of the Navy spy program suggested returning to the *Red Star* to do some silent salvaging, using C-4 explosives and a primitive version of today's ROVs (remote-operated vehicles) lowered by miles of cable from a stealthy American sub floating above. They were shocked when their plan was rejected and in its place the CIA proposed building a massive salvage ship to scoop the Soviet diesel boat whole from the ocean floor.

The CIA plan (code named Project Jennifer) went forward with hundreds of millions of dollars in contract payments going to Hughes, Lockheed, and Global Marine, an oil rig platform manufacturer, to build the gargantuan spy ship *Glomar Explorer.* Eventually, more than 4,000 people would be employed in the construction and operation of the *Glomar.* Outraged Navy men, including spy sub coordinator John Craven, quietly complained that the Nixon White House was using the CIA project to pay off its political patrons and California defense contractors before the 1972 elections. The fact that Howard Hughes had been a longtime secret contributor to Nixon's campaigns, as well as having provided a highly suspect loan to the president's brother, Donald, added weight to the charge. The public unveiling of the giant spy ship–cum–ocean-mining vessel on election day 1972 may have even reflected someone's cynical sense of humor.

Several possible cover stories for the *Glomar* had been considered, including the idea that it was going on a treasure hunt, looking for lost Spanish galleons full of gold. But the CIA worried that such a romantic tale, linked to a mysterious figure like Howard Hughes, might attract too much attention from congressional CIA oversight committees, among others. So, the cover story chosen was that of the manganese mining ship and, in the summer of 1974, it was launched on its "mining" mission.

Two weeks later some 5,000 delegates from 48 nations met in

Caracas, Venezuela, for the United Nations Law of the Seas (LOS) Treaty convention. The talks, which had been going on in a desultory fashion since 1958, went into overdrive as news of Hughes's half-billion-dollar ship heading out to sea hit the assembly with the force of a tropical cyclone. Many delegates were outraged at the idea that the *Glomar* might soon begin sucking up thousands of tons of mineral-rich manganese nodules from the ocean's depths. Those dark lumps were suddenly seen as a trillion-dollar godsend by the UN's poorer nonaligned nations organized as the Group of 77 (G-77). Looking to the 1970 UN resolution declaring the seabed "the common heritage of mankind," G-77 called for the establishment of a UN-administered international seabed authority labeled the "Enterprise" to participate in the expected mining bonanza. The Soviet Union, sensing a no-cost opportunity to align itself with the Third World and against the United States, quickly endorsed the G-77 plan (it would later abstain from a final agreement).

As the mining debate was heating up, the CIA salvage operation was turning into a costly bungle. On July 4, 1974, the *Glomar* arrived on station over the site of the sunken sub and began lowering a giant eight-fingered claw and steel netting attached to a three-mile tether of connected lengths of hardened steel pipe. Assembling the tether as they went, the ship's crew, made up largely of roughnecks from the offshore oil industry, dropped the claw through the *Glomar*'s wet well. It took several days before they reached bottom and were able to snag the submarine. Lifting it at six feet per minute, they managed to raise it more than a mile before the badly damaged vessel fell apart. In the end, they were able to recover only about 10 percent of the submarine and the bodies of six sailors, which they buried at sea. No missiles, code books, or encryption equipment were recovered.

Back at the LOS convention, the U.S. delegation was arguing that by producing new mineral wealth from the ocean's depths, private corporations such as Summa were contributing to the common heritage of mankind. It was an argument the majority of delegates vehemently rejected. The CIA could only take grim satisfaction in watching its cover story blow up into a major political cause célèbre. Hoping to return for a second salvage attempt (which never happened), the CIA continued to place mining articles in major media around the world, while the U.S. media ran feature stories on the *Glomar* in *Business Week,* the *New York Times,* and the *Wall Street Journal.* There was even a report to the U.S. Senate Commerce Committee projecting that the deep-sea mining industry would be worth more than a half-billion dollars by 1985.

With thousands of employees now working on Project Jennifer and whispers in Washington and Los Angeles of recent failure and boondoggle (on top of Nixon's Watergate scandal and resignation), it was inevitable that the true story of the *Glomar*'s mission would come out. The first exposé, with the run-on headline "U.S. Reported after Russian Submarine/Sunken Ship Deal by CIA, Hughes Told," appeared in the February 7, 1975, edition of the *Los Angeles Times*. This was followed by widespread coverage of the failed mission.

Oddly, despite the unraveling of the *Glomar* cover story, many of the world's leaders were by now convinced that large-scale ocean mining was feasible.

A number of mining consortiums had been organized by energy and mineral companies out of fear that Hughes's Summa Corporation would get the jump on them. Membership included the Sun Company, British Petroleum, AMOCO, Mitsubishi, Noranda, Kennecott, Union Minière, and International Nickel.

By the end of the decade, deep-sea mineral wealth and the question of who would benefit from it had become major sources of international tension, even though the practical costs of developing open-ocean dredging, transport technology, ports, and processing facilities (along with a decline in world metal prices) guaranteed that mining would remain land-based for the foreseeable future.

Michael Molitor, a former LOS official with both the United States and the UN, recalls a visit he made to the Canadian headquarters of International Nickel during this time. "They had a world map with small lights in Guatemala and Africa and all these places where they had mining rights, including a single light out in the middle of the Pacific. And there was a dial to turn that showed the price of nickel rising, and as you'd twist that dial all these lights would come on showing when the mines would become profitable. But no matter how far you turned the dial, that one light in the Pacific never went on."

Still, at the UN mining fever was running high.

"Deep-sea mining was one out of nine or ten issues on the table, and the only one that was not resolved to the satisfaction of the Americans," recalled Elliot Richardson, the former U.S. attorney general and ambassador to the LOS convention. Five years after standing up to Nixon during the Watergate crisis, the former Republican lawman was named by Democratic president Jimmy Carter to head the U.S. delegation to LOS. Carter hoped that Richardson would be able to untangle the diplomatic mess created by the mining issue.

By 1980 Richardson had worked out a compromise agreement that would see a mixed corporate-UN mining regime established, but in 1981 a new delegation appointed by the Reagan administration nixed any "giveaway" of deep-sea nodules, insisting that the ocean's resources belonged by right to those with the capital and technology to claim them.

"The Law of the Seas [treaty] would have been signed off by the Carter administration if he'd been reelected, but the conservative ideological baggage brought in by Reagan on the mining issue forced a shift and those negotiations were stranded," Richardson told me.

Although the LOS convention eventually established 16 solid agreements on freedom of navigation, maritime commerce, maritime law enforcement, marine environmental protection, and marine scientific research, the lack of a seventeenth provision on mining left everyone nervous. Fearing that Western corporations would soon begin mining off their shores, the nations of G-77, like a school of panicked mullet, quickly moved to assert control over nearby marine fisheries and oil, gas, and mineral reserves, declaring Exclusive Economic Zones (EEZs) that extend seaward for 200 nautical miles (230 statutory miles) from their coastlines.

While at the time it seemed like just another diplomatic squabble, the advent of the EEZ represented the first major redrawing of the world's ocean boundaries since the seventeenth century, when Queen Elizabeth I gave up on Church-negotiated boundaries and instead endorsed the Dutch concept of *mare liberum,* or free seas.

Domestically, the debate over this radical EEZ concept had been going on at least since the early 1950s, when Chile, Ecuador, and Peru claimed their own 200-mile fishing zones. The U.S. Navy, the State Department, and distant-water tuna fishermen formed a "freedom of the seas" coalition opposing EEZs, which they saw as a threat to global fishing and to the Navy's right of passage through potential trouble spots such as the Strait of Hormuz (the gateway to the Persian Gulf) and narrow channels surrounding Indonesia. In favor of enclosure were the domestic fishing industry and the National Petroleum Council, which wanted to move its offshore rigs into deeper water on the Outer Continental Shelf. The Interior and Commerce Departments backed this group. After the LOS negotiators recognized the right of free passage through strategic straits for military ships, the Navy abandoned its fishing allies, and the balance of special interests shifted in favor of enclosure.

Although the United States refused to sign on to the final LOS convention in December 1982, it wasted little time in following the example of other coastal states, with President Reagan declaring the world's largest EEZ on March 10, 1983.

Two weeks later Secretary of the Interior James Watt declared 70,000 square miles of this new ocean frontier open for mining. Wagons ho! Watt, who earlier had attempted to declare a billion acres of the Outer Continental Shelf available for oil leasing, was no friend of the marine environment, or the dry one for that matter. A Christian fundamentalist, he favored unlimited development of America's natural resources. Although personal faith should not be a factor in evaluating political appointees, Watt seemed to take pleasure in aggressively arguing his messianic beliefs as justification for what were essentially nineteenth-century frontier policies. Asked in a congressional hearing why he was so determined to see public resources developed, he responded that there was no point in long-term conservation because "I do not know how many future generations we can count on before the Lord returns."

Among the gaffes that would lead to Watt's forced resignation was his attempt to ban the Beach Boys, those wholesome muses of surf culture, from giving a free Fourth of July performance on the Washington Mall.

The EEZ territory Watt wanted to open up to mining was the Gorda Ridge, a recently identified site of deep-water volcanic chimneys, or "black smokers," off the coast of Northern California and Oregon. Like bumpy free-standing tea spouts, these superheated chimneys spew dark concentrations of percolating minerals, including zinc, iron, and copper, which form towers of so-called polymetallic sulfides that can stand up to 150 feet tall (researchers named the largest of these chimneys "Godzilla"). At the base of the towers can be found the same colonies of chemosynthetic clams, crabs, and strange feathery red and white tube worms that were first identified off the Galápagos back in 1977.

Reagan's hawkish secretary of the Navy, John Lehman, argued that mining these deep-seabed minerals would assure secure domestic sources of strategic minerals for future defense. Environmentalists countered that the proposed lease sale was a vast giveaway of a public resource based on little or no scientific knowledge, with the added risk of destroying newly discovered life-forms. The mining industry, watching the price of land-based minerals heading south, was even less enthusiastic about the proposed sale than the enviros. Within a year the lease plan had been put on hold.

The LOS convention required ratification by 60 nations before it went into effect. This took more than ten years. By then the United States and other Western nations had been talking with the UN about revisiting the mining provisions. This resulted in new terms more favorable to private development. On July 29, 1994, the Clinton administration, having achieved the deal that the Reagan administration demanded, joined what was by now 159 other nations in signing the Law of the Seas Treaty.

But North Carolina senator Jesse Helms, chairman of the Senate Foreign Relations Committee, refused to hold hearings that would allow the Senate to ratify the treaty. According to his staff member responsible for LOS (who refused to be quoted by name), the senator didn't want to join "a bureaucracy where the U.S. doesn't have a greater vote than anyone else."

Even after Helms left office, little progress was made. In 2004 Republican senator Richard Lugar of Indiana, the new chair of the Foreign Relations Committee, secured a 19-to-0 committee vote to take LOS to the full Senate for ratification. By then, everyone from the Department of Defense to the oil industry to environmentalists had endorsed the treaty. Unfortunately, this unanimity of support seemed to inspire the conspiracy-minded on the far right, who charged that the treaty aimed to undermine U.S. sovereignty by giving the UN authority over U.S. aircraft and spacecraft as they passed over the oceans, and would create a UN "blue hull" navy to enforce maritime law. They got the ultraconservative senator James Inhofe of Oklahoma to express "national security concerns" over the LOS Treaty (despite the Pentagon's endorsement of it). Senate Majority Leader Bill Frist then delayed calling for a floor vote so as to avoid alienating President George W. Bush's more extreme anti-UN supporters.

After the 2004 elections were safely in the past, Jim Connaughton, the head of the White House Council on Environmental Quality and the president's designated leader on ocean policy, claimed that the administration was working to convince "conservatives" that the treaty was a good thing. Since the Senate had appeared ready to ratify the LOS Treaty with at least 90 (out of 100) votes, had it been allowed to vote, it seemed clear by the end of 2005 that the Republican Party leadership had given the far right an effective veto over the treaty.

While the legacy and economics of ocean mining remain daunting, its promise of quick riches is periodically revived by techno-optimists. A 1990s cover story in *Time* magazine spoke of deep-ocean "oil and mineral wealth to rival Alaska's North Slope and California's Gold Rush."

Today Japan has a well-funded and ongoing commitment to developing deep-ocean technologies. At JAMSTEC (Japan Marine Science and

Technology Center) in Yokohama, the government and leading corporations such as Mitsubishi have leapfrogged two craft down to the bottom of the sea: the unmanned *Kaiko* ROV and the *Shinkai 6500,* the world's deepest-diving manned submarine. (In 1995 the *Kaiko* came within a few feet of the U.S. Navy's 1960 record dive site, almost seven miles down in the Pacific's Mariana Trench, where the robot's cameras recorded a sea slug and a shrimp. More than a decade later, however, the Navy's generation-old accomplishment remains unchallenged.) With few mineral deposits of its own, Japan's interests seem linked, at least in part, to a desire for resource independence through ocean mining.

For some time, the United States, Japan, France, Russia, and Germany have been granting "exploration licenses" to mining companies in the international waters of the mid-Pacific Clarion-Clipperton Fracture Zone, an area where manganese nodules have a fairly high mineral content. The U.S. claim alone in 2001 covered some 190,000 square miles. Recent interest has focused on black smokers and deep-water geothermal vents that run along volcanic submarine ridges, whose effusions have been found to be rich in gold, silver, and other precious metals.

Still, the future is rarely what we project it to be. Today, many Americans think that what is technologically feasible does not always translate into what is healthy or desirable. For more than a quarter-century Congress has prevented the oil and gas industry from carrying out new exploration or drilling off the East and West Coasts of the United States, including Alaska's salmon-rich Bristol Bay—not because those areas lack large reserves of oil but because popular pressure and changing environmental standards require that the extractors look elsewhere. Attempts in Congress to undermine these drilling moratoriums during President George W. Bush's second term in office have set off new environmental battles and increased public pressure to protect the public seas. Similarly, concern over preserving the ocean's health and genetic diversity, based on new scientific knowledge about the deep sea, may scuttle the "inevitability" of large-scale ocean mining.

Deep dredging or suction mining for manganese nodules even far out at sea could be expected not only to cause heavy mortalities among slow-breeding bottom dwellers, but also to suffocate surrounding benthic communities, according to a number of studies. Every 10,000 tons of nodules recovered each day would generate 40,000 tons of sediment in the water column. These sediment plumes, carried by currents, could remain suspended in the water anywhere from two weeks to 49 years (the time it takes for certain surface nutrients to settle on the deep bottom). The creation of this ocean smog could restrict light penetration and reduce planktonic growth that supports most life-forms in the ocean. It could also directly contaminate open-ocean fish stocks. Current mining claims overlap the migratory routes of yellowfin tuna and swordfish. Mining would also require centrally located mining smelters and onshore processing facilities in areas like Hawaii.

Hawaiian waters themselves have been found to overlie manganese crusts rich in cobalt. However, when the Department of the Interior's Mineral Management Service called a public hearing on leasing these manganese seabed crusts in 1992, close to 1,000 angry citizens turned out on the Big Island, some dressed up as whales and dolphins. From native advocates of Hawaiian sovereignty to tourist industry representatives, fishermen, flower growers, surfers, and retirees, they spoke out forcefully against any type of mining proposal, arguing that the ocean already provided them with an economy and a way of life they were unwilling to risk for some new mineral bonanza.

Abraham Piianaia, a native scholar of Hawaiian history, suggested that a careful harvesting of fish and new medicines would be a more respectful way of approaching the deep sea. "My people are a maritime people," he explained. "They looked upon the sea not merely as a body of water, they looked at the sea as a source of food, a pathway to another place. The sea provided medicinal things that they used. The sea provided recreation when they needed that. . . . And now you read a lot of stuff, of Western science that says the source of all life is the sea. This may be true. And yet these simple people found that out years ago."

Our deep oceans, once perceived to be a biological desert whose main value could be found in mining, dumping, and nuclear weapons testing, have more recently been identified as a key factor in ocean circulation, climate, and productivity (through nutrient upwellings) as well as a rich habitat for a wide and wondrous range of life. In terms of volume, 97 percent of the earth's livable habitat is in the oceans. But only now is human exploration of the middle- and deep-ocean frontier below 660 feet (the planktonic zone) beginning to yield a sense of just how much of that life we have yet to know or understand.

An observation camera rests on the deep-sea bottom off Monterey, California, recording the movement of sea cucumbers, mollusks, and clams gathered around a cold-water seep—a methane-rich chemical vent that creates a chemosynthetic ecosystem much like the scalding hot geothermal vents found elsewhere. A large seven-gill shark cruises by the camera. Thin spiderlike creatures float like mosquitoes around the pressure-sealed lights. What appears to be a rock will sit in front of the camera for months on end. Suddenly, over a period of days it will grow appendages and crawl out of view. Ethereal translucent jellies hover on the periphery of the lights, flashing bioluminescent signals at them like alien code.

Scientists estimate there are at least a million new species of life undiscovered in the deep oceans, not counting *Architeuthis,* the giant squid. Until recently much of our knowledge of this life came in the form of pressure-exploded fish and torn-up jellies lifted from the abyssal depths in trawler nets. ROV robot submarines now use specially designed slurp guns and pressure vessels to capture and preserve live specimens of deep-sea life for display at places like the world-famous Monterey Bay Aquarium.

"There are trends in oceanography just like in anything else. This area's now like the hot bar in a college town. For a while the place to work for a young scientist was Woods Hole in Massachusetts, then Scripps in San Diego. Now it's Monterey, Monterey, Monterey," says Bill Douros, who, as manager of the Monterey Bay National Marine Sanctuary, is not exactly an unbiased source. Still, his claim resonates with many people in marine science.

Looking out across the cool blue waters of Monterey Bay is like that first sweet shock of recognition when you fall in love. The heart of the world's second largest marine reserve (until the new Northwest Hawaii Sanctuary is designated), its near-pristine waters teem with life, from mobs of barking sea lions to spouting gray whales to shoals of shearwaters scudding across its surface like squall lines. Just offshore its submarine canyon contains sheer cliff faces more than 6,000 feet deep that gradually fan out onto 10,000-foot-deep abyssal hills.

But until the 1990s, maps of the canyon were not available to the public or civilian scientists, who believed that there was a lot yet to be discovered in the canyon. They also believed that the 1983 declaration of a 200-mile EEZ might lead to increased funding and access for ocean science, but the fulfillment of that hope would be delayed by almost a decade. "Beginning in 1983 we had run an EEZ mapping effort using multi-beam sonar ships," says Skip Theberge, a 38-year veteran of the NOAA Corps (the smallest of America's uniformed services, with some 280 members trained at the Merchant Marine Academy in Kings Point, New York). Theberge was in command of the NOAA research vessel *Mount Mitchell,* which mapped Monterey's deep canyon, a place that turned out to hide more than rockfish. "What we did was so accurate the Navy submarine community felt threatened, so it was all classified."

When the maps were declassified at the end of the Cold War, Monterey's deep waters began drawing scientists as chum draws gulls.

Gary Greene, a research scientist and former director of the Moss Landing Marine Lab (operated by the California State University system), has been on the scene since before it was a scene. He remembers his first submersible dive into Monterey's canyon back in 1970. He was on board the *Nekton*, a small steel sub, along with the pilot, Larry Headley. Headley sat upright in the conning tower as Gary, then a graduate student in geology, lay on his belly by the forward observation porthole, his legs sticking between Larry's feet. "We'd detected a deep hole. It turned out to be the bottom behind where a massive underwater landslide had filled in part of the canyon. We landed on the side of this steeply inclined mud and sediment dam about 1,000 feet down, at the sub's maximum depth. Then, as we tried to cruise along our tail began to drag. We assumed it was tangled up in a cable or something. You could unscrew the *Nekton*'s tail section and float free, but between me having to crunch up in the bow and Larry wiggling around with the wrench, our movement must have set off another slide. I was looking out the porthole and everything suddenly went black from this big mud cloud, and we could see the pressure and depth gauge rising as we were pushed downslope beyond the sub's limit. We were trying to blow ballast [with compressed air from a pair of scuba tanks] but nothing was happening. The prop was making a loud clanking noise, and then something fell out of the rudder. Then it started to get lighter outside and we were rising and I could see the mud cloud below us as we broke free."

I ask if they went back down again. "We dove again that day, but not in the same place." He pauses. "The strange thing is Larry got killed the following week in that sub. He was the observer and Rich Slater was the pilot. They had raised a Chris Craft that had sunk off Catalina, but then the line securing it broke and the boat sank back through the water column and hit their sub."

"It came tumbling down stern first and hit my porthole and cracked it and then, because of the pressure, the glass just imploded," recalls Rich Slater, now co-owner of *Delta*, a similar two person submersible. "I got hit in the face and knocked out. The sub filled up with water and went back to the bottom, about 260 feet down. When it hit I woke up underwater and got the hatch open, and we both got out of there real fast. I was unconscious when they found me near a kelp bed on the surface, my face all bloody, my eardrums blown out. I was deaf for months. They had to put a bunch of stitches in me. My face is still scarred from the glass." I notice the scars but they do not seem too bad; mostly they blend with the crow's feet and character lines accumulated during a life fully lived. "Larry was a better swimmer than me, but he had these rubber boots on that must have filled with water. We think that's why he didn't make it back up," Slater explains.

"I can appreciate the risk involved but it's also important to get down there," says Don Walsh. "The more we know about the ocean, the better off we'll be." Speaking from his ranch 30 miles inland from Coos Bay, Oregon, Walsh is one of just two men who have been to the very bottom of the ocean, 35,800 feet down in the Mariana Trench. That was in January 1960. No person has been back since, although the $50 million ROV *Kaiko* came close in 1995, sending video images of that slug and shrimp back to the surface through its control cable. (Because remote-control radio signals don't work well underwater, most robot subs have to be connected to the surface by a powered tether.) These ROVs operate alongside a growing number of chip-intensive self-guided AUVs, or autonomous underwater vehicles, now doing detection, defense, and scientific work in the world's oceans.

Walsh got to the bottom on board a far simpler vessel, the bathysphere *Trieste,* a 50-foot-long, gasoline-filled flotation hull atop a ten-ton steel observation chamber built by the Swiss inventor Auguste Piccard, who sold *Trieste* to the U.S. Navy (his son Jacques piloted the craft on its record-setting dive). The Navy later used *Trieste* to help locate the wreck of the nuclear submarine *Thresher,* which sank in the spring of 1963 with 129 men onboard.

Today you can see the *Trieste* at the Navy Museum in the Washington Navy Yards (although you'll need a special security pass post-9/11). Visiting this inner space craft at the museum's old converted armory building, I'm surprised how strangely fragile it seems, like a thin-skinned aluminum blimp above the heavy metal observation sphere with its tiny glass viewport. I accidentally pull a hose loose and quickly reattach it, glad we're on the surface. Compared to the *Spirit of St. Louis* or the *Gemini* space capsule at the Smithsonian Air and Space Museum, which are seen by some 10 million visitors a year, this pioneering vessel is a neglected relic of one of America's boldest explorations. This is particularly odd when you consider that hundreds of Americans have followed Alan Shepard and John Glenn into space, but only one American has ever been to the lowest point on the Earth's surface.

"There wasn't much of a Navy selection process," Walsh chuckles. "I was one of only two volunteers. When I went down there it was one of the last geographic frontiers on the planet, but today we don't see much interest in making the national investment needed to explore the deep oceans."

In October 1999, at age 68, Don Walsh went 8,000 feet down in the Atlantic to look at hydrothermal vents, aboard a Russian MIR submersible. "That was the alpha and omega for me," he says. "First seeing Earth recycling itself in the trenches back in 1960 and now seeing the Earth creating itself at these chimneys." When I again spoke with him in the summer of 2004, the 73-year-old Walsh was off to do some ice-breaker exploration and manned submersible diving at the North Pole.

A 2003 report from the National Research Council concurred with Walsh, saying, "The ocean is Earth's least explored frontier." Titled *Exploration of the Seas,* it went on to call for a new U.S. and international program of ocean exploration that could provide "economic, scientific and environmental benefits for all." It warned, however, that support for such a program could be lacking because "public awareness of the oceans' significance to the planet is extremely limited."

Scientists are only now beginning to appreciate what the deep ocean offers. Cold hydroseeps discovered in the Monterey canyon are being explored as sources of new bacteria and pharmaceuticals. The relation of these methane-rich seeps to earthquake faults is being studied by geologists from the United States and Japan, while fisheries experts are only beginning to understand the marine food web that we are rapidly depleting (midwater jellyfish, for example, appear to make up the bulk of the biological mass in Monterey Bay).

Other phenomena being studied include pollution dispersion and the role of the oceans in the creation of weather, in climate regulation, and as a carbon sink in a warming greenhouse world. A July 2004 article in *Science* magazine, for example, found that almost half of the carbon dioxide produced by the burning of fossil fuels and other industrial processes over the last 200 years has been absorbed by the seas. As a result the world's ocean chemistry is changing. The dissolved CO_2 reacts with seawater to form carbonic acid; this acidification depletes the calcium carbonate needed by corals, mollusks, and some plankton to produce their hard shells. To date most of this chemical alteration has occurred near the top of the oceans.

"The great thing about the canyon is that within an hour of leaving dock you can be in 3,000 feet of water," says Chris Grech from the pilot seat of his control room on board the twin-hulled $22 million ROV mother ship *Western Flyer.* A short, wiry man with mustache and goatee, he could easily pass for one of Sir Francis Drake's pirate captains who sailed these same waters some 300 years ago.

Until recently Grech was chief ROV pilot for the Monterey Bay Aquarium Research Institute (MBARI), one of 27 marine institutes now located along the bay's crescent shore; the *Western Flyer* is part of its fleet. Established in 1987 by the late David Packard, the management wizard who with partner Bill Hewlett founded the giant Hewlett-Packard (HP) computer corporation, MBARI has become the premier U.S. institute dedicated to creating new technologies for deep-water exploration. With $330 million of Packard Foundation money invested to date, its sprawling 153,000-square-foot oceanfront facility at Moss Landing, California, represents an emerging force in oceanography.

"When our father set up the family foundation, he challenged us to contribute to the world in some new way," recalls Julie Packard, a tall, slender woman with penetrating brown eyes. Since both she and her sister, Nancy, were marine biologists who shared their father's love of nature, it did not take long for them to suggest converting an abandoned sardine cannery in Monterey into a world-class aquarium that would bring the experience of the bay to the public. Once the aquarium, with its multistory kelp forest exhibit, surge machines, and in-house sea otters, became self-supporting (with more than two million visitors a year), David Packard decided to establish MBARI as a separate science institute. "Dad was very excited about the bay's deep water. He wanted to do something major as an engineering challenge; the challenge of getting down there intrigued him," Julie recalls.

The choice of whether to put development money into multimillion-dollar manned submersibles or into ROVs was the next issue he had to consider. It was a debate that earlier had divided the Scripps Institution of Oceanography (robots) from Woods Hole Oceanographic Institution (manned subs). While many scientists have favored use of America's aging fleet of climb-aboard submersibles, industry (offshore oil and gas, fiber-optic cable-laying, open-ocean aquaculture, and marine rocketry) has opted for tethered robots that can be loaded onto ships of opportunity and, when necessary, sent on "suicide missions" among the wrecks, blowouts, and other disasters that periodically befall offshore operations. "It's really not an either-or choice. It's more like a toolbox from which you should pick the right tools for the job," says Don Walsh.

Still, with his experience in the development of HP robots for manufacturing and hazardous duty (inside nuclear containment vessels), David

Packard decided to focus his resources on developing a new generation of ROVs. These would emerge from a collaboration of engineers, computer designers, and the marine scientists who would advise them on what they needed.

As I watch, Chris Grech scans a bank of monitors, a computer touch screen, and the slave controls that can adjust the movement of this 117-foot platform ship to those of an exploratory robot 12,000 feet below. I walk down a few steps into a large metal-walled room in the heart of the vessel and over to a hulking blue, green, and yellow ROV with the MBARI logo—a seven-gill shark—on its side. The ROV *Tiburon* stands seven feet tall, six across, and nine deep and is equipped with eyelike stereo video cameras, strobe lights, force-feedback gripper claws (which allow the operator to feel resistance), and slurp guns (for sucking in octopuses, jellyfish, and other live samples). It is suspended between an open moonpool for easy deployment and recovery and a huge spool containing 12,000 pounds of control wire.

The robot itself looks like a police tank sitting on top of a bear cage. This description doesn't please the *Tiburon* project director Bill Kirkwood. "The prototype was a 928 Porsche," he admits ruefully.

MBARI owns a second deep-diving ROV, the *Ventana*, which operates off the *Point Lobos* (a smaller ship known as the "Point Puke" to those who have to take it out in rough weather). Sailing four days a week, it uses a microwave relay to provide a live video link from its robot's underwater cameras to scientists and aquarium visitors back on shore, who get to share in a real-time exploration of the canyon.

In February 1991, Grech, working down the coast from Monterey, piloted the ROV *Ventana* to the newly discovered wreck of the USS *Macon*, a navy dirigible that crashed and sank in 1,450 feet of water in 1935. Built in 1933, the *Macon* was the largest aircraft in history, a 785-foot rigid-frame airship that also acted as a sky-based aircraft carrier for five Sparrowhawk biplanes. The fighter-spotter planes were stored in an internal hangar, much as the ROV *Tiburon* is stored inside the *Western Flyer*. They flew off and were recovered with an air hook hanging below the dirigible. The loss of the *Macon* to a violent gust of wind that drove it into the sea, killing two of its crewmen (81 others escaped by life raft) marked the end of the great age of American airships. Appropriately, its rediscovery marked a new era for underwater exploration by equally exotic craft.

"As we searched for the remains of the ship, we were microwaving live images to Dave Packard's house in Big Sur," Grech recalls with a grin. "He held a barbecue for his VIP friends and various scientists to show them what this new technology could do, and it worked perfectly. They saw it as it was happening, the debris field, the outline of the *Macon* planes. It was really cool and very strange, plus it kept the boss happy."

Monterey's submarine canyon is now yielding a bounty of new treasures. "We're discovering about five new species of animals a year with the ROVs," Grech says. One of these species, the *Calyptogena packardana* clam, is named after David Packard, who certainly contributed enough "clams." "The public doesn't have a concept, not a clue about all the animals down there," the ROV pilot smiles, shaking his head in amazement.

But the biotech industry does. In Monterey and across the blue frontier, the discovery of new life-forms has set off yet another wave of mining fever, this time involving bioprospecting for drugs, medicines, and microbes.

More than half of our present medicines derive from terrestrial plants and animals, including aspirin from willow bark, morphine from opium poppies, and penicillin cultured from a common mold. But as society abuses antibiotics, feeding them not only to sick children but also to cattle, chicken, and farmed fish, more resistant strains of bacteria have begun to emerge, posing a troubling new threat to human health. In addition, traditional threats from viruses, cancers, and many other maladies continue to frustrate medical science. And so, as Abraham Piianaia suggested, we have begun to look back to the sea.

For years, ocean science centers like the Woods Hole Marine Biological Laboratory (MBL) in Massachusetts and the University of Miami's Rosenstiel School of Marine and Atmospheric Science have used marine animals for biomedical research. MBL discovered limulus amoebocyte lysate (LAL), a blood derivative of horseshoe crabs that is used to test for bacterial toxins. They also use horseshoe crabs to study vision (the helmet heads have about 1,000 large rods and cones per eye versus the 300 million much smaller ones you are using to read this). Toadfish, with well-developed inner ears, are used to study balance. Two toadfish even got to ride along with John Glenn on his final mission into space.

At the University of Miami I'm led on a tour through a stucco warehouse full of sea hares (think guinea pig–sized frilly green sea slugs). Their big ganglia make them useful recruits for the study of brain and memory. I'm also shown pools of nurse sharks being raised for nonvoluntary hospital work (despite the media myth, sharks do get cancer, just not as often as smokers). Two widely used drugs—Acyclovir, which treats herpes, and AZT, which fights HIV—are derived from compounds first identified in marine sponges. More recently, orthopedic surgeons have discovered that porous hard corals make strong artificial bone implants that are not rejected by the body.

Between 1974 and 2004 some 20,000 biochemical substances were extracted from marine creatures. By the mid-1990s the National Cancer Institute's (NCI's) Natural Products Branch was rapidly expanding its marine life collections. Since Taxol, a compound that freezes cancer cell growth, was first derived from the bark of yew trees in the early 1990s, seven other compounds with similar effects have been identified. Six of them come from marine organisms, including soft corals. Other promising discoveries include anti-inflammation chemicals from sea feathers, virus-killing proteins from sea grass molds, painkillers from cone snails, and the bioremediation (toxic cleanup) potential of the bacteria *Beggiatoa,* which allows chemosynthetic clams and seaworms to convert hydrogen sulfide into energy.

The hardy microbes that thrive in the extreme conditions of heat and pressure around deep-sea vents and chimneys have become a favorite target of bioprospectors since the discovery and patenting of *Pyrococcus* (for DNA fingerprinting) in the late 1980s. Although these microbes hold great promise for drugs and industrial and agricultural processes, they are also hard to collect and hard to work with once they are brought to the surface.

"Of all these microbes, you can only culture around 1 percent of them. But you can take a beaker of water or sediment containing these microbes and [using genetic engineering] do gross DNA extraction," explains Dr. David Newman, of NCI's Natural Products Branch. "We can also take gene clusters from one of these organisms and, like those plastic pop-it beads from the 1960s, reassemble them in a different sequence and see what we get."

With only 1 percent of federal research and development money for biotechnology being directed to the marine environment (home to more than 80 percent of the planet's life-forms), a number of pharmaceutical companies have chosen to fund their own university-based ocean research. This has created situations rife with potential conflict of interest. Zeke Grader, the executive director of the Pacific Coast Federation of Fishermen's Associations, served on the University of California's Institute of Marine Resources Advisory Committee from 1983 to 1989, when he quit. "What finally got to me," he recalls, "I went to a meeting at Scripps, where the scientists were saying they weren't going to pursue a promising find involving marine plants because they couldn't patent it, and the research was being funded by the pharmaceutical companies. And I said, 'What if it's a cure for cancer? You're not going to study it 'cause they can't make money off it? You're a public institution!' "

With vast potential for profit as well as progress, marine microbes and other life-forms retrieved from public waters using taxpayer-funded tools (such as Navy-owned academic ships and submersibles) might be expected to provide a direct return to the U.S. Treasury—perhaps through some kind of royalty payment like those for offshore oil and gas. But to date there has been no discussion of this in Congress. If Congress does act, it likely will establish a token fee acceptable to the drug companies, given the huge sums industry spends to influence these kinds of decisions. In 2004, for example, pharmaceutical companies spent more than $96 million on lobbying. In that year's presidential and congressional elections, pharmaceutical and health products companies also contributed more than $27 million to the candidates, 68 percent going to Republicans and 32 percent to Democrats.

Another little-examined issue is the potential risks when genetically altered species developed for aquaculture and other purposes are introduced into the marine environment, like loose pop-it beads spilled on a dance floor. Researchers at the University of Alabama at Birmingham have cloned the gene for the blue crab's molt-inhibiting hormone (MIH). After blue crabs molt naturally (having outgrown their old shells), they briefly become soft-shelled and can be eaten whole. The researchers inserted the molt-inhibiting gene into insect cells in order to replicate large quantities of MIH. They hope to use this material to find a way to genetically block the hormone's release. If they succeed, they could force crabs to molt on command, providing a year-round supply of soft-shell crabs for the seafood industry. The risk, according to critics of the biotech industry, is that if such an MIH blocker gene got loose in the wild it could turn blue crabs into soft targets for predators and disease, spelling disaster for the crabs, the ecosystems they inhabit, and the fishermen who depend on them. Similar concerns have been expressed about the escape potential of farmed salmon genetically modified for fast growth.

While public policy discussion of these issues lags, technology-driven science and exploration leap forward with the exuberance of wild dolphins in a ship's bow wave.

"Nice weather," Wayne, the ship's walrus-mustached boatswain, says to me in a gravelly smoker's voice.

"For a fish," I agree.

We're 150 miles off Nantucket on the research vessel *Atlantis*, standing outside the main science lab on the weather deck watching white-capped 20-foot seas rolling across 8,000-foot-deep blue water. It is early fall 2001, and we're steaming west at 12 knots trying to avoid the brunt of Hurricane Erin, which the shortwave radio assures us is headed "safely out to sea" in our direction. I'm on the Deep East Expedition off the Atlantic seaboard, which includes a team of scientists hoping to develop a better understanding of newly identified deep-sea corals along with new species of life among the icy gas hydrates found in the miles-deep Hudson Canyon off New York.

Secure in its stern hangar, the submersible *Alvin* will not be diving today. First launched in 1964, the orange and white guppy-shaped *Alvin* is the only U.S. submersible able to get down to 4,500 meters (14,764 feet)—which still gives it access to only 65 percent of the world's oceans. A newer submersible capable of diving to 21,320 feet and reaching 99 percent of the oceans is scheduled to replace *Alvin* in 2008. I get a tour of *Alvin* in its hangar one night, climbing down a removable ladder through the orange conning tower, which floods during dives, and on through a thick hatch into a titanium sphere 6.5 feet across. I crawl into one of the two observer positions, each with its thick little acrylic window and camera-linked video screen. Inside, the sphere is about the size of a new VW bug if you removed the seats and steering wheel and replaced them with inch-thick Velcroed pads, an organized jumble of electronic and mechanical gear, an articulated arm, a joystick, toggle switches, monitors, and life-support systems.

"It's somewhat discouraging, all this fascination with that machine," grouses Peter Auster, a fish ecologist from the University of Connecticut, after I mention that *Alvin* is probably more famous than most of the scientists who have dived in it. "I mean, it's great engineering, but it's really about what it lets us look at. It's like going out onto the savanna to study elephants and writing about the jeep."

Our first morning out had been clear and warm with a score of dolphins leaping off our starboard side. At 8 AM *Alvin* had been deployed off the big blue A-frame on *Atlantis*'s fantail, its support swimmers then detaching its lifting line, as thick as my arm. They made sure the submersible was well clear of the big ship before *Alvin* dove, and then they scrambled back into their inflatable raft. Gavin, one of the swimmers, has an elaborate tattoo of a hammerhead shark etched across his shoulder and back. Hours later the sub resurfaced, its sample basket full of life from 4,500 feet down in Oceanographer Canyon. This included both multicolored and wedding-cake-white branching corals, one with a red brittle star twined in its limbs.

The scientists had been careful to take only "prunings" of corals, not whole organisms. I note how closely the cold, bumpy samples resemble the branch and fan corals I'm used to from diving on shallow tropical reefs. Like all life in the cold, nutrient-hungry depths, these colonial animals are slow to grow and reproduce. Today's samples may be decades old. Some three-foot-high corals may be 300–400 years old. Near Japan, collectors drag chains across the deep ocean floor to break up and snag pink coral, using the centuries-old remnants caught in their chains to make jewelry.

In addition to endangered marine life, the Deep East scientists are interested in deep-sea ice crystals that catch on fire when exposed to a flame. These methane hydrates are made up of natural gas molecules trapped in ice balls formed under great pressure. The ocean's store of these crystals may contain more than twice the energy of all the world's coal and oil deposits combined. Energy companies are interested in the potential for mining these deep-sea methane hydrates. The good news is that this fossil fuel has only half the planet-warming carbon dioxide found in petroleum. The bad news is that methane itself is a greenhouse gas ten times more powerful than CO_2. Like volcanoes and earthquakes, sub-seabed gas hydrates may also function as a major geological force, causing underwater landslides and slumps that can displace enough water to create massive tidal waves.

That evening I watch a lingering lemon and orange-sherbet sunset over the hidden canyon as the wind begins to rise. By the clanking, heaving morning, much of Deep East's work, including plans to dive on two unexplored seamounts, has been washed away by high seas and 40-knot winds. Disappointed that I now won't get to do a dive in *Alvin,* I drop out of the upper bunk in my three-man cabin and stagger/climb up to the bridge, with salt crystals from the rails sticking to my palms.

And soon, caught off guard like the rest of the world, I'm standing in the wheelhouse with Captain Gary Chiljean and Chief Mate Mitzi Crane, listening to a shortwave broadcast, a static-filled radio report on WINS 1010 out of New York, reporting live descriptions of the jetliner terror attacks on lower Manhattan and the collapse of the World Trade Center towers. There are additional reports of the attack on the Pentagon and a plane crash in Pennsylvania, and false reports of additional terror planes and a car bombing at the State Department.

Rebecca, one of the expedition members, lives three blocks from the trade center. We put her on the satellite radiophone and she gets through to her husband, Joe, who is okay, although a coworker of his in the south tower is missing. I go out on deck, where several people have gathered silently along the bulwarks. More dolphins leap off our starboard side.

The expedition's plan for a transfer of scientists at sea off Staten Island has been blown away, along with thousands of lives. The Navy (which owns *Alvin*) now cancels permission for the expedition to dive in the deepest parts of Hudson Canyon; we assume this means that they are moving nuclear submarines through there as backup for the aircraft carrier battle group that's been deployed off New York.

The night after the attack I'm watching some of the dive video taken in the dark, crushing depths of Oceanographer Canyon. There are beautiful corals in yellow, brown, orange, and white, also sponges, cutthroat eels, rattail fish, red crabs, luminescent and shimmering purple squid, and other life abundant amidst the descending marine snow. Someone tells me we now have TV reception. I go up to the lounge on the fo'c'sle deck to see for the first time, through a weak and snowy signal, images of the second jet hitting the south tower and of the towers coming down.

For the rest of my days I'll be stuck with those contrasting images of what we're capable of as a species—on the one hand, exploring and discovering new life in the most remote and challenging parts of our ocean planet; on the other, using modern technology to carry out mass murder in the heart of a city. Osama bin Laden, the leader of al Qaeda, the terrorist organization that carried out the attacks, first came to prominence fighting with the anti-Soviet resistance in Afghanistan. The Afghan mujahideen in turn were funded and backed by the CIA as part of America's Cold War with the Soviet Union. This fits a historic pattern of unintended consequences, also clearly apparent in all our attempts to extract wealth from the seas.

A few years earlier, University of Washington researchers using the Canadian ROV *Ropos* investigated volcanic chimneys on the Juan de Fuca Ridge, 200 miles out from Puget Sound. They sawed off the tops of several chimneys (now on display at the American Museum of Natural History), and one broke apart on the ship's deck. Inside, they found the glittering yellow flecks of chalcopyrite, known to an earlier generation of frontier prospectors as fool's gold.

Although the promise of quick and easy mining riches from the ocean's depths has not been realized, real treasure may yet be found as a result of the CIA's *Glomar Explorer* fiasco of the 1970s. This treasure may prove greater than military intelligence, copper, cobalt, microbes for the lab, or natural gas for cooking. For in recklessly laying claim to an ocean wilderness larger and rougher than any previous frontier in our nation's history, we have also stumbled on an opportunity to reclaim an important part of our past. The oceans that border and are a part of the United States remain—like Patriot's Bridge at Concord, the Golden Gate, Pearl Harbor, the twin towers, and New Orleans—an essential element in defining the people we are and the paths we choose to take.

CHAPTER 2

From Sea to Shining Sea

Sullen fires across the Atlantic glow to
   America's shore,
Piercing the souls of warlike men, who rise
   in silent night.
> — *William Blake,*
> America: A Prophecy, *1793*

"Give me your tired, your poor,
Your huddled masses yearning to breathe
   free,
The wretched refuse of your teeming shore.
Send these, the homeless, tempest-tost to
   me. . . ."
> — *Emma Lazarus,*
> *from "The New Colossus,"*
> *inscribed on the Statue of Liberty*

My best memories of childhood growing up on New York's Long Island Sound involve water—standing, brackish, and salty. I remember the swamp in Douglaston, Queens, where my friends and I used to play every day after school. We'd cut paths through the cattails and rushes that grew higher than our heads, startling rabbits and large pheasants that would burst into flight in front of us, setting our hearts beating to the flurry of their wings. Here we built reed forts and recreated the battles of Francis Marion, the Revolutionary War hero known as the Swamp Fox, using sticks and dirt grenades in place of musket and ball. In winter we would ignore adult warnings, sliding across the ice that formed where the swamp met the edging waters of the sound. One winter day two of my friends fell through the ice into freezing waist-deep water. After helping them crawl out, all three of us hid in the furnace room of one of their apartment basements, drying clothes and bodies and taking a pledge of self-protective silence lest our parents find out.

Our fourth-grade teacher, Mrs. Olson, was the daughter of a Long Island sea captain and used to bring to class mementos of America's maritime past, including a six-foot serrated bill from a giant sawfish her father had caught. Mrs. Olsen tried to instill in us a sense of what it meant to live on an American island, even one rapidly turning into a vast network of metropolitan bedroom communities.

Our town's class divisions were also marked by water, by whether you were a member of the Dock or the Club. The country club sat on a hill a few blocks in from the shore and was open to the community once a year during Strawberry Festival. Although this was a good time for pie-eating contests, carnival games, and razzing girls, it also took much of the mystery away from the Club. Having been given a chance to look over the tennis courts, mowed lawns, and chlorinated swimming pool, those of us who were members of the Dock knew we had the better of the deal.

The dock extended into Long Island Sound on creosoted wooden pilings from a narrow, rocky beach below a seawall. At its end was a raised platform connected to three pontoon floats. Here we'd practice cannonballs off the pilings or play dibble, diving after popsicle sticks that someone would release underwater or hide under a pontoon. Wading around the shallows was another kind of adventure, searching the muddy water with our feet for the primitive armored shapes of horseshoe crabs and then lifting them up by their spiky tails for closer inspection. Early on, our boys' culture divided between those of us who defended the rights of horseshoe crabs to be played with and skipped across the water and the older "hoods" who liked to imprison them in rock corrals and then smash their shells with heavy stones. I remember, after one fight in which by dint of numbers we vanquished a group of "hoods," a gray-haired eel fisherman coming over to congratulate us, explaining how sometimes you have to fight for creatures who can't fight for themselves.

I also remember Hurricane Donna, which swept up the Eastern seaboard when I was nine. My mother drove me and my sister down to a street overlooking the dock. We sat there behind the town's two police cruisers, with a hundred other townspeople in the whipping rain, watching the gray sound's white-capped waves smashing against the seawall, watching the dock swaying side to side, until finally the slashing winds tore the wooden slats and rails off their pylons, hurling them into the sky like a runaway fenceline. I thought it was the coolest thing I'd ever seen.

By the time I entered junior high school, the swamp had been filled in

and covered over by asphalt and red brick tract homes, and the newly
contaminated waters of the sound closed to fishing and swimming. My
memories of these natural pleasures lost are not unique. Rather, they are
the common currency of people raised along America's shoreline during
the second half of the twentieth century—a period of rapid transition on
our blue frontier, during which our sense of connection to the ocean
around us eroded like a walled-off beach turned to rock cobble. It wasn't
always that way, nor need it be in the future.

Beginning with its first human settlements, North America has been a
maritime culture. Fishing was key to a number of early settlers such as
the Lummi, Tlingit, and Chinook of the Pacific Northwest, who lived off
salmon and believed that humans came to the land on the back of a killer
whale. The Eskimos hunted in sealskin kayaks, while, more than a thousand years before European colonists began whaling off New England,
the Makah used 12-man canoes to harpoon gray whales that migrated
along the West Coast. In what would become California, the Miwok,
Yurok, Chumash, and other tribes traveled the coasts in wooden plank
boats gathering mussels and abalone along the marine terraces, warmed
themselves in sea otter fur, and hunted giant 16-foot sturgeon in the shallows of San Francisco Bay. Far to the east, the Penobscot, Pequot, and
Delaware fished the Atlantic's bays, islands, and estuaries, using wooden
fishtraps, spears, and hooks baited with lobster. The Narragansett of
New England were the first to fashion wampum beads for trading from
the dark, mother-of-pearl insides of quahog clamshells. Far to their
south, the Seminole and Calusa of Florida depended on the Everglades
pa-hay-okee (grassy water) as well as the clear, sparkling, low-nutrient
waters of Florida Bay for much of their sustenance, using nets, traps, and
hooks to catch sheepshead, sea trout, and drum.

Early European explorers and settlers were awestruck by the wealth of
fish, shellfish, seabirds, and marine mammals found along the Eastern
seaboard. When the English navigator Henry Hudson arrived in a great
wilderness harbor in 1609, he found local Indians fishing for shad off a
small sandy island they called Kiosk or Gull Island. The Dutch and
English later called it Oyster Island in tribute to its rich shellfish reefs,
while still later it would be known as Ellis Island, port of entry for more
than 12 million of America's future oceanic immigrants.

To the north, the Pilgrims were surprised to find Cape Cod and
Plymouth harbor alive with whales when they arrived aboard the
Mayflower in 1620. By then, fleets of European Basque fishing boats had
already been hauling cod off the nearby Saint Georges Bank for more

than a century. In 1649 the governor of New Amsterdam wrote home to Holland, telling of six-foot lobsters in the local waters around Manhattan, while an Englishman spoke of catching giant cod simply by lowering baskets weighed down with stones and hauling them back up. In 1699 Pierre Le Moyne, Sieur d'Iberville, his brother, and 13 others landed at what would become Biloxi, Mississippi, on the Gulf Coast. They found an abundance of game "and some rather good oysters," built a fort, and established the French colony of Louisiana, still renowned for its seafood.

From New England to the great bay the Indians called "Chesepiooc" (Chesapeake), whose oyster reefs posed a hazard to navigation, and on south to the parrot- and turtle-rich Georgia isles, the settlers were overwhelmed by the blessing and abundance of the seashore, which helped sustain them through rough, hardscrabble times.

The English colonial authorities were also much taken with New Hampshire's tall and majestic white pines, which made superior stock for the Royal Navy's masts and spars. Under the White Pine Acts of 1722 and 1729, the Crown established the "broad arrow policy," marking the best trees (those averaging up to 40 yards by 40 inches in diameter) with three blazes, thus creating for the Navy the first public land reserves in America. But lumbermen and mill owners among the colonists saw little profit in letting the Crown export raw logs to England to become ships' masts (also known as "skyscrapers" before buildings grew taller than ships). They cut 500 marked trees for every one that got shipped to the mother country. After the British surveyor General Daniel Dunbar tore down a mill full of blazed logs in the town of Exeter, New Hampshire, in April 1734, he and his men were set upon by a mob and driven away with small-arms fire, in a pattern of resistance that would repeat itself with increasing ferocity over the next 40 years. When the lieutenant governor appealed to the state legislature to punish the culprits, he was stonewalled by taciturn legislators—many of whom made their living in the local timber trade.

Much of this timber went to shipyards then being established along the Eastern seaboard. The colonial shipbuilding industry not only helped to stimulate local fishing and commerce but also spurred subsidiary industries that sprang up around the shipyards, such as tar, rope, barrel-making, and ironworks (producing anchors, chains, and nails). Seaports such as Boston, Newport, New York, Philadelphia, and Charleston became cultural and commercial centers for the colonists as well as centers of disaffection with English trade and conscription policies.

Although many colonists were dedicated sailors and watermen, they put up fierce, often violent resistance when it came to impressment, the Royal Navy's tradition of sweeping towns for able-bodied seamen. British captains were "mobbed," boats burned, and ships fired upon. Commodore Charles Knowles's efforts to sweep Boston Harbor for able-bodied men in November 1747 led to two days of heavy rioting. In 1764 there were riots and gunfire in Newport, Rhode Island, after a deserter escaped (the British ship *St. John* was also shelled by the colony's gunners at Fort George). That same year four fishermen seized off Long Island were released after the British ship's master was taken hostage ashore, and there was rioting in Norfolk in 1767 and again in Boston in 1768.

This physical resistance gradually mixed with talk of freedom, natural law, and unjust taxes as yeoman farmers, sailors, and fishermen gathered in their homes and around their hearths, ofttimes heated with broad arrow pine. In their discussions and debates over the meaning of freedom they formed a new American identity. Not surprisingly, one of the first martyrs to the American cause was an able-bodied seaman and former slave, Crispus Attucks, who was shot down in the Boston Massacre of 1770.

In 1775 Edmund Burke warned his increasingly frustrated and bellicose colleagues in Parliament not to underestimate the strength and spirit of these troublesome Americans. "Look at the manner in which the people of New England have of late carried on the whale fishery," he suggested. "Whilst we follow them among the tumbling mountains of ice, and behold them penetrating into the deepest frozen recesses of Hudson's Bay and Davis's Straits, whilst we are looking for them beneath the Arctic circle, we hear that they have pierced into the opposite region of polar cold, that they are at the antipodes, and engaged under the frozen serpent of the South. . . . Nor is the equinoctial heat more discouraging to them, than the accumulated winter of both the poles."

With the outbreak of the American Revolution in 1775 came the creation of a coastal and Great Lakes navy. This force, with the exception of John Paul Jones, who favored leading his crews into direct battle with the Royal Navy, spent most of the war practicing a legalized form of piracy known as privateering. American schooners, with letters of permit from Congress, attacked British merchant ships and seized their cargoes (some 600 in all), while striving mightily to avoid one-on-one confrontations with well-armed British warships. This type of maritime guerrilla warfare, while risky, never lacked for volunteers, as most of the American fishing and whaling fleets were bottled up in their home ports by British naval blockades.

With U.S. independence in 1783, the fleets were freed up for global commerce, including the ongoing trade in human chattel—the infamous triangular slave trade between Africa, the Caribbean, and North America, which would continue until 1808, when it was officially banned. This trade in human misery had by that time provided much profit for New England's burgeoning shipping industry.

In the wake of the Revolution, Massachusetts cod fishermen were guaranteed access to Canadian waters as part of the Anglo-American peace accord. What was not guaranteed was the new nation's right to a defensible marine boundary. In 1793 Thomas Jefferson, as secretary of state, announced a three-mile territorial limit for the United States (the standard range of a cannonball at the time, or so Jefferson claimed). Still, Britannia continued to rule the waves and to impress American sailors from merchant vessels. It was this practice of seizing sailors that led to the War of 1812, the British torching of Washington, D.C., and the 1814 siege of Fort McHenry in Baltimore Harbor. The last event inspired Francis Scott Key to write a resistance poem "by the dawn's early light," which later became America's national anthem.

During this period fishermen, sealers, and whalers from towns such as Nantucket and Gloucester, Massachusetts, and Stonington, Connecticut, began to gain fame as among the finest in the world. Having the world's richest offshore fishery in Georges Bank didn't hurt.

Before the discovery of petroleum, whale oil was used to light the world's better homes and streets and was the primary lubricant of the machine age. New England whalers became the leading hunters of "Leviathan" (as recounted in Herman Melville's classic American novel *Moby-Dick; or, The Whale*). Whaling was a mainstay of the U.S. economy through much of the nineteenth century; its impact was comparable to that of the post–Civil War railroads. By 1857 the town of New Bedford, Massachusetts, employed some 10,000 men working on 329 whaleships. Having emptied out nearshore populations of whales early on, New England's whalers began hunting along the coasts of Africa and Brazil (today these same waters are being prospected by offshore oil companies).

Fur hunters were among the first to round South America's Cape Horn and join Russian trappers operating along the Pacific coast of North America, killing sea otters in vast numbers and trading their skins in China for tea, spices, porcelain, and silk. In 1820 Nathaniel B. Palmer, a 21-year-old Connecticut sealer commanding the small sloop *Hero*, became the first person to spot the Antarctic continent while hunting the southern ice for fur seals. By the end of the 1820s Palmer and his fellow hunters had killed some three million fur seals, selling their skins in China as fake sea otter. The sealers soon overhunted themselves out of business but in the process opened up Antarctica's Southern Ocean to commercial whaling.

Yankee whalers also began heading west around Cape Horn and out into the Pacific. The Hawaiian Islands, under the rule of King Kamehameha, became a major provisioning center for whalers, who would stop there twice a year, once in the spring before heading north to spend the summer hunting on the Sea of Japan and again in the fall before heading south to cruise along the equator. By midcentury some 700 whaling ships were operating in the Pacific. Hawaii's tropical Polynesian culture with its less rigid sexual mores would prove to be both a revelation and great temptation for many sailors from cold, Puritan New England (who in turn would prove to be a source of syphilis, cholera, and other infectious diseases for the native Hawaiians). When Yankee sailors jumped ship in the islands, they were quickly replaced by young Hawaiians, lifelong watermen and trained artisans whose finely etched whale-tooth scrimshaw carvings can be found on display in maritime museums throughout the world.

Whaling was by its nature a boring, dangerous, and challenging profession in which small whaleboats from a mother ship were sent out on often rough seas to pursue and harpoon pods of whales. Harpooned whales often dragged the boats for miles in dangerous "Nantucket sleigh rides." Everything was expendable in pursuit of the whales—the harpoons, the rope, the line tubs, the whaleboats, even the whalers themselves.

Also onboard the whaling ships of the 1800s were large black iron kettles called try-pots, which were placed on a brick shelf or pile of sand and were used to "try," or render, whale blubber into oil while the ships were under way. In the western Pacific try-pots were recovered from storm-wrecked whaling vessels by cannibalistic Fijians, who used them to cook their victims. This later became the basis for the cartoon stereotype of the cannibal cooking a missionary in a big iron kettle.

Whaling competition with Britain, France, and Russia would eventually lead to increased U.S. settlement of the Hawaiian Islands and the overthrow of the Hawaiian monarchy, but by then whaling was an industry in decline. This decline can be traced in part to the first drilling for petroleum "rock oil" in Titusville, Pennsylvania, in 1859. (Kerosene, distilled from petroleum, proved far superior to whale oil for lighting lamps.) Other factors included the outbreak of the Civil War in 1861 (Confederate warships sank 50 Northern whaling vessels) and the Arctic ice disasters of 1871 and 1876, in which 45 New Bedford ships and hundreds of men were lost.

Maritime fortunes were also made and lost in trade and transportation, especially after the Mexican-American War of 1846–1848 and the discovery in 1848 of gold at Sutter's Mill, California, which opened up the West Coast to rapid Anglo settlement. While clipper ships spent months racing around Cape Horn during the gold rush, Cornelius Vanderbilt came up with a quicker method of transporting miners to California, establishing his Accessory Transit Company of fast clippers, stagecoaches, and riverboats cutting across the Central American isthmus at Nicaragua.

Safety at sea also took a qualitative leap forward in the 1840s, when naval officer Matthew Fontaine Maury published the first reliable U.S. wind and current navigation charts, based on the logs of whalers and other American seafarers. As hydrographer of the Navy from 1842 to 1861, when he defected to the Confederacy, Maury became known as "Pathfinder of the Seas." Equally impressive was the work of the civilian U.S. Coast Survey, which mapped the coastlines under the able leadership of Superintendent Alexander Dallas Bache.

One of Bache's surveyors wrote to him from the Florida Keys: "You ask whether the growth of coral reefs can be prevented, or the results remedied, which are so unfavorable to the safety of navigation. . . . I do not see the possibility of limiting in any way the extraordinary increase of corals, beyond the bounds which nature itself has assigned to their growth." Unfortunately, he was wrong. The live corals that comprised 90 percent of the Florida Keys reefs when his surveyor encountered them have declined to 10 percent as a result of human activities, including runoff pollution.

The 1840s also marked the first great wave of postcolonial immigration, made up mainly of Irish fleeing the potato famine, along with Germans and Italians fleeing the political turmoil that culminated in the European revolutions of 1848. Many of these immigrants arrived in steerage—named after the low-cost accommodations below deck by the stern rudder that steered the ship. Chinese also began arriving on the West Coast in response to news of the California gold rush. More arrived in the 1860s and 1870s to provide day labor as "coolies" (derived from the Chinese words *koo* and *lee,* which together translate as "rent-strength"). They would help build the western link of the transcontinental railroad as Irish immigrants worked on the eastern section.

This early Asian immigration reflected China's relative proximity to California as a closer source of trade and cheap labor than the U.S. East Coast in the days when you had to sail around the Horn. The railroads solved part of this transportation problem by establishing a national infrastructure for the movement of people, beef, and buffalo skins. Still, California continued to ship its grain by sail around Cape Horn to Europe until the end of the century. In 1881 no fewer than 559 ships assembled in San Francisco Bay to load grain bound for northern Europe. The Navy also felt hamstrung by its inability to quickly move ships from one coast to the other.

By the 1850s naval strategists and engineers in both the United States and Europe were beginning to discuss the possibility of a transoceanic canal, either in Nicaragua or through the Darién jungle on the Isthmus of Panama, which was then part of New Granada (Colombia). U.S. interest in the canal was delayed, however, by growing domestic turmoil and increasingly violent conflict as the nation was divided between free and slave states.

The American Civil War stimulated an industrial and technological expansion that included large-scale steel production, the growth of railroads, and the introduction of steam power, gun turrets, and metal armor on American ships of war. This last set of innovations led to the famous, if inconclusive, "brown-water" duel between the USS *Monitor* and the CSS *Virginia* in the shallows off Hampton Roads, Virginia, on March 9, 1862. This deafening battle of the ironclads marked the beginning of the end of wooden, wind-dependent warships and the rise of the heavy metal, engine-driven battleship fleets of the twentieth century. But in contrast with the rapid expansion of railroads into the arid Western frontier immediately following the Civil War, it would take the Navy's leadership another 30 years to appreciate the ironclads' potential to change the nature of warfare on the blue frontier.

In the post–Civil War era the railroad companies opened up the seashore to vast numbers of day trippers and urban expeditioners. Until then, coastal holiday retreats were largely the province of wealthy society types and robber barons, of Astors and Vanderbilts who built their massive summer "cottages" in Newport, Rhode Island, or similar enclaves such as Bar Harbor, Maine, and Avalon, New Jersey. Grand and elegant beachfront resort hotels like the Victorian Royal Poinciana in Palm Beach, Florida, and the many-gabled Hotel Del Coronado in San Diego—famed for the giant black sea bass that could be caught by surf casting from the hotel's strand—also drew the cream of society.

At the same time, America's urban working classes and nascent middle class discovered that, for the price of a train or trolley ticket, they too could escape the broiling cities, if only for a day, and make their way to New York's Coney Island or Atlantic City and Cape May on the 127-mile-long Jersey Shore. Coastal areas like Cape Cod, Massachusetts, long dependent on fishing and shipping for their livelihoods, suddenly began to realize new economic potential in ocean-oriented tourism. Joseph Story Fay, the businessman who gentrified the fish-rendering town of Woods Hole on Cape Cod, and Spencer Fullerton Baird, who established the first fisheries laboratory there, both arrived as railroad tourists in the 1870s.

On the Coney Island boardwalk, amusement parks with exotic-sounding names such as Steeplechase, Luna, and Dreamland would soon enter the American lexicon. In Atlantic City saltwater taffy became a popular treat identified with the boardwalk and the shore, while across the country, by San Francisco's foggy shore, the fantastic Cliff House hotel and glass-enclosed swimming pools of the Sutro Baths offered thousands an opportunity to enjoy the beach without actually having to enter the cold and treacherous Pacific.

Working with the post–Civil War railroad trusts, the Cleveland rock-oil refiner John D. Rockefeller, along with his close friend and colleague Henry Flagler, was able to create the Standard Oil monopoly, using railroad shipping rebates to undercut their competitors. Soon oil production was moved from Pennsylvania to east Texas and California, where the first ocean drilling took place off wooden piers in Summerland, a spiritual cult colony just south of Santa Barbara. In Louisiana the newly formed Gulf Oil Company began drilling in lakes and swampy coastal areas. As Rockefeller became more controversial, attacked by the press and investigated by Congress, he also became more philanthropic, establishing among other endowments the Rockefeller Foundation, which became a major funder of U.S. oceanographic research (which would create and field-test many of the deep-drilling technologies used in modern offshore oil exploration).

In 1884, as Congress started funding construction of new, heavily armed cruisers, dreadnoughts, and battleships, the Naval War College was established in tony Newport, Rhode Island. Among its first faculty was Captain Alfred Thayer Mahan, a student of the Royal Navy and its links to empire. Mahan rejected the U.S. naval tradition of commerce raiding and brown-water coastal defense as less than worthy of a great maritime power: America's navy, he argued, should be able to engage foreign fleets in direct battle. His book *The Influence of Sea Power upon History* (1890) electrified not only naval strategists but the public, including the young politician and future president Theodore Roosevelt, who became a lifelong advocate of Mahan and his theories.

The growth of a powerful blue-water navy became not only a tool of late nineteenth-century empire-building but also an excuse for it. The reasoning was that coal-fired battleships needed far-flung deep-water harbors and refueling stations. Also, the cost of maintaining a two-ocean navy could be greatly reduced by constructing a canal across Central America to facilitate rapid movement of the fleet.

In 1889 the idea of establishing a coaling station and naval harbor in Samoa almost led the United States into a war with Germany and Britain (until a typhoon sorted out the vessels of the three nations, leaving only the British warship unscathed). In early 1892, the United States came close to war with Chile over a barroom brawl in Valparaíso that left two U.S. sailors dead. Then, in 1893, with the support of the U.S. ambassador to Hawaii, John L. Stevens, American planters in Hawaii overthrew Queen Liliuokalani. U.S. marines off the heavy cruiser *Boston,* docked in Honolulu harbor, were dispatched to the royal palace to protect the coup plotters, and Pearl Harbor subsequently became the major U.S. naval base in the Pacific.

In 1894 a U.S. warship exchanged fire with Brazilian rebels blockading the harbor in Rio de Janeiro. In 1895 the United States threatened war with Britain over raids from British Guyana into Venezuela, which the United States saw as a violation of the Monroe Doctrine of U.S. dominance in Latin America.

Finally, in 1898 the Spanish went too far. A year earlier, while the Spanish colonial army in Cuba was suppressing Cuban nationalist rebels, the U.S. Naval War Board began planning a war with Spain, including an attack on the Spanish fleet in the Philippines. In January 1898 the Navy ordered the USS *Maine* to sail from Key West, Florida, to Havana, Cuba, on a "courtesy call." The wife of the *Maine*'s captain commented, "You might as well send a lighted candle on a visit to an open cask of gunpowder!" On February 15, 1898, the *Maine* exploded in Havana Harbor, resulting in the deaths of 253 men. Many of their bodies were returned home aboard her escort vessel, the USS *City of Washington*. It took the Navy a century of advances in forensic technology to determine that the sinking of the *Maine* was caused by an accidental detonation in its coal bunker and not, in fact, by a mine; at the time the Spanish were blamed and America went to war.

After several decisive naval victories, including the Battle of Manila Bay in the Philippines, the United States found itself in possession of an island empire incorporating Cuba, Puerto Rico, and the Philippines, where rebel insurgents, who had been fighting the Spanish for independence, were soon embroiled in a long and vicious guerrilla war against their American "liberators."

The end of the nineteenth century and the first two decades of the twentieth marked the second great wave of immigration to the United States, with the arrival of some 25 million of a total of 65 million immigrants who have come to America by ship since European settlement. Almost 90 percent of today's Americans are descended from shipborne immigrants, while another 10 percent were born elsewhere—part of a third great wave of mostly Latin and Asian immigration that began in the 1970s. (Another 1 percent of Americans came much, much earlier by way of the Bering Sea land bridge.)

Unlike the immigrants of the 1840s, the turn-of-the-century immigrants were mostly from southern and central Europe. Like their predecessors, however, they were fleeing poverty and religious and political persecution. They included Italians, Greeks, Austro-Hungarians, Russians, Poles, and Ukrainian Jews like my father, Max Helvarg. A not untypical immigrant, 11-year-old Max arrived at Ellis Island on September 22, 1922, with his eight-year-old sister, Sue, and their widowed mother, Liza. Refugees from the civil war that followed the Bolshevik Revolution, they had hidden in an attic with 20 other people for a week while Cossacks raped and killed the other Jews of their village. After the attack they fled toward Romania, hidden under the straw of a hay wagon. Max, nine at the time, and Sue, six, got separated from their mother at the Dniester River; the children were later smuggled across the frozen river ice. They had to climb a steep cliff on the other side and walk across the cold stubble of fall-cut wheat fields, Max carrying Sue on his back. The spiky stubble tore his shoes and shredded the soles of his feet so that he was leaving bloody footprints in the frost by the time they arrived in the village of Belz, where their mother was waiting for them.

They waited there two more years before traveling on to Bucharest and the port of Constantsa, where they sailed for the United States on the liner *King Alexander*. It took 30 days to make the passage through the Dardanelles to Constantinople (now Istanbul), past Athens and Gibraltar, and across the deep Atlantic to New York City.

Arriving in the harbor, Max searched for the Statue of Liberty, but all he could see in the fog was the electric Wrigley's chewing gum sign on the Jersey shore. The first black person the Helvargs ever met was the immigration inspector on Ellis Island assigned to question them. He smiled and spoke to them in fluent Yiddish. Max and Sue stared at him in amazement. When Liza's brother arrived, he took them on the subway to his home in Coney Island. Max and Sue were certain they would never get out of that hole in the ground. Then they were out of it and riding in the light as the elevated train took them above the buildings and the river, the bright seashore, and toward the promise of freedom.

The year of the century, 1900, was marked by patriotic celebrations of America's new maritime empire. Rudyard Kipling, the British poet laureate of imperialism, smitten by the recent American invasion of the Philippines, encouraged the United States to "take up the white man's burden." Subsequent U.S. Marine landings in Mexico, Panama, Nicaragua, Haiti, and the Dominican Republic suggested that some in political power found this idea appealing.

Along with jingoistic celebrations, 1900 also brought one of the costliest natural disasters, in terms of lives lost, in U.S. history. That September the wealthy Victorian port town of Galveston, Texas, built on a sandy barrier island, was devastated by a storm-driven sea surge that killed more than 6,000 of its citizens, about a third of the town's total population. In the wake of the disaster the citizens determined to stay and rebuild in harm's way. The Army Corps of Engineers, which had its origins in the construction of coastal forts and gun batteries, was enlisted to reinforce a ten-mile-long seawall erected to protect the town. The Corps would continue to defy and reengineer nature for more than a century to come, helping to set the stage for the tragedy of New Orleans in 2005.

In 1903 the Navy made it possible for the United States to help organize a secessionist rebellion in Panama. The U.S. gunboat *Nashville* and a battalion of marines kept the Colombian army at bay as the insurgents consolidated power. Within a few weeks the United States had recognized the "revolutionary" new government and negotiated a treaty that granted the United States sovereignty over a ten-mile-wide strip across the isthmus. French engineers had already spent years, fortunes, and thousands of lives in a failed attempt to excavate a transoceanic canal here, but ten years after beginning their work in 1904, American engineers had completed the canal. This was in no small part thanks to the work of Dr. Walter Reed in Cuba and Colonel William Gorgas in Panama, who identified malaria and yellow fever as mosquito-borne infections and fought to eradicate these diseases among the canal's workers

by eradicating the bugs and their breeding grounds. Still, more than
5,600 workers, mostly West Indians, died building the canal. If the
French construction effort is included, the death toll exceeds 25,000.
The completion of the Panama Canal was widely celebrated in the
United States, with Pan-American fairs and expositions in San Francisco,
San Diego, and other coastal towns, even as American troops began
shipping out for the Great War in Europe.

Shortly before completion of the Panama Canal, Americans' faith in
the technological wonders of their age was briefly shaken by the sinking
on April 15, 1912, of the White Star liner *Titanic,* owned by the
American industrialist J. P. Morgan. Carr Van Anda, the managing editor
of the *New York Times,* reflecting on the sudden cutoff of the *Titanic's*
radio signal after its collision with an iceberg, concluded that the ship
had sunk and put that out in the next day's edition. His educated guess-
work established the *Times* as America's newspaper of record.

As survivors reached New York on April 18, more than 40,000 people
jammed the city's docks to witness their arrival. They were swarmed by
press and newsreel photographers, their faces splashed across newspapers and shown in flickers—movies—on screens across the nation. In
the media frenzy surrounding the *Titanic* disaster still and motion picture
news photography came of age. Another result of the disaster was the
expansion of maritime safety regulations that mandated enough lifeboat
space for every passenger, regular evacuation drills, better lookout systems, and 24-hour radio watches.

Before long the *Titanic* tragedy was subsumed in the public consciousness by the horrors of World War I. The introduction of submarine
warfare and particularly the 1915 German sinking of the passenger ship
Lusitania (which, along with a number of American passengers, was carrying contraband ammunition to Great Britain) again changed the nature
of naval warfare. The end of World War I brought a disarmament treaty
that temporarily reduced the size of the world's navies, but the U-boat
ushered in more than 80 years of expanding submarine and antisubmarine warfare. The only comparable "revolution" in modern sea power
would come during the next war, when the Japanese attack on Pearl
Harbor and the Battle of Midway would establish the dominance of
warplanes and aircraft carriers over battleships and heavy cruisers.

The 1920s were marked by economic growth and prosperity across
the United States. Mass-production technologies and the coming of age
of the automotive and advertising industries helped to transform
America into a consumer culture. Radios, wristwatches, electric washers,

refrigerators, and processed foods sold through supermarket chain stores such as A&P and Piggly Wiggly helped create a national middle-class identity. By 1922 Clarence Birdseye was quick-freezing fish fillets near the Fulton Fish Market in New York, while the sale of cooked-in-the-can sardines skyrocketed. The popularity of this original "fast food," along with canned tuna, shrimp, oysters, or, if you were poor, inexpensive canned salmon from Alaska, kept fishing docks and processing plants busy from Juneau, Alaska, to Monterey, California, to Lubec, Maine. The introduction of gasoline and diesel engines on fishing boats also allowed the use of larger heavy-bottom drag nets called otter trawls, which created new fisheries for flounder, halibut, and other bottom-feeding flatfish. Catches increased rapidly, as did the number of fishermen. This fishing pressure, combined with environmental impacts from dams, water diversions, and other onshore activities, led to the collapse of a number of species. Some of them, like the Atlantic salmon and Chesapeake oyster, have yet to recover.

Separated from the U.S. Navy in 1919 and placed within the Treasury Department, the U.S. Coast Guard spent much of the Roaring Twenties chasing after Prohibition rum-runners, just as it would spend much of the 1990s diverting patrol boats, cutters, helicopters, and Falcon jets for the war on drugs. The year 1920 also saw passage of the Jones Act, which provided government subsidies to U.S. merchant and passenger ships as long as they were American-built and -crewed. This decision grew in part out of the vital role merchant ships had played as troop transports during World War I. By the end of the decade the United States Line, Presidents Line, Matson Line, Dollar Line, and other U.S. shipping and passenger fleets had become globally competitive, despite a decline in steerage business resulting from more restrictive U.S. immigration laws. American-flagged passenger ships were able to provide high-quality service across the North Atlantic and the Pacific, and south to the Caribbean and to Latin America, including small-ship service between Key West, Florida, and Havana.

At the same time, south Florida was becoming the target of a Roaring Twenties development boom that marked the first major landfill of coastal wetlands for nonagricultural purposes. (It also marked the age of the land scam, as far more swamp acreage was sold than was actually filled in.) Henry Flagler opened up Florida's east coast by building a network of railroads and hotels, including his famous "Flagler's folly" rail line linking the mainland and Key West, completed in 1912. Hundreds of workers died during its construction, including 300 men killed in a single hurricane in 1906. In 1935 another hurricane killed more than 400 retired World War I veterans and tourists being evacuated from the Keys as 50-foot seas swept their train off its elevated rail bridge. North of the Keys a dredged, terraced, and paved island known as Miami Beach was becoming renowned for its "millionaire's mile" of fabulous mansions.

It was during the flapper era that extended beach vacations became possible for significantly larger numbers of Americans. The expansion of middle-class culture led to the introduction of widespread travel advertising, the marketing of more revealing ladies' swimwear, the transformation of the suntan from a sign of outdoor labor to a symbol of beachfront leisure (a trend encouraged by designer Coco Chanel, among others), and, most important, the expansion of the U.S. highway system to coastal areas previously inaccessible by rail. One of the most popular roads built during this era was the Dixie Highway, running from Chicago to Miami, along which automobile trailer parks soon made their appearance.

It seemed that nothing could slow this reckless expansion of beachfront development, driven as it was by the burgeoning real-estate, construction, and tourism industries. In 1928, the year state engineers completed the Tamiami Trail through the Everglades, connecting the east and west coasts of southern Florida, a hurricane killed 2,400 Floridians. After the cleanup, survivors made a commitment to stand their ground and kept on building in harm's way.

Some scientists were beginning to warn of the vagaries of exposed coastal zones, tidal currents, maritime weather, and habitats. In the 1920s oceanography was still, from a practical point of view, a shore-based science, with few deep-water ships available for researchers beyond those temporarily on loan from the Navy for hydrographic sea mapping and oil exploration (the Navy was converting from coal to diesel fuel). Most oceanographers were trained in the biological disciplines—zoology, botany, and ichthyology—and engaged in limited studies of tides and marine plants and animals. In 1903 the Berkeley zoologist William Ritter set up a marine biological station out of a boathouse in San Diego with financial help from the newspaper publisher E. W. Scripps and his sister, Ellen. In 1925 Bill Ritter renamed his marine station the Scripps Institution of Oceanography. Its growing reputation would help establish ocean research in the mainstream of American sciences. He believed the job of marine scientists was to look at whole organisms and their relationships to their environment, a field of study later named ecology.

Up the coast in Monterey a wild and wildly innovative biologist named Edward F. Ricketts also was helping to introduce the idea of ecology to the study of the blue frontier. His book *Between Pacific Tides* (1939) emphasized the need to comprehend not only individual species but their interactions in the near-shore environment, where much of the ocean's productivity occurs. His collection of plants and animals from the submarine canyon and kelp forests, along with the work of Stanford University's Hopkins Marine Station, marked Monterey as a center for marine study. Ricketts's casual, party-friendly lifestyle inspired the character Doc in the 1945 novel *Cannery Row*, written by his close friend, Nobel Prize–winning author John Steinbeck.

In 1930, the Rockefeller Foundation, under the guidance of John D. Rockefeller's longtime advisor Dr. Wickliffe Rose, decided to establish an East Coast oceanographic science center to match the West Coast work being carried out at Scripps and Hopkins. Rose was convinced that marine fisheries could play an important part in global agricultural and food production, provided that enough scientific research was brought to bear. Along with new funding for Scripps and for ocean research at the University of Washington, three million dollars were earmarked for the establishment of the Woods Hole Oceanographic Institution, to be located in the village of Woods Hole on Cape Cod, where a government fisheries lab and the Marine Biological Laboratory already existed.

There were a few bright spots for ocean research in the 1930s, like the Rockefeller funding and the 1934 descent of biologist William Beebe and his friend Otis Barton one-half mile below the sea in a 2.5-ton bathysphere, which briefly inspired America.

On the waterfront, however, the Great Depression hit hard. Fish landings and international shipping trade declined steeply as the gross national product dropped by 25 percent. Among the hardest hit were merchant seamen and longshoremen. By 1933 an able-bodied seaman was earning $53 a month, down from $85 in 1920. But at least a seaman had steady if dangerous work. Longshoremen were earning around $40 a month, but only if they were able to survive the "shape-up," where crowds of desperate men gathered around a foreman who would pick a work crew for each ship to be loaded or offloaded. Often the only way to ensure a shot at the job was through bribery or strong-arm tactics.

As worker dissatisfaction grew, the International Longshoremen's Association of the American Federation of Labor began a union drive on the docks. Among its more effective organizers was a short, hawk-faced Australian named Harry Bridges. On May 9, 1934, Bridges led the San

Francisco longshoremen out on strike, demanding higher wages, shorter working hours, and a union hiring hall in place of the shape-up.

By July 3, with the strike still going strong, San Francisco's mayor decided to send the police down to the Embarcadero waterfront to "open up the port." This led to widespread rioting, with tear gas and bricks flying throughout the day. After a Fourth of July truce, the battle resumed on "bloody Thursday," when police opened fire with gas, pistols, and riot shotguns, killing two workers and wounding hundreds more. California's governor then ordered in thousands of National Guard troops to secure the port, and for a time Bridges thought the fight was lost. But after a funeral for the dead workers, attended by 35,000 mourners, the Bay Area's unions organized a general strike in solidarity with the longshoremen. Close to 130,000 strikers shut down San Francisco's and Oakland's stores, factories, and transportation system. Sympathy strikes shut down ports around the country. Under pressure from Franklin Roosevelt's administration to settle the dispute, the ship owners agreed to recognize the longshoremen's union and meet its demands. Later that year, facing the threat of another strike, they recognized the Seaman's Union and its demands for eight-hour at-sea watches, an eight-hour day in port, and improved pay.

As U.S. maritime labor became increasingly organized and effective, a new wave of ship construction got under way—not in the United States, however, but in Germany, Italy, and Japan. In 1936 President Roosevelt responded to this new maritime threat by expanding U.S. naval and merchant ship construction, calling it a public works project. The following year he appointed the Boston political fixer and post-Prohibition financier Joseph Kennedy as chairman of the U.S. Maritime Commission, with orders to speed up the shipbuilding effort. He'd tapped the right man for the job. "We are going to lay the keels for new fast ships. And we are going to do it now!" Kennedy pledged.

While Roosevelt saw the storm clouds of war and fascism rising in Europe and Asia and was convinced the United States would soon have to get involved, most Americans, including most military leaders, believed that the United States could remain neutral and isolated from the conflict, protected as it was by two vast oceans.

One newly arrived immigrant knew better. Even though she was only 16 years old at the time, my mother, Eva Lieberg, had seen the face of fascism. At age nine she had been interrogated by the Gestapo in her hometown of Ellrich am Harz, Germany. Her mother, Emi, was not allowed to be with her at the time. On November 9, 1938—Kristallnacht, the night of broken glass—Eva's father, Fritz, was taken off to Buchenwald concentration camp, where he was tortured for two months and put through a mock execution. About 250 of the men with him were murdered or committed suicide. In January 1939 he was let go. Many of the 30,000 Jews arrested on Kristallnacht were released at this time, only to be picked up with their families a few months later and murdered.

In the spring of 1939, after surrendering all their remaining cash to the Nazis, the Liebergs were finally able to make their escape to Holland. Fritz, Emi, and their three daughters were among the last German Jews to get out alive. From Holland they were able to procure U.S. visas and book passage on the SS *Rotterdam* on its final trip before the Nazis invaded. The night before they were to leave, another liner, the *Simón Bolívar*, hit a mine and sank. Dozens of the girls' young schoolmates drowned.

It took two weeks for the overcrowded *Rotterdam* and its seasick passengers to make it through the minefields and across the Atlantic to Hoboken, New Jersey. Once stateside, the Liebergs tried to arrange passage from Germany to Shanghai for Emi's older sister, Helene, but it was too late. She died in the gas chambers at Auschwitz. Her husband starved to death at the camp in Theresienstadt. Other relatives who had made it to England faced nightly bombing raids by the Luftwaffe.

The Liebergs had no illusions about their new American home being safe, but they did believe it to be strong. That strength would first be challenged, not by Nazi Germany, but by its Axis ally, Japan, on December 7, 1941. That day of infamy would not only bring America into World War II but also fundamentally change how the United States related to its ocean frontier for the remainder of the twentieth century and into the twenty-first.

CHAPTER 3

Oceanographers and Admirals

Only God Almighty and naval research can save us from the perils of the sea.

— *Senator John Warner at a Navy dinner*

If I'd seen a Russian footprint down there instead of a fish, we'd probably still be down there.

— *Don Walsh, retired Navy officer and one of only two humans ever to go to the deepest point on Earth*

Until quite recently few U.S. marine scientists and no major oceanographic centers had taken a leadership role in alerting the public to the environmental dangers facing America's blue frontier. This failure had little to do with any lack of insight on the part of scientists and their institutions and much to do with the hidden history of U.S. oceanography. It is a story of how science, which works best as a system of broad, open, and shared inquiry, can be distorted by single-source funding and state secrecy. It is a story of untold tales and classified secrets that, ironically, has its origins in one of the most recorded moments in American history.

Several years ago I had the privilege of interviewing a number of veterans of the December 7, 1941, attack on Pearl Harbor. Dick Fisk was a 19-year-old marine bugler on board the battleship *West Virginia* that morning, watching what he and a friend thought was a U.S. army plane making a practice run on their ship, launching its torpedo.

"We moved to the port side. We thought it was going to be a dummy torpedo until the explosion hit and then it seemed like this great big wall of water just washed us across the deck to the other side, which was 118 feet wide."

As the first wave of Japanese planes arrived over their targets, Commander Mitsuo Fuchida radioed a coded message, "Tora, Tora,

Tora," to let the Japanese fleet know that complete surprise had been achieved.

Joe Morgan was a third-class petty officer stationed on Ford Island that day. "When we ran outside to see what we thought was a plane crash, we saw a plane dropping bombs across the runway from our hangar, in the area of the patrol wing squadron.

"As the plane pulled out we could see the meatballs [the Japanese rising sun symbols] under his wings. I knew then that we were really in war, and I was afraid of being killed. About that time this plane came by flying slow, and I could see the goggles of the rear gunner. As he swung his gun around in our direction and started peppering our vicinity with machine gun bullets, I jumped behind a rear-wheel tractor for protection until after he passed.

"There was a plane that dropped his bombs over and around battleship row and was flying low across the landing field. As it started coming in our direction we all, nearly every gun in our squadron, was shooting at him. As he passed over our hangar with everyone shooting at him, he burst into flame. And instead of crashing in the water off the shoreline there, he landed right on top of the USS *Curtis* on the crane deck, and the whole top of the ship then burst into flames and that was one of the most memorable sights I still remember.

"So I'm seeing things going on all around, mainly looking for planes. As I happen to be looking out toward the *Curtis* again, I saw this little submarine come to the surface, . . . and was aiming at the *Curtis*, and so the *Curtis* gunner started shooting at him and put two five-inch shells right through his conning tower, and I actually saw the holes appear in the conning tower. And then about that time the USS *Monihan*, the destroyer, came dashing down the channel, heading to get out of the harbor, and they rammed it head-on, and then as they passed over dropped two depth charges on it. They had to be going so fast to keep from blowing off their own fantail in that shallow water, but they couldn't make the curve in the channel and they ran aground."

Within minutes of the attack local medical facilities began receiving heavy casualties. Dr. William Cooper, a civilian volunteer, arrived at Shipler Hospital, where he was introduced to the wartime practice of triage, choosing who should live and who should die. "It was a shock to see how much bullets could tear a guy apart. The first case that was put on the table for me to take care of didn't have any legs and had one arm gone and the second arm was just hanging . . . and I was going to start and give him some kind of assistance as he was still alive, but the triage gentleman said, 'No, take him off the table. Take him someplace else. We cannot take care of people like this. We only want you to help the ones who can fight tomorrow.'"

Dick Fisk, the marine bugler on board the *West Virginia*, had a brother working as a medic at Scofield Barracks. "Frank worked for over 72 hours straight. He said he never saw so many wounded people in his life and dead bodies up there. He finally collapsed going into one of the operating rooms and his white uniform was completely covered with blood, and so they thought he was dead, so they put him on a gurney, and they moved him into the morgue. And my brother said he slept for over 24 hours. He said it was the best rest he ever got. He said nobody bothered him except when he woke up he was awfully cold."

Battleship row ran along Ford Island for more than a mile. Of the nine battleships in Pearl Harbor that morning, seven were moored there, tied up to large white concrete piers known as dolphins. The *Nevada* was the only one to get under way during the attack, although it failed to reach the open sea. Next came the *Arizona,* moored next to the repair ship *Vestal.* The battleship *West Virginia* was behind it, moored outboard from the *Tennessee.* Beyond them were the *Maryland,* the *Oklahoma,* which later capsized, and the *California.*

After recovering from the shock of the first torpedo hitting his ship, Fisk resumed his battle station on the bridge of the *West Virginia.* "We took a total of eight torpedoes actually and four bombs, and then it was about twenty minutes after eight and one of the bombs came down. . . . We didn't see the shrapnel come over, but the next thing we knew, we saw Captain Bingham hit the deck. He let out a big yell and we looked over to him and most of his stomach was missing. He had a terrific hole in there. By the time they got him down to the boat deck, which was about 11 or 12 minutes later, he finally died.

"We fought fires and people were coming up on the decks. Most of them had so much oil stuck to them that they were on fire, and we were trying to roll on top of them to put the fire out. We stayed aboard ship fighting fires. And even then the bombing, the strafing was still going on and you could hear the machine-gun bullets whiz past you, but nobody seemed to pay any attention to it. I guess maybe we were in shock but we didn't pay much attention to that. We were just interested in getting our friends and buddies squared away.

"We saw this big bomb come down, and we all thought it was going to hit us. We were hurled up against the forepart of the navigation bridge, from the concussion of it, and then we got back up on our feet and we looked back and we just saw the *Arizona,* and it was just one tremendous ball of fire. It was the most devastating thing I've ever seen in my life. I never realized that a ship could blow up like that so fast. The bow just came completely out of the water, and when she settled down she was just one great big fireball, and we didn't realize it then but she had lost over 1,177. Right after the fireball I looked, and I remembered two of my friends that I went through high school with, James and Finley, and I was thinking to myself, 'God, I hope they're all right,' and come to find out later that they were killed in that explosion."

The explosion on board the *Arizona* that day, caused by a bomb striking its forward magazine, was the largest single detonation of World War II until atomic bombs were dropped on Hiroshima and Nagasaki. In all, 2,400 Americans died at Pearl Harbor on December 7, along with some 130 Japanese submariners and airmen. Of the 1,543 men aboard the *Arizona* that morning, 1,177 remain entombed in its wreckage, now a memorial. They represent every rank in the U.S. Navy from apprentice seaman to rear admiral.

The Japanese attack on Pearl Harbor was coordinated with military offensives against Malaysia, Hong Kong, Guam, Wake, Midway, and the Philippines. Militarily, the Pearl Harbor attack was a great but not unqualified success. Although the fleet was shattered, America's aircraft carriers were at sea and escaped destruction and would soon hammer the Japanese fleet. The failure to hit Pearl's power plant and fuel supplies allowed the U.S. Navy to rebuild quickly. But more important than military considerations, the Japanese ruling circles completely misjudged the American public's response to the attack. Rather than undermine the U.S. will to fight, December 7 unified a divided nation in its commitment to total war against Japan and its fascist partners.

In the wake of Pearl Harbor, the nation rapidly mobilized its military and civilian resources. At Woods Hole, Scripps, and other marine stations, scientists joined the war effort. Scripps helped organize a University Division of War Research at the Navy submarine base on Point Loma in San Diego, which was overseen by Scripps geologist and Navy lieutenant Roger Revelle, a tall, personable man who would soon become the first oceanographer of the Navy. Among his colleagues were the physicist Carl Eckart and a young Austrian-born graduate student named Walter Munk.

Until then marine research had focused primarily on the sea's living resources—fish, invertebrates, and marine mammals—and their interactions in the water and along the shore. "Now physical oceanography, the study of acoustics, water temperature, currents, the bottom structure, visibility, all things that might affect submarine or ship operations, came into their own," recalls Walter Munk.

While Revelle's people were working on acoustics for sonar, Munk and Scripps director Harald Sverdrup taught the Navy how to predict swell and surf conditions for amphibious landings in North Africa, Italy, and Normandy.

On the East Coast, Woods Hole director Columbus Iselin and investigator Maurice Ewing discovered how underwater sound location was influenced by temperature and salinity, identified the sonar interference caused by snapping shrimp (called the deep scattering layer), and found deep sound channels within the sea—all major breakthroughs for submarine warfare. One of Iselin's students, the future Woods Hole director Paul Frye, worked on underwater explosives, while Allyn Vine and other scientists developed portable depth-finding and temperature devices, underwater cameras, antifouling paints, and improved weather forecasting, all of which helped the Navy win the war at sea.

Late in the war Revelle, now the oceanographer for the Navy's Bureau of Ships, was traveling frequently between the Pacific theater, California, Woods Hole, and Washington, D.C. In 1944, seeing the promise of postwar work for his colleagues, he set in motion what would become the Scripps Marine Physical Laboratory (MPL). The MPL was an acoustics lab that functioned as part of the University of California but also conducted top-secret antisubmarine warfare research for the Navy. Other Navy-funded university weapons labs included the applied physics labs of the University of Washington, Johns Hopkins University, Pennsylvania State University, and the University of Texas at Austin.

The end of World War II quickly segued into a Cold War with the Soviet Union, including the testing of U.S. atomic weapons in the Pacific. In the winter of 1945, Revelle was put in charge of oceanographic studies for Operation Crossroads, a test firing of two nuclear weapons against Navy ships at Bikini Atoll in the Marshall Islands. "When the task force arrived, a lot of people from Scripps and Woods Hole came out. We had most of the oceanographers in the country out there. There weren't so many in those days." Revelle half smiled, recalling the scene for me some 35 years later. "The most striking event, the most vivid event that nobody really expected, which was quite frightening, was this phenomenon called the bay surge from the underwater explosion—the second test. All the ships had been moved outside the lagoon except the target ships, and we were watching and saw what looked like a huge wave about 100 or 150 feet high moving rapidly out from the center of the explosion toward the beach. This thing only went partway and then stopped, and then it lifted off the water. You see, it really wasn't a wave at all. It was just a cloud of mist and spray about a mile across that lifted from the lagoon. Then it began to rain on us from this cloud. . . . All the ships got badly covered with radioactive water. For days thereafter we had the crews trying to clean up the ships. A lot of the radioactivity stuck to the paint. We never really did get any of the ships decontaminated."

In August 1946, President Truman signed a bill establishing the Office of Naval Research (ONR). The original idea was that this would be the nuclear propulsion center for the Navy. ONR quickly began funding university-built nuclear accelerators, but the Bureau of Ships seized the initiative to develop nuclear propulsion for the Navy, handing it off to a young lieutenant named Hyman Rickover. (Rickover went on to become a highly efficient but autocratic admiral, the J. Edgar Hoover of the nuclear Navy.)

With its original purpose undermined, ONR shifted focus to wider support for basic science that might be of interest to the Navy. Under Vice Admiral Harold Bowen, Revelle became director of ONR's Geophysics Branch, which oversaw oceanography, and he helped establish the contract language for its university research grants. In 1948 he left ONR to help run Scripps and was replaced by geophysicist Gordon Lill. It was Lill who oversaw the reorientation of marine science from a living-resources to a physical-engineering perspective. By 1949 ONR was spending more than 75 percent of its basic science budget in the physical sciences and only 15 percent in biological and medical sciences. "The value of research in nuclear physics is more obvious to the navy than is the value of research in the life sciences," noted *Scientific American* in February 1949.

The ONR's $43 million in contracts in 1949 represented 40 percent of the nation's total science spending. ONR provided millions of dollars and surplus ships to the Navy's friends at Woods Hole (Iselin), Scripps (Revelle and Eckart), and Columbia University's Lamont Geological Observatory (established by Maurice Ewing). Lill also began seeding the coasts with new ocean centers, creating or expanding programs at the University of Washington, the University of Miami, Oregon State, Texas A&M, and the University of Rhode Island, where he handpicked John Knauss to direct the program. (Knauss, who studied under Walter Munk, would later head NOAA—the National Oceanic and Atmospheric Administration—under the first President Bush.)

"We were the major player in determining what went on with oceanography. It was fun being there," recalls Art Maxwell, a former Navy man and graduate student under Revelle who joined ONR as Lill's assistant and later succeeded him.

"By the 1950s Gordon Lill is in effect the Navy czar of civilian oceanography," says Gary Weir, chief of the Contemporary History Branch at the U.S. Naval Historical Center. "A generation of scientists now depend on their friends in the Navy to keep them afloat, Woods Hole more than the others [since it has no university funding].

"Because the research is Navy-driven, biological oceanography and biology are neglected," Weir continues. "Physical oceanography and geology and chemistry are brought to the fore. The heads of the oceanographic institutions are aware this is a problem, but they also know they have to pay a price for what they're getting, and that price is to place the emphasis where the Navy wants it to be. . . . If you're Columbus Iselin at Woods Hole, you know 70 percent of your budget comes from ONR. You're not going to lie to Gordon Lill, and if you do he'll know it because you've been friends for years and drink together and go out to sea together."

Although Congress established the National Science Foundation in 1950 as an alternative source of research funding (under the leadership of ONR's chief scientist, Alan Waterman), the Navy continued to provide two-thirds of all federal spending on marine science into the 1970s.

"The job of people like Lill and myself was to convince the rest of the Navy that anything we supported in oceanography was also good for the Navy," recalls Art Maxwell. That job was made easier after civilian oceanographers helped the Navy get into the nuclear weapons game.

In the early days of the Cold War, the Army and Navy saw themselves confronted by an enemy that terrified them, making them fear for their very survival. This was, of course, the Air Force with its monopoly on nuclear bombers and its ongoing work developing long-range ballistic missiles (with the help of former Nazi rocket scientists like Werner von Braun).

In 1949 Secretary of Defense Louis Johnson came out in support of the procurement of B-36 long-range bombers capable of dropping nuclear weapons on as many as 70 Russian cities. "B-36 Can Blast 70 Red Bases, AF Says," was the headline the Washington Daily News ran after classified documents were leaked to UPI. At the same time, Johnson rejected Navy plans for a "supercarrier" capable of launching long-range atomic bomb–toting aircraft. Shortly thereafter, Congress received an anonymous document claiming funding irregularities in the B-36 program. This led to a series of hearings at which high-ranking Navy officials complained to Congress about having their feelings hurt. The press dubbed this the "revolt of the admirals."

The Air Force's bombers and growing missile program continued to represent America's primary nuclear strike force throughout the 1950s. After the Soviet Union developed its own bombs, America's first-strike plans evolved into a strategy called MAD, for mutually assured destruction. During this period the Army and Navy were reduced to working on tactical nukes—atomic land mines, artillery shells, torpedoes, and depth charges.

In 1955 Roger Revelle and MPL's chief scientist, Al Focke, chose a deep-water site 450 miles southwest of San Diego for Operation Wig-Wam, the Navy's test-firing of a nuclear depth charge. The blast was not supposed to break the surface, but it did. Two days later, on May 16, 1955, a spike of radiation passed over San Diego. "Those bomb tests made an anti-weapons man out of me," Revelle later admitted. "I feel very strongly about it. I don't think anybody should be developing nuclear weapons. Believe me, no one who's seen one of those things go off ever wants to see another one."

Still, in 1956 Woods Hole hosted the Undersea Warfare Committee of the National Academy of Sciences. Dubbed Project Nobska (after a local lighthouse), the summer-long retreat, held at the Whitney estate, included the nation's leading oceanographers and some outside scientists including Edward Teller, the "father of the H-bomb." Out of this woodsy idyll came three volumes of proposals for new approaches to naval warfare, including the idea of firing nuclear-tipped missiles from submerged submarines, using small warheads, solid-rocket fuels, and advanced guidance systems. By 1960 the submarine *George Washington* had test-fired a Polaris missile at sea, and the Navy was able to claim the third leg of what became known as America's strategic nuclear triad: Air Force bombers, land-based missiles, and Navy "boomers" or missile submarines. For the next 30 years the Navy would be dedicated to protecting the boomers while going after Soviet subs using satellites, helicopters, surface ships, and, of course, other submarines.

The civilian oceanographic centers by 1960 were top heavy with physical oceanographers and physicists with high-level security clearances and big money contracts, not only from the Navy but also from the Air Force, the CIA, and DARPA (the Pentagon's Defense Advanced Research Projects Agency). "The physical oceanographers became the directors of all the stations, and the marine biologists felt like they were now second-class citizens," explains Deborah Day, the senior archivist at Scripps.

The growth of physical oceanography made significant contributions to the earth sciences by establishing the theory of plate tectonics (continental drift) based on the work of Walter Pittman, Bruce Heezen, and Marie Tharp at the Lamont Geological Observatory and Harry Hess at Princeton. Roger Revelle also made a major contribution by linking rising levels of carbon dioxide in the atmosphere to industrial greenhouse gas emissions from the burning of fossil fuels.

The institutes were also blessed with a growing fleet of Navy-funded blue-water research ships and vessels including Woods Hole's *Alvin* (named after the pioneer researcher Allyn Vine). Delivered in 1964, *Alvin* was a three-person submersible capable of diving more then a mile down. In 1966 it was used to locate an H-bomb lost off the coast of Spain (after a B-52 collided with its air tanker during refueling). Among Woods Hole's Navy liaisons was a young ONR ensign named Bob Ballard, who would later use *Alvin* to locate the wreck of the *Titanic*.

Unfortunately, oceanographic biology, marine ecology, and work in the nearshore environment were badly neglected during the Cold War. One exception was the California Cooperative Oceanic Fisheries Investigations (CalCOFI), funded by the state of California after the 1947 collapse of the sardine fishery. For more than a half century CalCOFI has provided ongoing data on the California current and its living resources.

In 1951 Rachel Carson, then an employee of the U.S. Fish and Wildlife Service, also managed to break through the martial drumbeat of the times with publication of *The Sea around Us*. This natural history of the oceans sold more than one million copies, introducing the public to what were then obscure concepts such as the marine food chain, ecosystems, and the biosphere. It inspired an Academy Award–winning documentary and a follow-up book, *At the Edge of the Sea*. In 1962 Carson shifted focus to the dangers posed by DDT and other pesticides with her most famous book, *Silent Spring*, which in turn provided a major boost and inspiration to the growth of environmental protest in the United States.

In 1970, during the height of the Vietnam War and protests against the war, Mike Mansfield, the Democratic House majority leader, pushed through an amendment to a military spending bill that limited ONR funding to work that had direct application to the Navy's mission (to help win an unwinnable war). This marked a transition point, after which the National Science Foundation became the major funder of oceanographic research. Still, the priorities of the field would remain in the hands of physical oceanographers and military physicists, people like longtime Scripps director Bill Nierenberg, a former assistant secretary general of NATO, and Woods Hole director Craig Dorman, a retired Navy admiral in charge of antisubmarine warfare. The Navy also retained a monopoly on funding in two areas it saw as critical—acoustics and, oddly, marine mammals.

"After Maurice Ewing discovered the deep sound channel, the Navy decided this was so important that acoustics kind of went behind a curtain for twenty years, and the ocean community had little to do with the acoustic community," says Walter Munk. "In retrospect, we would have been better off without such heavy security."

While the Navy was using its sound surveillance system (SOSUS) hydrophones to listen in on Russian submarines, the audio "garbage" it was trying to filter out proved to be a treasure trove for discerning scientists with top-secret clearances. "You look at when SOSUS was opened up [for civilian use] in 1993. All these scientists were surprised that the number of marine mammal sounds and underwater volcanoes were an order of magnitude greater than they'd been recording," says Navy historian Gary Weir. "All except people like Munk, who had been using it for years."

"We had a kind of treaty with ONR, where if we didn't identify the location or aperture [of the SOSUS arrays], we could use the information we collected," Munk recalls. "Still, some science journals turned our work down, saying if you can't identify your sources of information, we won't publish your work." This had to be frustrating for scientists with access to the Navy's secret sound systems, satellites, submarines, and sea maps—like being allowed to take an open-book exam on the oceans while everyone else has to guess the answers, but then not getting to see your grades posted on the bulletin board.

Former Woods Hole geologist and Navy commander Bob Ballard used his access to the Navy's top-secret tools to realize a lifelong ambition. According to an article by Laurence Gonzales in *National Geographic Adventure* magazine, Ballard used the NR-1, the Navy's miniature ten-man nuclear spy submarine, to survey the wreckage of the USS *Thresher* in 1984. This gave him the vital clue he needed to locate the *Titanic*.

"Suddenly it all became clear," Gonzales wrote of Ballard. "To find a deepwater wreck, you don't look for a hull a few hundred feet long. You look for a trail of debris a mile or more long. And when you find it, it will take you directly to the heaviest debris, the ship itself."

Because Ballard discovered the debris scattering effect (reflecting the difference between crush depth and bottom depth) on a top-secret Navy mission, he was able to keep the technique to himself. This knowledge came in handy a year later, in 1985, when he used the same approach to locate the wreck of the *Titanic* in a part of the North Atlantic where numerous other search efforts had failed.

Eventually the Navy's interest in acoustics and echolocation would lead it into a very different realm of secret research involving the most sophisticated sonar operators in the world, even if they lacked opposable thumbs.

"No Dogs Allowed Including Military Working Dogs. Code 35 Authorized Persons Only. Code 35 Marine Mammal Program," reads the sign on the gate inside the San Diego sub base on Point Loma. It's a warm fall day with the temperature in the low eighties as longtime Navy public affairs man Tom LaPuzza guides me onto a wooden pier that smells of creosote and fish. Open to San Diego Bay are a series of 30-foot-by-30-foot enclosures holding dozens of dolphins, and a pair of white beluga whales from the Arctic swimming about in their own double-wide enclosure. A few pelicans and a snowy egret are hanging around as trainers feed fish from a bucket to a couple of their charges. A monarch butterfly flits by. The dolphin closest to me is lolling on the surface looking, if I may anthropomorphize, bored silly. Just beyond the dock a Boston Whaler is pulling up next to one of the corrals.

"We're going to tone test some of the dolphins before exposing them to noise generators," LaPuzza explains. "Then we're going to retest them for tone response to see if they've experienced any temporary hearing loss."

"What?"

He looks to see if I'm making a joke. I realize this is about low-frequency active sonar (LFA). The Navy plans to deploy a $350 million system that would project 215 decibels of sound (what you'd hear standing next to a jet engine) into the water and bounce it off enemy submarines (Iranian, North Korean, whatever). Environmental groups and a growing number of marine scientists object that loud underwater noises could prove harmful to marine mammals. The Navy's dolphins have been volunteered to test this theory.

Initial testing suggests that it is a problem in shallow as well as in deep waters. In 1997 and again in 2000, beaked whales usually found in deep water stranded themselves following Navy and NATO testing of active sonar in the Bahamas and the Mediterranean. Initially the Navy denied any link, but tissue damage found in the dead whales' ears proved the connection. Other reported strandings include 16 dead whales washed ashore on the Canary Islands during NATO naval exercises (including the use of active midrange sonar) in 2002 and 2004. Additional strandings and signs of distress by several hundred whales and porpoises in Washington state and Hawaii immediately followed U.S. Navy sonar exercises in 2003 and 2004.

A 2003 article in the science journal *Nature* suggested that sonar may cause decompression sickness in whales and dolphins. Scientists reported that sonar signals disorient the animals, forcing them to surface too quickly, which can generate damaging nitrogen bubbles like those found in the body tissue of some of the Canary Islands whales.

The Navy's response has been to get a permit from NOAA, the lead U.S. civilian agency for the oceans, that would allow it an "incidental take" (killing) of 12 percent of all marine mammals. Sued in California federal court by the Natural Resources Defense Council, the Navy in late 2003 accepted an injunction limiting its use of LFA. Still, it continues to press for broad congressional exemptions from the Marine Mammal Protection Act that will allow it to deploy the system more widely.

In speaking with a number of people familiar with antisubmarine warfare and remote sensing, I gained the impression that the United States remains fully capable of detecting even the most stealthy subs with existing technologies developed during and since the Cold War. I was also told of rapid advances being made in satellite and airborne multichannel hyperspectral imaging, which can make the oceans transparent to a depth of at least 100 feet, with future improvements quite likely. This passive surveillance approach could be used off P-3 Orion and other sub-hunting aircraft in preference to deploying expensive warships with arrays of high-intensity loudspeakers. It's rather like the choice you might make when approaching a dark cabin where you think a bad guy is hiding. You could look for him using night-vision goggles, or you could fire a shotgun into the building hoping to hear a scream.

Still, the Navy isn't spending $20 million a year on the care, feeding, and transport of 75 dolphins, 25 sea lions, and 2 beluga whales in order to see if they'll scream or bark or click. Many critics, from animal-rights activists to congressional budget hawks, wonder why they *are* spending the money.

It is hard to grasp the extent to which the Navy has been involved with marine mammals since the 1960s. Through ONR it has employed or provided grants to almost every major scientist involved in work on dolphins and sea lions, including the late John C. Lilly, the popularizer of research on dolphin intelligence and the author of *Man and Dolphin*. It has worked closely and traded animals with a number of schools and ocean theme parks, including the University of California at Santa Cruz, the University of Hawaii, the New England Aquarium, Sea World, and various dolphin petting zoos in the Florida Keys. Even the *Sierra Club Handbook of Whales and Dolphins* had its origin as a Navy technical report. The Russian Navy also used to own dolphins but shut down its program in 1998 when it realized that it had barely enough herring to feed its own sailors.

The U.S. Navy's original interest in dolphins was based on the animals' short-range high-resolution sonar and hydrodynamics, but researchers soon began viewing these highly sociable animals as potential seagoing K-9s.

"The fleet animals are the operational animals," LaPuzza tells me. "We've used them in mine hunting exercises around the world. They're also very effective at swimmer defense. When you send a dolphin out, the dolphin tells our guys there's a swimmer in the area, then the dolphin is removed from the scene and the guys deal with it."

In 2003, at the beginning of the Iraq War, a number of San Diego–based dolphins and sea lions were deployed to help clear mines from the waters off the southern port of Umm Qasr, and to guard U.S. ships in Bahrain. Bottlenose dolphins including K-Dog, Loma, and Fathom detected a number of mines and searched for suspicious swimmers in order to allow humanitarian aid shipments to get through to Iraq and to keep terrorists from targeting ships and piers in the Bahrain port of Mina Salman. Along with showing off their dolphins, the Navy held a press demonstration of sea lions chasing divers and placing clamps with attached lines on their legs so the divers could be hauled out of the water backward.

Back in 1987–1988, during the Iran-Iraq War, the U.S. Navy was escorting oil tankers through the Persian Gulf, and used its dolphins in a swimmer defense system off Bahrain. At the time, the Reagan-Bush administration was providing satellite and perhaps other intelligence to Saddam Hussein.

"At Bahrain a commander drinking at a party said the killer dolphins are coming, and no one swam in that harbor again, so they certainly have a deterrent value," LaPuzza grins. "But there never really were killer dolphins in Vietnam or elsewhere. That's a lie."

That is not the story I've been told.

In 1971 six Navy dolphins were flown from Kaneohe Bay, Hawaii, to Cam Ranh Bay, Vietnam, where enemy divers were sabotaging U.S. ships. Once in-country, the dolphins were housed in an elaborate flotation craft built in San Diego. A dolphin would scan the bay waters with its sonar. If the water was clear, the animal would push a normal response paddle. If it sensed an intruder, it would hit a second paddle that opened its pen gate.

Here's where the stories diverge. According to the Navy, the dolphin would then clamp a marker onto the swimmer and alert its trainers. According to former Navy and CIA dolphin specialist Michael Greenwood, however, who gave 150 pages of closed-door testimony to Frank Church's Senate Intelligence Committee in 1975, the dolphin would run its beak into a padded cone placed in a water-level weapons rack. The cone's tip contained a heavy-gauge hollow-point needle attached to a carbon dioxide cartridge, a weapon developed by the Navy as an antishark device. The dolphin would then swim to the diver and plunge the needle into him. The carbon dioxide gas would explode the diver's organs from within, floating the corpse to the surface for recovery by the dolphin's trainers. This was known as "swimmer nullification."

Articles in *Penthouse* and the *Christian Science Monitor* in 1977 claimed that the Navy's dolphins killed several dozen Vietnamese divers and two Americans who strayed into restricted waters. James Fitzgerald, who helped develop the swimmer nullification program for the CIA, told *Parade* magazine that the Navy's dolphins "blew up" a number of frogmen. In 1984 I interviewed a retired Navy scientist who confirmed that killings took place during the early part of the dolphins' deployment but said that later on the dolphins made "live captures." He requested anonymity, saying he didn't want to "give the Navy a black eye."

Ken Woodal, a former Navy SEAL I interviewed in Fort Smith, Arkansas, said that he worked for six months as an underwater demolitions man with dolphins in Vietnam, carrying out top-secret raids against North Vietnamese harbor facilities. The animals he worked with were not used for swimmer nullification but rather to place mines.

"The three dolphins I worked with were quite effective in attaching light mines to enemy wharves and piers," he told me. "We'd transport them from Cam Ranh Bay by C-130 aircraft and river patrol boats. They were never sacrificed. They were trained to detach from their mines and return to their pickup boats. The thing that still sticks with me after all these years is the intelligence of those water mammals. You'd listen to them in their pens or working together in the water and swear they were talking to each other."

Later, during the Reagan administration's defense buildup, the Navy program expanded to some 140 animals. "We got a national defense exception to the Marine Mammal Protection Act that allowed us to capture wild animals [in the Mississippi Gulf]," LaPuzza says.

But even as plans were being made to deploy animals to guard Trident nuclear missile submarines in Bangor, Washington; Savannah, Georgia; Groton, Connecticut, and elsewhere, a few trainers began questioning the safety and reliability of the program.

"When I came into the program in 1985, they'd updated the dolphins' nose cones with a .45-caliber bullet ejector, like an [antishark] bang stick," recalls former trainer Rick Trout. "They'd practice ramming divers and dummies in the water in order to 'nullify' them."

In 1987 Trout participated in a weeklong nighttime dress rehearsal for the dolphins being deployed to the Persian Gulf. "I volunteered to play an enemy diver that they were supposed to detect, find, and nullify, only nothing went right. Mostly they'd run off to play with the wild dolphins in San Diego harbor or else spook and return to their pens and refuse to come back out. Finally, Toad, a female, used her sonar to locate me in about 20 feet of black water. Only, as she approached, she tossed her weapon, swam up to me, and lay her chin on my shoulder. The next day I went up to the program director and said, 'This doesn't work anymore, does it?' He said, 'We know that.' 'Then why are we here?' I asked. 'It's just a deterrent,' he said." After talking to reporters in 1988, Trout was fired and threatened with federal prosecution for revealing classified information.

In 1990 new charges were made by another trainer, David Reames, who had worked with the Navy's sea lions. Reames claimed that the animals often failed to respond to trainer commands. While trying to maintain his security oaths, he gave several examples of animals bumping "potentially dangerous classified objects" (the .45-caliber weapons) against scuba tanks, trainers, and boats. On at least one occasion when an armed sea lion jumped into a training boat, its human handlers jumped into the water to get away from it.

Today the Navy insists that its marine mammals are highly effective operatives. These last military draftees remain "operational" in large measure because of the Navy's expanded interest in mine warfare. This includes what the Navy calls its "Very Shallow Water/Mine Counter-measures": a detachment of Navy SEALs, marines, and dolphins working together to scout out and clear amphibious landing zones, bays, and harbors. Despite the development of a new generation of mine-detecting robots and autonomous underwater vehicles, the Navy says that it needs to hang on to its animals "for the foreseeable future."

Still, you don't see the Air Force supplementing its Predator drones with camera-wielding bald eagles, or the Army deploying tigers to guard its forward bases. War is essentially a human activity that we really don't need to share with our fellow mammals.

The deployment of dolphins in the nearshore waters of the Middle East is just a small part of a gradual shift in the Navy's theater of activity from the high seas to what it calls "the littoral regions of the world."

The *American Heritage Dictionary* defines *littoral* as "referring to a coastal region or shore." Throughout the Cold War, the Navy (and U.S. ocean science) focused on the open seas or "blue water," where Soviet nuclear submarines were seen as the major threat to U.S. national security. With the loss of this global maritime threat and the beginning of base closures and defense budget cutbacks in the early 1990s, the Navy and the Marine Corps had to find a new strategic justification for their existence and funding. In September 1992 the Navy and the Marine Corps published *From the Sea*, followed two years later by *Forward . . . From the Sea*, arguing that they must be ready to project power from the continental shallows or "brown waters" of the world onto any shoreline where regional conflict (or stateless terrorism, though they didn't think of it at the time) might require or inspire intervention by the world's last superpower.

"We spent a lot of time looking at the deep ocean because that's where the major threat was [during the Cold War]," says Rear Admiral Paul Gaffney, the head of ONR from 1996 to 2000, referring to Navy-sponsored research. "Now with the increase in mine warfare and diesel subs, smaller, quieter subs that can be obtained by Third World countries or any number of nations, you get into the shallows, and it's a more complex environment. On the deep ocean bottom, on the abyssal plain, processes tend to be very gradual. The shallows by contrast change quickly. You can see differences taking place a meter apart, and to try and predict them is very difficult."

That is one reason the admiral remained a strong backer of continued funding in basic oceanographic research, even as Congress continued to hand him buckets of money for applied military research. ONR's 2000 budget was around $1.5 billion, of which Gaffney was able to sequester $400 million for broad-ranging basic research.

"Really I can't imagine an ocean topic not of use to the Navy and Marine Corps," he tells me when we first meet, at ONR's glass and concrete headquarters just outside D.C. in January 2000. "For example, we want to characterize maritime environments; reefs, seagrasses, barrier islands, mangroves. . . . We want to understand the processes taking place in these different [nearshore] environments so if we're going [to war] somewhere, and if there is not a comprehensive oceanographic survey that's been done [of that location], we'll still be able to see what's gong on there, we'll have a reliable model of what takes place in that environment. That's our goal."

I can see why this charismatic officer won the admiration of so many marine scientists, even those not applying to him for grants. His friendly brown eyes and beagle-like cheeks give him an engaging demeanor that counterbalances what might otherwise be an intimidating intellectual fleetness of mind as he pursues what he refers to as his "vocation": seeking to understand the blue frontier, first for America's maritime warriors, and today as president of New Jersey's Monmouth University and a recent member of the U.S. Commission on Ocean Policy.

Since his days at the Naval Meteorology and Oceanography Command in Stennis, Mississippi, Gaffney has worked hard to declassify Navy data that might be useful to civilian scientists, policymakers, and the public, while pursuing research partnerships with a number of other federal agencies. And, of course, the purse strings he has controlled looked like massive towing cables to civilian researchers. "Watch Gaffney at a meeting and see all the people form in his wake, like remoras following a shark," suggested one observer of the phenomenon.

The admiral takes a sheet of paper and folds it into three parts. He reopens it and writes "land" on the first third and "ocean" across the other two thirds. "This is pretty close to how the planet's divided," he explains. He then draws a thin double line along the land's edge, shading it in. "We're now six billion people, and 50 percent of us live within 50 miles of an ocean. In our lifetime we've seen twice as many people living on the coast. And this creates environmental problems of pollution, and this creates conflicts. And if the sea level rise increases, that will also affect people."

I mention that half the world's people are also living in cities for the first time in human history.

"Yes, urban warfare becomes more important," he agrees. "We need to understand what's going on here." Gaffney runs his finger along the thin line dividing paper land from paper sea. "This is where the Navy and Marine Corps operate, in this area that's also under the most stress."

I think of America's long-neglected frontier waters, including its 95,000 miles of exposed and degraded coastline, and don't feel reassured. It's become axiomatic that the military is always preparing to fight the *last* war. The 1991 Gulf War was fought with the overwhelming military strength the United States had built up preparing to fight the Soviet Union on the plains of Europe during the Cold War. After 9/11, Washington declared a "war on terrorism" and after going after Al Qaeda and the Taliban in Afghanistan, declared war on Iraq—a nation state with few known links to terrorism, but one that the U.S. had an operational plan to invade, if not occupy.

In the twenty-first century, depending on military strength to control scarce natural resources and respond to increasing global stresses linked to environmental crisis may be the very definition of fighting the last war, whether by land or by sea.

CHAPTER 4

A Littoral State of War

The steel decks rock with the lighting shock,
  and shake with the great recoil,
And the sea grows red with the blood of the
  dead and reaches for his spoil –
But not till the foe has gone below or turns
  his prow and runs,
Shall the voice of peace bring sweet release to
  the men behind the guns!

>   —John Jerome Rooney,
>   "The Men behind the Guns," 1900

For two centuries, geography has been America's biggest
security asset. With oceans to the east and west and friendly
neighbors to the north and south, the United States has been
untrammeled by enemy boots on our ground. Those carefree
days are now over.

>   —Stephen Flynn, America the Vulnerable, 2004

The U.S. Coast Guard's motto, *Semper paratus* ("Always ready"), was
put to the test on September 11, 2001, when, following the Al Qaeda
attacks on New York, some half a million people were evacuated by
water from lower Manhattan in the largest maritime rescue in U.S.
history.

  As soon as the second plane hit the World Trade Center, the captain
of the port, Coast Guard admiral Richard Bevins, ordered the harbor
closed to all vessel traffic. Small Coast Guard boats loaded with armed
boarding parties were launched from bases in Staten Island and New
Jersey. After the towers collapsed the Coast Guard put out a second call
for all vessels in the harbor to go to Battery Park and begin evacuating
people.

Brendan Brewer, based at Coast Guard Station Battery Park, saw the second plane fly above him close enough that he could look into its windows. He described a scene of mass panic after the towers fell, with blinding ash clouds and mobs of people trying to get over the station's razor wire. "Things only began to calm down once the tugboats, ferries, and other rescue craft started arriving at quayside," he recalls.

Coast Guard quartermaster Bruce Dickenson, in addition to working at Battery Park, was also a volunteer fireman. As soon as the first plane struck, he ran to the towers six blocks away and worked with firefighting crews until the buildings fell. Barely escaping with his life, he headed back to the water and got on board the Coast Guard Cutter *Hauser,* a 65-foot tug that was the first command vessel on the scene. From there he helped evacuate civilians, transport emergency workers, and direct water traffic. He then transferred to his old patrol boat, the *Adak,* to do armed security work. (Five years earlier he had been aboard the *Adak* when it was the first to arrive at the site of the TWA 800 crash off Long Island that killed 230 people; he took the original video of the burning fuel and floating debris. In 2003 the 110-foot *Adak* was one of a number of Coast Guard vessels shipped off to the Persian Gulf to patrol the waters near Iraq.)

On maps showing the locations of Coast Guard vessels on September 10 and two days later on September 12, you see what looks like a belt being cinched tight around the continental United States. In Washington, D.C., Coast Guard cutters closed down the Potomac as the Pentagon burned on 9/11. In Boston Harbor they refused to let a liquid natural gas tanker dock for fear it might be used as a weapon of mass destruction. In Los Angeles, Houston, New York, and San Francisco, port security units armed with M-60 machine guns took to the waters on highly maneuverable 25-foot Boston Whalers.

Since then the Coast Guard, like much of society, has been transformed.

Scanning the slate-gray waters of San Francisco Bay on an overcast spring day, I spot more eider ducks and gulls than barges or ships. We're patrolling past Alcatraz in a 41-foot Coast Guard utility boat that's almost as old as its blue-eyed 30-year-old coxswain, Chuck Ashmore. This old workhorse, with its aging marine radio and Vietnam-era machine gun, is operating on the cutting edge of a revolution in homeland—or, I should say, home-waters—security.

Long the threadbare cousin of the Navy, the Coast Guard has redefined its mission since 9/11. Then, just 2 percent of Coast Guard resources were directed at security, but in the immediate wake of the attacks, security work commandeered 58 percent of its resources. By 2005 that had dropped back to around 25 percent, but the net gain still represented a dramatic shift of focus. As did the transfer of authority over the Coast Guard from the Department of Transportation to the Department of Homeland Security

Our greatest geographical vulnerability may be along our 95,000-mile coastline, where 14 of the nation's 20 largest cities and more than half the U.S. population are located. With some 17 million privately owned boats and 10,000 commercial and cruise ships plying U.S. waters each year—carrying 2 billion metric tons of trade goods to and from some 360 U.S. ports—building a taut security net is a daunting project.

"If a container has some nasty stuff in it, once it gets to this port it's already too late," says Tay Yoshitani, the executive director of the Port of Oakland, one of the nation's busiest shipping-container ports. "You want to go back to the source."

San Francisco Bay is also home to a major Coast Guard station on Yerba Buena, a pine- and lupine-covered island that divides the two sections of the Bay Bridge. At the top of the island, in a prefab structure beneath a field of microwave and radar antennas, resides command central, and at its heart, the Vessel Traffic Service. The equivalent of an airport control tower, the system consists of more than two dozen computer and video terminals that are manned 24/7 and that daily track some 350 to 400 vessel transits, both on the bay and under the Golden Gate Bridge at the mouth of the estuary.

In the past officers read information about boats entering the harbor off the system's radar screens and then wrote the ships' vital statistics on index cards. Today operators use digital chart overlays of processed radar video imagery to track vessels, then color-code them by type and size. Visiting here, I read some of the ships' names off the screens: *American River, General Villa, Eagle, Raccoon, Trig Lund.* If any one of them attracts an operator's interest, he or she can call it up in the database, which describes the size, tonnage, ownership, and other vital aspects of every vessel that has come into the bay since the mid-1990s.

Before September 11, incoming ships had to give the Coast Guard 24 hours' notice before entering the bay. Now ships are required to notify the Coasties 96 hours in advance and must provide more detailed information—such as where the ship originated, its most recent port of call, crew lists, and cargo manifests. That data is sent to a new office within the Coast Guard—the National Vessel Movement Center in Martinsburg, West Virginia—where it is checked against criminal and intelligence databases.

In the future, tracking global maritime trade and gleaning real-time intelligence may get more efficient. Under new rules adopted by the International Maritime Organization, a UN agency responsible for maritime law, by 2010 the vast majority of oceangoing commercial vessels will be equipped with a transponder that broadcasts information on the ship's ownership, cargo, and schedule, as well as its global positioning system–derived position, course, and speed. Any ship lacking this technology will immediately become a high-interest target for the Coast Guard.

Among those who might greet such a vessel are new Maritime Safety and Security Teams who patrol a dozen key harbors around the United States aboard 25-foot Defender-class response boats. These dedicated groups of armed officers include boat operators and gunners in marine blue camouflage who—like waterborne SWAT teams—can be deployed to any number of ports in case of an attack or natural disaster. The Navy has also shifted 13 highly maneuverable, 170-foot Cyclone-class coastal patrol ships to the tactical control of the Coast Guard. "We're going to bring our littoral warfare resources into domestic waters," claimed Rear Admiral Richard West, then oceanographer of the Navy. (But while the Navy giveth with one hand, it taketh away with the other: the Coast Guard's six 110-foot patrol boats, normally used for fisheries enforcement in U.S. waters, have been redeployed to support the war in Iraq.)

Even with beefed-up patrols, U.S. port security remains an area of deep concern as ever more ships bring a growing mountain of trade goods to America without a concomitant increase in resources and personnel needed to screen them. Once a vessel is cleared to land its cargo, that shipment may or may not be scrutinized in port. Nearly 8 million cargo containers are shipped to U.S. shores each year, but just 5 percent of these huge metal boxes are physically examined (up from 1 percent in 2000). Other tactics are being employed to take up the slack: since 9/11, for example, some 100 U.S. Customs agents have been stationed in foreign ports to prescreen United States–bound cargo ships; high-risk containers are identified and inspected. In a future innovation, special "smart seals" will be applied that electronically indicate whether a container has been tampered with in transit.

Meanwhile, cargo inspectors here at home are getting a boost from a truck-mounted machine that resembles a heavy-duty cherry picker. Called the Vehicle and Cargo Inspection System, it shoots low-intensity gamma rays (generated by the radioactive isotope cesium-137) at shipping containers, offering inspectors a partial view of what's inside. Gamma rays are more effective than X-rays for this job because their shorter wavelength is more energetic. As a result, they are less easily absorbed by solid material and can penetrate through more than four inches of steel.

Customs Service Chief Inspector Steve Baxter and I are sitting in the cab of one of these machines. It backs down a line of parked trucks on San Francisco's Pier 80, its double-jointed arm systematically moving over shipping containers just offloaded from a Latin American cargo vessel. "Without this machine, that's our main technology," Baxter says, pointing to a pair of red heavy-duty bolt cutters and a pry bar lying on the cement quay.

The gamma-ray machine operator peers at a screen displaying an image of the first 20-foot container. Resembling a medical film, it shows a dark mass resting atop a more open matrix. He colorizes the image to enhance the contrast. "The dark area is dense," he says. "They're saying it's empty wooden boxes, but that density on top is a problem. Density equals mass." I'm struck with the odd thought that if that mass were conventional explosives about to blow up, the radioactive cesium used in this detection system would turn the container into a so-called dirty bomb.

A giant-wheeled front loader called a Port Packer lifts the container off its truck carriage, and four burly customs inspectors force it open. Inside, they find that the "empty" wooden pallets have been covered with sheets of old plywood. The unreported plywood was what showed up as density on the operator's monitor. The inspectors now go to work drilling holes in the plywood, checking for empty spaces where other sorts of dense materials—drugs or explosives, for instance—could be hidden. "With inspections like this you don't get much complaint," Baxter says as the battery drills whine. "Now, with expensive furniture shipments . . ." He gives me a smile and shrugs.

Some of the most unusual security efforts in San Francisco Bay are taking place underwater, where a series of shore and dockside instruments and bottom-anchored sensors record the estuary's shifting winds, tides, salinity, and currents. They report this information to shipmasters every six minutes over the Web and by dial-up voice mail. Called the Physical Oceanographic Real Time System (PORTS), this sensory array was originally deployed in response to one of the worst bridge disasters in U.S. history: in 1980 the freighter *Summit Venture* rammed into the

Skyway Bridge in Tampa, Florida, during a blinding squall, killing 35 people.

The PORTS system has since shown that it can help mitigate this and other types of disasters. After a 1996 oil spill in San Francisco, PORTS, which now operates in nine major U.S. harbors, tracked the slick and, through computer models, predicted its trajectory. If terrorists released biochemical agents or other toxins into the water, PORTS could potentially track those substances as well. In addition, PORTS data tells Coast Guard officials which parts of the harbor are navigable at any given time.

Like a small, nimble, go-fast boat, the "multi-mission" Coast Guard has responded to the changing needs of changing times by reorganizing rapidly. The Navy, on the other hand, changes direction as ponderously as one of its glacier-sized aircraft carriers. More than 15 years after the end of the Cold War and some five years into an ill-defined war on terror, the Navy recognizes that the glory days of deep-water Soviet sub-chasing and practicing for nuclear Armageddon have drawn to a close, but it is only slowly refocusing on the strategic coastal regions of the littoral. Its slowness is especially frustrating to the oceanographers and marine scientists who see the littoral as the frontline for today's most urgent environmental challenges.

In a March 2005 meeting with retired Navy Admiral Conrad Lautenbacher, now head of the National Oceanographic and Atmospheric Administration, I mention how a high-tech U.S. Ocean Observation System proposed by NOAA, along with giving real-time information on the marine environment, might also have military applications.

"I wish the Navy saw it that way," he groused. "Then we might get the kind of support we need."

Despite a huge expansion of American oceanographic power during the Cold War, as measured in terms of people, ships, and dollars, the public interest was not well served. The civilian oceanographic stations became so much a part of the Navy's blue-water world that they failed to identify and alert the public to the blue frontier's nearshore living resources at risk. They failed to let us know that coral reefs, seagrass meadows, salt marshes, mangrove swamps, barrier islands, beaches, watersheds, estuaries, and the once abundant marine wildlife that depend on them were in danger of collapse. The responsibility for this may be limited, but we are all sharing in the consequences.

"The irony is that environmental scientists are now the ones who have the global view," says Scripps Institution of Oceanography director Charlie Kennel. "As the Navy sees itself fighting wars in close waters, however, its interests should link up with our concerns. The Navy will find itself with technologies that match our new environmental needs," he argues. "If the Navy is sampling water, diagnosing it for signs of biological weapons, that kind of detection method can also be used for tracing pollutants or other scientific sampling. Resource management is also likely to promote conflicts in the future. And our job is not to turn our thoughts away from that, but to think it out. We will need real-time observation systems to cover environmental security issues like global climate agreements that have to be monitored for CO_2 reduction."

"The Cold War was the driver of oceanography. One of the new drivers may be found in population concerns," adds Bob Gagosian, the director of Woods Hole Oceanographic Institution. "If our population doubles to 12 billion and our coastal population triples in this century, it's not going to be enough to protect the oceans. We're going to have to learn how to manage and use them wisely, which means understanding them far better than we do today."

Kennel, who was appointed director of Scripps Institute of Oceanography in 1999, and Woods Hole's Gagosian, appointed in 1994, represent a post–Cold War transition that is taking place in American oceanography. Kennel previously directed NASA's Mission to Planet Earth and has helped promote Scripps as a center for the study of climate and climate change. Gagosian, an organic chemist, is interested in global change research and human impacts on the marine environment

"Everyone says the future of oceanography is now in biology," explains Deborah Day, Scripps's archivist and institutional memory. "The future is in air-sea interactions and understanding climate change, and understanding the biological consequences of the breakdown in ecosystems and fisheries. How will we cope with this, and what are the consequences of the deaths of coral reefs and of cods?"

"What we're now doing is a bit like the exploration of the American West," Kennel tells me in an interview, with the blue waters of La Jolla cove glittering just beyond the picture windows of his waterside office. "One hundred and fifty years ago explorers caused massive biological reorganization of the continent [killed off the wildlife and chopped down the trees]. And behind these trappers came the scouts from the biological labs in England cataloguing the biological wealth, studying it as they were destroying it. One hundred and fifty years later we don't know what's out there on the ocean frontier. Our scientists think most ecologies are collapsing. Look at the fish. On land, buffalo provided food for whole Indian cultures, and now the buffalo are gone. The same's happening with our fisheries." He pauses long enough for me to think that perhaps this is his vision: oceanographers as obituary writers, recording the passing of a living sea. Then he rallies a bit. "Personally, I feel an ethical pull with these environmental problems. I find it very attractive to want to do something that might matter."

One thing Kennel has done is to allow the outspoken marine conservationist Dr. Jeremy Jackson and his wife, Dr. Nancy Knowlton, to set up the Center for Marine Biodiversity and Conservation at Scripps. With major funding from the National Science Foundation, the Center is helping take Scripps back to the ecological perspective its founder, Bill Ritter, helped pioneer more than 80 years ago.

Still, much of the cutting-edge work in biological oceanography has shifted from the big marine science centers, which were structured and funded for deep-water science during the Cold War, to smaller coastal programs and cooperative enterprises such as the Monterey Bay Crescent Ocean Research Consortium (MB-CORC), made up of more than 27 small- to medium-sized institutes linked by modem and mobility.

In the recent past many believed that the end of the Cold War would see a huge "peace dividend," including the opening up of military and intelligence research to the larger scientific community. That dividend quickly turned into a deficit, as the fate of one promising project shows. In 1991, following the collapse of the Soviet Union (which the CIA failed to predict), Republican CIA chief Robert Gates and then–Democratic senator from Tennessee Al Gore consulted about a possible new role for the spy agency: studying global environmental change. One approach they agreed on was to start declassifying intelligence data useful for research in areas such as climate change and the collapse of marine ecosystems. A special task force was established to oversee MEDEA (Measurement of Earth Data for Environmental Analysis). Its 35 to 40 members would include people from the intelligence community and from the Navy, and civilian scientists with higher than top-secret security clearances.

Linda Zall has piercing blue eyes, straw-colored flyaway hair, a preference for bright red lipstick, and a kind of nervous animated personality (at least in the presence of a reporter). She is MEDEA's executive director and was the technical director of the CIA's Environmental Center before it shut down in 2000. Established in 1997 and housed in the directorate of intelligence, the CIA's short-lived ecocenter assessed the potential political and economic impacts on U.S. security interests of environmental events such as the climate-linked forest fires in Indonesia during 1998's El Niño, and China's coal-driven energy expansion.

Zall chose the MEDEA acronym to honor Medea, the mythic princess and sorceress who helped Jason and the Argonauts steal the Golden Fleece. (JASON is also the name of a long-established science group that advised the Pentagon on its weapons systems but whose funding was revoked in 2002.) Of course, the mythical Medea also bore Jason children and then killed them to avenge his infidelity—and that was before the CIA was even operational. During the 1990s MEDEA began providing science institutes with some limited information based on Navy oceanographic data and spy satellites operated by the Department of Defense and the National Reconnaissance Office (NRO). Still, "only minimal resources were made available," according to Congressman Curt Weldon, who sits on the House Armed Services Committee.

"I'm unhappy with the pace of it [declassification]," the Republican representative from Pennsylvania tells me. "There's also the issue of trust and polarization from the past. In the past you were either pro-environment or you were pro-defense, but I see a natural linkage. We can do things for the ocean's benefit with spin-offs from defense." His aide interrupts him to say there's a vote in two minutes. He excuses himself, leaving for a House floor vote. I check out the models of different weapons systems on top of his office TV—an A-1 Abrams tank, a fighter jet, an Osprey tilt-rotor aircraft, a pilotless spy plane.

"I can take ocean research into the defense agenda," he tells me on his return. "They don't see me as a threat, so I can convince them to do more. But I also blame the ocean research community for not doing enough. They think this [information and technology transfer] should take place just because it makes sense. But this town is also about perception, about how you make your case."

To date, MEDEA has released only two out of more than a dozen reports it has produced (along with some spy satellite photos of Antarctica). One was "Scientific Utility of Navy Environmental Data," and the other was on the effects of Soviet dumping of chemical munitions in the Arctic environment. Although that report concluded that the risks to the Arctic seas are minimal, at least the matter was studied. So far the U.S. Navy and other government agencies have refused to conduct a thoroughgoing study of impacts from nuclear and chemical dumpsites off America's own coastlines. These Cold War atomic relics contain tens of thousands of barrels of radioactive and hazardous waste from the Navy and the Atomic Energy Commission (later the Department of Energy). They are mostly scattered and unmapped in what are now National Marine Sanctuaries off Northern California and Massachusetts.

Some progress has been made. Among the once-classified military tools that have become available to science are the SOSUS (sound surveillance system) arrays, certain Navy ships, mapping technologies, Navy sea-surface gravitational measurements (satellite altimetry), and sub-Arctic ice studies.

In 1998 and 1999 the Navy also provided one of its nuclear submarines, the USS *Hawksbill,* to civilian scientists, who used it to travel under the Arctic ice and set up a polar surface camp. From the submarine they were able to study the thinning of Arctic ice associated with rapid climate change. On their second journey they surfaced at the North Pole for a memorial ceremony, scattering the ashes of Waldo Lyon into the frigid Arctic sea. Lyon was the civilian founder of the Navy's Arctic Submarine Laboratory and a longtime advocate of polar exploration. Woods Hole's Al Vine got a similar and fitting sendoff back in 1995, when *Alvin* took its namesake's ashes down to the depths of the Mid-Atlantic Ridge, some 13,000 feet below the surface, where they were deposited along with a plaque in his honor.

With the decommissioning of the *Hawksbill* in 2000, however, the Navy announced that it could no longer provide nuclear subs for scientific research—except for NR-1, for which shipwreck explorer Bob Ballard seems to hold the pink slip.

This lack of interest in environmental research is not limited to the Navy. Despite a Clinton-era presidential directive stating that "environmental issues are significant factors in U.S. national security policy," less than 1 percent of the NRO's reconnaissance satellite time is dedicated to environmental data collection.

Nevertheless, the old institutional players are not averse to using the public's growing concern over the state of the blue frontier to advocate for more big science projects in the deep oceans. The idea of a real-time Global Ocean Observation System (GOOS), using fiber optics, miniaturized tracking devices, autonomous underwater vehicles, sampling buoys, and satellite links, has become a major goal of academic scientists and administrators. Along with the directors of Scripps and Woods Hole, Admiral James Watkins, the former chief of naval operations and chair of the U.S. Commission on Ocean Policy, has been a major proponent of this technology. Interest is also growing among the Four Ns of ocean science: the Navy, NOAA, NASA, and the National Science Foundation.

Although gaining a better understanding of ocean processes is always useful, a key question is not being asked. Without far stronger links between science and public policy, how can such an ocean observation system function as anything more than a high-tech version of those nineteenth-century biological scouts who collected interesting samples on a dying frontier?

The Cold War may be over, but the Navy continues to thrive in a world of uncertainty, stateless terrorism, and cost-plus contracting. Its budget for 2005 was $119 billion, part of a $417.5 billion defense appropriation—roughly 12 times the budget of the other two major ocean agencies, the Coast Guard and NOAA, combined. Even so, the Navy, like almost all bureaucracies, continues to insist that it needs more money to carry out its mission. And no vessel in its fleet is more symbolic of the Navy's ability to project power at all costs than the aircraft carrier.

I'm sitting inside a noisy narrow fuselage facing backward, feet up and arms crossed over restraining gear and a life vest. Two crewmen in insect goggles and helmets wave their hands frantically to signal the time has come. There's a sudden yank and I'm watching my peripheral vision shrink as I feel the pull of three Gs, like getting sucked over the falls backward on some 40-foot monster wave. Time slows down during the two seconds in which the steam catapult accelerates us from zero to 150 miles per hour before tossing us off the lip of the USS *John C. Stennis*. But unlike an F-18 Hornet, which would goose its afterburners and streak near vertical toward the heavens, streaming white contrails off its wingtips, our two-prop COD (Carrier Onboard Delivery) aircraft seems to drift like a freed balloon, banking gently to port.

The last few days have been a fun and deafening experience, getting to see how a million dollars a day of our tax money is spent maintaining the smooth functioning of the $3.1 billion CVN-74—one of America's 12 aircraft carriers, which, along with their $20 billion battle groups, ensure America's ability to project power anywhere in the world. The *Stennis* is named after a Mississippi senator who, as head of the Armed Services Committee, never saw a Navy budget he didn't like, even as his state consistently rated forty-ninth in the quality of its children's education.

I arrived on the *Stennis*, some 50 miles off the coast of Southern California, in a mixed group made up of members of the Young Presidents Organization—top corporate types under the age of 50—and four guys from the Tailhook Association, the naval aviators group that gained infamy following its sexually predatory 1991 convention in Las

Vegas. Fittingly, one of the outcomes of the Tailhook scandal was the Navy's accelerated program to qualify female combat pilots: women like Beth Creighton, a red-haired, self-confident flyer in a patch-covered jumpsuit I meet in the officer's mess. Flying the F-18 Superhornet FA 122, she has run a number of combat patrols over Iraq. Most of the pilots on the *Stennis* this week are not veteran flyers, however, but trainees doing their first at-sea landings and takeoffs or CQs (carrier qualifications).

The *Stennis* weighs 95,000 tons (about 20,000 tons shy of a super-tanker full of oil), has a 4.5-acre flight deck, and can carry a crew of 5,100. It is more than 24 stories tall from the top of its mast to the bottom of its hull, including 18 decks of ladders. It is also about the length of the Empire State Building if you laid that building on its side, with the power to blow up the Chrysler Building, Rockefeller Center, and the United Nations.

Even more incredible, from my point of view, is the fact that every year the weighty equivalent of 900 of these ships is taken out of the world's oceans by commercial fishing fleets. "And yet fishermen are still losing their jobs," the captain comments when I mention this to him. Captain Richard K. Gallagher is a lanky, narrow-faced man in his forties, with a clipped mustache, receding brown hair, and a forthright manner that leaves little room for irony.

We're standing that evening on the darkened bridge of the *Stennis*, silhouetted in the red glow of night operations lighting, watching the double white disks of F-18 afterburners flare periodically as Hornets are catapulted off the deck below us, their onboard fly-by-wire computers controlling the initial seconds of flight. A former commander at the Top Gun school at Miramar Naval Air Station, Gallagher (flight name "Weasel") also commanded the antimine warfare ship USS *Inchon* in the Adriatic during the war in Yugoslavia.

The *Inchon* is an example of the Navy's stepped-up focus on nearshore operations. A converted helicopter assault ship, it carries ten large mine-hunting CH-53 helicopters, two Seahawk spotter-rescue choppers, and four explosive ordnance dive teams, each made up of 32 divers with fast RIBs (rigid inflatable boats) and mobile (flyaway) decompression dive lockers. It also carries ROVs and occasionally works with the Navy's marine mammals. (In the near future the Navy may forward-deploy its dolphins and sea lions on ships like this.)

"Each CH-53 helo could lift 30 to 40 tons," Gallagher tells me. "So we flew food from Tirana Airport in Albania, moved food into refugee areas. Remember, we feared hundreds of thousands of people might starve to death. It was a war tactic of Milosevic to drive these people across the border, and there was lots of worry about people starving and a big concern to get refugee camps going before winter."

"Which is now all part of littoral warfare?" I ask.

"Well, we've been operating in the [Persian] Gulf for some time," Gallagher replies by way of an answer. "I was ExO [executive officer] on the [aircraft carrier] USS *Eisenhower,* operating in the Red Sea when Iraq invaded Kuwait [before the Gulf War]. We've been training for years to operate in these more restricted waters. It hasn't taken us by surprise."

The Navy plans to fight more coastal engagements with a diverse fleet of specialized craft. These include Virginia-class shallow-water submarines equipped with cruise missiles and contingents of SEAL teams and AUVs (autonomous underwater vehicles). It will also have more 35-knot-plus Cyclone-class coastal patrol ships, missile-firing arsenal ships that bear a striking resemblance to giant Civil War ironclads; fast electric-drive destroyers; and new marine amphibious ships carrying tilt-rotor Osprey airplanes, air cushion landing craft, and well-armed and armored amphibious assault vehicles. And there will be a new generation of carriers for over-the-beach air support (the General Accounting Office does not believe that they need to be nuclear-powered but the Navy insists they should be). The fighting will be coordinated through real-time battlespace intelligence generated by sub-launched robot aircraft and satellite imaging in 3-D high-definition TV. This will allow all the ships and planes, in the words of the former chief of naval operations Admiral Jay Johnson, to "distribute firepower in new and exciting ways."

The only thing that will not change is people getting blown up and dying in wars, although sensors woven into the body armor and underwear of young men and women could tell medics where they have been hit and how quickly they're bleeding out. If more than 20 percent of the casualties of these future conflicts involve combatants rather than unarmed civilians, that too will mark a dramatic change from late twentieth-century warfare. So far, the invasion and occupation of Iraq suggests that this is not to be.

"There is a mindset change taking place," Captain Gallagher tells me. "Now we're not sure who's interesting, who's the next threat, where's the next hot spot, and how to prepare, because there are some good weapons systems proliferating out there."

"We sell a lot of them," I point out, going on to suggest that at least we have a monopoly on aircraft carriers.

"Well, the Russians have one, though I'm not sure if it's operational or could be made so. The French also have one that's supposed to come on line [the *Charles de Gaulle* became operational in 2001]."

"How about the British?" I offer helpfully. "We've fought them twice."

I'm not sure if it's something I said, but my stateroom that evening is changed to directly below the night-launch catapult. Unable to write or sleep to the *whoosh-bang* of jets landing, the roar of afterburners, or the steam scream and clanging subwaylike return of the cat cable, I decide to head up to the air control tower.

Housed in the superstructure, the highest enclosed space on the ship's island, this roost is the domain of air boss Mike Allen and miniboss Baron Asher. Close to a dozen of their people also crowd around. I look out to see an F-18 miss all four arresting wires, its tailhook scraping the deck and sending up a shower of sparks before the pilot uses his afterburners, pulsing like a pair of white-hot dragon tails, to drive the 25-ton plane back off the deck. "That's called a bolter," Baron explains to me. "Really chews up the deck. We have to continually resurface."

The next aircraft, an A-6 Prowler, makes a good landing, getting yanked to a stop by one of the arresting wires. The deck crew quickly pushes the plane to the black-water edge of the flight deck to turn it around, as its wings begin to fold upward. "We've got limited acreage to work with," Mike Allen explains. "The way the planes land is they watch a set of lights off the side of the carrier. The center light is called the meatball. It gives the pilot a target, a 13-by-13-foot box from his eye to the deck. If he goes in too low, he hits the fantail; too high, he misses the wire; too far right or left, he hits other aircraft. In five days of these CQs we'll do 700 of these landings."

"How many launches?" I ask, scribbling furiously in my notebook.

"We try to make our launches and landings even." He grins hugely.

Mike is big, jut-jawed, and clean-shaven, with a rough dinosaur look about him, a 20-year career man. Baron is shorter and slighter, with a light beard, glasses, and 18 years in the service. They can handle as many as 47 aircraft and 200 crew moving on the deck at any time. Tonight 15 planes are launched and recovered.

"Attitude," crackles the radio. It's a signal officer talking to an SA-3 pilot, who adjusts his wings and makes a rough landing. His landing space is 800 feet long.

An SA-3 bolts it. An EA-6 Prowler bolts it. An F-18 Hornet is shot off the catapult, afterburners flaring.

"How much fuel do planes like that burn?" I wonder.

"An F-14 Tomcat can burn 300 gallons a minute with its afterburner. It can burn its fuel in eight minutes or two hours, pilot's choice," Mike says. "When our air wing's operational, we burn 200,000 gallons a day. We have about 20 million pounds of jet fuel on board."

Another jet rockets off the deck.

"What are the worst sea conditions you'll launch in?" I ask.

"We'll fly with a 200-feet ceiling and half-mile visibility during operations," Mike replies. "We've launched with water coming over the catwalks of the deck [60 feet up]. We wait on the swell till the bow is through the trough, and shoot on the upswing. We've done it here and in the South China Sea on the backside of a typhoon."

The next afternoon I'm back in the tower. It's jammed with reps from Shamrock Squadron 41 out of San Diego's North Island Air Station, trying to get Mike to qualify their people. "Name is Breckenridge, sir. He needs two more traps at a minimum." "Three-thirty-six bolted, boss."

Planes are coming in every 45 seconds now. "Check it out," Baron says, glassing the horizon with his binoculars. All I can see is one of two Seahawk search-and-rescue helicopters waiting on station, and then I spot the vapor blows and curving backs of gray whales. At 20 knots we quickly pass the pod. "We were seeing a lot of whales earlier this summer," he tells me. Later I ask Lieutenant Nick Fiore, one of the chopper pilots, if he enjoys spotting marine life. "Well, you're circling out there for hours," he says. "If you see whales or dolphins, that's fun for like fifteen minutes. Then you want to take a gun to your head. You're always circling."

I'm back in the tower that evening. I figure this is where the action is. Mike and Baron haven't left, of course. Number 242 is coming in for a landing. Baron explains the psychology of a night landing. "Once you get past the idea that you're hurling yourself at the water at 500 feet a second, it's not so hard to land."

Mike is staring at the approaching plane: "Hummm, humm, humm." Baron laughs. "Boss is sending out good vibes." Number 242 makes the trap and is quickly shoved aside by the deck crew. .

As 227, an F-18 Hornet, is launched, one of its engines blows out with a bang—then, a second and a half later, relights. There's silence in the tower, followed by a noticeable break in the tension. "It's an air burp from hesitation in the fuel-air mix, maybe a feedback from the catapult steam," Baron explains. "It's hard to distinguish it from an engine failure is why the concern."

Even with the obvious professionalism of carrier ops, this is still a high-risk enterprise. Since its first deployment in 1998, the *Stennis* has lost an S-3 pilot and navigator, killed when their plane dropped off the bow, and has had two deck crew mutilated, one losing part of a leg, the other an arm that was surgically reattached, after a blast deflector crashed down on them.

The next plane coming in drags and sparks its tailhook before bolting back off the deck. "725 bolter," says a young sailor with a clipboard.

"A new voice heard in the tower." Baron smiles at the sailor, who beams back as though his dad just brought him a new baseball glove.

"336, 727, 362, touch and go, 53, touch and go," Mike instructs. They're taking them around a racecourse pattern, giving them a new play.

They wave off a plane coming in too low that had bolted a couple of times during the afternoon. "Mr. Breckenridge storms onto the night stage," Baron notes wryly.

You can't help but like guys like this, the air boss and miniboss working well together with a kind of casual discipline, controlling both ends of the deck simultaneously, fully confident of each other's calls, moving a deafening carousel of prancing, bolting, jolting high-performance jets like so many high-strung Lipizzan horses going through their paces.

Back down below deck I find two pilots talking in the passageway outside my stateroom, too pumped to sleep. Dave Bigg and Bryant Medeiros are both 29. Bigg made his first carrier landing on his first try, then bolted twice tonight. "You come down at 150 miles per hour and see a little carrier box in a big black ocean, and you're looking into a geometric cone [he creates one with his hands], and you hook it to your eye, and by the time your eye is over the ramp it's a three-foot cone, and every foot your eye is off puts you 15 feet further down the deck."

"I did a touch and go, two bolters, and a trip," Medeiros, an S-3 pilot, volunteers. "I bounced over the four wires on the touch and go. That scared me." Bigg tells him of an acquaintance of theirs whose wing blew up on a recent landing with the landing gear shooting through it. "But he climbed out okay and may get to fly again after the incident investigation."

"Night landings are not fun. It's the hardest thing you can do," Medeiros says.

"But you did it."

"Honestly, you forget the carrier is there," Bigg jumps in. "You're concentrating so hard. You're looking at the stupid ball [center light] and the white line [flight deck center line] between your legs. That's it." He shakes his head. Medeiros grins. I retire, leaving them to talk out their adrenaline jag.

The next morning I go up on the deck with a new group of VIPs— Republican congressional aides from Washington. We move single file behind our guide. Even with our Mickey Mouse–style ear protectors, the place is roaring, with A-6s, SA-3s, and Hornets slamming the deck and all sorts of catapult steam, loud noise, and unburned fuel odors hitting us with the rush of jet exhaust, and young sailors directing planes and giving each other high fives. The average age on deck is 19, and the kids seem to love their jobs: young guys with goofy short haircuts, and pretty girls draped in tie-down chains and greasy camo pants. In between the launches and traps we are moved back to the arresting wires, ducking under a jet's tail on the way. An F-18 turns and we're all waved into a crouch as its powerful exhaust whips over us. Seeing a half-dozen congressional aides forced to their knees makes the whole trip seem worthwhile.

Although not allowed to see the nuclear reactors, encryption room, or weapons magazine (which we're told is "inconvenient"), we still get a pretty good Cook's tour: visiting the Combat Direction Center, air ops room, pilots' ready room, the hangar deck (where a step aerobics class is under way), overcrowded crews quarters, jet engine shop, cryogenics plant, and rudder stems (the rudders are 60 tons each). I ask to visit METOC, the meteorological and oceanographic office, where I talk with the senior chief, Glen Picklesimer, about tactical exploitation of the environment.

Despite the Navy's major impact on civilian oceanography, Picklesimer's specialty—determining weather and ocean conditions for ship operations—has not attracted many recruits. His top boss's job, oceanographer of the Navy, has historically been an undervalued command. Until recently the position was seen as a dead-end job for two-star admirals not expected to make their third star.

But the tougher new requirements of coastal warfare have begun to turn things around. "It's a lot more challenging getting into the littoral," Picklesimer explains. "We used to chase subs in blue water with 10- to 15,000-feet depths. Now we get up near shore, and it's like being in mountain ranges with biologics [animals], waves, bottom sound, ice, all these interesting noises. All our oceanographic ships are spending their time doing surveys in the littoral these days."

At lunch the assistant propulsion engineer tells me of pumping radioactive waste water into the sea. "But at no more than background levels, no different than this," he assures me, holding up a glass of water with a lemon wedge and ice.

This reminds me that I want to talk to the ship's environmental officer. Lieutenant Commander Paul Kratochwill, who takes care of all nonnuclear engineering equipment, is as close as the ship has to an environmental specialist.

"When I joined [in 1985] we threw anything and everything over the side 12 miles out," he tells me. "Then in January 1997 you had the international convention on dumping go into effect [which bans the dumping of plastic at sea]. All our food products come in plastic. We serve 18,000 meals a day. So what we do now is rinse and wash the plastic and use these 400-degree ovens to make plastic pucks." He takes me to see the ovens and piles of giant pizza-sized pucks. "We produce around 150 pounds a day," he tells me.

"We had a ship that dumped some medical waste overboard a few years ago, and that had bad publicity value for the Navy, so things have begun to change. With paper, we mulch it and turn it into a slurry that goes over the side. Cardboard is burned in this incinerator." He shows me the sealed room next door where a sailor is using a heavy metal rod to load the blazing incinerator. "Join the Navy and see the world?" I ask. "It's not a nice job," Kratochwill agrees. "That's why we only make them do it three months at a time.

"Burlap bags of glass and metal are dumped over the side," he continues. "Thousands of arresting wires [greasy inch-and-a-half-thick cables] litter all the sea bottoms. We get rid of them after a hundred recoveries [of aircraft]. Oily wastes we dump out beyond 50 miles."

The sewage for the *Stennis*'s 5,000 people is mulched but not treated before being pumped over the side three miles or more offshore. "I'd say 30- to 40,000 gallons a day would be a low estimate." Kratochwill calculates the *Stennis*'s "black water" sewage production. Many cruise ships, by contrast, which are in almost constant operation and might carry 3,000 to 5,000 passengers and crew, are equipped with secondary sewage treatment facilities.

"Have you seen the sewage plants on those cruise ships? They're big and labor-intensive things," complained Rear Admiral Andrew Granuzzo when I interviewed him shortly before his retirement in 2000. Granuzzo oversaw the Navy's environmental and occupational safety programs from offices in Crystal City, Virginia. "We've tried sewage treatment plants," he said. "I got one on my amphibious ship [one that he used to command]. It went well, but they're highly technical and take a lot of care and feeding for our big ships. The tradeoff in size and weight kept us from going after them.

"We are investing in new incineration technology instead. We hope to have self-contained membrane technology to revolutionize waste disposal and think it can also work for bilge and oily water waste. It also appears to be applicable to black and gray [sewage and shower] water. So then we can incinerate it all. We're developing the environmentally sound ship for the twenty-first century. In the next 15 years we'll build ships with zero discharges," he claimed.

"We used to dump stuff without thinking, but times change," Lieutenant Commander Kratochwill muses, back on the *Stennis*. "When I was an ensign in 1986 I took a boat over to the Thirty-second Street Naval Station [in San Diego], and there was nasty dirty stuff in the water, oil and solids, and today you can see the bottom there, no garbage or oil at all."

Things may have improved, but because the Navy was exempt from most environmental laws during the Cold War and operated with little concern for the impacts of toxic paints, solvents, antifouling agents, munitions, or low-level radiation, the bottom sediments in military ports and shipyards are among the most toxic in America. A 1998 NOAA study of sediment toxicity in 22 harbors found San Diego to be the second most polluted after Newark, New Jersey, with major hot spots located in the sediments around North Island Naval Air Station and the Thirty-second Street Naval Station.

During the late 1990s, port dredging for the arrival of the *Stennis,* the first of three Nimitz-class nuclear carriers to be permanently stationed in San Diego, was halted when the sand being used to replenish an eroding beach in the north county town of Oceanside was found (by curious children) to contain unexploded munitions, including 20-millimeter shells and 50-caliber rounds.

The Navy's use of offshore islands for bombing and live-fire exercises has also generated controversy and prompted the Navy to begin changing its ways. Kahoolawe island in Hawaii was returned to the state and is now being cleared of ordnance. Vieques island, off Puerto Rico, became the focus of widespread protests following the accidental killing of an island resident by a Navy bomb in 1999. By 2004, the island had been returned to its residents and the surrounding waters surveyed by a company contracted by the commonwealth of Puerto Rico. The company, Underwater Ordnance Removal (UOR), found some areas where the reefs were dramatically rebounding and others where unexploded ordnance needed to be removed. Ex-Navy demolitions man Jim Barton, the founder and CEO of UOR, told me that he was hopeful of cooperation from the military in cleaning up the former bombing range.

I ask Lieutenant Commander Kratochwill about the *Stennis*'s airborne emissions from burning 200,000 gallons of jet fuel a day off the coast of Southern California. "No one ever asked me about that before," he admits. That is not surprising, as the Navy has never had to concern itself with emissions. In negotiating the Kyoto Treaty on greenhouse gases (later rejected by the Bush administration), the United States insisted that military bunker fuels and strategic (non-shore-based) forces be exempted from any reductions. The Navy is also exempt from the 1990 Oil Spill Prevention Act, the Marine Pollution Act, the Aquatic Nuisance Act, and Superfund legislation.

However, the Navy's internal handling of fuel and oil spills (as opposed to sewage) has won praise from the Coast Guard, NOAA, and other observers. Its strict reporting rules on discharges stand in marked contrast to Royal Caribbean and other foreign-flagged cruise ship operators who have faced multimillion-dollar fines for illegally dumping oil and hazardous chemicals in U.S. waters.

I go back on deck to watch the U.S. Navy ship *Pecos* extend its hoses across the blue swells and begin pumping 1.5 million gallons of jet fuel to the *Stennis*. From across the flight deck I can see the bridge of the 400-foot supply ship rising and falling with the ten-foot swells, which are hardly detectable from the surface of the giant carrier. Looking back over the stern, I watch our wake leaving a wide bright aquamarine trail in the ocean.

I walk over to talk to a young maintenance crew gathered around a plane, including avionics specialist Laurie Hale. She is proud of the EAB-6 radar-jamming planes she works on. "They can show a bunch of our planes on an enemy radar screen, even if there's really just one," she explains.

I wander over to where the *Pecos* has just disconnected its fuel lines.

"It's kind of sad," says John Barbour, a member of the Young Presidents group. Barbour is a thick-set Scotsman and owner of a toy company; with his camera gear and shooter's vest he looks more like a war photographer than many a war photographer I've known.

"What's sad?" I ask.

"The redundancy and the waste. It's impressive, but you think of the poverty and the shitty education kids get in this country, and this all seems too much."

Just then, as the *Pecos* drops back, the *Stennis*'s sound system starts playing U-2. "I have run, I have crawled, I have scaled these city walls, only to be with you." With the oiler slipping behind in the steely blue sea, it's a strangely moving moment. "But I still haven't found what I'm looking for. But I still haven't found what I'm looking for."

If what the Navy's looking for is a good fight, I have no doubt of its ability to inflict murderous punishment on the United States' declared enemies and to do so more effectively than any seaborne military force in history. If, however, it's looking to be an environmentally responsible member of the ocean planet on which it operates, it still has a long way to go.

The ocean rolls; the smell of jet fuel briefly lingers in the air. Those hydrocarbons are the combustible sinews of industrial civilization. Modern war and the power to make it depend more than anything else on that single product—a product that, like the U.S. Navy itself, continues to transform what is happening on, above, and below America's blue frontier.

CHAPTER 5

Oil and Water

It was pioneering . . . and also our people were pioneers. I felt
we were in on the early stages of a marvelous business.

> — *Former president George H. W. Bush*
> *on offshore oil drilling in the 1950s*

Well, the oil revenues are—they're bigger than we thought
they would be at this point in time. I mean, one year after
the liberation of Iraq, the revenues of the oil stream is pretty
damn significant.

> — *President George W. Bush*
> *at a press conference, April 13, 2004*

I'm staring into the 400,000-gallon main tank at the New Orleans
Aquarium. It's swarming with tarpon, redfish, snapper, stingrays, alligator gar, sea turtles, sawfish, nurse sharks, black drum, and horse-eye
jacks, all swimming through the metal legs of a recreated offshore oil
platform. The sign off to the side reads, "Gulf of Mexico sponsored by
Amoco, Shell, Exxon, WMP, Chevron, Kerr-McGee and Tenneco."

Flying out of Venice, Louisiana, the next morning, I'm not sure if that
sign referred to the exhibit or the real thing. From our Bell 412 four-rotor
helicopter, a kind of buffed-up version of a Huey, we pass over shredding
islands of brown spartina, or salt grass, cross-hatched with canals and
studded with oil tank transfer stations. A flock of large white egrets flies
over the water beneath us, like stately extras from some *National
Geographic* documentary.

We pass over the southwest channel of the Mississippi and a breaking
surfline the color of chocolate mousse. As we fly beyond our first cluster
of platforms the water turns a strange jade green. Soon we're some 50
miles offshore in deep blue water. Looking out across the horizon you
realize there's no point at which you can't see oil platforms. There are
some 4,000 platforms operating in the Gulf of Mexico today. Offshore

drilling accounts for more than 30 percent of U.S. domestic oil and more than 25 percent of its natural gas production. Despite heated debate over drilling off California, Florida, Alaska, and North Carolina, 93 percent of offshore production continues to take place here in the Gulf. In the early 1990s some reports said that the Gulf might be a "Dead Sea," tapped out after 50 years of exploitation, but that was before deep-water drilling technology took off. Today more than 65 percent of oil extracted from the Gulf comes from wells drilled in depths of 1,000 feet or greater.

Soon we're circling a flat-topped platform called Pompano. Owned by BP-Amoco, it is the second-tallest bottom-fixed structure in the world, drilling into the ocean floor 1,310 feet below the surface. About 700 feet wide at its base, it is taller than the Empire State Building (or the aircraft carrier *John C. Stennis* standing on its tail). Drilling is moving much deeper, though, with newer tension leg platforms (TLCs), giant water-filled spars to aid stability, semisubmersible platforms like the five-billion-dollar stadium-sized Thunder Horse platform (which was knocked off-kilter by Hurricane Dennis in June 2005), and proposals to bring into the Gulf double-hulled production ships moored to seafloor wells 10,000 feet down. In 1998 the old CIA spy ship *Glomar Explorer,* leased from the Navy by Global Marine and converted to a drilling ship, sank a well in 7,718 feet of water. In November 2003 the drillship *Discoverer Deep Seas* set a new record when it sank an exploration well in 10,011 feet of water—and drilling is rapidly moving toward the two-mile-deep mark. As the rush into ultradeep water continues, most predict that deep-water drilling will produce more than 25 billion barrels of Gulf oil in the next fifteen years—about as much as the total taken out since the industry went offshore back in 1947.

We land on Pompano's helideck 12 stories above the water. Even with the copter's rotors stopped, the sea winds continue to whip against us at 30 knots. We climb down two levels past some rigid enclosed lifeboats to the living quarters, walking on cookie-cutter grating that lets you see all the way down to the swells breaking against the platform's legs. Entering the crew structure, we pass a three-button panel marked "Abandon Platform/Fire/General Quarters." The TV room–galley, with its cafeteria-style service, metal tables, bug juice dispenser, video player, and thick couches grouped around the oversized TV, reminds me of a number of workboats I've been on, minus the sense of movement.

"It's just like an aircraft carrier in that the platform has to be completely self-sufficient," Hugh Depland, BP's public relations guy, tells me. He then goes off with a three-man video crew that is shooting a company-sponsored spot for the Chicago Museum of Science and Industry. Oddly, all three of them are named Mark.

So is one of the two helicopter pilots who flew us out. Mark Stearns is a short, bright-eyed oil-patch veteran with a snow-white mustache and 16 years of experience in the Gulf. Cathal Oakes, his lanky, younger Irish colleague, is studying for his final pilot's exam. They both live in California and work in the Gulf, 14 days on and 14 days off. Most rig crews work seven and seven.

"There are probably 150 to 200 aircraft in the air at any one time out here, moving people on and off the platforms," Mark tells me. "And the DEA [Drug Enforcement Administration] watch us all, track us by transponder. If you go south of a certain point in the Gulf or if your tracker is turned off for any reason, your company gets a call right away."

When not flying for ERA, one of the petroleum helicopter services, Mark does water bucket drops for the U.S. Forest Service. He fought the big Florida fires of 1997–1998, caused by the El Niño drought. "Watching rainforest burn is pretty amazing," he says. "Those palmettos really burned hot."

I ask him if helicopters are less safe than airplanes, as I have always believed, and he reassures me that, hour per air hour, what they do is as safe as flying a commercial jet. This despite the fact that I was advised not to wear my steel-toed boots on the flight out (they weigh you down in the water), and just about everyone out here seems to have a crash story.

Preston Smith and Shelby Williams were both on a Bell 407 that crashed on September 18, 1997. "All five of us survived," Preston tells me. He is a thickset white man, probably in his late fifties, bald, with silver glasses, a flushed face, and a nervous hand tremor. "We'd just left 826 platform when we hit the water. . . . We all got hurt. I had bruising in the chest around my heart and my back was hurt, my knees, and I still have numbness in my lower back. It's also caused me some mood swings and stuff I'm still not over. I'm on light duty out here."

Was he willing to ride copters after that? "No, but this is the only kind of work I know how to do, so I have to support my family. I just have to face forward and sit by the door is the only way I can ride them now."

"We were ten minutes into the flight and just heard a loud bang. The tail rotor had broken off and sliced into the boom," recalls Shelby Williams, a handsome, broad-cheeked, brown-eyed African American in his thirties, with closely cropped hair under a Bud Lite bill cap. "We angled over steeply, breaking left at 140 miles per hour, and then started looping down. We went in nose forward and hit the water at about a 75-degree angle. But the pilot hung on to that joystick even seeing this wall of water coming at him. He was really good.

"No one ever yelled as we went down, we just followed our training, which says don't panic," he continues. "When we hit, the blades were still turning. There was a big buzzing from where the radio went out and then we went under the water, and the pilot deployed the floats and we popped up again. We threw the life raft into the water, pulled it back by this long lanyard, and stepped into it and just floated away. About 15 or 20 minutes later a copter spotted us, then two more came, and later there was a workboat. It took us to the platform and then another chopper took us to Jefferson Medical Hospital. I'd been flying backward and took the crash force from behind. My ligaments took the impact. It felt like someone was shoving needles into my back." Having since made his peace with helicopter flight, Shelby goes on to tell me how the next few years "are really going to be happening here in the Gulf," thanks to the industry's new deep-water discoveries.

Normally operated by a crew of 12, Pompano is crowded this month with 22 extra men reconfiguring the platform for the return visit of a drilling rig. After five years of operation, its production has declined from around 68,000 barrels of oil a day to about 46,000 barrels (and 63 million cubic feet of gas). Not bad, at more than a million dollars' worth of product every 24 hours, but it can do better, and will. Using 3-D seismic imaging and computer-controlled sensors, the oil companies are now able to find oil- and gas-laden sands that they used to miss. For older platforms such as Pompano, they use what they call 4-D seismic studies, incorporating past production patterns into computer analysis of where additional hydrocarbons might be found.

Down in the highly automated multicontrol center (MCC) I meet George Yount, the operations supervisor. He's wearing a tan Carhartt work coat and a BP hard hat and looks like a beachmaster elephant seal, thick-throated, well-padded, but strong, with a scraggly mustache and a three-day growth of beard. He's been 25 years in the industry, starting as a rig deck roustabout. Also working here is Wendy Lemoine, a thin, blonde assistant engineer. While the oil patch has been racially integrated for some time, it is well behind the Navy when it comes to women. Wendy is the only female among some 80 men on the two platforms I visit, a not untypical ratio. A chemical engineer on temporary duty, Lemoine says that while she doesn't mind the work, she's definitely looking forward to getting back to her base in Houston.

After making sure that I have a hard hat and earplugs, George takes me down to the well bay to see the Christmas trees (well pipes). On the way I look over the side and spot about 200 good-sized fish schooling around one of the yellow platform legs. A little farther out the torpedo-shaped bodies and yellow tails of a pair of dolphin fish (mahimahi) streak by. Later in the day we spot a big manta ray cruising the area, its nine-foot wingtips clearing the surface of the water like sails. Although platforms have not been shown to increase fish productivity, they do tend to concentrate fish, as does any structure in the ocean. The growing surfaces they provide for algae, corals, and barnacles attract small fish, which attract larger fish, which in turn attract recreational fishermen, who have become major advocates for the rigs.

Back in the 1980s some oil platform crews would reel in large amounts of redfish, snapper, and other commercially valuable species, loading hundreds of pounds of fillets into big ice chests and taking them back on crew boats to shore, where they'd sell them illegally to commercial fish houses. But a crackdown by the feds and the companies (after complaints from commercial fishermen) put an end to the practice.

The Christmas trees on Pompano are 23 vertical well pipes (plus two water reinjection pipes) married to small chokes and connectors so the oil can be separated through heater-treater processors and the gas dewatered before being pumped into big 12-inch pipes running to "the beach." George turns on a small caffe latte–type spigot to show me the raw crude, a light-colored mix of oil, water, and gas that he lets run over his fingers. BP, which used to dump its processed water over the side, now reinjects it into the wells to keep the head pressure up. In the 24 hours before I arrived, Pompano produced 46,641 barrels of oil, 63,887,000 cubic feet of gas, and 15,692 barrels of sub-seabed water.

Along with wells drilled from the platform, Pompano has a tieback pipeline to eight subsea oil wells in 1,850 feet of water four and a half miles away, which were drilled and installed by ship. A new platform under construction will have a 30-mile subsea tieback. Having showed me the drill deck (living quarters) and production deck, which also houses the electric generators (the platform operates on 3.2 megawatts of power), George takes me down to the subcellar, where the fire pumps, hydraulics, and utility equipment are located. There I get to check out the large gray pipes that drop to the seabed before running the oil and gas ashore. The bottom of the Gulf is spider-webbed with tens of thousands of miles of pipes like these, along with underwater well heads and production complexes.

"A platform like Pompano costs around $350 million to build and operate," Hugh Depland tells me. On the horizon we can see Chevron's $750 million Genesis Spar (supported by water ballast and mooring lines), operating in 2,600 feet of water. Mark Moore, the video cameraman, tells me how while he was shooting an industrial video about the construction of Texaco's half-billion-dollar Petronius platform, its derrick barge accidentally dropped the crew quarters, worth $70 million, which quickly sank out of sight.

That evening we eat a tasty dinner of jambalaya, crawfish étouffée, cornbread, french fries, and ice cream. Rig dining may not be heart healthy, but at least none of the guys out here appear to be undernourished. I ask George about accidents on the rig, and he embarrasses one of the kitchen crew by recounting how the fellow injured himself zipping up his pants, and how the catering company required George to write up an accident report. Not done having fun, George turns to Hugh and says, "In the book he's working on," pointing at me, "he's writing about the Navy. So I told him how he can make the connection to this place. Write about the Navy, then the Coast Guard, then oil spills, then us." Hugh the PR man smiles wanly.

We go to sleep in double-stacked steel shipping containers converted to crew quarters (bunks, plumbing, and a washer-dryer). The next day we take the 15-mile helio-hop from Pompano over to Amberjack. I learn that rigs are named after their lease sales, which, for security reasons, are given theme-based designations by the oil companies' secretive exploration departments. That way if some drunk is overheard in a Houston bar mentioning how many millions his company bid on Bullwinkle or Nirvana, it won't mean anything to the eavesdropper. Lease sale themes have included rock bands, country-western singers, types of cows, booze, game fish, and cartoon characters. To date, none have been named after famous woman authors or environmental heroes.

Amberjack is the ultimate Tinkertoy. An active drilling rig, it towers 272 feet from the waterline to the top of its bottle-shaped derrick. Its density of utilized space is a structural salute to human ingenuity. The rig contains a four-story metal crew building, helipad, flare-off tower, tanks, processors, compressors, a drill deck with 8,300 feet of piping stacked 12 feet high, 1,000 barrels of drilling mud, mud shakers, cement, two big yellow cranes, an office shack, lifeboats, and hundreds of flow-pipes, tubes, racks, gears, lines, and computerized systems hanging out over either end of its legs on wide, thick steel shelves. You know that whoever designed this thing does not waste closet space at home. Still, from the air, Amberjack looks small and somewhat fragile set against the vast, white-capped expanse of the Gulf's deep blue waters.

The winds are howling close to 40 knots today, the swells are about 12 feet, and with an extra half-million pounds of drilling gear on board, you can feel some sea movement on this platform. Once inside we are given a safety lecture and told to remove rings and Velcro watchbands to avoid "degloving injuries," where the skin and muscle can be ripped off your hands. We're introduced to Cary ("Call me Bubba") Kerlin, the red-faced, spherically shaped "company man."

"Might look a little dirty," he warns us. "We've been getting a lot of gumbo mud while we've been drilling." Gumbo is a heavy, clay-thick, gray black mud that is hard to wash off.

As a drilling supervisor, or company man, Bubba has been around the oil patch, having worked Colombia, California, and Alaska, as well as in the Gulf. Before that he spent 12 years with the U.S. Fish and Wildlife Service doing environmental assessments on oil company dredging canals, "till they made me an offer to get out of government and into industry, and I became oil trash," he grins.

Under the company man is the tool pusher, or rig manager. Then there's the driller, who controls the drilling console; the skilled rough-necks who work for him; and the less-skilled roustabouts, or general assignment workers. There's also the mud man, or fluids engineer, who runs the lubricating muds (polymers, clays, dirt, and additives) that cir-culate down the pipe string. Several stories above them all stands the der-rick man on his monkey board, a small catwalk from which he handles the high end of 42-foot sections of pipe. As the pipe tilts up toward him, he leans out almost horizontal in his harness to grab the top of the pipe and align it with the heavy rubber fill-up tool that adds drilling mud to the pipe string.

Bubba takes me up to the drill deck. It's a noisy, thrilling scene; a cho-reographed dance of steel pipe, muscle, and machine. The cranes lift the pipe to the roughnecks and roustabouts in their hard hats and steel-toed boots, who manhandle it into position below the derrick with its massive yellow top drive and block. I stand near the console on the water-slick deck watching the crew work the hydraulic tongs around the pipe stem and thread it into the hole with a creaky slow rotation before the top drive begins its work. At this point, they're down to 8,387 feet. With more than 36 other wells down there, it's a directional driller's night-mare. This hole is being drilled at a 45-degree angle, although they are capable of slant drilling like a boomerang, going down and then up again. One of the crew has a T-shirt that reads, "New Rig, New People, New Records."

Another 42-foot section of pipe is chain-winched onto the derrick floor like a skidder-pulled log coming up a clear-cut hillside. I move forward and begin taking pictures of the red-helmeted derrick man as he leans out from his monkey board like a trapeze artist to grab the $13\frac{3}{8}$-inch pipe top and begins shifting it around to line it up with the rubber mud hose dropping down on him from above. I'm carefully lining up my shot when one of the roughnecks sneaks up behind me and slaps my ribs, letting out an animal howl.

I turn around quizzically. He's grinning happily. "I can't believe you did that," another guy semishouts to be heard. I didn't jump at the prank because I knew there were no howling predator animals lurking on this rig—other than these guys, of course. On the way back to the helicopter I spot the crane operator on a break, standing on the catwalk outside his cab, licking an ice cream cone and staring off into the blue frontier.

For more than a half century the leasing of offshore oil and gas has been one of the linchpins of U.S. oceans policy. In 1896, less than 40 years after the first rock oil derrick was drilled in Titusville, Pennsylvania, the first offshore drilling piers were built out from the newly established spiritualist center of Summerland, California.

Soon the more secular oil men were at war with each other, hiring armed thugs, sabotaging each other's piers, and racing to suck up as much oil as possible before the wells lost pressure and had to be abandoned. Abandoned wells and badly managed gushers soon led to widespread oil pollution and fouled beaches. "The whole face of the townsite is aslime with oil leakages," reported the *San Jose Mercury News* in 1901. The resort town of Santa Barbara, just up the coast, quickly moved to ban oil piers, fearing their impact on tourism and beach life. By the 1920s the state of California had made several feeble attempts at regulating offshore drilling by charging a 5 percent royalty, but this legal structuring had the unintended effect of creating a rush of lease applications by oil companies tired of the wildcatting competition. As charges of corruption and evidence of pollution mounted, the state legislature was forced to take stronger action, placing a moratorium on all new offshore lease sales in January 1929. By then the Standard Oil Company had developed slant-drilling technology, which allowed it to tap into state-controlled "submerged lands" from its onshore rigs in Huntington Beach (a practice later ruled illegal).

Louisiana was going through a similar oil boom in its southern swamps, lakes, and marshes, but with its thin coastal population and lack of recreational opportunities along much of the flood-prone Mississippi Delta, there was little resistance to the blowouts, fires, and other pollution taking place there. In fact, many of the region's settlers had always made their living through economic exploitation of the swamp—from fishing and trapping to market hunting of ducks and logging of old-growth cypress, which resulted in the near extinction of the trees just around the time the oil companies arrived. (Today the small cypress trees that have grown back are being cut down and sold for garden mulch.)

"Oil provided an alternative," writes University of Southwestern Louisiana professor Robert Gramling, "and the shift from one exploitative use of the region to another seemed natural and unproblematic." In the 1930s Gulf Oil and other companies, having developed drill barges for use in the swamps, began dredging hundreds of miles of canals to access their claims. These canals and associated erosion and subsidence became major contributors to Louisiana's subsequent land loss.

South Louisiana has been losing around 35 square miles a year in recent decades, about a football field every 15 minutes, due to both flood-control levees and oil canals that speed Mississippi River sediment—which normally builds up the delta—out into the deep Gulf. Along with these hydrologic speedways, ground subsidence (partly due to drilling) and sea-level rise, from the burning of fossil fuels, also contribute to land loss.

Unfortunately, a joint state-federal plan to invest $14 billion to restore the delta, which could be both a wildlife-rich ecosystem and a powerful storm barrier, had gained little support by the time Hurricane Katrina devastated the region in 2005.

By the late 1930s it was becoming clear that individual onshore salt domes and other geological features associated with oil extended well offshore. But the oil companies were not free to pursue them out to sea. The world refused to recognize national claims to economic resources beyond the three-mile limit. But World War II changed all that. As early as 1943 President Roosevelt, agreeing with Secretary of the Interior Harold Ickes, wrote that the three-mile limit "should be superseded by a rule of common sense. For instance, the Gulf of Mexico is bounded on the south by Mexico and on the north by the United States. In parts of the Gulf, shallow water extends very many miles offshore. It seems to me that the Mexican government should be entitled to drill for oil in the southern half of the Gulf and we in the northern half of the Gulf. That would be far more sensible than allowing some European nation, for example, to come in there and drill."

By the end of the war, seeing no naval powers likely to challenge U.S. claims, Ickes wrote a proposal that asserted the United States' right to drill for oil on the submerged lands of the continental shelf—the shelf of land that surrounds the entire U.S. coastline, extending out to where the deep seafloor begins. The State Department strongly opposed this breaking of a legal precedent, which went back to the 1609 essay *Mare Liberum* by the Dutch lawyer Hugo Grotius that (with the backing of Queen Elizabeth and the British Navy) established the principle of open seas.

But Roosevelt's secretary of state, Edward Stettinius, had bigger fish to fry with the upcoming Yalta conference, which would determine how postwar Europe was to be divided. As a result, Ickes was able to get a less experienced State Department official to sign off on his plan. In March 1945 a gravely ill Roosevelt gave final approval to the Ickes plan. Following Roosevelt's death, the atomic bombings of Hiroshima and Nagasaki, and the unconditional surrender of Japan marking the end of World War II, President Harry Truman announced America's claim to its Outer Continental Shelf (OCS) oil on September 28, 1945. This became known as the Truman Proclamation.

The political power of big oil was already well known, from the breakup of the Standard Oil trust and the Teapot Dome scandal to what became the first scandal of the Truman administration, resulting in the resignation of Ickes in February 1946. Ickes resigned to protest Truman's nomination of former Democratic Party treasurer Edwin Pauley as undersecretary of the Navy. In that position Pauley would control U.S. naval oil reserves. But Pauley was known as a bagman for the oil companies, and during the war he allegedly told Ickes and Roosevelt that if the federal government did not challenge state claims to offshore oil (where the companies felt they would get a better deal), the oil companies would make major contributions to the Democratic Party. According to Ickes and other witnesses, Pauley continued to push this idea on the train returning from Roosevelt's funeral. With the press hot on his trail, Pauley withdrew his name from nomination.

By the end of World War II, the Texas and Oklahoma wildcatting oil-boom days were long gone. The postwar industry was consolidating its political and economic power, as graphically illustrated by the oil derricks pumping on the front lawn of the state capitol in Oklahoma City.

This left a small independent company founded by the former Oklahoma governor Robert S. Kerr and his friend Deane McGee with little chance of securing any top-grade land leases. So Kerr and McGee decided to gamble with some new technologies.

The end of the war had brought home experienced Navy men and surplus landing ships, or LSTs, to America's coastlines. In 1946 the Magnolia Petroleum Company (later part of Mobil and then Exxon-Mobil) used Navy veterans to begin a drilling operation in the Gulf five miles off Louisiana, on a platform made of wood and steel. Surplus Navy ships housed the crew on the leeward side of a nearby island, and shrimp boats transported them back and forth. Because it drilled a dry hole, history has tended to ignore Magnolia's breakthrough effort. Credit for starting the offshore industry usually goes to Kerr-McGee, which established a platform anchored by Navy surplus ships 12 miles south of Terrebonne Parish in the fall of 1947. Two and a half weeks after it began drilling in 16 to 18 feet of water, a roustabout called his boss on shore and told him that oil was collecting in the drilling mud. "Well, skim it off," his boss replied. "Skim it off. Hell. There's barrels of it," the oil worker declared, announcing one of the great frontier energy booms in American history.

Conflicts between coastal states and the federal government over who could claim royalties from this bonanza escalated in the courts and in the press until 1953, when Congress passed the Submerged Lands Act. This gave states control out to the three-mile limit and the federal government jurisdiction over all OCS submerged lands beyond.

With the rules firmly established, investors and speculators headed offshore, including one George Bush: the son of an Eastern senator, a veteran war pilot, and a future president. Bush was among what *Fortune* magazine called the "swarm of young Ivy Leaguers" who descended on the "isolated west Texas oil town" of Midland in the early postwar years, anxious to make new fortunes apart from those they were already in line to inherit. Bush and his partners formed Zapata Oil, after the Marlon Brando movie *Viva Zapata!* then playing in a Midland movie theater.

George Bush later recalled, "Hugh Liedtke and I got in the offshore drilling contracting business and worked out a deal with LeTourneau and built three-legged rigs back in the mid-fifties. And they went on to become prototypes for drilling equipment that sat on the bottom. Our timing was good. We suffered a couple of setbacks. The first rig bent a leg or did something, had to be hauled into Galveston to be reworked. And the third or fourth one, the third one, disappeared in a hurricane, just vanished. I went out. I've never felt my eyeballs actually ache. I was flying in a single-engine plane with Hoyt Taylor. We were looking for any sign of it. We'd taken the people off and it was gone. A six-million-dollar investment, that would be more like $76 million today. I loved the business. It was pioneering, the LeTourneau design, and also our people were pioneers. I felt we were in on the early stages of a marvelous business."

Offshore drilling would also prove to be a marvelous cash cow, generating more than a trillion dollars for the oil industry and more than $125 billion for the federal government during the second half of the twentieth century. Today, offshore oil and gas royalties and lease sales contribute around six billion dollars a year in state and federal revenues. About a third of that goes to Louisiana, Texas, Alabama, California, and Alaska. The remaining four billion dollars make up the U.S. Treasury's second largest source of revenue after taxes (in close competition with customs tariffs).

There was some local resistance to drilling in the Gulf, but it quickly gave way. *Thunder Bay,* a 1953 movie starring Jimmy Stewart as an oil exploration geologist confronting suspicious shrimpers in Louisiana's bayou country, reflects the dominant view at a time when progress and industry were thought to be synonymous. It ends with the happy sight of an oil gusher promising new wealth for the misbegotten Cajuns and a bright future for all. Today a gusher is seen as an ecological disaster, while the Cajun heritage and other regional identities are highly valued in our increasingly homogenized culture.

By the late 1950s a number of shrimpers, including Edison Chouest, had converted their vessels to oil industry crew boats and began building the largest offshore fleet in the world. The Edison Chouest Company is best known today for its specialty boats such as the Antarctic research vessel *Laurence M. Gould.*

The construction of an oil and gas infrastructure in the Gulf also had unprecedented physical and environmental impacts, with the appearance of fabrication yards, ship channels, roads, pipelines, and onshore production facilities, including 18 major oil refineries in Louisiana alone. Over the last generation, 136 polluting petrochemical complexes and six refineries located between New Orleans and Baton Rouge gave this 90-mile stretch of the Mississippi a grim but not inaccurate nickname, "Cancer Alley."

Another downside to America's marvelous new business became apparent on January 27, 1969, when a Union Oil platform off Santa Barbara, California, had a blowout. Less than a year earlier the Department of the Interior had sold drilling rights to 71 OCS tracts in the Santa Barbara Channel for $603 million. This was done over the objections of Santa Barbara residents, whose opposition to offshore oil traced back to the turn-of-the-century Summerland spills. By the time Union Oil started drilling from its Platform A in January 1969, it had gotten federal waivers permitting the company to reduce the length of its primary ocean floor drill-pipe casing to 15 feet and the secondary casing to 238 feet—instead of the 500 feet and 861 feet normally required for oil-spill prevention. On their fourth well the drillers hit a snag, and suddenly oil and gas exploded up the pipe string. In a choking spray the crew managed to cap the well, but then oil began leaking below the shortened casings and through surrounding geologic fault lines. Within days, some three million gallons had come ashore, turning 150 miles of beach to goo and ocean waves into a sludgy pulse.

"Get oil out!" became a local, and then a state and national, rallying cry. Pictures of dying oil-soaked birds and the ineffective spreading of hay and cat litter onto the sand to soak up the oil inspired the beginnings of what would become a national environmental movement targeting industrial air and water pollution. President Richard Nixon came to look at the beach under the silent gaze of thousands of angry residents. For months afterward few people ventured onto Santa Barbara's fouled strand, except for a few hard-core surfers willing to follow up a session in the waves with a stinging turpentine bath—the only way to remove sticky oil and tar balls from their skin, eyelids, and hair.

Santa Barbara was only the first of a string of disasters. On February 11, 1970, a Chevron rig in the Gulf of Mexico caught fire and began spilling oil. It burned for weeks before being blown out with explosives by famed oil fire fighter Paul "Red" Adair. The platform was found not to have been equipped with a storm choke, a device designed to cut off oil flow in an emergency. A subsequent investigation ordered by Secretary of the Interior Walter Hickel found that hundreds of rigs were operating without chokes. The feds indicted Chevron on 900 counts. The company was found guilty and fined one million dollars.

In 1979 the Mexican-owned and U.S.-operated Ixtoc platform in the Gulf of Mexico exploded, gushing 150 million gallons of oil in a fiery uncontrolled spill (several men died trying to control it) that lasted ten months and fouled the beaches of Texas, including the Los Padres National Seashore. Although some coastal communities were up in arms, the oil-dependent state government kept notably silent during the ongoing ecodisaster.

In 1982 Secretary of the Interior James Watt, less concerned about oil spills than charges of fiscal mismanagement, established the Mineral Management Service (MMS) to administer offshore oil leasing and collect royalties. Through most of the 1980s Watt and his successor, Don Hodel (now cochairman of the Christian Coalition), attempted to lease a billion acres of the OCS for new oil development, arguing that if Congress prevented them from moving forward with their plan they would, in Hodel's words, "be putting a sign on America that says we're willing to blindfold ourselves to our God-given resources and place ourselves at the tender mercies of OPEC."

Their attempts to lease huge expanses of the blue frontier, from fishery-rich waters off Alaska, New England, and North Carolina to the coral shallows of the Florida Keys and the chill waters off the scenic redwood and pine bluffs of Northern California, sparked massive protests. Public outrage led to annual congressional drilling moratoriums that ended up excluding 85 percent of the U.S. coast from new leasing. The oil industry objected to the moratoriums, arguing that without more offshore platforms and pipelines the United States would become increasingly dependent on oil tanker traffic, which posed even greater risks of disaster.

In his 1976 ode to Alaska, *Coming into the Country,* author John McPhee recalls meeting local people worried about the Trans-Alaska pipeline then being constructed to link the North Slope oil fields on Prudhoe Bay to the port of Valdez. "There is the real problem," he quotes one local, "not the possible spills on land but the spills that could happen in Prince William Sound."

It was a fear repeatedly expressed by fishermen out of Cordova and other fishing ports on the sound. As early as 1971 they filed a lawsuit seeking to block the pipeline and what they called the "inevitable major" oil spill that would result from a tanker accident in Prince William Sound. They lobbied for laws that would require the oil companies to establish baseline environmental studies of the sound and implement spill-prevention and response measures, including tanker escorts, double-hulled tankers, and cleanup contingency planning, but by the time the tankers started sailing in 1977, few of these precautions were in place.

Meanwhile, for years the oil industry had been making cutbacks in tanker crew size and training, constructing fleets of very large and ultralarge crude carriers (VLCCs and ULCCs), and resisting calls for double hulling. So it seemed a self-fulfilling prophecy when the *Exxon Valdez* spilled its oil in Prince William Sound in 1989 because Captain

Joseph Hazelwood, after drinking ashore, let an inexperienced crewman run his ship onto Bligh Reef.

More than 15 years later it's still hard to grasp the extent of the 11-million-gallon spill. Americans saw images of oil-soaked bald eagles, dead otters by the hundreds, a stunned and oil-blackened grizzly bear padding along a rocky shore. Moon-suited cleanup crews worked futilely to scrub or steam-soak 1,200 miles of oil-covered wilderness coastline or skim 3,000 square miles of water stained with toxic rainbow sheens. With the herring and salmon seasons ruined, fishermen and Native American communities faced futures of economic uncertainty and social dislocation. John Mitchell, a former editor at *National Geographic,* described returning to these same communities ten years later and finding people still unable to get beyond the trauma of it, "just not able to let it go." A 2003 study published in the journal *Science* found that the ecosystem was also unable to let go, that patches of persistent oil from the spill continued to lower the survival, reproduction, and growth rates of local fish and wildlife.

If a similar spill occurred on the West Coast of the lower 48 states it would stretch from Mendocino, California, 100 miles north of San Francisco, to the Mexican border. On the East Coast, it would spread from Cape Cod, Massachusetts, to below Cape Hatteras, North Carolina. So far this hasn't happened, yet every year less dramatic spills and discharges from many sources—offshore operations and coastal refineries, oily water illegally pumped from ship bilges, unburned gasoline from two-stroke outboards, motor oil dumped down storm drains, leaking fuel from underground storage tanks, roadbeds, and parking lots, along with other petrochemical runoff—put the equivalent of one and a half *Exxon Valdez* spills into America's coastal waters.

Just before I visited the BP platforms there was a "minor" spill of 47,000 gallons of oil from a Chevron pipeline near Grand Isle, Louisiana, which created a four-mile oil slick and fouled a small barrier island. On my first day offshore natural gas blew out at the Apache Well platform, resulting in two injuries and lots of damage to the drill deck. A month later 94,000 gallons of oil spilled when a drilling rig anchor was dragged across an underwater pipeline, creating a seven-mile slick 75 miles offshore. According to figures from the MMS, every year of the 1990s saw an average of 243,650 gallons of spilled oil fouling the Gulf's waters. As a result of 2005's Hurricane Katrina, more than nine million gallons of oil were spilled along the lower Mississippi and in the Gulf.

In the wake of the *Valdez* spill, Exxon agreed to pay a billion dollars into a state and federally administered oil-spill trust fund. Much of that money has gone to purchase or protect a half-million acres of wildlife habitat around Prince William Sound. In 1994 a federal jury in Anchorage awarded fishermen and affected communities an additional five billion dollars in punitive damages. More than a decade later Exxon is still appealing that ruling.

The year after the Prince William Sound spill, other major oil spills occurred in Arthur Kill off Staten Island, New York, and off Texas, New England, and Huntington Beach, California. Passage of the *Valdez*-inspired Oil Pollution Act of 1990 (OPA 90) had some salutary effects, however. Making shipowners responsible for damages and cleanup costs for oil spills and removing limits on their liability in cases of gross negligence and violation of safety rules seemed to get their attention. In 1991, tanker spills in U.S. waters dropped to their lowest level in 14 years. An industry-sponsored study documented improved safety inspections, awareness, and prevention procedures in the face of this tough new liability law.

The main provision of OPA 90 called for double hulling of all oil tankers operating in U.S. waters by 2015. But recently the oil industry began warning that 25 years may not be enough time to get ready, even though the average lifespan of an oil tanker is only 20 years. "People are not knocking down our doors placing orders [for double-hulled tankers]," says the American Shipbuilding Association president, Cynthia Brown. "There's no sense of urgency, and if they don't order soon, shipyards won't be able to deliver on time. I think this is an intentional strategy by the oil companies to delay. And then they'll all order at once. And when the yards can't deliver, they'll ask Congress for relief."

The oil industry was certainly relieved when in early 2000 the Supreme Court ruled in favor of the International Association of Independent Tanker Owners (INTERTANKO) in its suit against Washington state. INTERTANKO argued that states do not have the right to create safety standards tougher than those established under OPA 90. Under Washington state's "best achievable protection" regulations, vessel operators had to get approval for oil-spill prevention plans from state authorities as well as the Coast Guard. The court found that federal laws take precedence, even where those laws may not be sufficient to safeguard the environment.

A second suit was brought in the U.S. Court of Claims by Maritrans, Inc., a tank barge company, arguing that OPA 90, by shortening the economic life of its single-hulled oil barges, was an unconstitutional taking under the Fifth Amendment. The company demanded a billion dollars in compensation. The U.S. Court of Claims is a popular venue for "regulatory takings" claims by corporations that do not want to comply with maritime safety regulations, coastal developers who are prevented from building in hurricane zones, and mining companies denied permits to dig up salt marshes.

Part of the Fifth Amendment states, "No person shall be . . . deprived of life, liberty, or property, without due process of law; nor shall private property be taken for public use without just compensation." Today, when the government condemns land to build a highway or commercial port, the Fifth Amendment guarantees that the landowner be paid market value for lost property, but there is a body of law that helps define what constitutes a taking.

In 1887 the Kansas beer brewer Peter Mugler argued the first case for a regulatory taking, claiming that a prohibition law passed in his state was a taking under the Fifth Amendment because it devalued his property, putting him out of business. The Supreme Court ruled against him, stating that "a government can prevent a property owner from using his property to injure others without having to compensate the owner for the value of the forbidden use." This "nuisance clause" is the basis on which the government has been able to establish health and safety regulations, zoning, labor codes, and consumer and environmental standards.

More than a century of this precedent has tended to show that for every form of regulatory taking, there are far more government-initiated "givings" that benefit the public. The land-use plan (a taking) that prevents a corporate hog farm from dumping manure into an upstream river may be seen as a "giving" by coastal residents whose beachfront is saved from being smothered by a bacteria-rich, nutrient-fed algae bloom and fish kill. However, the oil industry's advocates for regulatory takings compensation are not looking to legal precedent to advance their positions, but to the political and judicial legacy of the Reagan administration.

In 1985 Richard A. Epstein, a professor at the University of Chicago Law School, wrote *Takings: Private Property and the Power of Eminent Domain,* in which he argued that the Fifth Amendment requires the government to pay property owners compensation whenever regulations or laws limit the value of their property. He went on to claim that along with environmental laws and building permits, income taxes are a form of taking. Epstein's eccentric interpretation of the Constitution found favor in the Reagan administration, particularly with Attorney General

Ed Meese and his advisors. The Reagan appointee Loren Smith, who was chief judge of the U.S Court of Claims and remains on the court, numbers Richard Epstein among his philosophical heroes. Other members of the court share Smith's views, which attracts takings plaintiffs to their chamber like hungry sharks to a dead whale.

Of course, it is still far easier for the oil industry to score extra billions from Congress than from the courts. Despite growing concern over fossil-fuel-fired climate change and U.S. dependence on Middle Eastern oil, Congress continues to provide more than $12 billion a year in federal subsidies to the oil industry. To keep this federal largess coming, the oil and gas industry is willing to prime the pump, spending more than $440 million in Washington, D.C., between 1998 and 2003. Of this, about $381 million was spent on lobbying and $67 million on political contributions, with 73 percent of that money going to Republicans. The three biggest individual recipients were President George W. Bush, House Energy Committee Chair Joe Barton (R.-Texas), and former House Majority Leader Tom DeLay (R.-Texas). Nor does it hurt the industry cause that the current president, his father, his vice-president, and his secretary of state are all oil-industry alumni.

For three years oil lobbyists were also able to delay passage of the American Oceans Act—the law that established the U.S. Commission on Ocean Policy to study the state of America's blue frontier and recommend changes. "The petroleum industry presence was definitely felt on the Oceans Act," says Jim Saxton, the Republican representative from New Jersey who was one of the bill's cosponsors. "We got the bill out but it never got through the Senate."

"So why would the oil industry oppose it?" I wonder.

"An industry doesn't like rules changed when they feel like they're getting what they want. They had their soldiers here in Congress doing their work. I'd ask them what they objected to in the bill, and they'd keep saying one thing and then another, and soon it became clear they were just out to scuttle the bill. They just like the way they're doing business now." (The Oceans Act was finally passed in July 2000, with the ocean commission reporting back to Congress four years later).

Other benefits the oil and gas industry won in the 2005 Energy Act include royalty holidays for deep-water drilling and for going after deep gas in shallow waters of the Gulf.

"The number of leases went up with the Royalty Relief Act," Hugh Depland tells me. Aside from his job with BP, Depland is also the public relations chair for the National Ocean Industries Association (NOIA), which represents offshore energy companies. "The technology was moving forward independently but this brought some new players into deep water, and certainly was of some assistance to us."

I understand. It certainly would be of some assistance to me if I could get Congress to pass a bill giving me a major tax break to encourage literary innovation and reduce America's dependence on foreign authors.

I wonder about the effects of future oil spills that inevitably will occur in deep water, just as they have following every past industry innovation, starting with those 1896 pier platform gushers in California. Little is known about conditions that exist in the depths of the Gulf below 8,000 feet. In 2000 a deep diving expedition using Woods Hole's submersible *Alvin* discovered powerful "abyssal storms" scouring the bottom at 1.5 knots (typical currents in deep water run only about one-tenth of a knot). Along with this never-before-witnessed phenomenon, the divers found unique plants and animals living near benthic gas seeps and deep-sea mats of marine bacteria. Recent research has found that the Gulf's deep waters also attract hundreds of endangered sperm whales, which concentrate in areas where seismic survey ships are using noise-generating airguns to hunt for new pockets of oil and gas. The MMS recently committed the underwhelming sum of $5,900 to a two-year study of how these loud underwater noises might affect the whales.

And no one knows much about what happens when oil and gas are released in the extremely cold, high-pressure environment of the deep sea. "It's a frontier area," admits Bob LaBelle, the chief of the Environmental Division of MMS. "Finding, tracking, and remediating [spilled oil] will be very challenging. Where it will surface, when it will come up, and what it will look like are all big questions."

Among the 51 rigs destroyed and more than 110 damaged by Hurricane Katrina was Shell's *Mars,* a $550 million deep-water platform that looked like it had lost a battle with Godzilla. On Dauphin Island, Alabama, where I visited a few weeks after Hurricane Katrina, I got to see the wrecked jack-up rig *Ocean Warwick,* which had been blown 65 miles before coming ashore. Of the more than nine million gallons of oil spilled in the Gulf and along the Mississippi, the Coast Guard knew of none from deep-water drilling sites.

An unplanned test of deep-water spillage occurred when the oil tanker *Prestige* broke up off the Spanish coast in November 2002. After spreading some 70,000 tons of fuel oil along the Galician shoreline, killing more than 300,000 seabirds and shutting down the tourism and fishing industries, its stern section sank with some 20,000 tons still onboard.

While some industry people predicted that the oil would solidify under the intense pressures of the deep, the *Prestige,* now 12,000 feet below the surface, continued to leak 120 tons a day before a French minisub was able to plug some of the holes in the wreck. In an innovative multiyear salvage effort, a Spanish company removed much of the remaining oil by drilling new holes, allowing the oil to drift up into 98-foot-tall double-lined plastic bags, which were then floated to the surface. This project cost about $120 million.

Whatever the risks, environmental concerns are unlikely to slow the latest offshore energy boom. Since James Watt created MMS in 1982, the agency has never canceled a lease sale based on an oil-spill risk assessment. "It's hard to make or break something as big as a lease on one issue," explains Bob LaBelle. Even if we were to take a more cautious approach, oil-spill impacts on America's and the world's marine ecosystems will continue so long as massive amounts of oil and salt water remain separated by mere inches of metal piping and tanker hull.

Growing numbers of climatologists, ecologists, and economists have begun to argue that it's time to begin a shift to cleaner energy technologies that, unlike carbon-rich fossil fuels, don't contribute to global warming. Interestingly, John Browne, BP's CEO, was the first leader of a major oil company to acknowledge that the science on climate change is sound. Looking to the future, BP has begun calling itself an energy company rather than an oil company, and runs ads saying that the company's name (an abbreviation of British Petroleum) now stands for "Beyond Petroleum."

"We see a shift to lower-carbon energy," Hugh Depland tells me. "The world is moving from coal to oil to natural gas and then to carbon-free hydrogen." Looking out at the rigs scattered across the Gulf, he acknowledges that this won't be an easy transition. As technologically challenging as the search for deep-sea oil and gas has been, the shift to new energy sources such as photovoltaics, wind turbines, biomass, hydrogen fuel-cells, and marine tidal, wave, and thermal energy will make today's oil-patch innovations pale by comparison.

For now, however, the Gulf's roughnecks and roustabouts continue to practice their dangerous and challenging craft with the same professional pride as America's nineteenth-century whalers, who, by extracting leviathans' living oil, lit and lubricated an earlier industrial age until they too passed into history.

CHAPTER 6

A Rising Tide

On that day all the fountains of the great deep burst forth,
and the windows of the heavens were opened.
            —Genesis 7:11

My greatest concern is that what we saw in the summer of '04
in Florida and the summer of '05 in Louisiana is no longer the
exception—it's the new rule.
            —Dr. George Crozier, Dauphin Island Sea Lab director
            and coastal policy expert

Clouds, snow, rock, and water as hard as black marble is all we can see approaching the end of our four-day, 900-mile journey from Punta Arenas, Chile. Up on the bridge of the *Laurence M. Gould*, Robert, the first mate, is playing Led Zeppelin and talking on the radio with Palmer Station. "Never been this far south without seein' ice," he says in a lilting Cajun accent.

"That's 'cause we cleared it for you," the base's radioman jokes. "Went out in our Zodiacs with blowtorches." We round Bonaparte Point, and there it is, set in a boulder field below a blue white glacier— Palmer Station, Antarctica.

Palmer, one of three U.S. Antarctic bases run by the National Science Foundation, is where I got to spend six weeks one austral summer (the northern winter of 1999). Palmer is located on Anvers Island, 38 miles of granite rock covered by ice up to 2,000 feet thick. Anvers is part of the Antarctic Peninsula, a 700-mile-long tail to the coldest, driest, highest continent on Earth—a landmass bigger than the United States and Mexico combined, containing 70 percent of the world's fresh water and 90 percent of its ice. The peninsula, where polar and marine climates converge, is also a wildlife-rich habitat that researchers refer to as "the banana belt." And that was before global warming.

While docking, we're greeted by a small welcoming committee of people, Adélie penguins, skuas, and elephant seals. Palmer Station has the look of a low-rent ski resort next to an outdoor equipment dealership. It is made up of a group of blue and white prefab metal buildings, with two big fuel tanks, front loaders, snowmobiles, and Milvans scattered around. The two main buildings, Biolab and GWR (garage, warehouse, and recreation), are separated so that if one burns down the other can act as a refuge for the 20 to 40 scientists and support personnel who work here year-round.

The short oblong pier on the inlet with its giant rubber fenders is where the *Gould*, our 240-foot supply and research vessel, docks every six to eight weeks during the summer. January and February's summer temperatures may drift between a balmy zero and 40 degrees Fahrenheit, with 23 hours of daylight to enjoy the views. The weather is variable, with sun, clouds, wind, rain, snow, and gale-force winds, often on the same day, kind of like the San Francisco Bay Area on steroids. Next to the pier is the boathouse and its string of black and gray Zodiacs: Mark 3s and Mark 5s. Fifteen to 20 feet in length, they provide the main means of transport at Palmer, along with thick Sorel boots and ice crampons. We'll get to operate these fast rubber rafts in the subfreezing, island-studded waters on days when the winds drop below 20 knots.

Since 1970 climatologists have predicted that global warming, as it kicks in, would occur most rapidly at the poles, a fact now confirmed by scientists in Alaska, Canada, and Greenland, at the North Pole, and here on the Antarctic Peninsula.

Bill Fraser, a rangy, sun-weathered 50-something ice veteran from Montana is the chief scientist here at Palmer. "The Marr glacier used to come within 100 yards of the station," he tells me, pointing upslope. "Its melt water was the source of our fresh water." Today the Marr is a quarter-mile hike from Palmer across granite rocks and boulders. Skua birds now splash in the old melt pond, while the station is forced to use a saltwater intake pipe and reverse osmosis desalinization to generate its fresh water. Periodically, the artillery rumble and boom of moving ice alerts us to continued glacial retreat and spectacular views of irregular ice faces collapsing into Arthur Harbor, setting off a blue pall of ice crystals and a rolling turquoise wave beneath a newborn scree of chunky brash ice.

"When I was a graduate student we were told that climate change occurs, but you'll never see the effects in your lifetime," Bill says. "But in the last 20 years I've seen tremendous effects. I've seen islands pop out from under glaciers, I've seen species changing places and landscape ecology altered."

While global temperatures have warmed an average one degree Fahrenheit over the last century—paralleling increased industrial output of carbon dioxide and other greenhouse gases—the Antarctic Peninsula has seen a jump of more than five degrees in just 50 years, including an incredible ten-degree average warming during its winter months.

One way that we know there is more carbon dioxide in our atmosphere today than at any time in the past 650,000 years is through ice core samples taken from Siple Dome, Vostok, and other sites in the Antarctic interior. These cores contain trapped bubbles of ancient air that have been isolated, dated, and chemically analyzed. They also show that climate is far less stable than we've imagined, and that the past 10,000 years—the period that has seen the rise of human civilization—has also been a period of atypical climate stability.

The Antarctic Peninsula has also been making news over the last several years as huge pieces of the Larson-B ice shelf, including one iceberg twice the size of the state of Delaware, began calving off its eastern shore. Scientists are now discussing the possibility that the Western Antarctic ice sheet adjacent to the peninsula could experience a sudden meltdown, raising global sea levels by 18 to 20 feet (instead of the two to three feet currently predicted by 2100). While most experts believe this melting will occur sometime after the current century, by the time they know for sure it will be too late to do anything about it.

So I can argue that I'm learning a survival skill when the first thing I do after helping unload the ship's "freshies" (fresh fruits and vegetables for the station) is to learn how to operate one of the Zodiacs and take it for a test drive. Steering the 15-foot rubber boat through floating fragments of brash ice, I spot a leopard seal lazing on an ice floe. As I maneuver around to take some photos of the snaky, blunt-headed predator, a panicked penguin jumps into the boat, tripping over the outboard's gas can. We exchange looks of mutual bewilderment before it leaps onto a pontoon and dives back into the icy blue water.

A few days later I'm out with Bill Fraser and his "Schnappers" (the boat-radio moniker for his seabird researchers, in honor of a Wisconsin polka band). We tie off our bow line on the rocky edge of Humble Island. Removing our orange float coats, we walk up to a wide pebbly flat past a dozen burbling 1,000-pound elephant seals lying in their own green waste. One of them rises up just enough to show us a wide pink mouth and issue a belching challenge that means "Stay back or I might have to rouse myself from complete stupor in order to attack you." The elephant seal population, once restricted to more northerly climes, is now booming along the peninsula because of warming conditions.

Their belching and grunting are soon complemented by the hectic squawking, flipper-flapping, and cow-barn odor of 3,000 Adélie penguins and their downy chicks, which occupy a series of rocky benches stained the color of Georgia red clay by their krill-rich droppings. Brown gull-like skuas, looking for a weak chick to kill and feed on, glide majestically overhead.

"These penguins are the ultimate canaries in the mine shaft. They're extremely sensitive indicators of climate change," Bill tells me as we walk past a group of two-foot-tall adults waddling up from the sea, their bellies full of krill.

Tiny shrimplike creatures, krill are the most abundant animal on Earth in terms of their total biomass. They make up the broad base of Antarctica's food chain and are consumed in vast quantities by penguins, seals, and whales (a single blue whale can eat four tons a day). But without access to sea ice, krill shrink, lose weight, and are vulnerable to early death.

"The bottom of the ice is where 70 percent of krill larvae are found," explains Dr. Robin Ross of the University of California at Santa Barbara, a prim and cautious scientist who'll spend the research season onboard the *Gould* trolling for krill and plankton. "The ice is like an upside-down coral reef with lots of bumps and crevasses and caves for them to hide in," she continues. "But in the early nineties the cycles of high and low ice began to fall apart. This year's winter sea ice was the lowest on record."

This year's trawls are also bringing up more salps than krill. Salps are open-water jelly creatures called tunicates, which look like floating condoms, foul the bow lines of our Zodiacs, and are prey for only a limited number of birds and fish. Unlike krill, salps reproduce in open water— and may soon fill the ecological niche created as shrinking sea ice leads to a long-term decline in krill. A decline in krill of course would wreck much of Antarctica's living ecosystem.

Rising temperatures also increase precipitation—which in Antarctica takes the form of snow. Excessive spring snow has disrupted the nesting and breeding of Adélie penguins, leading to the extinction of many of their island colonies.

Back on Humble, I'm waving off a dive-bombing skua while Bill is conferring with Rick Sanchez of the U.S. Geological Survey. Rick is carrying a portable GPS (global positioning system), along with a satellite antenna sticking out of his backpack and a magnesium-shelled laptop strapped to an elaborate fold-down rig hanging from his waist and shoulders. He's trying to walk off the perimeter (he calls it the polygon) of an extinct colony of Adélies in order to confirm Bill's observations linking increased snowfall to their declining numbers, but a burbling pile of elephant seals is blocking his mapping venture. If he tries to move them, they might stampede and crush still-living penguin chicks from an adjacent colony. Such are the quandaries of high-tech research projects in Antarctica.

While Adélie populations are crashing and the species could go extinct, more adaptable species like chinstrap penguins (which eat fish and squid when krill are not available), elephant seals, and fur seals are increasing their numbers. These newcomers to the area are threatening to displace sea ice–dependent animals like Weddell seals, crabeater seals (which are actually krill eaters), and leopard seals (which also eat krill, penguins, crabeaters, and the occasional Zodiac bumper).

What these changes in the Antarctic Peninsula suggest is that rapid warming could speed up a global chain reaction of extinctions. This process—thanks to the impact of humans—is already under way and has been labeled the sixth great "extinction pulse" in planetary history (the last one, a meteor-based event, took out the dinosaurs some 60 million years ago).

In a warmer world, "weedlike" species that are highly adaptable to disrupted habitat (pigeons, rats, deer, algae, and chinstrap penguins) will displace more specialized creatures (tigers, monarch butterflies, river dolphins, coral polyps, and Adélie penguins) that depend on unique ecosystems such as rain forests, tropical oceans, and the Antarctic ice shelf. Rising temperatures may also kill off certain plant species.

Tad Day, a sandy-haired, boyish-looking professor from Arizona State University, who drives his Mark 3 Zodiac "Lucille" like a Formula One racer, has been studying Antarctica's only two flowering plants, hair grass and pearlwort. Hair grass, the dominant species in Antarctica, is being displaced by pearlwort, a mosslike plant. The main study site he and his "Sundevils" use is Stepping Stone Island, a surprisingly green, rocky isle several miles south of Palmer around the rough chop of Bonaparte Point. "Step" is surrounded by pale blue icebergs, a rumbling blue white glacier, and other rocky islands and outcroppings—including Biscoe Point to the south, which, with the retreat of the Marr glacier, has now become Biscoe Island. Amidst nesting giant petrels—albatrosslike scavengers the size of eagles—and a friendly skua named Yogi, Tad maintains two gardens, fenced to keep out fur seals, containing more than 90 wire plant frames surrounding banks of hair grass and pearlwort growing not in true soil but a close approximation made up of glacial sand and guano.

Day has found that warming improves the growth of pearlwort but appears to have a negative impact on hair grass. "Global warming," he explains, "has the capacity to shift the competitive balance of species in ways that, until we get out there and do the research, we don't understand yet, and that could have important consequences on our ability to produce food and fiber."

Increasingly reliable climate models now predict a three- to ten-degree planetary warming in this century (by contrast, the last ice age was only five to nine degrees colder than today's average temperatures). This will result in shifts in agricultural production; the spread of tropical insects and diseases; increases in extreme weather events, flooding, and droughts; more intense coastal storms and hurricanes; erosion of beaches; coral bleaching; rising sea levels; and changes in ocean chemistry, with the world's oceans becoming more acidic—all of which has already begun.

Still, it's hard to maintain a sense of gloom and doom on the last wild continent, at least for more than a few hours at a time. Along with nightly discussions over Pisco sours with glacier ice at the Penguin Pub (the open bar located above the machine shop in GWR), I manage to distract myself with simple sojourns on the southern ocean. You need at least two people with radios to take out one of the Zodiacs, so on the days when I'm not working with the Schnappers or Sundevils I spend time looking for a boating partner. Doc Labarre, the station's big, balding, fatalistic physician, who used to work in the emergency room in Kodiak, Alaska, is among those regularly up for an adventure.

One day we cruise past Torgersen Island, where I take the Zodiac up "on platform" (as you speed up, the bow drops down, giving you greater visibility and control), and head toward Loudwater Cove on the other side of Norsel Point. The following seas allow us to surf the 15-foot craft past the rocky spires of Litchfield Island and around the big breaking waves at Norsel. We then motor around a few sculptural apartment-sized icebergs, crossing over to a landing opposite the glacier wall, where we tie off our bow line, watching a serpentine leopard seal sleeping on an adjacent ice floe. Dumping our float coats, we climb several hundred feet up and over some rocky scree and down a snowfield splotched with red algae, to the opening of an ice cave. In the cave it's like a dripping blue tunnel with slush over a clear ice floor that shows the rocky piedmont below. Hard blue glacier ice forms the bumpy roof, where icicles hang like stalactites and delicate ice rills form pressure joints along its edges.

Outside we hike the loose granite, feldspar, and glacial sand until we encounter a fur seal hauled up several hundred yards from the water on the sharp broken rocks. He barks and whines a warning at us. Nearby ponds and 100-year-old moss beds have attracted crowded colonies of brown skuas, who soon begin dive-bombing us. I get whacked from behind by one of the five-pound scavengers. It feels like getting slapped hard in the back of the head by a large man. We quickly move away from their nests, climbing back over the exposed glacier rock, past middens of limpet shells, and down a rock chimney to where our boat is tied up. The leopard seal is awake now, checking us out as we take off. I notice blood-stains on the ice where he's been resting.

We next drop by Christine, a big bouldery island where we walk past a large congregation of elephant seals hanging out opposite a colony of squawking Adélies. Crossing the heights we find mossy green swales with ponds full of brine shrimp. We stretch ourselves out on a rocky beach at the end of a narrow blue channel, sharing the space with two elephant seals about 500 and 1,000 pounds each. The southern ocean is crystal clear; the sun has come out and turned the sky cobalt blue. It feels almost tropical as we lounge to the sound of the waves rolling and retreating across smooth fist-sized stones. Farther out are several flat islands with big breakers crashing over them, sending spray 50 feet into the air. The elephant seals are blowing snot and blinking their huge red eyes, their black pupils the size of teaspoons for gathering light in deep-diving forays after squid. A fur seal comes corkscrewing through the channel's water before paddle-walking ashore and scratching itself with a hind flipper, a blissful expression on his wolfy face. And there we are, just five lazy mammals enjoying a bit of sun.

Driving the Zodiac back to the station, we're accompanied by a flight of blue-eyed shags (also known as royal cormorants) and squads of leaping penguins in the water. Doc steers while I keep an eye out for whales, like the minke that bumped the boat I was riding in a few days earlier (a real Melville moment, watching its huge brown back roll out from under us). The sky has again quilted over with clouds, turning the water the color of hammered tin; with the buck and slap of the boat and the icy-cold saltwater spray in our faces, it feels like all's right with the wild.

Antarctica is vast and awesome in its indifference to the human condition. Yet it is also a world center for scientific research and has provided us fair warning about the human impact on climate. The message from the ice is as plain as the penguin bones I found scattered around a dying Adélie colony: their world and ours, Antarctica's southern ocean and America's blue frontier, are more closely linked than we imagine.

Nearly anywhere you go on our blue planet such messages are being sent. While Antarctica is a continent surrounded by ice, the Arctic is an ice sheet surrounded by land—but not for long. Since 1979, 20 percent of the polar ice cap has melted. In 2001 the U.S. Navy held a two-day symposium on "Naval Operations in an Ice-Free Arctic." The Office of Naval Research, one of the sponsors of the symposium, believes that summer sea lanes in the Arctic will be open to shipping by 2015 and that the summer ice cap could disappear entirely by the end of the century.

In November 2004 a three-year collaboration of scientists from eight nations with arctic lands, including the United States, concluded that the Arctic was warming at nearly twice the rate of the rest of the planet and could be as much as 13 degrees warmer by 2100, melting the Greenland ice sheet, accelerating sea-level rise, and leading to the extinction of polar bears in the wild.

After Antarctica, I'm sent on assignment to Australia's Great Barrier Reef and to the island state of Fiji to look at the impact of climate change on coral reefs. While the trip is an adventure, what I discover in these warm-water realms is a bummer. Even if we fix all the problems related to polluted runoff, overfishing, and physical damage, we will still lose at least half the world's tropical reefs to heat-induced coral bleaching from carbon dioxide already released into the atmosphere. In addition, acidification of the ocean will make it more difficult for shell-forming creatures such as coral polyps to extract from seawater the calcium carbonate they need to regenerate reefs.

Not long after that South Seas trip I'm standing under tall and stately palm trees with members of the Alliance of Small Island States from Fiji, Samoa, and Micronesia. They're concerned that rising sea levels might submerge their tropical nations. Soon another island resident arrives to lead us on a tour. She explains how her island, which has seen its surrounding waters rise a foot in the last century, will be affected by the additional two- to three-foot sea-level rise predicted in this century.

Dr. Vivien Gornitz, a diminutive, plainspoken scientist and native New Yorker from NASA's Goddard Space Institute at Columbia University, then leads our group out from under the palm trees in the Winter Garden atrium of the World Financial Center, heading over to lower Manhattan's Hudson Pier. We're about to take a ferry ride to Hoboken, New Jersey. The group is followed by a television camera crew and producer Andrea Torrice, who is shooting a PBS documentary, *Rising Waters,* about the impacts of climate change on Pacific islanders.

Gornitz points to the green algae tidal marks halfway up the seawall that runs below Battery Park City. "This area was pretty much under water during the eight-foot storm tides of the big nor'easter of 1992," she explains. "I spoke to a man on Wall Street who was stuck in his office looking down as his Porsche sank. I asked him what he did. 'Wait for the tide to go out,' he said. In this century, 100-year storms like that one will begin to occur every decade or so. In areas like lower Manhattan they'll raise the seawalls. There's too much valuable real estate here to let the sea take it. Of course that's not feasible for parts of Long Island, North Carolina, Florida, or Louisiana."

Boarding the ferry, Torrice and her crew herd the tour group onto the exposed upper deck, into the teeth of a cold March wind. "But we'll freeze up there," Gornitz protests. As the boat pulls away, affording a stunning view of the Statue of Liberty and the city, climatologist Pene-huro Lefale of Apia, Samoa, takes a look back at the World Financial Center. "You have some really amazing architecture here," he tells me, smiling. "That building alone has to be worth more than the budgets of all our small island nations."

(Badly damaged on 9/11, the Center's Winter Garden reopened one year later. These days when I look at the lower Manhattan skyline, once dominated by the twin towers, I wonder why so many people, knowing what we're capable of doing to each other, are still unable to believe what we're doing to our ocean planet.)

Dr. Gornitz, who lives in upper, dryer Manhattan, is part of a National Science Foundation–funded team assessing climate change impacts in the metropolitan East Coast (MEC) region—part of a national assessment of climate change impacts on the United States. She has focused on lower Manhattan, Sea Gate, and Coney Island in Brooklyn, Westhampton and Freeport on Long Island, and parts of New Jersey, trying to go from understanding the macro effects to understanding the micro effects of climate change.

In Hoboken Dr. Gornitz takes us through the marine terminal and down the stairwell to the commuter PATH trains. "During the '92 storm these stairs became waterfalls as the river surged in," she explains, pulling out photos to illustrate. She then shows us a map of how a ten-foot surge, typical of the more extreme storm events predicted in the coming decades, could flood all of New York's subway tunnels and three major airports.

"Here the waters cover the concrete. At home they flood our taro fields and take away our food plants and houses," says Masao Nakayama, the UN ambassador from Micronesia, recounting how during the big cyclone of 1991 people on Truk had to get in their canoes and paddle as the storm surge covered the entire island.

Soon the group is back on the Manhattan riverfront esplanade, walking south toward the vulnerable areas of the South Street Seaport and lower Wall Street. "Are people who live here aware of the sea-level problem?" Penehuro Lefale wonders.

"Not for the most part," Gornitz admits. "We live on an island in Manhattan, but we're cut off from the sea in our daily lives and don't think about the water all around us. The irony is just as we're beginning to rediscover our waterfront and rebuild on it, it's at risk."

Penehuro, who lost his family home and grandmother's grave to a savage storm, nods his understanding. "For us the sea and the land are very much about who we are," he tells her.

"That's great," Torrice interrupts. "But could you both say that again? We had a problem with the camera battery."

A month later I'm back in New York for a follow-up meeting with Gornitz. The NASA Goddard Institute for Space Studies at Columbia is located in a university building above Tom's Restaurant, an easy-to-spot landmark at the noisy, traffic-congested corner of Broadway and 112th Street.

"I don't know what else I can tell you," she tells me in her surprisingly quiet office. "We're working with the Army Corps [of Engineers] in terms of their beach nourishment programs in New Jersey and how rising seas will impact that. . . . We know 70 percent of sandy beaches around the world are eroding. Global coral bleaching was at an all-time high in 1998 [as sea temperatures warmed]. Oceans are rising one to two millimeters a year according to the IPCC [the UN's Intergovernmental Panel on Climate Change]. The rate of sea-level rise over the last century is much faster than over the last several thousand years. Places already seeing sea-level rise include Chesapeake Bay, Florida, and Louisiana."

The findings of Gornitz's study, published in 2001 and based on what are now seen as conservative estimates, suggest that by 2100 New York City will have as many 90-degree days as Miami does today. Sea-level rise will contribute to regular flooding or permanent inundation of many of the city and region's coastal areas, including lower Manhattan. Severe droughts that once occurred on a 100-year cycle may begin to occur every 3 to 11 years. Heat, flooding, and drought also will facilitate the spread of insect-borne tropical diseases such as West Nile virus, which first appeared in New York City in 1999—the hottest, driest summer in a century—and has since spread across the nation.

Just off 117th Street in Miami, inside the entry gate to Florida International University, is a low reinforced-concrete and steel building with roll-down hurricane shutters and an array of satellite dishes and microwave masts rising like palmettos from its flat roof. If the antennas come down in a storm, two buried fiber optic cables will keep the operational core of the building connected to distant weather stations, with uplinks to geosynchratic NOAA and Navy satellites. All the building's entrances are under 24-hour video surveillance. The entire fortresslike structure, completed in 1995, is elevated on a dirt berm five feet above the surrounding campus. I figure this has to be the right address for NOAA's National Hurricane Center (NHC). I get buzzed in through a sealed metal door.

The NHC's pressroom is the building's last protective ring before the core operations center. It has glass doors leading into the ops center, a briefing podium, and a producer's console for live video feeds. Just beyond the glass is a large TV monitor and a desk facing outward toward the pressroom. "We use this as a TV set with the director sitting up front, explaining things to the pool camera," Frank Lapore, the center's press guy, explains to me. Behind the big props the ops center is divided between eastern Pacific and Atlantic sectors, shown as computer-generated maps on various terminals and monitors. Hurricane specialist Dr. Jack Bevin is seated with a cup of coffee, keeping an eye on the Pacific this morning, as Dr. James Franklin works storms in the Atlantic.

Off to the right and out of view of the pressroom is NOAA's Tropical Prediction Center, where the Tropical Analysis and Forecasting Branch develops aviation and marine forecasts, churning out more than 50 charts a day for, among other clients, helicopter companies such as Mark and Cathal's, which make daily flights to and from oil platforms in the Gulf of Mexico. I notice that the Weather Channel is playing on a TV monitor suspended from the ceiling. "We want to make sure our information is getting out and being presented accurately," Lapore explains.

A polar satellite display on one computer screen shows swaths of different-colored earth; another shows swirls of red, gray, and blue, the blue representing the cold tops of clouds. Still another shows aviation zones in the Caribbean with an overlay map of country outlines. I pick up an "Ash Advisory" statement from Montserrat, a small island with ongoing volcanic eruptions. "That's important. Can't fly a jet well with its engines full of silicate," he notes.

We walk back into the ops center. It's midsummer but still early in the hurricane season. "Must be a slow news day. They called asking if this low could be a storm in the making," Jack Bevin reports, pointing to one of his monitors as he hangs up the phone.

"During a hurricane we might have half a dozen people working in here and a couple of dozen straphangers, including the tribal elders [retired forecasters], hanging around, imparting their wisdom. Everyone is pumped up. It's exciting. You should come back during an event," Frank offers.

I consider doing so in August 2004, when Hurricane Charley is approaching Tampa with winds up to 145 miles per hour, before it jags inland and across the peninsula. By the time I call the airlines, however, all flights south have been cancelled. Later, when Hurricanes Frances, Ivan, and Jeanne come barreling toward the state, I don't bother. My friend Carl, who shoots the network pool camera inside the hurricane center during the storms, tells me the scene is actually quite boring.

Charley eventually left 27 dead and more than eight billion dollars in damages in its wake. Some two million people evacuated at its approach, and close to three million did so when Frances and Ivan approached. Frances, a lumbering, Texas-sized giant, soaked much of the state, leaving six million people without power, ten dead, and some ten billion dollars in damages. Ivan killed people in the Panhandle, along the Gulf coast, and on up through Appalachia, leaving at least another ten billion dollars in damages from wind, floods, and tornadoes. Just behind these three came Jeanne, flooding and battering Puerto Rico (seven dead), devastating the impoverished nation of Haiti (more than 3,000 dead), then slamming into Florida as a category 3 hurricane—hitting the same part of the coast struck by Frances three weeks earlier and leaving at least five dead. Total damage from the four hurricanes topped $42 billion with a U.S. death toll of 59. One in five homes in the state was damaged.

Three million people hit the roads when Floyd approached five years earlier, making these events—Floyd, Frances, and Ivan—the largest civilian evacuations in U.S. history, along with Katrina in August 2005 and Hurricane Rita the following month, when more than three million people fled from Texas and western Louisiana. Of course, Katrina's one million evacuees didn't get to return home after a few days.

Like Charley, Floyd veered from its projected path and missed Florida but went on to inundate North Carolina with several feet of rain. Giant hog farm manure lagoons along the Neuse and Tar rivers collapsed and overflowed into waters already filled with hundreds of thousands of dead hogs and chickens, propane tanks, gasoline and chemical slicks, and floating coffins from supersaturated graveyards.

When Charley reached North Carolina in 2004, it had downgraded considerably, averting the extensive damage suffered when Hurricane Isabel came ashore in 2003. But Ivan just kept on going, causing flooding and tornadoes in 13 states from Alabama to New Jersey, while Jeanne added yet more rain to the supersaturated ground of central Florida, Georgia, and the Carolinas.

During my visit to the NHC I asked Frank Lapore about people who might choose to remain behind in coastal high-rises and ride out the increasing number of hurricanes that are predicted in coming years.

"Some new technologies suggest we've been underestimating hurricane wind speeds by 20 percent," he told me. "So now we're thinking that vertical evacuation for high-rises may have some problems. You run them up the first few floors from the storm surge, but then you put them into higher wind speeds. So now we're saying, don't take them above the fifth floor. Just look at what happened to Burger King World Headquarters [in Homestead, Florida, during 1992's record-setting (pre-Katrina) $35 billion Hurricane Andrew]. The storm surge took out the first two floors and the wind just took out everything above that. All that glass just got ground up like a big Mixmaster."

"So in terms of climate change's growing impact—"

"Ask our Virginia Key lab. Our job [at the NHC] is to provide 72-hour forecasting." I take his advice.

If you're going to be a meteorologist, you ought to have a name like Dr. Chris Landsea. Wearing a Florida tan, shorts, sandals, and a faded aloha shirt, this 30-something meteorologist works at the Atlantic Oceanographic and Meteorological Laboratory on Virginia Key, just past the Seaquarium on the causeway leading to Key Biscayne. His cluttered office includes an aquarium full of fish from the black-water lagoon over which the lab is built, and a brightly colored toy parrot. Something of a rare bird himself, being a native Floridian, Chris received high school class credits for working at the lab. When he'd finish his assignments, he would go wind surfing on Hobie Beach just down the causeway. After getting his meteorology degree at Colorado State, he came back to Miami to work full-time for NOAA. His job description includes riding into hurricanes every fall aboard Gulfstream jets, P-3 Orions, and Air Force C-130s—the famous "vomit comets" based out of Fort McDill in

Tampa, which take internal readings of approaching hurricanes. "I have a weak stomach so I wear [anti-nausea] patches," he tells me.

"The last years have been the busiest on record for tropical hurricanes in the Atlantic," he goes on. Between 1995 and 2005, eight of ten hurricane seasons were above average in terms of activity.

When I ask him if he thinks this is related to climate change, he says, "I was on a panel, an IPCC follow-up, and we found that areas of hurricane activity won't change, but a French team came out proposing a small change overall in increased frequency of hurricanes. I'd go along with that."

"And intensity?" I ask.

"The maximum intensity of wind speed might go up 5 to 10 percent. That also agrees with published work out of Princeton University. So the intensity will increase for the strongest storms."

If 5 to 10 percent doesn't sound like a lot, consider what Dr. Steven Leatherman, a leading coastal scientist from Florida International University, has to say. Recalling that in 1992 Hurricane Andrew caused $35 billion worth of damage, he suggests that "if you had increased that storm by 5 or 10 percent in its sustained wind speeds, those numbers would have probably popped up into the $90 billion to $100 billion category."

But there are also feedback patterns within the ocean that may help mitigate such effects, according to Chris Landsea. "The current mixing that takes place in big storms brings upwellings of cooler water that weaken storms after moist, warm, ocean-generated air has started them up. So, in a sense, the ocean has a foot on the accelerator with moist warm air and a foot on the brake with cool water upwellings."

"And what role will rising sea levels play?"

"Sea surge from storms will affect Miami. Most of this county is below ten-foot elevation. So if there's a one-meter sea-level rise by 2100," he pauses, "we should really begin to assess the risk of living here. . . . Personally, I love living here and I'll take the risk, but where I live in Pinecrest we're 15 feet above sea level. That's nosebleed country for Florida. Plus I have hurricane shutters. I'm prepared."

He adds, "But I don't think people in Iowa should have to pay for our property here." (By 2004 the federal government was providing $301 billion of federal flood insurance coverage for Florida real estate that the private insurance industry refused to handle.)

Chris explains how, even in the absence of rapid climate change, local storms come in 25- to 40-year cycles linked to a one degree Fahrenheit warming of the North Atlantic. "We saw this in the 1940s to 1960s, when we averaged three major storms per year. Between the 1970s and the early 1990s [during the largest home construction boom in Florida history], the average dropped to 1.5 storms." He brings up an ocean map on his computer screen. Red splotches appear and disappear as he runs his program through a time line. "We've got good sea surface temperature and storm records going back to the 1870s, and based on this 120-year record, it looks like things will be getting very active over the next 25 years."

Just to add a little complexity to the story, he tells me that El Niño events, which are expected to increase in frequency and intensity with global warming, actually cut down on Atlantic hurricane activity. "It [El Niño] creates vertical sheer over the Atlantic in the upper troposphere that makes it harder for hurricanes to organize themselves. In 1997, for example, all these other factors were overwhelmed by the El Niño effect."

"So when we get battered by El Niño in California, that's good for Florida?"

"Better," he agrees with a grin.

According to NOAA the 1997–1998 El Niño cost the U.S. economy $25 billion. A recent study by Swiss Reinsurance, one of the world's largest insurance companies, estimates that global losses from climate change impacts will run around $150 billion a year by 2010. The largest property reinsurance company in Britain projects that, unchecked, climate change impacts could bankrupt the global economy in 65 years.

On average the United States currently experiences around four billion dollars per year in hurricane-related damages. (Charley, Frances, Ivan, and Jeanne upped the price to $42 billion in 2004.) Within a $10 trillion economy, that is not considered a great deal, but what happens when the United States begins experiencing hurricane seasons like 2005, with impacts from what emergency planners call "$100 billion city-busters"? The costs from Hurricane Katrina alone are estimated to run toward $300 billion.

My Miami friends Carl and Kathy Hersh lost their trees and ground cover to Hurricane Andrew back in 1992 and again to Wilma in 2005. Their home suffered little structural damage, but the impact on their psyches was enduring, as Kathy relates. "Because most of the private insurance companies pulled out afterward, we're now way underinsured." South Florida was really traumatized by Andrew. People strip store shelves like it's Armageddon whenever a storm approaches now. . . .

Andrew's winds were just devastating. If there'd also been a water surge, many more people would have died. But the winds were extraordinary. They left 200,000 people homeless overnight. Then after Wilma we were camping out. People were without power for weeks. It creates stress. Child abuse, spousal abuse, divorce all increase in the wake of disasters."

Another friend and colleague, Mark Schleifstein of the *New Orleans Times-Picayune,* wrote about the risk of a category 4 or 5 hurricane striking his city for so many years that his editor started calling the stories "disaster porn." Just before Katrina struck, Max Mayfield, director of the NHC, called Mark at work and asked nervously, "How high's your building and what's its structural integrity?"

"Are you saying what I think you're saying?" Mark responded. After two days of working and living out of his office during the great storm and the flooding that followed, Mark and the other staffers had to evacuate. "We got out of the building in these big-wheeled newspaper delivery trucks, with all of us in the back and the water up to the grills," he recalls. They drove to Houma, where they put out an online edition of the newspaper. Mark's home in the Lakeview section of New Orleans was under ten-plus feet of water for more than two weeks, making it, along with tens of thousands of other homes in the city, uninhabitable. He now lives with his wife and four colleagues in a house in Baton Rouge.

After my visits to the Hurricane Center and weather lab, I check out South Miami Beach with Orlando, a young British visitor who's spending the summer apprenticing in video production with Kathy and Carl. Orlando and I saunter past South Beach's neon-bright clubs and restaurants: the Casablanca, Majestic, A Fish Called Avalon, Scandals, Rendezvous on the Beach, and Wet Willie's. As Ocean Avenue begins to crowd up, we sit down to eat and watch the passing parade: young women in tank tops and platform sandals, guys with pet pythons, open silk shirts, sleeveless tees. Classic cars cruise by, low-rider vans, a neon-lit motorcycle attempting to compete with the neon-lit Art Deco buildings. Just yards across Flamingo Park and a low-lying wall is the wide sandy beachfront, compliments of the Army Corps of Engineers and its contract dredgers. We get some frozen fruit bars. The Breakwater club is jamming, its street-side stage featuring live music by Luis Menia and a flamenco dancer who moves like quicksilver in a glass.

What transformed South Beach from a low-income Jewish retirement community into a gay mecca and a vibrant social scene is its fabulous architecture. The classic Art Deco apartments were built following the 1926 hurricane that leveled the city of Miami and its artificial barrier island; thousands were left homeless and 114 were killed. It's estimated that a similar storm, striking today, would cause more than $80 billion in damages. Nine years later, in 1935, a hurricane hit the Florida Keys, killing 427 people.

At the time only 3,000 people lived between Miami and Key West, about one one-thousandth of today's population. Many of those early residents were swamp rats, settling around what former Governor Napoleon Bonaparte Broward labeled "that abominable, pestilence-ridden swamp"—the Everglades.

In 2000 I attend a press conference being held at the Willard Hotel in Washington, D.C., to promote the eight-billion-dollar, 20-year state and federal plan to restore the Everglades. The idea is to redirect fresh water, long diverted by the Army Corps of Engineers for flood control and agriculture, back into the "river of grass." Among those attending are Allison Deflour, Governor Jeb Bush's policy coordinator for the Everglades, and representatives of various environmental organizations. After initial statements by politicians and state and federal officials, the floor is opened to questions.

"With sea-level rise projected at up to three feet, what makes you think the Everglades won't become a saltwater estuary in 50 years?" I ask.

"I think I'll take a pass on that one." Jeb Bush's man smiles, turning toward the enviros. They all express concern, but some argue that restoration of the 'Glades will help mitigate some of the impacts of climate change.

The environmentalists are not alone in failing to address the issue. The Army Corps of Engineers, assigned the lead role in restoring the Everglades water flow that it originally diverted, has not bothered to incorporate sea-level rise into its master plan schematics.

About a month later, I drop by the Everglades National Park's headquarters and its Visitor Center in the sultry fry heat of July. The center is a nice, low-slung shady building sitting by a swampy pond. (The previous center was destroyed by Andrew.) At 1.5 million acres, Everglades National Park is only about half the size of the historic Pa-hay-okee river of grass. Many of the Everglades' old marl prairies are now residential developments in Dade and Broward Counties, home to some of south Florida's seven million residents. Coastal areas such as Palm Beach were also flooded every year, and not just by millionaires jetting in for the season. All these drained and built-up areas, plus the state's freshwater aquifer, remain vulnerable to sea-level rise and saltwater intrusion.

"The highest point in the park is only eight feet above sea level," ranger Rick Cook tells me, spreading a map in front of us. "A foot or two rise would affect almost everything in green"—which appears to be most of the park map, not counting Florida Bay, which is already underwater.

Of course, there are places at even greater risk. On the approach into New Orleans Airport you fly over Lake Pontchartrain and its levees, and on the far side of the lake, down below the level of its brown water, you can see curving tree-lined suburban streets, homes, lawns, kids on bikes, and parked cars. Atlantis Gardens would be a good name for this development, I think at the time.

New Orleans itself averages eight feet below sea level, surrounded by protective levees. From parts of the French Quarter you can look up and see freighters sailing past at high tide. Only the poor are buried here beneath the damp ground, where they might rise again; elevated mausoleums keep the city's rich dry as bone. New Orleans also has a system of massive pump stations that have been operating continuously, 24 hours a day, for the past 100 years, pumping five million gallons of subsurface water back into the lake. In 1718 the early French settlers who called this the Isle of Orleans were immediately hit by a hurricane. Today (this was written in 2000), "the town that care forgot" and the 1.3 million people living in and around it are considered by the Federal Emergency Management Agency (FEMA) as a worst-case scenario for a hurricane strike.

The city is still buffered by 20–40 miles of marshland between its levees and the Gulf of Mexico. Every few miles of that marsh is said to absorb a foot of storm surge. But with the present rate of land loss, New Orleans is expected to be a coastal city within 30 years.

Johnny Glover, a fishing guide and resort owner down on the coast, has seen the change, watching land eaten away around Terrebonne Bay. "Between subsidence and sea water rising all around the world, I don't keep too much on the ground that can't be moved," he tells me. "September a year ago we had twenty days with water over my land. Our parking lot was underwater for all but maybe five days that month."

A comprehensive restoration effort for the Mississippi Delta has been proposed under the rubric Coast 2050, which calls for a $14 billion local, state, and federal funding effort over the next several decades. Mark Davis is executive director of the Coalition to Restore Coastal Louisiana, a citizen activist group that has played a key role in promoting Coast 2050. "We know Louisiana is experiencing sea-level rise, but it still has the capacity to create new land where the delta's natural systems are allowed to operate intact," he explains

Davis and I meet near the French Quarter, in a surfers' bar that, with its quiver of boards hanging on the wall and big-wave videos playing on TV monitors, strikes me as weirdly out of place, like a tiki bar in Omaha.

"The Army Corps has given us a levee system that's traded periodic Mississippi river flooding for permanent coastal flooding, and that to me is a bad deal," Davis says. "We buy insurance out of fear of injury or disease, not because we know it's going to happen. It's the same thing here. We have to act because the costs if we get it wrong are too high."

Does that mean that he believes he can mobilize enough popular will to turn around the forces of sprawl and development, not to mention the Army Corps, oil drilling, and canal building that contribute to subsidence and land loss?

"If our advocacy is inadequate to the task," he warns, "then a hurricane will make the case for us." In August 2005 Katrina makes that case.

On the West Coast, sea-level rise is only one of the climate factors that have begun to alter the marine ecosystem. Others include the increased frequency and severity of El Niño storms, loss of fisheries from a warming Pacific, and loss of wetlands and hardening of the coast in response to rising seas.

Projected increases in the number and intensity of El Niño Southern Oscillation (ENSO) events—involving warming Pacific sea surface temperatures—are based on computer modeling and the dozen El Niño events that were recorded in the twentieth century. These include the severe El Niño events of 1982–1983 and 1997–1998. The latter was the strongest ever recorded, causing global bleaching of coral reefs along with drought-induced rainforest fires in Indonesia, Brazil, Central America, and West Africa.

Along with California coastal storms and increased runoff from flooding, the El Niño effect has been marked by dramatic shifts in offshore biology.

More disturbing, the 1970s saw an abrupt jump in water temperatures off California that persisted into the new century. The warmer temperatures were accompanied by reduced mixing in the water column,

reduced upwelling of nutrients, and widespread declines in algal productivity along the coast. Although water temperatures cooled again in
2003, zooplankton at the base of the food web did not recover. There
have also been dramatic declines of seabird populations, including a 90
percent decline of sooty shearwaters, declines in a range of fish species,
and declines in their marine habitat.

A projected sea-level rise of one foot in the San Francisco Bay and
Sacramento Delta, along with increased storm surges (which have been
recorded since 1970), is expected to turn 100-year flood events into ten-
year floods. During the 13 years I lived in the San Francisco Bay Area,
the Russian River, just over 100 miles north of San Francisco, experienced three "100-year floods." One predictable response to this
increased flooding activity will be increased demand by coastal property
owners and Delta farmers for more levees and protective seawalls. While
providing temporary relief, such measures also will speed up erosion and
prevent wetlands and other natural systems from adapting to the coming
change.

On the Atlantic coast, rising waters in Chesapeake Bay have reduced
Maryland's Smith Island, a small crab-fishing community of 300 people,
from ten by six miles to eight by four, and it continues to lose 11 to 12
feet of shoreline a year. State policy advisors point to Smith Island as an
example of how sea-level rise has to be taken into account in regional
planning for bay restoration and cleanup. But now that one-third of
Maryland's bayfront property has begun to collapse, including the lawns
of middle-class neighborhoods in populous Anne Arundel County, state
legislators have begun to reexamine antierosion efforts, including the
building of seawalls, breakwaters, and other stone and concrete barriers
that were abandoned years ago.

In trying to stem the tide by armoring the coasts, these legislators
would be choosing a scientifically discredited yet widely popular
approach. Even as the risks from hurricanes and rising seas increase,
more and more Americans are moving to the beach. Developers, ever
attuned to market trends, are building them ever-grander castles made of
wood and stucco. And all this high-risk behavior is being supported and
encouraged by a government that hasn't learned how to just say no.

CHAPTER 7

Paradise with
an Ocean View

World-class beach house with boat dock. Fish right from your
own 125-ft. dock. See dolphins playing right before your eyes
while you lounge in your gazebo.

> — *Real estate ad for $2,650,000 estate on
> North Captiva island, before Hurricane
> Charley devastated the island*

What the sea wants, the sea will have.

> — *Sailor's saying*

Barrier islands are like geology on amphetamines. Unarmored, they tend
to move, by the decade, year, season, or sometimes in a single stormy day
like August 13, 2004. That's when Hurricane Charley created a 450-
yard-wide ocean channel that split North Captiva, Florida, in two, just as
a 1921 hurricane had split North Captiva from Captiva.

It's a natural process that can be strikingly beautiful, even awe-inspir-
ing, provided you haven't just closed on a $2.7 million beachfront dream
home in a place where it's happening. Unfortunately, more and more
wealthy Americans are moving to or buying vacation homes in places
like Fire Island, Easthampton, Hilton Head, Sea Island, Ocean Reef, or
Captiva. Other folks are buying high-rise condos in Ocean City, Myrtle
Beach, Gulfport, Coronado, and Honolulu or flocking like lemmings to
new housing developments built on filled-in marshes and floodplains all
along the coastline. And although lemmings don't actually jump off cliffs
and drown themselves in the sea, if they did, there would undoubtedly be
government programs offering them flight insurance and full coverage
for any water damage.

More than 155 million people, about 53 percent of the U.S. population, now live within 50 miles of a marine coastline, with more than a
million new arrivals showing up every year. Every day some 2,000 new

homes are built along our coasts. Fourteen of America's 20 largest cities are coastal, as are 17 of America's 20 fastest-growing counties. Every week 8,250 new people arrive in California's coastal regions and 5,750 in Florida's. The nation's coasts (excluding Alaska) are now three times as densely populated as the rest of the country. And while various government reports have expressed concern about associated problems of erosion, sprawl, marine pollution, loss of wetlands, wildlife habitat, and human safety, federal programs continue to encourage people to move to the beach.

"You might need somethin' to hold on to, when all the answers they don't amount to much." Bruce Springsteen sings on the car's CD player as I drive past cherry trees in bloom, old clapboard houses, and corner groceries, across railroad tracks and down to the beach in the Boss's old hangout of Asbury Park, New Jersey. Since 1999 there's been talk of revitalizing this area, but with its eroded tax base and absentee landlords, it looks more like the beachfront in Gaza, dominated by abandoned dance halls and a skeletal, unfinished high-rise. There are weedy lots, boarded-up stores, and streetlights left on in the middle of the day. Now construction crews have begun tearing down some of the older waterfront buildings to make way for high-density townhouses and condominiums.

But there is a long Jersey tradition of mixing concrete and corruption, and one of the key players in Asbury Park's waterfront redevelopment— also a major contributor to the disgraced former governor Jim McGreevey—pleads guilty in August 2004 to tax and other criminal charges. The developer Charles Kushner has been implicated in a witness-tampering scheme, including allegations that he spent $25,000 to hire a prostitute to seduce his brother-in-law (who was cooperating in a federal investigation of him) and then had the tryst videotaped. Meanwhile the governor, before resigning over an adulterous homosexual affair linked to allegations of blackmail and financial cronyism, signed a law making it easier for real-estate developers like Kushner to build along the Jersey shore by "fast-tracking" the environmental review process.

I climb a fence and go out on the warped boardwalk, beyond which rock jetties jut out into the sea. A guy in a wheelchair and an army pea-coat is the only other person in sight. As I make my way across the sand, gulls fly around looking for a handout or something newly dead. There's a "No Swimming" sign on the beach, which is being scalloped out between the jetties. For years people built rock groins and jetties like these to retain sand in front of their homes and hotels, while eroding the beaches downdrift.

The people on those beaches would in turn build their own jetties to capture waterborne sand carried in the nearshore current, until eventually you'd have an ugly series of rock piles ending in a stretch of severely eroded shoreline. At that point seawalls were often erected, only to collapse in a few years as increased wave energy generated by their steep hard surfaces undermined the walls' own foundations and drove any remaining sand back out to sea. There's a term coastal geologists use for this process of hardening the shore. It's called *newjerseyization*.

Driving through Asbury Park, I pass the Stone Pony, where Springsteen and his band used to play. Fallen into disrepair in the late '90s, it reopened in 2000 as a premier musical venue. Northward along Ocean Avenue the scene quickly shifts to one of mansions, private beach clubs, and condos, the ocean lost to sight behind them. When the view reappears in Long Branch, it is of a large seawall. On the mainland side of the road are the modest homes, shops, streetside bars with Bud Lite banners, sandy sidewalks, and chain convenience stores that have become iconic of American beach towns, or, in this case, wall towns.

In Monmouth Beach, the next town up the Shore, I park at a bus stop and climb wooden stairs next to a shelter that's marked "Public"—the first public access sign I've seen in five miles. Unfortunately, all the side streets have "No Parking" signs warning that if you are not a resident your car will be towed. The cobble-rock-and-cement wall is about 15 feet high and 12 feet across the top. There are numerous other stairways up and down this taxpayer-built wall, but they're all marked "Private— Keep Out." On the other side of the wall is a bermlike dune and wide beach recently pumped onto shore by the Army Corps of Engineers. I'd like to check it out but am afraid a cop might come along and ticket my illegally parked car. If there's ever been a less user-friendly beach I can't imagine it, except perhaps Normandy on D-Day.

I put up that evening at the MiraSol Motel on the 150-yard-wide coastal strip of Sea Bright between the Shrewsbury River and a newly created beach that I can see over the wall from my second-floor room. Sea Bright, some 25 miles south of New York City, is the starting point for the largest and costliest "beach nourishment" project in the United States. It is an Army Corps of Engineers operation (65 percent federal money, 35 percent state funds) designed to build up beaches along the entire 127-mile length of the Jersey Shore. Begun in 1994, the project is estimated to cost as much as $9 billion by completion, or more than $60 million per mile. Similar projects are under way in south Florida, Mississippi, and Texas.

Even though 150 feet of beach is expected to disappear for every foot of sea-level rise, and FEMA officials estimate that one out of four houses built within 500 feet of the water will be lost to erosion by 2050, Sea Bright's new strand could last for decades, provided there are no major storms. But storms have already washed away Monmouth's new beach three times in the past decade, making it what the Corps' engineers call an erosion "hot spot."

Sandy Hook, the curling spit of sand just north of Sea Bright, is covered in dry grass, cattails, scrub oak, and pine. I follow directions to its old Spanish-American army fort, which, like San Francisco's Presidio, is now one of America's glories, a coastal park. This one comes complete with a Coast Guard station, a national marine fisheries lab, a flock of Canada geese, and, along captains' row, the offices of the Littoral Society, a nonprofit beach and coastal conservation group with some 6,000 members, mainly in the New York–New Jersey and Delaware area.

I enter the 100-year-old officers' quarters by the kitchen door, where I encounter the society's director, Dery Bennett, steaming clams on an old four-burner stove. At 68, Dery stands six feet, three inches, more gristle than fat, with skin like salted salmon leather, curly gray hair, and brown eyes that can go from mournful to mirthful, depending on the light and the topic. Taking the clams from the pot and placing them in a china bowl of hot water, he cracks them open and starts to eat.

"I live in Fairhaven. Moved there in 1968. They closed the clam beds 32 years ago and reopened them last year, so this is the first time I've gotten to try these," he says while chewing and crunching.

"How is it?"

"A little overcooked and sandy." He dips another clam in the hot water. "Not bad. Things have improved. They got the owners to compost the manure at Monmouth Park Racetrack. Reduced the farm runoff. I just raked these on the riverbed yesterday, the second-to-last day of the season. When they opened the beds last year, guys were in there taking six to eight bushels a day, that's six to eight hundred dollars. That fishery was rebuilt over 30 years but they've hammered it back down in a hurry."

He finishes his clams and leads me upstairs, past walls filled with stuffed fish—wahoos, rays, striped bass, bluefish, a swordfish with a Santa cap, a big hammerhead shark. In his equally cluttered office Dery shows me a map of dredged channels and drowned rivers behind New Jersey seawalls built in the 1930s and 1940s. He begins talking about the Corps beach project, and I try to pay close attention though I can't quite take my eyes off the goosefish skull hanging on his lamp like a wide-brimmed hat. "They plan for 50 years' protection," he tells me. "Earlier seawalls were put up to protect towns like Sea Bright, and the direct result was the loss of the beach. The Corps' pumping and then maintaining the sand. It's supposed to last seven years. So they'll redo it every seven years."

The day I met with Dery, Congress passed the six-billion-dollar Water Resources Development Act (WRDA), the annual funding mechanism for dredging ports and harbors, building levees, and pumping sand. Dery is not a fan of pumping sand.

"You've got a tough fight if what you're saying is, don't save the beaches," I point out.

"I think if there's winners and losers, I'm on the side that's losing right now," he admits. "New Jersey just voted up to $25 million a year for beach sand pumping, but not a nickel for improved public beach access. Of course most of the money still comes from the feds. That's why the states like it, 'cause of the pork, the salt pork. It's welfare for the rich and the damp."

"To say this only benefits the rich is disingenuous. There's no question all of society in coastal states benefit from opportunities for recreation," counters Jim Saxton, the environmentally concerned Republican congressman from New Jersey's Third District, which includes much of the Shore. "Economists have told me that tourism accounts for 50 percent of New Jersey's gross domestic product. So it's in our interest to make an investment in beach nourishment and replenishment. We have families that save to rent a cabin or condo for a week or two during the summer. You'll see hundreds of them in a single block along the shore. We also have day trippers who'll come to the beach for a day in the summer. I just think it's short-sighted to say this only benefits a few big homeowners."

Across the New York bight from Sea Bright, on Long Island's south shore, sand replenishment has clearly benefited a few big homeowners, along with some unscrupulous real-estate developers. Following a 1962 Ash Wednesday storm that destroyed a large number of homes, the Army Corps of Engineers (New York District) began a 15-year project to replenish the sand at Westhampton, building 21 groins—480-foot-long rock spurs, running perpendicular to the beach. Since the nearshore sand transport ran east to west, the way to minimize the erosion effect these structures would inevitably create would have been to build them west to east, which is what the Corps planned to do. But, according to a 1983 *New York Times* account, wealthier property owners on the east end "used their political influence . . . and the county told the Corps of Engineers that it would not pay its local share unless the project was changed to go from East to West." That change ensured that the richest homes would be the first to get storm protection, even at the cost of starving the residential beaches westward.

As a result, during a series of storms in the early 1990s a new inlet formed across the erosion-narrowed western end of the barrier island at Dune Road. Two hundred and fifty homes were cut off from the rest of the island, but only 90 of them were still standing after the storms had passed. In order to strengthen a class-action suit against the county, state, and federal authorities, 150 property owners from the area incorporated as the Village of West Hampton Dunes. In 1994 they won a legal settlement in which the federal government, along with the state and county, agreed to fill in the newly formed channel and build a 400-foot-wide beach along the vulnerable Dune Road at an estimated cost to taxpayers of $75 million.

In the five-part series "Shoreline in Peril" published in *Newsday* in August 1998, reporters Thomas Maier and John Riley showed how the mayor and other West Hampton Dunes officials quietly bought up a number of the town's sunken lots from desperate property owners, roughly tripling their investment once the government sand was in place and new construction started on vacation homes worth a million dollars and more (which also qualified for cheap federal flood insurance).

"What we're doing here is permitted by law and is moral and legal," claimed the newly prosperous mayor, Gary Vegliante, who went on to suggest, "What happened in West Hampton Dunes is a model for the nation on coastal policy."

Perhaps, but when I visit West Hampton Dunes on the way to the beach with friends in July 2003, it looks like a corridor of super-sized box houses has sprouted from the sand, blocking our view of the Atlantic but providing lots of opportunities to admire the Humvees, Mercedes SUVs, and other status rides parked in their carports.

An alternative model of coastal development exists along 1,500 miles of Massachusetts' ocean beaches and bays where, since 1978, the state has banned construction of seawalls and jetties. "We lost half our wetlands up 'til '78 and have lost very little since," says Jim O'Connell, the former state coastal geologist who now directs the Woods Hole Coastal Research Center. I'm sharing a bench with him along the Shining Sea Bike Path overlooking Nantucket Sound on Cape Cod.

"Natural erosion creates bays, estuaries, and barrier beaches," he explains. "But if you armor your uplands you lose your beaches and wet-lands. If you put seawalls up along the Cape Cod National Seashore it would disappear in less than a century." A white-haired woman in pink cotton pants and a striped shirt stops on the path in front of us. "I love to see people sitting there. My husband and I, this was our favorite spot to sit here and watch the ocean." She resumes her power walk. I notice a bronze plaque on the bench back, "In loving memory of Bill Port 1919–1997. Shirley."

"Thank you, Shirley," I call out. She turns her head, smiles, and continues on her way.

I'm swimming in warm, milky white waters just off Miami Beach. The water's cloudiness comes from suspended silicate not yet settled out of the sand slurry that's being pumped a few hundred yards south at Government Cut. Scooping some sand off the bottom, I find it grainy and thick with shell. Offshore is a big four-legged dredge platform owned by the Great Lakes Dredge and Dock Company; a large sand pipe comes ashore at a fenced-off area near the shipping channel, where Jetskis and cigarette boats are buzzing around and young Haitian teens are jumping off a high wooden fishing pier. The pumping of sand slurry (about 85 percent water and 15 percent sand) has stopped for the day, and a Caterpillar dozer is spreading the sand in a rampart down along the water's edge.

This 13-mile stretch of beach, part of 150 miles of Army Corps of Engineers beach projects in Florida, is the nation's second largest sand nourishment program after that of New Jersey. Miami Beach once had a natural strand but seawalls built by hotel owners eroded that away, and now the Corps is bringing in sand from offshore to maintain this new beach. There is only one problem.

"We're exhausting the last offshore sand in Dade County," says David Schmidt, the chief of the Coastal Navigation Section for the Corps' Jacksonville District. "So we're looking to aragonite [sand] either upland or barged in from a foreign country. In the Bahamas and Turks and Caicos, aragonite precipitates out of the water. But the Bahamas won't give us any because they're in competition with Miami and want tourists to come to their nice white beaches. The Turks is willing, but the American dredging industry doesn't like the idea of foreign sand. They think the work will go to foreign companies. So they got Congress to pass a law saying foreign sand can't be used where there's American sand available."

It sounds like protectionism to me, although not the kind that protects our coasts.

Pumping offshore sand to the beach also can pose a danger to offshore reefs, which can be easily buried. About 25 miles north of Miami are some of the most northerly living reefs left in Florida, located, oddly enough, right off the crowded beach at Fort Lauderdale, a boomtown best known for its spring break rowdiness. Based there is a small but determined citizens' group called Cry of the Water, working to document and protect several hundred acres of staghorn and pillar corals located in an area the Army Corps has identified as holding potential sand resources for beach replenishment.

On another trip to Florida—officially to attend Reef Awareness Week 2004 in Key West—I take advantage of a five-hour layover in Fort Lauderdale to meet with Cry of the Water founders Dan and Stephanie Clark, and get a little time in the water. From my window seat as we descend, the turquoise sea and cobalt sky of south Florida are still awesome to behold. But it's impossible to ignore the urban seawall of high-rise glass and steel condos and hotels marching down the beach, the sprawl of suburbs laced with brown-water canals, and the algae-choked marina outlets lining the coast. Former real-estate developer turned governor Jeb Bush lauds this metastasizing growth in the name of jobs and progress.

Shortly after my plane lands, Stephanie picks me up and we drive across the Intercoastal Waterway down to Sunrise Boulevard and the beach. Here we meet Dan and some members of the local "kayuba" (kayak and scuba) club. I strip down to my bathing suit and put on snorkel gear; accompanied by kayakers towing an extra craft, we swim out beyond the high-rises and construction cranes, the distractions of thong bikinis and hot sands, to a surprisingly live reef they've been telling me about, just over 1,000 feet offshore. We swim through several acres of branching staghorn corals, habitat for swarms of small fish. Then we climb in the extra kayak and paddle over to another site, where a healthy pillar coral is being investigated by a curious French angelfish and some bright green parrotfish. Aside from their other virtues, reefs are a major source of natural beach nourishment in the tropics, thanks in part to parrotfish, which eat coral and poop copious amounts of sand.

After we have bobbed around on the surface for 15 minutes, the *Sea Experience*, a 42-foot glass-bottom boat, makes its rendezvous with us. We're invited aboard for sodas and sandwiches and to meet several research scientists, grad students, and local activists who are working with Dan and Stephanie to study and protect this northerly Florida reef. Besides the threat of Army Corps sand pumping, they are concerned about plans for new offshore gas pipelines, the laying of fiber-optic cables, and other underwater development facilitating the runaway onshore development. After 40 minutes aboard the *Experience,* we motor over to an outer swim buoy, where Stephanie and I step off the stern and swim back to shore. After a quick beach shower she drives me back to the airport in plenty of time before my connecting flight to Key West. I figure this has to beat hanging out at the airport newsstand for four hours.

Along with its activities in flood control and beach replenishment, the Army Corps of Engineers also dredges some 400 million tons of sediments a year for shipping channels, marinas, harbors, and ports—about three times the amount of earth moved to build the Panama Canal. Most of this dredge spoil is dumped into rivers, bays, and estuaries or used for landfill (on which to build those waterfront developments). Some 60 million tons goes to 100 ocean dumpsites selected by the Environmental Protection Agency (EPA).

While most shipping channels leading into America's major ports contain fairly clean muds or sand and seagrass bottoms, some inner harbors—particularly in older cities and military ports—contain sediments contaminated with high levels of mercury, heavy metals, PCBs, and dioxin. For years the EPA refused to dredge at a dioxin-contaminated Superfund site off Palos Verdes, California, for fear that disturbing the bottom would stir up the contaminants. At the same time, it approved dredging and ocean dumping for the Port of Newark's inner harbor, even though testing showed the area to be highly contaminated with dioxin from an old Agent Orange factory. This led to a series of protests, lawsuits, and a 1997 decision by the state of New Jersey to ban the disposal of contaminated sediments off its shores. The EPA agreed to shut down its ocean dumpsite, which by then had grown into a subsea mountain 1.5 times the size of Manhattan.

The Littoral Society, Clean Ocean Action, Coast Alliance, and other marine conservation groups later released a report titled *Muddy Waters: The Toxic Wasteland below America's Oceans.* The report compared the EPA and Army Corps of Engineers' ocean dumping of untreated sediments to "a medieval man tossing the contents of his chamber pot out the window." Rather than simply put out bumper stickers reading, "Save the Mud," the coalition proposed a number of practical solutions. These were based on the idea of combining pollution prevention (not allowing any new contamination) with cleanup technologies being tried out in the New York–New Jersey Harbor area by government and commercial enterprises. These techniques include chemical, pressure, and thermal treatments in which contaminated sediments are run through big rotary kiln incinerators or mulched with wood chips, compost, and manure to form commercial soils, which can then be cleaned by cattails and other wetland plants that absorb heavy metals. Other treatments involve the use of recoverable solvents that remove pollutants from mud or the locking of contaminated sediment slurries into cement or glasslike materials useful for aggregate, landfill, and roadfill.

Of all the coalition's proposals, the one that would seem easiest to implement—avoiding any unnecessary dredging in ports—may prove to be the most difficult. This is because of the increasingly unbalanced relationship between America's ports and the globalized shipping industry.

Today, more than 97 percent of America's non-NAFTA trade goods, about a billion metric tons per year, are carried by ships across the blue frontier. And while West Coast trade is fairly concentrated in three major port areas—Seattle-Tacoma, Oakland, and America's largest container port, Los Angeles–Long Beach—there are literally dozens of East Coast and Gulf ports being played off against one another by the world's shipping companies. Boston, New York, Philadelphia, Baltimore, Norfolk, Charleston, Savannah, Jacksonville, Miami, and Galveston-Houston are among those vying to become megaports, dredging ever deeper and wider channels in the hope of accommodating a new generation of container ships called Post-PanaMax. These are freighters too large to fit through the Panama Canal (or into most existing ports).

In 1956 a revolution in shipping occurred when Malcolm McLean, a North Carolina trucker turned entrepreneur, introduced "the box," a reinforced truck trailer with its wheels removed. He put 58 of these boxes on the *Ideal X,* a ship he modified and sailed from New York Harbor to Houston. That voyage marked the beginning of the end of net-loaded break-bulk cargo.

The longshoremen's union, still led by San Francisco's Harry Bridges, recognized that containerization would mean fewer men working the docks. Rather than fight the technology, they negotiated contracts that allowed their older members to retire with their benefits intact. This allowed the union to maintain control of the remaining jobs (crane and forklift operators, yard truck drivers, and so on). The continuing power of the union was demonstrated during December 1999's "Battle in

Seattle," when longshoremen staged a one-day shutdown of West Coast ports in solidarity with the anti–World Trade Organization protesters.

Another demonstration of how changing technologies have strengthened the union took place in the fall of 2002, when shipping companies locked out the dockworkers in an attempt to win job-reduction concessions. But containerization, computerization, and globalization have led to the replacement of most warehouse inventories with "just in time" delivery systems. This means that everything from Chinese toys for Wal-Mart to car parts for General Motors are slated to cross oceans and docks to reach end users just as the old parts run out. The lockout caused a backup of goods clogging the ports, like that *I Love Lucy* episode where the assembly-line chocolates tumble out of control, only on a planetary scale. Even with a sympathetic Bush administration in Washington, the shipping industry was forced to back down within weeks when the lockout began to threaten the whole U.S. economy.

Containerization and intermodel transport (linking shipping docks to railroad spurs and highways) have dramatically decreased costs and increased speed of delivery of global marine commerce. Shipping costs have become so cheap that a growing number of giant gantry cranes, those superstars of the ports, are now built in China and shipped whole from Shanghai. These cranes lift and load what are called 20-foot-equivalent-unit (TEU) containers, although most are actually twice that size (40 and 45 feet). Modern container ships can carry as many as 5,000 TEUs, both within their hulls and stacked up to 12 high on their decks.

But even as the oil transport industry has reduced the number of supertankers in the wake of various maritime disasters, the shipping industry—unconstrained by any major public outcry over dredging and accidents—continues to expand the size of its container ships. In 1998 Denmark's Maersk Shipping sent its aircraft carrier–sized 6,000-TEU ship *Regina Maersk* on an East Coast tour of the United States. It had to stop first at the natural deep-water port of Halifax, Canada, to offload part of its cargo so it could ride high enough to fit through New York's 40-foot-deep shipping channel and dock at Port Newark. An alliance of Maersk and Sea-Land, whose leases with New York were scheduled to end in 1999, offered to move their business (350,000 TEUs per year) to whatever port offered the best incentives, including dredging to 53-foot depths.

The ports could have refused to accept these hard-to-handle megaships, or they could designate a single deep-water hub and a series of feeder ports. Instead, they reverted to form, trying to steal each other's business. Maryland and the Port of Baltimore put together the largest financial incentive in the state's history, trying to lure away New York's leases. In the end Maersk and Sea-Land opted to stick with the Big Apple, having squeezed as much juice out of it as they could.

Beginning in 2003, a Hong Kong shipping company launched the first of eight 8,063-TEU ships, and there is talk of possible 10,000-TEU ships that will require even deeper ports.

In an article for *Container Management* magazine, Lillian Borrone of the Port Authority of New York and New Jersey (who would go on to serve as a member of the U.S. Commission on Ocean Policy) bemoaned the fact that as the shipping industry consolidates and sets the terms for doing business, ports, which are mostly public enterprises, continue to favor cutthroat competition over alliance-building that could improve their bargaining position. One result of this competition has been more than seven billion dollars in new deep-channel dredging and expansion projects over the past five years.

Many maritime nations have national port authorities, but a 2004 National Research Council (NRC) study found that federal responsibility for marine commerce and transport is widely dispersed, decentralized, and poorly coordinated. Despite our dependence on shipborne trade, which is projected to double in the next 20 years, there is no equivalent to the Federal Aviation Administration for our ports and shipping. Which is why the U.S. Commission on Ocean Policy has recommended that Congress designate the Department of Transportation as the lead federal agency to at least begin working on planning and oversight for marine transport.

Many of today's dredging projects are hard to justify from either an environmental or an economic point of view. Attempts by the Georgia Ports Authority to deepen the river channel into the Port of Savannah, the nation's eighth largest container port, have generated opposition from the municipal government, the local business community, and conservationists. According to hydrologists, deepening the channel would allow a saltwater ridge to flow upriver, which could kill up to 10,000 acres of the 27,000-acre Savannah National Wildlife Refuge, located just across from the town's riverfront tourist district. Businesses that withdraw water from the river are also worried about silt and salt intrusion, as is the city, which fears it might have to relocate its water treatment plant.

When the U.S. Fish and Wildlife Service, which runs the refuge, objected to the dredging, Republican representative Jack Kingston, a dredging supporter, went ballistic. A leaked Georgia Ports Authority note reads: "JK [Jack Kingston] needs us to kick F&W's ass in the paper. . . . Don't let rinky-dink agency beat us."

The 1999 Water Resources Development Act bill authorized $230 million to deepen the Savannah harbor from 42 to 48 feet, but the money never got spent. Economic projections for the port showed that dredging and expansion would work only if Savannah could steal business away from the ports of Brunswick, Georgia; Charleston, South Carolina; and Jacksonville, Florida, which are also expanding. By 2005, business in the Port of Savannah had improved thanks to better ground transportation connections and increased Asian imports. The Georgia Ports Authority and the Corps of Engineers were still trying to sell the dredging plan, but support was fading at a time when things seemed to be going fine without it.

A significant conflict of interest is built into the mandate of the Army Corps of Engineers: along with dredging ports, the service (together with the EPA) is responsible for protecting wetlands and approving permits that allow wetlands to be filled in or altered. More than half of America's coastal wetlands have been lost to development over the life of the republic, including 95 percent of California's, with the greatest losses occurring in the 1970s and 1980s. After the first President George Bush pledged "no net loss of wetlands" back in 1989, the rate of loss slowed but didn't stop. Under George W. Bush, wetland losses appear to have increased again owing to lax enforcement and easing up on development permits. It's hard to tell because the Corps and the EPA have failed to generate definitive data.

For generations, wetlands were perceived as dank and dangerous swamps, home to snakes, alligators, and the occasional philosophical possum. Since World War II some 50 million acres of farmland have been paved over by urban and suburban development, while some 53 million acres of wetlands have been filled in for agricultural use. This was considered a reasonable tradeoff until science began identifying wetlands as key habitat for migratory birds and wildlife, a nursery for 75 percent of our marine fisheries, a protective barrier against coastal storms and hurricanes, a pollution filtration system, and a natural recharger of freshwater aquifers.

Coastal wetlands and estuaries often trail off into seagrass meadows, which help secure the nearshore bottom, reduce turbidity, and provide vital habitat for juvenile fish and shellfish. But significant losses of seagrass have occurred as a result of sediment and nutrient runoff, vessel wakes, and scarring from dredges, anchors, and shallow-draft vessels including personal watercraft.

Visiting the Georgia coast south of Savannah, I'm overwhelmed by the soft beauty of its salt marshes. About one-third of the entire Eastern seaboard's total are located along this narrow 120-mile coastline. For a fellow from California, where a reedy duck pond near the ocean is considered a maritime treasure, the sight of extensive live-oak hammocks and Spanish moss draping over the banks of coastal river marshes that meander as far as blue herons can fly is just too nice. The locals attribute their coast's relatively pristine condition to eight-foot tides (which make building difficult), wealthy carpetbaggers (who bought up barrier islands as family retreats), tree farms (which dominate the local economy), and insects (the biting kind).

They are also thankful to Savannah's Jim Williams, the accused murderer in the best-selling book *Midnight in the Garden of Good and Evil*. It was his sale of Little Tybee Island to Kerr-McGee for a planned phosphate mine back in the 1960s that outraged Georgia citizens and inspired them to establish one of the strongest coastal wetlands protection laws in the United States.

Still, even here people worry that their natural coast may not stay that way for long. "If we don't do the right things now, we'll be like Florida," warns Robert DeWitt, a blue crab wholesaler in Darien. "Right now we don't have a coastal population, we've got sand gnats." The same can't be said for urban areas like New York, Miami, and Los Angeles, where people outnumber sand gnats and the last remaining coastal wetlands are highly valued—by real-estate developers.

The year of the millennium, 2000, saw construction begin for phase one of a multibillion-dollar "dream city" called Playa Vista (Spanish for "beach view") on the last undeveloped coastal valley in Los Angeles. The 1,087-acre Ballona Valley lies north of Los Angles International Airport and south of Marina del Rey. Longtime community opponents of Playa Vista, whose planning began in the early '90s, have pointed out that LA has the lowest ratio of parks to pavement of any major city in America and called for restoration of the entire valley as a tidal wetland and city park. They have also objected to inevitable traffic and air pollution from the 200,000 additional car trips per day Playa Vista is expected to generate.

Ballona Valley escaped Los Angeles's postwar building boom only because it had already been bought up by Howard Hughes. For years, the mysterious Mr. Hughes was content to maintain a single 60-acre aircraft factory on the valley's far eastern end, even as Marina del Rey and other developments sprang up along the edge of the valley's coastal wetlands. In 1947 the Hughes aircraft factory completed production of its most famous work, the Spruce Goose, a seaplane so large it could barely rise off the water.

Hollywood's DreamWorks studio, which dropped out of the Playa Vista development in 1999, brought early media attention to the project. DreamWorks' principals include the movie titans Steven Spielberg, David Geffen, and Jeff Katzenberg. During the 1996 presidential campaign Geffen hosted a $25,000-a-head party that raised $3.5 million for President Bill Clinton. Spielberg, Geffen, and Katzenberg also personally contributed more than $1.5 million to the Democrats between 1990 and 1997. President Clinton then selected Playa Vista as one of five Partnership for Advancing Technology in Housing communities promoted as models of sustainable development. Critics saw this as a payoff to the administration's Hollywood supporters. When Vice President Al Gore's staffers called local enviros to see how they'd react if he came out to LA and personally endorsed Playa Vista, the Sierra Club threatened to picket Gore. He never made the trip.

Playa Capital, the development group, went on to build 3,200 housing units and 1.5 million square feet of office space on the Ballona site, with plans for 2,600 more townhouses and 350,000 feet of additional retail and office space. In the process they dug up methane seeps from old oil drilling sites, more than 300 human remains from Native American burial sites, and two World War II bomb canisters. (The Los Angeles Police Department bomb squad called in the Army, which declared them nonexplosive.) In 2003, under pressure from environmentalists and community activists, the state of California bought up 540 acres of the Ballona wetlands west of Lincoln Boulevard, which will be protected and restored, while development east of Lincoln is expected to continue apace.

Reporting on the conflict several years ago, I was impressed by the bizarrely contrasting visions that Los Angeles can conjure up for a visiting journalist. It was raining and misty on my first day as I stood on the Westchester Bluffs looking a mile west toward Marina del Rey and the ocean. Large sheeting pools of water in the still green valley provided easy pickings for white-feathered egrets and insect-hungry frogs, whose crickety trillings carried on the wind. Soon I was down at ground level climbing through a broken hurricane fence with the activists Marcia Hanscom and Bruce Robertson. My running shoes quickly soaked through as we wandered among the pickleweed, cattails, and chest-high foliage, spotting a hovering kite, the fuzzy tail end of a rabbit, and a half-dozen great blue herons foraging along the edge of a brackish creek before lifting off in a great beating of three-foot wings.

I asked the activists if they thought they could win their battle to save an ocean-view valley in the heart of Los Angeles. "Well, it's kind of like a Spielberg movie," Hanscom grinned, "where the little guys take on the huge corporate developer."

The next day was bright and sunny as I rode upvalley on an old two-lane tarmac road with Doug Gardner, the friendly architect turned site manager for Playa Vista. The first animal we spotted was a large African elephant rearing up on its hind legs next to a moving van. One of Howard Hughes's old aircraft hangars had been converted to a movie studio where they were shooting *George of the Jungle.* Inside we wandered through several acres of fake rainforest and softly yielding earth made of potting soil and wood chips. There were klieg lights and big 35-millimeter cameras on dolly mounts and craft service caterers scuttling around with trays of straw-studded coconut-shell drinks for the cast. I recognized a unique kind of dream magic taking place here: Hollywood's always seductive ability to suspend our belief, whether creating a tropical rainforest in an aircraft hangar or pitching the idea that the only way to save the last coastal wetland in Los Angeles is to build a new city on its shore.

Most of today's wetland losses are not big and controversial and played out in the media, but small and little noted. It's an acre here, two acres there, usually permitted by the Corps of Engineers without inspection. A whole new consulting industry has grown up to help developers navigate government regulations and permit requirements on what they refer to as "environmentally challenged sites." By "environmentally challenged" they mean (George Orwell would appreciate this) pristine coastal wetlands and forested islands containing endangered species.

In 2000 the *Washington Post* ran a series of articles by reporter Michael Grunwald exposing internal plans by the military commanders of the Corps to increase the Corps' budget 50 percent over five years through rapid expansion of its water projects. This was to take place apparently without regard to the economic necessity or environmental impact of the works.

"Oh my God, my God. I have no idea what you're talking about. I can't believe this," the civilian assistant secretary of the Army, who was then supposed to be overseeing the Corps, told Grunwald when asked to comment on the plans. The Corps' military "green shirts" (as opposed to its civilian employees) seemed to be in thrall to some primal force beyond their control, a spirit half warrior and half beaver. Five years later, in 2005, little seemed to have changed, with the Corps again caught up in multibillion-dollar controversies over plans to dredge, dam, and replumb the Columbia, Missouri, and Mississippi rivers and questions about the structural integrity of New Orleans's failed flood walls.

Meanwhile, America's coastal wetlands continue to decline as tidal flows are cut off by roads and houses, and Spartina (sea hay) is gradually replaced by the prettier but less beneficial swamp grass called Phragmites ("frag"), which often indicates a disrupted habitat.

The same process of fragmentation and loss that is happening to wetlands can also happen to coastal cultures when traditional fishing towns, beach communities, and waterfront cities fail to maintain their civic vigilance. That's when they can morph into dangerously overbuilt urban seawalls like Atlantic City or Gulfport, Mississippi, driven by casino, condo, and real estate values that measure life on the blue frontier based solely on the dollar value of oceanfront footage.

Unfortunately, prime beachfront real estate tends to be transitory in nature. In 1968 the Federal Emergency Management Agency (FEMA), worried about the disaster risks faced by new beachfront residents, came up with a plan. If homeowners met certain basic safety standards in beachfront construction (such as putting houses on stilts), they would qualify for a newly created National Flood Insurance Program (NFIP). FEMA convinced Congress that this would reduce individual risk while shifting the burden of hurricane disaster relief onto policyholders. They would guarantee a large insurance pool by making the rates so inexpensive that lots of people would buy the policies.

This idea worked for a while—about as long as the historic lull in Atlantic hurricane activity persisted through the 1970s and 1980s. As soon as Hurricanes Hugo, Andrew, George, Fran, Floyd, Isabel, Charley, Frances, Ivan, Jeanne, Dennis, Katrina, and their ilk started coming ashore, the program turned into a huge money loser and the largest financial exposure the federal government now faces. By the summer of 2005 FEMA had insured more than $763 billion worth of property against flooding, about half of it in the Gulf region that includes low-lying, hurricane-prone Florida.

The greatest impact of NFIP has been to fuel the coastal construction boom of the past four decades, which makes the Western land rush of the nineteenth century pale by comparison. As Cornelia Dean points out in

her book *Against the Tide,* until NFIP came along it was almost impossible to insure beachfront property against flooding. As a result most
bankers refused to issue mortgages, so beachfront homeowners had to
pay cash and tended not to build bigger than they could afford to lose.
But once the feds started offering beachfront flood insurance (for an
average $300 annual premium), real-estate developers found mortgage
bankers more than willing to lend them money, setting off a tsunami of
new coastal construction.

When Hurricane Frederick struck barrier islands off Alabama in 1979,
for example, shattered beach cottages at Gulf Shores were quickly
replaced by 5- to 15-story fully mortgaged condominiums, many of which
were then destroyed by 2004's Hurricane Ivan. "We'll clean it up for next
summer and make it better than ever," promised Gulf Shores' police chief,
surveying Ivan's devastation. Plans included a new 66-acre barrier island
shopping center, which, according to Gulf Shores' mayor (and local real-
estate developer), will transform the area from a one-time "Redneck
Riviera" into a more desirable "Gulf Coast resort destination."

Federal flood insurance covers up to $250,000 for property damage to
homes and $500,000 for businesses. Storm-battered beach communities
are also eligible for low-interest small business loans; federally funded
reconstruction of highways, roads, and bridges; and sand replenishment
courtesy of the Army Corps of Engineers.

"The problem is the government won't operate like a business. It
won't cancel policies or increase premiums when a house is destroyed
like a real company would," complains Steve Ellis, a maritime specialist
with the Washington-based Taxpayers for Common Sense. "Erosion and
sea-level rise aren't even factored into their rates."

FEMA insurance also allows policyholders to make repeat claims,
encouraging people to rebuild in harm's way. ABC-TV correspondent
and free-market champion John Stossel aired a *20/20* piece on FEMA's
insurance program after his weekend beach house in Westhampton was
washed away in a storm. "It was an upsetting loss for me, but financially
I didn't lose a penny. National Flood Insurance paid for the house and its
contents," he explains, lounging on the beach. "And now that you're
paying to replenish my beach [with taxpayer-funded sand], it's possible
that my neighbors and I will build our houses again and you'll insure us
again. Thanks." He then flashes his trademark smirk for the camera.

Although Stossel appears to be critical of the program (while still taking money from it), popular novelist Nicholas Sparks defended FEMA
flood insurance in a *New York Times* editorial following 1999's Hurri-

cane Floyd. His home, built on Bogue Banks, a North Carolina barrier island, has been repeatedly damaged by storms. His argument, however, is that in a major storm surge the houses of poor people on the mainland would also be destroyed. "That's the real reason for the subsidy," he claims. "It protects large numbers of people who are not rich, whose homes are worth less than $250,000." Of course, those are the home-owners least likely to file repeat claims, their houses being far less exposed to flood damage than properties on high value–high risk beaches like Bogue Banks, Westhampton, Hilton Head, and Captiva.

Although they represent only 2 percent of NFIP-covered properties, 40 percent of federal flood insurance payments go to repetitive loss claims. For example, a commercial property on Fire Island, New York, collected $96,000 in 1991, $203,000 in 1992, $42,000 in 1993, and $250,000 in 1994. A beachfront property on Topsail Island, North Carolina, collected $457,713 for losses from eight different storms between 1981 and 1996. With repetitive claims costing the program more than $200 million per year, President Clinton's FEMA director, James Lee Witt, gave a 1998 talk proposing that insurance be denied to homeowners who file two or more claims that total more than the value of their house. The speech was immediately attacked by the National Homebuilders Association, and FEMA staged a quick retreat from what could only be described as an already overly cautious proposal.

Six years later, in 2004, President Bush signed the Flood Insurance Reform Act, a similarly cautious law that will provide assistance to repeat damage claimants to elevate or move their homes or, if they refuse, make them pay full-market rates for their coverage. Predictably it took Congress another year to provide funding for the reform act, which it finally did in May 2005.

As early as 1982 Congress began to see the folly of promoting dangerous coastal development, so it passed the Coastal Barrier Resources Act (CBRA, pronounced "Cobra"). The act excludes some three million acres of flood-prone undeveloped barrier islands and sand spits from federal subsidies. This does not mean that property owners in these areas can't develop their land, only that they can't bring in Uncle Sam as their real-estate partner.

"I travel the coast, and the CBRA units are not being developed and you have to ask why? Well, you can't get flood insurance and other federal money, and that clearly suggests that federal insurance and beach replenishment and road and bridge construction must be encouraging development," says Woods Hole's Jim O'Connell.

Having passed some good legislation, Congress quickly went to work tampering with it. Beginning with the 104th Congress, the House and Senate have passed dozens of "technical corrections" to CBRA in order to remove constituents' properties from CBRA's subsidy-free zones. These "corrections" relate to properties that were already developed or being developed in some way when they were included in the act. Typically, in the final days before the 1999 Thanksgiving break, Congress rushed through a number of "technical corrections" restoring federal subsidies to properties in Delaware, North Carolina, and Florida's North Captiva Island, one of the wealthiest places in America. The changes were requested by Republican representatives Michael Castle of Delaware, Walter Jones of North Carolina, and Porter Goss of Florida. (In 2004, just weeks before Hurricane Charley cut North Captiva in two, Goss would be named by President Bush to head the CIA. If nothing else, Goss's efforts on behalf of his wealthy constituents showed that he knew how to act covertly.) By 2005 there were four bills in Congress aiming to exempt more than 50,000 acres from CBRA protection in coastal Georgia, Texas, and Florida.

In another case from the late 1990s, about 12 acres on the exclusive Ocean Reef Club in North Key Largo and the 25-acre Pumpkin Key just offshore from it won "technical corrections." The Berry family, which owns Pumpkin Key, wanted to develop a dozen homesites on the small island property, where nearby homes and condos start at a million dollars.

I call Terra Cotta Realty (Florida), which is actually located in Crystal Lake, Illinois. Speaking with Bob Berry, Terra Cotta's vice president, I ask to visit Pumpkin Key. He says he'll call back, and when he does, he tells me they would be happy to send me their congressional testimony, "but our attorney doesn't think it would be appropriate for you to visit."

I later run into Representative Pete Deutsch, the liberal Democrat from south Florida who got the two properties exempted from CBRA. "The fact is they shouldn't have been included," he tells me. "I went out there to Pumpkin Key, and there are roads and plumbing hook-ups. And the Ocean Reef property was fully developed [and occupied by multimillion-dollar homes]. It was a technical issue. Based on the legislation, it was a mistake."

He looks around, seeming uncomfortable even in his nicely tailored suit, and begins to talk to a reporter from the *Miami Herald* about Cuban exiles confronted by the Coast Guard on the water off Florida.

He complains about the federal government returning illegal immigrants to Cuba, "the last dictatorship in the Western Hemisphere." In south Florida speaking ill of Fidel Castro has never hurt a politician, nor has speaking out for real-estate interests.

I look at the House testimony of Bob Berry's father, George, who bought the low-lying island in 1973 and has since put five million dollars into his private paradise (not counting $100 a day in cut flowers when his wife is there). More interesting, however, is the testimony of Terra Cotta's chairman, Tom Hayward, before the Senate Committee on Environment and Public Works on September 22, 1998. On the very day that Hayward asked Florida senator Bob Graham and others to pass a law restoring the Berrys' development subsidies, Ocean Reef and the Keys were being evacuated because of Hurricane George. George left a billion dollars of damage in its wake, including $250 million to the Keys. Still, the Berrys had their subsidies reinstated.

"We still purchase federal flood insurance," Bob Berry tells me when we talk again. "We were looking into not purchasing it, but you can't get homeowner's, liability, or any other type of insurance unless you have it." Tom Hayward joins the conversation. "CBRA would have impacted on our marketability. Without flood insurance you wouldn't be able to get a mortgage if you wanted to buy a house there [on Pumpkin Key]."

"We're not interested in being part of any book," Bill Hackelton, the director of communications for Ocean Reef, tells me when I call to inquire about a visit. The 4,000-acre gated community has 1,600 residences, plus golf courses, tennis courts, hotel rooms, private restaurants, a small airport, and a large yacht basin. Incorporated as a private club in 1993, Ocean Reef has membership rates of $117,000 and $300,000. The higher rate gets you discounts on food, beverages, and golf. Either one lets you buy properties ranging from studio condos for $280,000 to waterfront mansions for seven or eight million dollars. This has made it prime winter-golf habitat for Kathy Lee and Frank Gifford, Whitney Houston, George Bush Senior, various corporate CEOs, and the occasional Kennedy or two.

"Don't you sometimes hold conventions?" I ask.

"We hold conferences, not conventions. We don't invite retired postmasters in. We have senior management retreats and CEO meetings."

"So reporters aren't welcome?"

"Not unless you're a guest of one of our members."

Or go in with the service guy who scrapes the barnacles off their yachts. But as with the Douglaston Country Club when I was a kid, once you've seen Ocean Reef it's hard to get too excited. It is a suburban dream writ large: wide meandering streets, apple-green golf courses, Spanish-accented rooflines (and service employees). The street traffic is mainly scooters and golf carts occupied by white guys wearing Lacoste shirts.

We swing past the marina and over to Snapper Point, where I walk to the water's edge and pull out my binoculars. Thirteen hundred feet away is Pumpkin Key. I could swim out to it, but the warm soupy brown water of Card Sound doesn't look too inviting unless you're a manatee. Plus I'd be trespassing. But I can see there's infrastructure in place, a gray building sticking out of low-lying mangroves and a dock with a 70-foot yacht pulled up to it. My tax dollars at rest.

Still, despite the risks from hurricanes, rising seas, and golf carts blocking emergency vehicles, alternative models for coastal development do exist, even in Florida. In the movie *The Truman Show,* Jim Carrey is raised in a utopian beach town that he discovers is really a domed TV set. Although it was altered for the film (computer graphics added a curved horizon, fake river, and tall buildings), the real-life town of Seaside, Florida, made a convincing set because it is something of a visionary beach community.

Seaside is located on the sugar-white sands and blue green waters of the Florida Panhandle about halfway between Pensacola and Panama City. Founded in 1980, the development has grown to 400 beach cottages and shops on 80 setback acres of scrub, live oak, magnolia, and pampas grass, picket fences, and pastel-painted homes, many with steeply inclined tin roofs and screened-in porches, and all linked by rain-porous cobble streets and sandy footpaths. Its "neotraditional" style and low-impact design have won praise from *Time* magazine, *Architectural Digest,* and the Florida Audubon Society.

When Hurricane Opal hit the Panhandle on October 4, 1995, with high winds and a 15- to 20-foot storm surge, towns such as Destin and Dune-Allen, just a few miles from Seaside, were devastated. But all 280 of Seaside's Old Florida–style frame homes came through unscathed. "They protected the dunes and the dunes protected them," explained Donna M. Dannels, the FEMA official sent to assess the damage. Aside from building behind the beach's protective sand dunes, Seaside also used tough building standards designed to withstand 150-mile-per-hour winds, sank its foundation pilings deep into the ground, and planted lots of native trees and grasses to secure the dunes and buffer the houses. Cheap, modern building materials such as vinyl and strandboard siding were rejected. "If it didn't exist before 1940, we didn't feel it was proven," says Robert Davis, the founder of Seaside. "As a kid I spent summers with my family in simple, expendable beach cottages near Panama City, where they later built bulkheads and put large buildings behind seawalls, and you can guess what happened next," Davis says. "They've had to take some of those buildings down after the beaches went away. . . . It used to be everyone built well back from the beach. That was before federal flood insurance made stupidity feasible.

"What washed away [during Hurricane Opal] were slab houses built on bulldozed sand, really stupid construction," he continues. "We'd all be better off to let hurricanes do what they do and take the proceeds from the insurance and buy somewhere else, but I suspect we'll just keep shoveling against the tide."

I ask him if he sees Seaside as part of a trend toward more careful coastal developments.

"This is less of an exception than it used to be, but calling it a trend may be overly optimistic. . . . I built Seaside not just for its environmental advantages, but because I thought it would be more pleasant to build low density. We've created land values two blocks from the beach that exceed the beachfront condos around here. People will pay huge amounts for access to unencroached-on wilds and beaches. The more coastal protection the state of California enacts, the higher its coastal property values climb.

"Good developments are done with long-term greed as their operating principle," Davis argues, "but there's still more short-term greed at work. We make piles of money and show our colleagues you can make money slowly and not rape and pillage the land. We try and share the idea of building lightly on the land [and by the water]."

The city of Hilo, Hawaii, is another example of how stepping back from the edge can work to the benefit of both local residents and the economy. After losing dozens of people and its downtown waterfront district to tsunami tidal waves in 1946 and again in 1960, the city came up with a new plan called Kaiko'o ("rough seas"). Downtown commercial development was moved inland behind a 350-acre bayfront park and fish market. Today the landscaped park (designed to take the brunt of the next tsunami) includes Japanese gardens, picnic grounds, and a palm-landscaped Coconut Island. Creating this recreational space also inspired a movement to clean up the bay and got surfers, boaters, and kayakers back into the water. Hilo, with its refurbished waterfront, has become a popular destination for both out-of-state visitors and other Hawaiians, who see it as the last traditional *aloha* city. Real estate overlooking the park and bay now sells for far more than the old waterside properties.

While maintaining natural setbacks like these makes good environmental and economic sense, there's a more troubling reason why some people choose to turn their backs to the ocean. According to a recent report from the National Academy of Sciences, marine life in more than a third of U.S. coastal areas is being killed off by nutrient-fed algae blooms. At the same time, more beach closures are occurring and more coastal health advisories are being posted than ever before—more than 20,000 in the summer of 2004.

"In 1987 and 1988 we had a disaster with our coastal economy because of beach closures, algae blooms, medical waste, and dolphins washing up dead on our beaches," recalls Representative Jim Saxton of New Jersey. "We made a lot of needed changes in response to that kind of point-source pollution. But a more difficult challenge is still ahead of us."

CHAPTER 8

Flushing the Coast

The beach is open. Only the water is closed!
>— *Surf-shop owner Michael Ali, on the 1999*
> *closure of Huntington Beach, California,*
> *due to bacterial pollution*

Aging, overrun sewage treatment and septic systems; runoff
from irrigated fields and lawns doused with fertilizer and
pesticides; and storm water runoff from streets and rooftops
caked with sediment, motor oil, and animal waste. . . .
>— *August 2004* U.S. News and World Report,
> *explaining reasons for beach closures*

I'm diving through the warm blue green waters of Conch Reef, seven
miles off Key Largo, Florida. Below me appears something resembling
the underwater lair of a James Bond villain. Actually, it's a 48-foot cylin-
drical habitat called Aquarius, the last underwater research station in the
world. It seems to rest weightless on its four steel legs, its yellow body
rusting to orange in spots and encrusted with weedy growths grazed by
roving schools of fish. On a platform just off the entryway is a white six-
sided gazebo with an air pocket—Aquarius's temporary rescue hut
should it need to be evacuated in a hurry. As I swim by one of the habitat's round viewports, a scientist inside looks up from his laptop and
waves, a can of salted peanuts by his side. I turn around and notice three
big tarpon shadowing me. The largest fish has to be at least 150 pounds.

Running from the habitat across the 60-foot-deep sandy bottom and
onto the reef is a spaghetti mat of cables, enough to power a Lolla-
palooza concert. In this case, the cables end at two acrylic domes and a
tripod-mounted stereo camera rig. Under one of the domes is a brain
coral, its respiration being measured as part of this month's mission to
evaluate the condition of North America's greatest living reef.

Coral reefs are the most diverse ecosystems on earth (25,000 species and counting) and serve as the nursery for more than half our tropical seafood including lobster, red snapper, grouper, and drum. They also act as coastal storm barriers and provide epic adventure for sport fishermen, kayakers, snorkelers, and, of course, divers.

Steve Miller, the director of the University of North Carolina's National Undersea Research Center, which administers Aquarius, leads me under the skirt of the habitat. We slide through the low-slung entryway to the wet room, popping up next to two researchers from the New England Aquarium about to make their way out onto the reef. A school of yellowtail snappers huddle discreetly toward the back of the wet well. Waist deep in water, we strip our gear and climb up a short ladder with the assistance of Jay Styron, one of Aquarius's two live-aboard support staff (out of a crew of six). In his spare time, Jay, a former charter boat crewman, acts as Clara Barton for barracudas, grabbing the ones who got away by stray line and leader and, holding them under one arm, removing the hooks from their mouths.

The inside of the habitat is cramped but comfortable, with blue industrial carpeting, a lab, a kitchen, and two sets of triple bunks. For Dr. Mineo Okamoto, a visiting scientist from JAMESTEC (Japan Marine Science and Technology Center), it's a dream come true. "In seven years studying coral from boats I could never do what I'm doing here," he says, his voice squeaky from the increased atmospheric squeeze on his larynx. Saturated with highly compressed air to compensate for the pressure, he and the other aquanauts will live inside Aquarius for eight days, scuba diving up to nine hours a day and spending much of the rest of their time monitoring their reef subjects, as they themselves are monitored from a wireless watch desk back at Mission Control, a gray stilt house in Key Largo. Mineo appears to be slightly giddy, not from nitrogen narcosis—that drunken feeling too much nitrogen in the bloodstream can give you—but from having stayed up all night reading the respiration rate of his coral as it appears on his laptop computer, which is secured by bungee cord to a narrow shelf on the far wall. He shows me a color graph running across its screen that means bupkis to me. He then hands me his business card. I apologize for not having thought to bring my own.

Unfortunately, as surface interlopers, Steve and I have only a little over an hour of visiting time before the nitrogen beginning to build up in our body tissues might cause decompression sickness, or the bends. At the end of their stay the Aquarius crew will go through a controlled 17-hour readjustment to surface air pressure, with the habitat itself acting as their decompression chamber. After they are brought back up to ambient surface pressure, they'll step into a smaller lockout chamber, the space between the wet well and living area that includes a toilet, a shower, and some camera shelving. Here they will be quickly repressurized to depth in order to return to the surface via the wet well, as if they had just been down on a five-minute dive.

On a subsequent visit with a video crew from *National Geographic*, I check out the seascape surrounding Aquarius, and realize one of the reasons this undersea lab is located where it is. Despite the fish drawn to the habitat (as to any underwater structure, be it a shipwreck, oil rig, or barrel of nuclear waste), this reef is dying. Branching corals that once grew here remain only as skeletal sticks in bleached rubble fields. Many of the abundant rock corals are being eaten away by diseases that have spread in an epidemic wave throughout the Keys. The names of the diseases tell the story: black band, white band, white plague, and aspergillus, a fungus normally found in terrestrial soil that can shred fan corals as moths shred Irish lace. The corals are also being smothered under sediment and algal growth linked to polluted runoff and are periodically bleaching white as a result of warming ocean temperatures.

"The story of this decade is one of coral decline," says Miller. Coral reefs, while grand in appearance, are actually fragile structures, living within a narrow range of clarity, salinity, and chemistry, so that even a slight increase in the ocean's temperature or increased carbon dioxide put into the ocean from the burning of fossil fuels can cause stresses. Bleaching is occurring more often; the reef experienced major bleaching events in 1987, 1990, 1997, 1998, and 2005. Increases in water acidity can also slow the growth rate of the corals, which strain calcium out of seawater to build their limestone castles. With some 70 percent of the world's coral reefs now losing productivity, it has become a global crisis and a scientific mystery with one prime suspect. Reefs found to be at greatest risk of dying are those closest to human development. And no reef line in the world is closer to urban sprawl than the 126-mile-long Florida Keys reef.

With diving, boating, and recreational fishing offered at every mile marker, the Keys are a major contributor to south Florida's $15-billion-per-year tourism industry. Unfortunately, the Keys are also downstream from seven million south Floridians and their urban and agricultural runoff, including runoff from Florida's huge sugar industry. Nutrient-rich phosphorus and nitrate fertilizers, pesticides, and herbicides used in the sugar industry's 300,000-acre Everglades Agricultural Zone have been identified as major polluters of both the historically low-nutrient Everglades and the Keys' historically low-nutrient bay and reef system. And the politics of sugar have tended to play a dominant role in both Florida's and Washington's responses to the problem. Even while calling for pollution reduction, the federal government continues to provide costly subsidies to Florida sugar producers. The pattern goes back to the 1960 embargo of Cuban trade with the U.S. in sugar and other commodities, part of an ineffective attempt to undermine Fidel Castro.

Still, the reef's problems cannot be traced to a single source of pollution such as sugar, which means that there is no silver-bullet solution to save the reef. Along with agricultural sources of nitrate and phosphorus runoff, Florida is also home to phosphate mining companies and their wastewaters. New construction and oily runoff from paved streets, driveways, and shopping malls throughout south Florida add additional silt, nitrogen, and hydrocarbons to the water, as does air pollution when it rains out. Studies of the Gulf of Mexico suggest that phosphorus and nitrogen runoff from the Mississippi and several Latin American rivers also has found its way onto the reef.

Nitrogen is essential for soil productivity, but too much of a good thing can be a bad thing, as anyone who has ever had a hangover will attest. According to various studies and reports in *Science* and *Scientific American,* synthetic fertilizers developed after World War II and the burning of fossil fuels doubled the global nitrogen cycle between 1960 and 1990. Along with natural nitrogen found in air, soil, and lightning, the added nitrogen input is too much for the land to handle, and the surplus is washed off into the world's rivers, estuaries, and oceans, where it ends up feeding giant algal blooms.

Corals, in their most productive state, need clean, clear, low-nutrient waters to thrive. By contrast, algae love sewage and other nutrients, and in their presence will bloom into a green light-obscuring soup that sucks the oxygen out of the water as it decays, killing off massive numbers of reef creatures, while suffocating the living coral polyps.

In addition to these global factors, more than 80,000 residents and 2.5 million annual visitors to the Florida Keys rely on septic systems that flush untreated waste through the islands' porous limestone—the skeletal remains of previous generations of coral—and into nearshore waters, changing their color from aquamarine to lime Jell-O. Key West, with the only municipal sewage plant on the islands, shut down its beaches during the summer of 1999 because of high bacterial counts as city workers dug up leaky pipes for replacement. But their effort paid off. With a citizen-supported construction bond the city upgraded its system and built an advanced waste treatment plant that, unlike traditional sewage plants, strips nutrients from its wastewaters. The town also reduced and cleaned up its stormwater runoff. Key West is now negotiating with the cruise ship industry, asking the nine big ships that visit every week to pump their wastewaters into the new sewage system rather than dump nutrient-heavy wastes onto the reef line.

In 1994 I produced a PBS segment on the locally based activist group Reef Relief. During the shooting I stood on the bridge of the group's cabin cruiser while a NOAA diver prepared to test the waters around the city's sewage outfall: before going down he donned a drysuit and protective hood, gloves, boots, and mask, which were then sealed with gaffer's tape. Back on board afterward, he ladled antibiotic solution over himself before removing his hood and gloves.

Ten years later, in 2004, I was able to revisit the site, now a municipal marine park for snorkelers. In its clear, clean waters I swam among new coral growths, sea grasses, and abundant fish life including big jacks, tangs, rays, and barracuda—proof that practical solutions to marine pollution can be enacted. Unfortunately, Key Largo and other parts of Monroe County (which encompasses the Keys) have yet to make a similar commitment to nutrient reduction even though reef tourism generates some $1.8 billion per year for the county's economy

"You can emphasize but not get bogged down by the complexity of the reef environment," suggests Steve Miller. "What we have to do is consider those things we can control that may have a negative impact on the reef. We can control overfishing [of lobster, parrotfish and other grazers that target algae], we can control nearshore pollution, and maybe some of those nutrients. But it can't all be done locally. What Midwest America dumps on its streets and adds to its soil ends up in the Mississippi and the Gulf of Mexico, which ends up on our reefs. People have to begin to understand that you may live in Iowa but you're also living on an ocean planet."

He says this with a kind of affable gentility. Steve, with his bearded smile, twinkling chestnut eyes, and slightly nerdy oblong glasses, is, after all, living the good life. He manages the National Undersea Research Center from a Key Largo canal complex that has the feel of a water-rat frat house, but with the added adult pleasures of home, wife, and family just down the road.

He shows me the extra decompression chamber parked in the flood

zone under the gray stucco stilt house. I look in through the window at
its two molded fiberglass benches that seat seven.

"Looks pretty uncomfortable."

"When the alternative is death it's comfortable," he says, and then
grins. "Hey, that's pretty good. You going to use that in your book?"

Late that evening I'm kicking back at the watch desk upstairs with
several of Steve's staff, including Craig Cooper, the operations director
for the program. A big man with blond hair blending to a white beard
and cool blue eyes in a sun-reddened face, Craig gives an impression of
solid competence—which is what you want for the frontier challenges
this former oil rig diver has to face every day. Right now he's videocon-
ferencing with Jay inside the habitat, discussing a pinging sound on their
shared computer net and a carbon monoxide default on one of the new
sensors they installed. They agree that the sensor needs to be reset and
watched.

"We have to figure these things out as we go along," Craig explains.
"There's no habitat store to go to and pick up an extra whatever." Two
nights earlier, Aquarius's air conditioner had failed; instead of pulling the
huge unit, Craig had improvised a way to get glycol (antifreeze) down to
the habitat in a sealed hose.

"Last year the power went out and I had to decompress inside the
habitat for 17 hours with a scientist. The temperature was 95 degrees
with over 95 percent humidity. That was the worst decompression I ever
went through."

Bottom time in the habitat can get boring for the regular crew, so
they've found ways to amuse themselves. When recreational divers used
to come into the area, Craig would play the theme music from the movie
Jaws on the underwater hailer. "Some of them were all right and came to
the window and would pretend to get pulled under. Others were clearly
nervous when they heard it."

I ask him how he got into the business. He says he read a magazine ad
for commercial diving and ended up in Houston for six months at a
commercial dive school, training for the most dangerous profession in
America. While working for Taylor Divers in 1977, he was offered
$1,000 a day to work 1,000 feet down on the construction of Shell Oil's
Cognac platform but turned the offer down. One diver who volunteered
for the job told him he saw 1,200- to 1,500-pound groupers down there,
"real sea monsters."

For $500 a day he did saturation diving in 600 feet of water, reweld-
ing pipeline housings with bad swivel joints. "We'd pull the pipes off the

bottom and drop these huge hydraulic frames and put a 16-by-16 housing over them and dig our way in underneath, working out of a diving bell. Once inside the hut you'd take your [tethered] dive helmets off to work, but you worried because the ship up top was using dynamic positioning to stay in place and if that fails, your helmet will be dragged off, leaving you behind."

Craig had a roommate and several friends who were killed while diving, including a buddy in the water with him at the fiery 1979 Ixtoc oil platform blowout in the Gulf of Mexico. Such experiences have made him a stickler for safety and quick response. His go-fast boat tied to the quay outside can be at the habitat in 20 minutes. I ask if there have been any close calls with Aquarius.

"Four of us got stuck on the top barge [later replaced with a buoy] during a storm named Gordon," he recalls. "We were stuck on the barge for 28 hours, then had to evacuate the habitat in 15-foot seas. The Coast Guard wouldn't help 'cause they said it wasn't a life-threatening situation, but we needed to decompress the scientists and get them out. Our generators had gone down and one had caught fire. So they were down there using battery power for the CO_2 scrubbers, with no functioning air conditioning. We finally got back out to them on a 50-foot catamaran owned by a local dive company. We established a down line in zero visibility by crawling down the umbilical [power and communications line] and then taking the rescue line back up to the cat. We'd send two men up the line and then motor toward them and shut down the engine. As soon as you powered down you'd start turning broadside to the waves, though. A few times I thought the boat was going to go over. Six of us would grab the divers out of the water and power back up before the wave took us. We used everything but gaff hooks hauling those guys out of the water like tuna.

"Hurricane George had five-knot currents 80 feet down. It broke one of the four support legs on the habitat. The buoy was recording 28-foot waves, and the top of the habitat is only 34 feet down, so it was lucky no one was aboard that time. We stayed here on the canal rather than evacuate the island. The water was two and a half feet above the dock with 90- to 100-mile winds. That was another close one."

It wasn't the wildness of life on the blue frontier but the absence of life that Dr. Nancy Rabalais of the Louisiana Universities Marine Consortium noticed, in the course of making a historic discovery. Diving on an abandoned oil rig 25 miles off the coast of Louisiana, she was surrounded by shoals of fish, including sheepshead, drum, and yellowtail snapper. Going deeper, she passed through a kind of hazy shimmering layer about 30 feet down and then, looking around, noticed a strange change. Suddenly there was nothing but empty murk as far as she could see. Sometimes while diving you can sense a presence, something lurking in the water just beyond your field of vision. It is a not uncommon feeling, whether you're looking out into the borderless azure blue of the open sea or swimming cautiously through brown coastal waters that can reduce visibility to feet, sometimes even to inches. Fish will often scatter moments before a big shark or other silent predator swims into view, sending your heart racing.

Rabalais looked up, but the fish above were still visible through the murk and shimmer, schooling and seemingly unconcerned. She dove on, looking for life in the normally teeming water, but found none. On the muddy bottom 70 feet down, however, she did find a lifeless crab and then a brittlestar and white seaworms that had crawled out of their holes in the mud before they stopped crawling at all. That's when she knew, with a certainty that sent a shiver racing across her flesh under her wetsuit, that her calculations and studies had all been correct—she had finally entered the Dead Zone.

Fifteen years later, thanks to the work of Dr. Rabalais and her colleagues, much more is known about the nutrient-fed Dead Zone that lurks unseen below the Gulf of Mexico's surface. Amoebalike in structure, it appears seasonally every spring and summer, stretching and writhing like some stealthy creature. First studied in the 1970s, it doubled in size following the great Mississippi River flood of 1993. In 1998 it shrank in length but expanded in depth. In 2002 it reached a record size of more than 8,000 square miles, larger than the state of New Jersey. In the summer of 2004 it receded to 5,800 square miles, about the size of Connecticut. In 2005 it threatened to grow larger than ever before.

What makes a dead zone is lack of dissolved oxygen (DO) in the water. At least five milligrams of DO per liter makes for good life-supporting water. When it drops to two milligrams per liter, the water is called hypoxic and is a risk to shrimp, fish, and shellfish. "Anything that can't move out eventually dies," says Rabalais. At less than one milligram the water is anoxic, or without any means of supporting life. The whole deadly process of creating this nutrient-rich, oxygen-poor water is called eutrophication. As the scientific understanding of the Gulf's eutrophication has become more focused, the economic consequences have vastly expanded.

The Mississippi watershed drains 41 percent of the continental United States into the Gulf, including 52 percent of farms that during the 1950s and 1960s became increasingly dependent on synthetic chemicals. These commercial fertilizers and pesticides, promoted by the government, the American Farm Bureau Federation, and the Agricultural Chemicals Association (since renamed the American Crop Protection Association), boosted production but undermined the long-term viability of the soil. They also tripled the nitrogen load carried by the land.

Today, in states such as Illinois and Iowa, corn farmers, caught up in a cycle of chemical dependence, typically apply 150 pounds of fertilizer per acre. In addition, corporate feedlots for cattle, hogs, and chickens generate tremendous amounts of largely unregulated methane, ammonia, and nitrogen. Every spring, rain and snowmelt deliver much of this nutrient-rich brew (along with urban and industrial runoff) into the Mississippi River. The river discharges its spring flow of fresh water across the top of the saltier Gulf, where it is warmed by sunlight and fed by surplus nitrogen and phosphorus, causing massive algal blooms to appear. They attract tiny crustaceans called copepods and other needle-point-sized critters that graze on the algae. The dead algae, along with copepod waste, sink to the bottom to become food for bacteria. In the process of feeding, these bacteria suck up most of the oxygen, dropping the water's DO levels to around two milligrams. Then, in a final voracious feeding frenzy, like cable news pundits during a major crisis, they consume the last oxygen, suffocating even themselves.

To date, the Dead Zone has had mixed impacts on the Gulf's sea life and its billion-dollar seafood industry, representing about 40 percent of U.S. production. Benthic communities of seaworms and shellfish (which provide prey for other creatures) have been able to recolonize after the seasonal environmental insults subside. Commercial shrimpers have been able to target the edges of the Dead Zone, sometimes benefiting when great swarms of shrimp flee directly into their nets. But many worry that if the Dead Zone continues to grow there will be no place left to feed or to flee.

In the summer of 2004 several people were bitten by sharks along the upper Texas coast. Terry Stelly, an ecosystem biologist with the Texas Parks and Wildlife Department, told the BBC that shark numbers had increased noticeably in local nearshore waters during recent years. "The chances are good that sharks were looking for higher dissolved oxygen in the water," he said.

Global blooms of jellyfish are also blamed, in part, on the growing number of oceanic dead zones. Sea nettles and moon jellies in the northern Gulf of Mexico, for example, have been found to be thickest where oxygen levels are lowest.

There have always been some natural algal blooms and small hypoxic areas resulting from siltation and plant litter in the Gulf of Mexico, whose rich brown waters have long been known as the "fertile crescent." Mobile Bay, Alabama, flushes some 50 billion gallons of water a day into the Gulf, making it the fourth largest freshwater flow in the nation (after the Mississippi, Yukon, and Columbia rivers). Records going back to the 1860s document periodic hypoxia events, called "jubilees" by local residents.

"That's when the shrimp and bottom fish are driven out of the water and throw themselves onto the land to get some oxygen, providing a free feast for the locals," explains Jonathan Pennock of the University of Alabama's Dauphin Island Sea Lab. "People put bells on the beaches that they can ring when this happens."

Pennock, who has silver hair, a trim mustache, and a somewhat fastidious manner, helped write a University of Alabama (UA) report, funded by the Fertilizer Institute, that focused on factors other than fertilizers contributing to the Gulf's Dead Zone. Among the factors highlighted were dredging of navigation channels, loss of wetlands, and unusually heavy rains that put more carbon into the water. Although not well received by other scientists studying the problem, the report was highlighted in a *Forbes* magazine article titled "Hypoxia Hysteria" penned by Michael Fumento, a conservative think-tank author who had previously written about "the myth of heterosexual AIDS." *Dakota Farmer* magazine also found the UA report highly persuasive, as did the Farm Bureau (a not-for-profit advocacy group and insurance provider heavily invested in agrochemicals).

"Nancy [Rabalais] and me are being put in opposite positions by the media, which is unfair and putting our friendship at risk," worries Pennock. "People with the Farm Bureau and some other farm interests misused our information, claiming the UA report said carbon was the issue. But in my mind there should be movement to reduce nitrogen inputs upriver but also keep looking at these other inputs. . . . I think in 15 to 20 years from now farmers will do all they can [to reduce nutrients] and the major inputs will be from coastal growth, from you and me using autos, fertilizing our lawns, spraying rose bushes. We're still a notch away from that, but it's going to happen."

To get to Cocodrie, Louisiana, you take Highway 56 out of Houma past the airport, oil tank farms, and sugar cane fields, the shrimp and off-shore workboats tied up by the canal; past Dan and Cyndi's Minnows and Our Lady of Prompt Succor. Pretty soon you're driving past houses and house trailers jacked 15 feet off the ground, with wetlands and water all around and (if you like good music) your radio dial tuned to the Ragin' Cajun. Cocodrie (fractured French for "crocodile") may not be the end of the world, but when you think you're getting close, look off to your right and you'll see what appears to be a small tan airport on concrete pylons. This is the Louisiana Universities Marine Consortium, or LUMCON. Rather than commuter jets, several large workboats are docked off to one side, including the 105-foot steel-hulled RV *Pelican*—Dr. Nancy Rabalais's research vessel.

"I have two rules for the media—film me before I get wet and no butt shots," says Dr. Rabalais. But when I later look at newspaper and TV clips featuring her, I'm reminded that you just can't tell the media what to do. In her fifties, Rabalais is slim with wavy brown hair, bright green brown eyes, and a sweet tentative smile behind a Texas twang unaffected by years in Louisiana. I mention Jon Pennock's statement that his work has been misused by farm interests.

"Jon was pretty naive to take their money and not think they'd use that report how they wanted," she replies.

Nancy Rabalais first began studying the Gulf's nutrient runoff problem back in 1985, along with colleagues Gene Turner (whom she later married) and Bill Wiseman. She pulls out offshore charts, showing me research transect sets (study tracks) going back a generation. Most of the lines are compass straight except for the first two, which curve oddly. "That's where we were trying to stay close to the oil platforms," she grins. "The first year out I had a 21-foot Boston Whaler to work off of, which I kept close to the platforms so if the weather got rough we'd have someplace to run to. Then we got a 45-foot boat and later began doing our summer research cruises off the *Pelican*."

Like many marine scientists she creates her transects by taking water samples at a series of established sites, lowering a CTD rosette on a winch. The rosette is a long, cage-like array of pipes and fittings holding CTD (conductivity, temperature, and depth) instruments. She also measures chlorophyll, suspended sediments, and active (light) radiation, and pulls bottom samples. In addition to monitoring a permanently moored instrumentation package, she oversees monthly day cruises and an extended summer research cruise that includes boat-based and dive operations.

Her work, along with that of scientists like Cornell University professor Robert Howarth, gained the attention of top officials in the Clinton administration and led to the establishment in 2000 of a White House "Action Plan for Reducing, Controlling, and Mitigating Hypoxia in the Northern Gulf of Mexico." Implementation of the plan has gone largely unfunded during the Bush administration, however. Even though it is the kind of "voluntary, collaborative environmental effort" the president touts—all the agricultural states along the Mississippi River agreed to and have participated in the plan—the administration's attitude remains, at best, one of benign neglect.

By 2005 NOAA was reporting that more than 50 percent of U.S. estuaries were suffering from nitrogen overload, and the United Nations Environment Programme identified 146 coastal dead zones as an emerging global problem, with nearly a third of them located off the United States

I ask Rabalais if she's faced a lot of criticism for her science work. She tells me of a presentation she gave in Davenport, Iowa. "There were agricultural interests there; the Phosphorus and Potash Association, the Fertilizer Institute, the Farm Bureau. . . . I very seldom turn down requests to talk, so I've become a kind of target for them. I've been told I'm too much of an advocate. But I don't state policy. I say what's happening in the water. I'll talk to anyone who's interested because this is important.

"I think a lot of farmers are really concerned about their land and the impact they have on it. The stuff you hear, the attacks, are mostly out of the lobbyists and the big agricultural groups. We were on a radio show in Illinois and had a farmer call on his cell phone from his fields and talk about the problems he faces in terms of the economic pressures and costs for chemical treatment, and he was really caught between a rock and a hard place and we didn't have any answers for him."

But Tony Thompson, a fifth-generation Minnesota farmer with 1,850 acres of corn and soybeans, has at least a few answers. "We farmers are often applying more nitrogen than we need. We can reduce nitrogen without suffering yield loss," he told *Newsweek* magazine. Thompson, like many innovative farmers from Maine to California, is combining traditional ecological methods of soil management, including planting buffer strips along rivers, protecting some prairie and wetlands, and raising organic crops as well as using high-tech methods such as global positioning system (GPS) satellite mapping, which targets where and how to use herbicides and fertilizers sparingly. The result is far less waste in the form of nutrient runoff from Thompson's fields.

Along the central California coast local farming and ranching interests have joined with the Monterey Bay National Marine Sanctuary to form the Agriculture Water Quality Alliance, which uses a range of strategies to reduce runoff. Over the past five years their efforts have prevented 450,000 tons of topsoil from washing out to sea.

Unfortunately, this kind of careful, targeted approach tends not to work well for large-scale industrial farming, including the factory farming of hogs and chickens that exploded in the 1980s and 1990s under the sponsorship of Murphy Family Farms, Tyson, Perdue, and other large agrocorporations.

The worst case of agroindustrial pollution to date took place in North Carolina. It was there, in 1990–1991, in the warm, slow-moving river waters of the eastern coastal floodplain, that Dr. JoAnn Burkholder first discovered *Pfiesteria piscicida,* the so-called cell from hell. The aquatic microbe Pfiesteria, which spends most of its existence buried in the mud as a harmless cyst, has a chameleon-like life cycle of at least 24 stages, in one stage disguising itself as a green plant and during four stages turning into a deadly predator.

Stimulated by excess nutrients, Pfiesteria in its most toxic stage can strip the flesh off fish within three minutes, leaving fatal lesions the size of half-dollars. Humans who have been exposed have lost consciousness and suffered memory loss, fatigue, nausea, vomiting, diarrhea, bloody sores, painful muscle contractions, and respiratory distress, among other symptoms. While working in a poorly ventilated lab, both Dr. Burkholder and her assistant were exposed to airborne Pfiesteria spores that led to months of debilitating neurological disorders.

Dr. Burkholder's work in the early 1990s paralleled the growth of the North Carolina hog industry, which grew from about two million to some ten million swine between 1990 and 1997. With hogs producing four times the amount of excrement as humans, this meant upward of 20 million tons of annual hog waste that factory farmers keep in huge untreated lagoons or spray on fields incapable of absorbing all the manure they're hit with. Along with runoff, additional waste vaporizes as ammonia and then rains out into the water.

In 1995 a hog lagoon spilled 22 million gallons of waste into the New River. Millions of fish died there and in the nearby Neuse River, which was also struck by hypoxia. Along the coast, massive Pfiesteria outbreaks killed as many as a billion small and medium-sized fish. At the same time, Burkholder's credibility came under attack from the governor's office and the state Department of Environment, Health, and Natural Resources. These often personal attacks took place even as her research was being published in *Nature* and other prestigious science journals. The reason for the attacks became apparent when the *Raleigh News and Observer* ran an investigative series by reporters Pat Stith and Joby Warrick. The series, "Boss Hog," revealed how the state's powerful hog industry (including former state senator and hog operator Wendell Murphy) convinced the state government to go easy on environmental controls for the sake of corporate profits. The newspaper series went on to win numerous awards, including a 1996 Pulitzer Prize.

Burkholder's reputation was further redeemed when in 1997 she became the subject of an admiring book, *And the Waters Turned to Blood* by Robert Barker, and was asked to advise the state of Maryland on how to respond to a new Pfiesteria outbreak. That summer Pfiesteria-linked fish kills were reported on several Maryland rivers that feed into Chesapeake Bay. Although the "cell from hell" never entered the bay proper, consumer fears resulted in some $40 million of lost seafood sales for Chesapeake Bay fishermen.

One of the most documented sources of nitrogen and phosphorus runoff into the bay is the huge chicken production complexes on the Delmarva Peninsula (shared by Maryland, Delaware, and Virginia). Contract growers there get their feed and chicks (close to a billion a year) from major poultry companies including Tyson, Perdue, Allen Family Foods, and Mountire Farms. When the chicks have grown to full-sized broilers, the companies pick up the birds, leaving the contract farmers with more than one million tons of manure to dispose of.

The EPA has called for "comprehensive nutrient management plans" for these large-scale confined animal feeding operations, or CAFOs. The idea is to treat factory farms the same as municipal sewage plants. But the EPA plans remain voluntary; plans for eventual mandatory controls were rolled back by the Bush administration in January 2003.

In Maryland, state legislators and then-governor Parris Glendening demanded immediate nutrient reduction under terms that would make the major poultry companies legally responsible for disposing of, excuse the expression, all their chicken shit. Poultry titan James Perdue sought to play the victim, complaining, "What about all the septic tanks, and people fertilizing their lawns, and municipal sewage plants? How come nobody's looking at them?"

Meanwhile, back in North Carolina, the state finally began inspecting its factory farms, finding hundreds of health and safety violations, poisoned drinking wells, and dead waterways. In the spring of 1999, reversing his previous course of inaction, Democratic governor Jim Hunt proposed phasing out the state's hog waste lagoons and removing them from the coastal floodplain. Unfortunately, his proposal came a storm season too late. Within months, Hurricane Floyd struck. The flood that resulted sent a witch's brew of animal and human waste, dead livestock, and toxic chemicals into the 1,700-square-mile Pamlico Sound, the country's second largest estuary after the Chesapeake. Algae grew and decayed at ten times the normal rate, creating a massive new dead zone more than 350 square miles in size, with anoxic DO levels of one part per liter.

Dying coral, oxygen-starved dead zones, and a microscopic cell from hell are only three of a growing list of science fiction–like horrors from the flushing of our coasts. Woods Hole and other marine science centers are monitoring the growth of harmful algal blooms (HABs). These include naturally occurring red and brown tides containing toxic algae that have, quite unnaturally, more than doubled in number in the past 30 years. HABs now threaten every coastal state and territory on the blue frontier.

In 1995 more than 300 manatees, an endangered species, were wiped out by a red tide of one-celled dinoflagellates off the coast of Florida. In 1996 hundreds of dolphins and brown pelicans washed up dead along the Mexico-California coastline, killed by toxic one-celled diatoms. In 1997 a red tide killed millions of fish off South Padre Island, Texas, and sent tourists fleeing with hacking coughs from poisonous algae aerosolated by the surf. In 1998 more than 400 sea lions died in California's Monterey Bay after eating anchovies that had consumed toxic algae. In 1999 red tides again hit Florida, causing new fish kills, dolphin die-offs, and eye and respiratory irritations in humans. And in the summer of 2005, following heavy spring runoff, a massive early-season red tide shut down New England shellfishing and threatened to spread south along the mid-Atlantic coast.

In Alabama scientists met in 2000 to discuss possible links between nutrient runoff, global warming, and global increases in jellyfish blooms. The big problem for Alabama was a dramatic increase in the number of stinging jellyfish just off the beach at Gulf Shores and other tourist destinations. Ouch.

In 2002 a large mass of black water, hundreds of square miles across, appeared off the coast of Florida and then broke into large dark patches. State scientists identified it as an unusually colored algal bloom and said it did not appear to pose a threat to marine life, but commercial fishermen claimed it was killing fish and bottom-dwelling species and, like a mild acid, stripping plant life off their lines and gear.

In the summer of 2003 nearly half the water in Chesapeake Bay was so oxygen-depleted it could no longer sustain life. A third of the bay's underwater grasses died as pollution blotted out their sunlight. Ironically, that same summer Maryland's Republican governor, Robert Ehrlich, abandoned rules set by his predecessor, Parris Glendening, that held poultry giants such as Tyson and Perdue responsible for cleaning up their chicken waste. Saying that he would find ways to clean up the bay "without excessive government intrusion," Ehrlich proceeded to add a $2.50 homeowner surcharge or "flush tax" to upgrade the state's aging sewage plants—a way to share the pain, though not among his corporate supporters.

By the summer of 2004 several feet of stringy macro-algae slime, or "green gunk," was matting the bottom and fouling the crab pots and lines of Chesapeake watermen in the upper bay, threatening their livelihoods and the environment. It was a mystery how this could be taking place when the Chesapeake Bay Program—a 17-year-old state and federal EPA compact that was supposed to clean up the bay—was reporting that it had reduced the flow of major pollutants into the bay by 40 percent. The *Washington Post* solved the puzzle in July 2004 when it compared the computer model used by the program with actual water monitoring data, which showed that there had been no real decline in nitrogen and phosphorus flowing into the bay. The computer models being used as proof of the voluntary program's success were "too optimistic." In 2005 Cornell's Robert Howarth reported that in the wetter weather expected as a result of climate change, nitrogen flow from the land into Chesapeake Bay could increase another 17 percent by 2030 and up to 65 percent by the end of the century.

In the Pacific Northwest more frequent appearances of toxic dinoflagellates have increased cases of diuretic shellfish poisoning (DSP) and potentially lethal paralytic shellfish poisoning (PSP). A Seattle-based fisheries cop gave me a vivid demonstration of what PSP looks like. He grabbed his throat so that his face reddened, filled his mouth with his tongue as if it were swollen, and began choking, gurgling, and flopping around on his desk quite convincingly. It made me much more careful about when and where I buy my oysters.

One place I will not buy shellfish is on the beach in Los Angeles. Santa Monica Bay's waters have improved, thanks to sewage treatment upgrades completed in the 1990s (they were originally ordered in 1972), but are still not what you would call swimmer friendly. For years Los Angeles argued that because it could pipe its wastes directly into deep water off its sloping coast, it deserved a federal waiver from the Clean Water Act, which requires cities to decontaminate and filter human wastewater. Eventually, Los Angeles agreed to upgrade its four treatment plants after high bacterial counts and human viruses were discovered in coastal waters off Southern California and at some of the area's most beautiful beaches, including Topanga, Malibu, and Laguna. San Diego, by contrast, still hasn't upgraded its sewage treatment.

In 1999 Huntington Beach, just south of Los Angeles, was closed to swimmers and surfers for most of the summer as a result of high bacterial counts. "The beach is open. Only the water is closed!" argued surf-shop owner Michael Ali, one of hundreds of retailers who saw their beach businesses hammered.

Immortalized as "Surf City, USA" by the singing duo Jan and Dean, Huntington Beach has had more than its share of environmental insults. In 1990 it was hit by a major oil spill, inspiring local surfer activists to protest, "No way, dude! We don't want your crude!" In 1995 its Republican surfer representative, Dana Rohrabacher, played a key role in an attempt to defang the Clean Water Act. House Resolution 961—labeled the "Dirty Water Act" by its detractors—would have, among other things, eliminated the EPA's water-quality monitoring program and exempted sewage discharges into the ocean from existing clean-water standards. And in September 1999, just as the bacteria counts declined, more than a thousand used hypodermic needles washed up on Huntington Beach, restricting a planned annual beach cleanup for children and adults.

Finally in 2002 the Orange County Sanitation District voted 13 to 12 to invest some $450 million to upgrade its sewage treatment. The minority argued that this was too much to spend without definitive proof linking beach closings to waste disposal. But one need only take a casual walk along the waterfronts of Orange County towns like Newport Beach, Laguna Beach, or San Clemente to grasp the benefits of improved sewage treatment: billions of dollars' worth of private real estate whose value is based largely on having a clean ocean to enjoy.

Not surprisingly, visits to beaches in the Los Angeles area have declined by 50 percent since 1983, reflecting public unease with the area's water quality. Despite some sewage cleanup, people are justified in their concern. A 1996 study of Santa Monica Bay found that one out of 25 people swimming near stormwater drains became sick with pollution-related illnesses, mainly stomach flu and upper respiratory infections. Their risk of infection was at least 57 percent greater than that of people who avoided those sections of the beach. One positive effect of the study was the passage of a new California law that requires regular water testing and public warnings at all of the state's swimming beaches. Still, the waters flowing from the concrete-jacketed Los Angeles River and Los Angeles's 1,265 miles of storm drains continue to pose an ongoing threat to human health.

"Storm water is lighter than seawater and creates a plume, a kind of liquid lens that sits on top of the salt water and doesn't mix well. Most aquatic life is not in the top of the water. People swimming and recreating are in the top of the water, which is why this is such a human health threat," explains Judy Wilson, recently retired as the director of the Los Angeles Bureau of Sanitation. On the challenge of managing pollution in a megalopolis, she says, "It's much easier dealing with nonpoint pollution if you know it's from a dairy farm because you can deal with the cow manure, but when you're dealing with a city of nine million people, all with extremely bad habits, it's a lot more difficult."

Geography and climate are key factors in why Los Angeles has the worst urban runoff in the country, Wilson notes. "We have the Santa Monica Mountains to our north. In the winter, rain runs down to the coastal plain where it used to flood all the time. To address the flooding problem the Army Corps used concrete and straightened out the lines of the LA River to get this water to the ocean as rapidly as possible. We now have an underground freeway taking this water to the sea. Our beaches basically are the dumping ground for our storm drains. We call the first big storm of the winter the first flush. That's when all the paper, plastic, and everything that collected all year in the storm drains just gets whooshed down to the ocean, and you get tons of trash on the beach, along with oil and grease that's collected on the freeways during the dry season, and also your dog poop, the chemicals used on your lawn, everything people use to wash their cars . . . it all runs down the driveway and finds its way to the ocean.

"It's very difficult to educate people about this issue," she admits, "especially in such a diverse community with people speaking something like 43 languages.

"Remember when we started talking about seat belts, how they reduce deaths, and we also talked about tobacco not being good for you? It took a whole generation to realize that if you don't use seatbelts you'll fly out of your car and if you chainsmoke Camel unfiltered you'll probably die of lung cancer. So our first need is to make sure the public knows what's going on."

There are a few things Wilson has been able to handle on her own. In

2000 she got the Los Angeles City Council to approve a project in which water flows from storm drains known to have high bacterial counts would be diverted from the beaches to the city's wastewater treatment plants.

"The thing is, we just have to keep all the bad news on the front page." She smiles without humor. "You [reporters] have to keep writing all these horror stories; I'm serious. That's the only way we're going to be able to move our programs forward."

That and lawsuits. In August 2004, after six years of litigation and millions of dollars of legal fees, the city of Los Angeles agreed to the demands of the activist group Santa Monica Baykeeper. The Baykeeper group insisted that the city repair its dilapidated sewer system pipes (following repeated sewage spills in poor neighborhoods) and improve the stormwater program Wilson had initiated. Then-mayor James Hahn called the settlement under the Clean Water Act a "win-win" situation for everyone, but failed to explain why the city had spent $5.6 million fighting the lawsuit. The two billion dollars required to upgrade the system may raise residential sewer rates from $21.00 to $29.75 a month over five years—about the cost of a revival screening of, say, *Creature from the Black Lagoon*.

Judy Wilson still worries that not enough is being done about urban runoff. "Let's use copper as an example. Copper in our effluent [sewage] pipes has come down dramatically but copper in the water has climbed astronomically. That increase is all from urban runoff. We need to go back to the automobile industry and say to them, listen, copper brake linings [on Los Angeles freeways] are resulting in pollution. You need different ways of doing brake linings, different types of products that don't break down in the environment. But that's a hard group to lobby, so people are either going to have to get awfully sick, or there's going to have to be a huge new green [or blue] power movement in this country."

If history provides lessons, the Clean Water Act could serve as a model for how to mobilize that movement. After its passage in 1972 many politicians realized that the new law was not just about plugging the industrial pipelines polluting America's waterways. It was also a chance to launch new public works projects for any district that had an outmoded municipal sewage plant or outfall in need of upgrading. It provided politicians with a chance to cut ribbons and be seen as friends of public health and the environment.

As a result, Congress has been willing to allocate more than $40 bil-

lion in grants for new sewage systems over the past three decades. More
work still needs to be done to get rid of outmoded combined storm and
sewer systems such as the one in Washington, D.C., which backs up and
pollutes local waters every time there is a heavy rain. Still, dramatic overall improvements have taken place. Water quality and wildlife habitat
have been restored and recreational opportunities expanded for thousands of the nation's lakes, rivers, and coastal communities.

If many of these gains are now being reversed by the poisonous
nutrient-heavy flushing of our coasts, at least we know that realistic
models of restoration are possible. All that is needed is the political will
to fight for our watersheds and our blue frontier.

Senator John Kerry of Massachusetts has been one of a handful of
Washington politicians who understand the frontier values of America's
living seas, as he demonstrated long before his failed run for president. A
decorated former Navy combatant, antiwar veteran, and dedicated
windsurfer, the tall, silvering politician has been jokingly referred to as "a
new-wave Democrat." Among his efforts on behalf of our coasts, he
helped get Boston a two-billion-dollar wastewater treatment plant on
Deer Island in Boston Harbor. By improving the city's water quality, the
Deer Island plant has also spurred a multibillion-dollar physical and cultural revival of the historic harbor and its adjacent coastline.

I catch up with Kerry at a Trade Center luncheon overlooking the harbor on a bitterly cold January day, with drifts of accumulated snow
blowing between the slate-colored water and an achingly bright cobalt
blue sky. He is here to encourage some 300 businesspeople to give their
time and money for the restoration of the state's wetlands. He grabs people's shoulders, gestures expressively, and tells a slightly shaggy story
about General Francis Marion, the "Swamp Fox" who fought the British
by retreating into Carolina's salt marshes to conduct guerrilla warfare,
using the calls of swamp animals to signal his friends and confound his
enemies. "And that," Kerry concludes with an engaging grin, "is how we
owe our freedom to the wetlands." The crowd chuckles and applauds
appreciatively.

"The Clean Water Act and past cleanups have lulled some people to
sleep," he tells me after the speech. "Now we have to rekindle a sense of
emergency. When you look at what's happening downwater in our bays
and estuaries and salt marshes and how at risk they are from contamination, we need to reeducate people and reenergize people.

"Leadership can put this on the table, and there's a huge constituency
waiting to act on it," Kerry believes. "I grew up on the ocean and spend

as much time as I can out on Buzzards Bay [Cape Cod]. If I didn't love it as well as I do, I probably wouldn't be as involved as I am. It's my touch-stone, my sense of being and place to reenergize. But it's also a fragile system that needs to be capable of regeneration for itself."

As Kerry and almost every ocean lover and fisherman in America knows, the continued flushing and fertilizing of our coasts could easily spell death for our oceans' living marine resources. Scientists like Steve Miller, Nancy Rabalais, and JoAnn Burkholder have sounded the alarm clearly and eloquently. It's now up to the rest of America to heed their call.

Of course, when it comes to the blue frontier's once vast and diverse fisheries and the birds, bears, marine mammals, and people who depend on them, runoff is far from the only threat. For groupers, swordfish, shark, salmon, and thousands of other species, coastal pollution and habitat destruction, as bad as they are, are only half of an increasingly deadly equation.

The Last Fish?

My concern's for the fishermen facing those high seas.
I haven't seen a Steller's sea lion that's voted for me yet.

> — *U.S. Representative*
> *Don Young (R-AK), 1999*

If we don't manage this resource, we will be left with a
diet of jellyfish and plankton stew.

> — *University of British Columbia*
> *scientist Daniel Pauly, 2003*

I meet Scotty Doyle by the Staten Island Ferry Terminal at 3:45 on a cold, dark, drizzling morning. He introduces me to Tommy Graham, a short, swarthy New Yorker. Scotty is taller, with curly gray hair under a bill cap, thin frame glasses, and green eyes. He wears the bulky shape of a Kevlar vest under his shirt and black shell jacket and carries a 10-millimeter automatic, marking him as a fed. He's a National Marine Fisheries Service (NMFS) enforcement agent, but don't call him a fish cop. He doesn't like that. Tommy, in his worn khaki uniform, is with New York's Department of Environmental Conservation (DEC).

We approach the Fulton Fish Market across misty, rain-slick streets. There's a mobile white inspection booth set on a corner where dozens of tractor-trailer rigs, box-reefer (refrigerated) trucks, and vans are parked waiting below the FDR Drive, within a stone's throw of the Brooklyn Bridge and the East River. Company names are written on their sides: Tico Transport, Ameri-Cana, F&B Mussels, Ecuadorian Line. This is the market as it has existed for 184 years, before its 2005 move to a huge new warehouse next to a prison barge in the Bronx.

Fulton used to be heavily mobbed up until former New York mayor Rudolph Giuliani set up some controls. Trucks coming from different locations used to have to pay kickbacks to different mob families in order to get their product offloaded. With city inspectors checking manifests, the kickbacks declined. Of course, that has little to do with how much of the billion dollars per year of fish moving through the market is contraband.

"We usually target specific dealerships with CIs [confidential informants]. Word goes fast when we show up," Scott explains. "We or state guys like Tommy try and get down here two or three times a week. Of course we could be here every night and still stay busy.

"Me and [NMFS agent] Jimmy MacDonald on Long Island try and cover the tri-state area, including the three airports," he continues. "We're looking for black-market lobster, bluefin tuna [which can sell in Japan for $30 a pound], that sort of thing. We recently caught two fish at JFK [airport]. They were out of North Carolina and worth about $60,000."

Scott suddenly stops next to a puddle reflecting squiggly light from a nearby lamppost. "You ever seen *Guys and Dolls?*" he asks, grinning. "It's exciting like that with the wet streets, the fresh rainy air, the hi-lows unloading, and all the characters around here."

I look around as we walk into the market. The streets are full of hard-working men and freshly killed fish—boxes, crates, handtrucks, and forklifts full of fish, and half the guys carrying wooden-handled metal hooks over their shoulders or in loops by their hips. There are open displays of big tilefish, king mackerel, fresh and frozen squid, and yellowtail flounder the size of serving trays; boxes marked Wisconsin farm sturgeon, farm-raised striped bass, and tilapia; along with baskets of clams and scallops, small red mullet, and yellowtail snappers in fading colors of red, yellow, sky blue, and green. A couple of guys cover crates of crabs with a blue tarp. Scott and Tommy and the dealers are acting friendly, greeting each other with tense nods and smiles.

"Want to keep it professional, never let it get personal," Scott mumbles. Tommy stops and checks the paperwork on some haddock and pollack. Scott pulls out a gauge to check some lobsters for size, measuring from the back of the eye to the beginning of the carapace. A short old man in a torn cotton sweatshirt is introduced as Herbie. "How ya doin'? Nice to meet ya'. S'cuse me, but right now I've got a lot of stuff to do," he says in a gravelly voice.

"Herbie's company does $68 million in annual business." Scott tells me, as the old man wanders into a narrow cubicle marked M. Slavin & Sons. His company is one of five wholesalers later charged with buying illegally caught fish.

We pass 100-pound halibut from Maine on display outside other narrow streetside fish stalls, including that of M. V. Perretti Corporation,
another of the five accused wholesalers. In December 1998 a New Jersey
fisherman, Ronald Ingold, pleaded guilty to illegally catching and selling
fish from PCB-contaminated waters under the George Washington
Bridge off Manhattan. In court a year later, assistant U.S. attorney Joseph
DeMarco claimed Perretti bought nearly 100,000 pounds of this tainted
fish from Ingold and other fishermen.

"Everyone knows me here. If we want to do undercover work, we
bring someone from outside," Scott explains. Between the iced fish and
drifts of rain, a bone-chilling cold has set in. Forklift derbies are going on
under FDR Drive. I ask a dealer about some odd-looking red fish.
"They're silkies out of Brazil, a kind of snapper," he tells me. There are
also piles of dead parrotfish, their colors, so dazzling when you see them
munching coral on tropical reefs, now faded to a dull algal green. "The
West Indians buy them," the dealer tells me. "They go for $2.70 a
pound."

DEC Lieutenant Tim Duffy joins us, a friendly, square-jawed cop with
erect posture and a clipped military-style mustache. We pass Pickle Barrel
Seafood, a company recently assessed $80,000 for dealing in unreported
fish. NOAA will later reduce this to a $2,000 fine and a ten-year ban on
trade in federal fish. A young guy pushes a handtruck past the DEC
cops, singing, "You must have been an ugly-ass baby, 'cause baby look at
you now." They smile coolly.

Big groupers are on display, possibly imports. Almost all the large
groupers have been fished out of Florida and the Caribbean. We pass a
50-pound bulbous-headed Louisiana buffalo fish, tagged clams, and
Florida jacks. There's a big tuna—a yellowtail out of Vietnam—bunches
of New Zealand clams, and greenshell mussels. More snapper and small
Atlantic swordfish, each maybe 80 pounds before their heads and tails
were removed. Twenty-five years ago they averaged more than 260
pounds, but the longline fishing fleets, both U.S. and European, fished
out all the big ones and began taking immature fish too young to breed.

We enter a shed-covered area called the Tin Building, where I spot a
big swordfish, about 250 pounds. "That's the way they should all be,"
Scott says. I admire a big-eye tuna, which looks like a fat torpedo. The
dealer has laid it flat on one fin. Since it was caught its skin has not
touched a deck or floor. The Japanese buyers do not like bruised flesh.
"This one's 158 pounds, worth about $550," the dealer tells me. "It's
from Ecuador."

Tommy thinks he found some bags of undersized clams and pulls out a one-inch gauge. If they slip through they're illegal, but these prove to be legit, if just barely.

As the two state cops are checking the clams, Scott stands back and scans nearby stands to see if anyone is trying to move anything out of sight. A dealer strikes up a short conversation with him. "That's what's called a distraction strategy," Scott says wryly after the guy moves on.

"See, they're fine," the dealer with the clams grins. "You know me. I'm here 44 years."

"You're due," Scott replies, the hard cop.

Meanwhile, Tommy explains "stovepiping" to me. "You have to dig through the bags 'cause they'll use a metal stovepipe to load undersized clams in the center, fill in all around with legal-sized clams, and then pull it out."

Frank Giammarino, the owner of Seahorse, comes up to Scott to complain. "I got a $50,000 fine 'cause I didn't even know I needed a federal permit, but those boats in Montauk, they got $1,500, $2,000 fines. It's not fair. When I hear what they got, I'm upset. I want to appeal."

"Call me, I'll give you our attorney's number. The one who handled your case," the agent tells him.

"He had 14,000 pounds of summer flounder he shouldn't have had," Scott tells me after the dealer is placated, "from a boat that didn't exist."

On July 17, 1996, a Boeing 747 that had just taken off from New York's Kennedy Airport plunged into the ocean, killing all 230 people on board. The TWA Flight 800 disaster, initially believed to be the result of a terrorist bomb, led to a massive search and salvage operation in the waters off Long Island that continued for the better part of six months. Federal, state, and local agencies including the Navy, the Coast Guard, NOAA, and New York DEC were used in the search for clues and bodies.

During the search, with state officers off the docks and the Coast Guard not doing fisheries patrols, reports began filtering in of widespread pirate fishing taking place off Long Island and black-market product moving through the Fulton Fish Market. When Scott Doyle, Jimmy MacDonald, and other agents checked Seahorse's summer flounder records against paperwork in Montauk (on the eastern tip of Long Island), they discovered a fictional boat named *Magpie* working with the unpermitted dealer. Several boats had been overfishing, including a 76-foot trawler named *Perception*, whose owner, Bill Grimm, and operator, Bill Braun, created "*Magpie*" as a cover for their taking of summer flounder out of season. Crates of these fish would appear on the dock in the middle of the night with a note written from *"Magpie"* crew, instructing Seahorse to leave envelopes of cash pinned to a spot on the wall of the dockhouse.

In the year following the September 11 attacks, with the Coast Guard focusing many of its resources on port security (and its fisheries enforcement down 38 percent), widespread pirate fishing was again reported.

Another dealer now comes up to Scott to complain how "the fishermen are going fucking crazy with all the rules and regulations. Could you tell me if it's okay to use fishtraps on tilefish right now or not? How are these guys supposed to know all that crap?"

"I couldn't tell you, but if you called me, I'd look it up and let you know. I'd never not get back to you," Scott promises, "and if I'm a tilefisherman I will know the rules on my fish, 'cause that's my business, that's how I make my living, so I will."

"You got a point," the dealer concedes. "Who do you work for?" he asks me. I tell him I'm working on a book but also write for different outlets such as *Sports Afield*. "Oh, yeah, all those rich recreational fishermen who are trying to put us out of business. They're anti–commercial fisherman."

"I also do stuff for *Marketplace* radio. You're not anticapitalist, are you?"

"Fuck, no, I'm a capitalist. I'm the best capitalist in the world!"

"Better than Herbie?" Scott wonders.

"I'm a capitalist, not a crook," he responds.

Tommy tells me how New York DEC cops like himself cover everything environmental, from fish on the waterfront to toxic waste to endangered species. They recently took a mountain lion out of a Brooklyn apartment. "It was in the bedroom. We staked out the place after a tip and went in with Emergency Services. It was a full-grown female. We tranked [tranquilized] her and now she's in a wildlife protection park somewhere upstate. We had another mountain lion sting where we bought a lion from a guy in the park. People seem to like the big cats."

We pass some Australian yellowtail, some octopus and live crabs, sea urchin roe and skate wings, catfish and grunts, whiting, and butterfish. Still, the Fulton Fish Market is tiny compared to others like Tokyo's Tsukiji. What they all have in common, though, is globalization, the creation of a world market for anything indigenous to the sea. The urchin caught in California, Maine, or Alaska one morning could have its gonads removed and served in a Tokyo nightspot the next evening. A bluefin tuna caught off Louisiana will definitely end up in Tsukiji, as will most black cod (sable) caught off the West Coast. A white abalone from California could be the centerpiece of a $450 dinner in Hong Kong, which is why there are only about 2,000 of this threatened species of sea snail left in the ocean. Giant geoduck clams caught in Puget Sound have been smuggled into Canada for shipment to Asia, just as polluted "black clams" have been smuggled from Mexico into the United States for sale in East Lost Angeles. Marine creatures once considered useless or inedible—baby eels, skates, dogfish, horseshoe crabs, sea urchins—all now have their markets.

The global fish trade is also keeping many Americans ignorant about what's happening in their own waters. People who order fish and chips in Boston may not realize that the white fish they eat is pollack from the Bering Sea off Alaska instead of overfished New England cod. The blue crab ordered in Baltimore may come not from nearby Chesapeake Bay but from Indonesia, where the pickers work for $15 a week. And that expensive "wild Alaska salmon" sold in upscale New York markets is most likely from fish farms in Chile, Canada, or Norway, according to an investigation by the *New York Times*. More than 75 percent of the seafood Americans now eat is imported. Meanwhile, Pacific Northwest salmon that once spawned by the millions are slowly going extinct— river by dammed, logged, and diverted river.

In 2002 some 80,000 spawning salmon died on the shores of the Klamath River in Northern California, threatening the livelihood of commercial fisherman and Indian tribes. The die-off was attributed to low water flows after the Department of the Interior (DOI) diverted water north to Oregon farmers. Although scientists from NOAA and the DOI had argued that this was an unwise move from both environmental and economic points of view, it turned out that the decision had more to do with politics. Before the water diversion was ordered, President Bush's political advisor Karl Rove met with 50 top DOI managers, telling them that the administration sided with the farmers and that "we need to support our base." Klamath farmers, it turned out, were in the eastern (heavily Republican) part of Oregon, a swing state in the upcoming 2004 presidential elections, while downriver California tribes and fishermen were mostly Democratic. And of course fish don't vote. (Oregon would nevertheless go with John Kerry, the Democrat, in 2004.)

Moreover, in 2004 the administration announced that under no circumstances would it remove four marginally productive dams from the Snake River, even though its own scientists said this would be the best way to assure the survival of wild salmon on the Columbia River (which the Snake feeds into). Instead the administration proposed counting hatchery-bred fish as wild salmon in order to avoid the legal protection requirements of the Endangered Species Act. This would be akin to introducing packs of Irish setters into the wilds of Idaho and saying they were the same as wolves. Again, the eastern Washington dam users were Bush voters while the downriver tribes, fishermen, and residents of towns like Portland, Oregon, who supported dam removal, tended to vote Democratic.

By now it's 6 AM and the market's beginning to clear out. It won't be active again until after midnight. As we head back to our cars, Scott dumps some old coffee and a cardboard cup down a storm drain. Tommy and Tim give him a weird look.

"Of all the fish caught in the U.S., how much is being taken illegally, and how is that figure incorporated into the stock assessments the government uses when it decides if a species is overfished?" I ask our federal litterbug.

"The number of illegal fish is never going to be counted in the estimates," Scott replies. "Not with industry making all the rules." It's a complaint I'll hear repeated often by enforcement agents, scientists, environmentalists, and even a number of fishermen who recognize that the present system of industry-dominated management is broken, probably beyond repair, and that a new approach has to be taken if America's sealife is to survive.

Today 37 percent of U.S. commercial fisheries are overfished, according to the National Marine Fisheries Service. This is a slight improvement from 1999, when 43 percent were listed as overfished. But along with 230 commercial species whose status NMFS is able to rate, there are another 674 species whose status is unknown to them, the service admits.

While managing fisheries one species at a time may help in tracking commercial landings, it provides no basis for understanding the complexity of saltwater ecosystems and how the removal of one type of marine animal can affect others. What is known is that, in the middle of a global extinction crisis, the world's aquatic species are going extinct at a rate five times faster than land animals.

One problem is that fisheries managers are failing to account for the impacts of fish taken illegally or as bycatch (caught and thrown back over the side because they are not the fish being targeted). Another is illustrated by a recent study finding that some 5 percent of fish are being taken by recreational fishermen and -women, and that managers aren't effectively tracking the impact of these catches either. For example, in the 1990s investigators realized that the fisheries management plan for geoduck clams in Puget Sound was underestimating the diver take by 100 percent. For every one of the giant bivalves harvested legally, another was being pirated and shipped off to Asia via Canada, threatening the species' survival. Luckily NMFS agents were able to close down the black market. Today, a significant part of Asia's geoduck demand is met by two Washington-based aquaculture companies.

Northwestern crabs have also been heavily targeted by poachers. A team of fisheries enforcement agents and I are passing through fields of crab pot buoys on the cold, slate-green waters of Boundary Bay in northern Washington, below a bruise-colored, rain-saturated sky. "It's like a minefield trying to walk across this bay if you're a crab," says Pete Choerny of NMFS, flashing a ready smile as he squints out across the water at three small fishing boats, lifting his binoculars for a closer look.

We're approaching latitude 49, the invisible line in the water that separates the United States from Canada. Craig Carlisle of the Washington Department of Fish and Wildlife checks landmarks along the coast against the GPS monitor on the bridge of the *Gauntlet*, a 46-foot state-owned cabin cruiser. "They're over a quarter mile south of the line," he notes, bringing the wheel about.

"They're taking off like a covey of quail," Choerny agrees, as the three boats scatter, the *Gauntlet* going to full throttle to chase after the closest one, a 24-foot aluminum skiff with two men aboard. "This is a typical day on the line," Choerny half-shouts over the roar of the engine. The powerful outboards on the skiff we're chasing throw up a roostertail of water ahead, and the skiff jags to keep its stern to us, hiding the Canadian registration number on its side. After entering Canadian waters in hot pursuit but failing to gain on his quarry, Carlisle powers down and turns his boat around. Choerny, Carlisle, and David James, a fisheries enforcement officer from the Lummi Indian reservation, begin pulling up the pirate traps south of the line.

"What would you have done if you'd caught them?" I ask. "Seize their boat and put them in jail," says Carlisle.

Knowing that the possibility of jail exists tends to make poachers and pirates uncooperative. Some years ago the *Gauntlet*, with another state officer and NMFS agent Andy Cohen on board, was pursuing another illegal crab boat.

"We came alongside during a chase in heavy four-foot seas," recalls Cohen, a father of two with curly, dark hair. "I stepped on board and moved to turn off their engine. That's when one of them grabbed a meat cleaver off the transom. I pulled out my .357 revolver from my shoulder holster, backing up against the wheel. He moved forward, lifting the cleaver over his head. You know how with a revolver trigger there are two clicks before it fires. I had it pulled two clicks back. The state officer had his gun aimed from the other heaving boat, and I remember thinking, if he fires it could hit any of us. The guy with the cleaver was ready to swing down on me when he decided to drop his weapon. He saved his life and saved me from ruining my life by his choice."

Along with poaching, bycatch seriously threatens the ocean's limited reserves of life. On a shrimp trawler on St. Simon Sound off Georgia, I watch three "try-net" sets. The small try nets are used to test the waters before big commercial nets are deployed. The first set brings up a pile of white shrimp (which wholesales for four dollars per pound) and a larger pile of bycatch, including whiting, silver eels, tonguefish, squid, butterfish, silver perch, and weakfish, plus a rare, spiny-looking sea robin and some bay anchovies. These all get separated out and shoveled back over the side. On the next dip we get about one-third shrimp along with much the same bycatch mix, plus some blue crabs, ocean catfish, baby flounder, and whelks. When this bycatch is swept off the deck the baby flounder, whiting, and tonguefish are grabbed off the surface by flocks of cawing seagulls that have descended on the boat like frat boys at a tailgate party. The third set brings up a big flounder that the crew keeps, along with a big stone crab, spotfish, pigfish, silver eels, tonguefish, and whiting.

In the Atlantic, Southeast shrimpers get three to four pounds of bycatch for every pound of shrimp they catch. In the Gulf it's more like seven to nine pounds of bycatch per pound of shrimp. NMFS estimates that bycatch from the U.S. shrimp fishery is close to a billion pounds a year, a waste of edible protein (unless you're a seagull) equal to 10 percent of the total U.S. catch. Non-target species that are killed and tossed overboard make up around 25 percent of the total U.S. catch.

Drowned sea turtles used to make up a significant part of shrimpers' bycatch until NOAA required them to add escape-hatch turtle excluder devices (TEDs) to their nets. Today the five endangered species of sea turtle found on America's blue frontier are making a modest comeback, while the shrimpers are making more money than ever. The use of TEDs was delayed for years, however, because of opposition by industry-friendly politicians including Representatives Tom DeLay of Texas and Billy Tauzin of Louisiana (now a lobbyist), and Representative (later Senator) John Breaux of Louisiana, who got the House Appropriations Committee to cut funding for TEDs research. Today many of the same politicians who opposed TEDs are fighting a proposal to develop and deploy BRDs (pronounced "birds"), or bycatch reduction devices, even though some of the most innovative BRDs have been crafted by fishermen themselves.

As incredibly complex as the crisis of America's fisheries may seem, it can be broken down into three basic problems: the destruction of fish habitat, overcapitalization of the industry, and built-in conflict-of-interest in fisheries management.

"For years we've said, 'How can you address fisheries without addressing fish habitat?'" says Zeke Grader, the director of the Pacific Coast Federation of Fishermen's Associations (PCFFA), which represents some 1,800 small-boat operators on the West Coast. "The problem is you got the Farm Bureau and the oil industry saying NMFS has no business looking at essential fish habitat. And NMFS doesn't have the stomach to take on dam builders and developers in order to protect fish."

Along with the loss of rivers, wetlands, and productive coastal estuaries, recent studies identify certain kinds of fish farming and even fishing equipment itself as additional causes of habitat destruction.

With consumer demand for fish growing and wild captures declining, aquaculture—the farm rearing of aquatic plants and animals—has taken up the slack, expanding some 9 percent annually in the United States. Today 30 percent of the fish Americans consume comes from aquaculture, and by 2030 half the world's fish production is expected to be farmed. Most catfish and trout, along with about half the shrimp and salmon we consume, are from farms, as is a large proportion of the tilapia, striped bass, sturgeon, abalone, oysters, crawfish, and seaweeds. Right now most U.S. domestic production comes from ponds in Mississippi, Louisiana, Idaho, and Appalachia. Many of these aquafarms have been able to develop effective waste control systems. Offshore shellfish farming actually improves water quality, because the farmed oysters, mussels, and other bivalves pump up to 50 gallons a day through their shells, filtering excess nutrients out of the surrounding water.

In contrast, netpen farming of salmon in the slow-moving waters of coastal bays and harbors can damage marine habitat. High-density salmon farms pollute shoreline ecosystems with their excess feed and feces. Because the fish are so concentrated, they are more susceptible to sea lice and diseases such as infectious salmon anemia, which can spread to wild fish. And the antibiotics used to treat these farm fish can prove fatal to surrounding aquatic life. Fish chow and additives used to give farmed salmon their reddish color (which wild salmon get from krill and other open-ocean prey) also have raised health concerns. Several peer-reviewed studies in 2004 found that farmed salmon contained higher levels of PCBs, dioxin, and flame retardant than wild salmon. In addition, Atlantic salmon used throughout the industry escape on a regular basis. The fear is that escapees will spread disease, displace endangered wild Pacific salmon in their native rivers, or breed with wild salmon and weaken their genetic instincts to migrate and spawn.

Recent responses to these problems have been to move fin fish aquaculture offshore into open ocean waters or, conversely, inland into warehouses. Private companies are now raising fish for market several miles off of Puerto Rico and Hawaii in submerged net cages shaped like giant tops. These 50-foot-tall-by-85-foot-wide "ocean spar" nets hold hundreds of thousands of cobia, moi (threadfin), and amberjack in depths of 90 to 150 feet. Similar projects are working on raising cod, haddock, and Atlantic halibut. Fast-moving offshore currents disperse the fish wastes in the water column so that pollution doesn't build up in the immediate area.

Other companies (and university projects) have begun raising baramundi, cod, and striped bass in standardized indoor tanks, using purification and recirculation systems adapted from wastewater treatment plants and public aquariums to grow profitable crops of fish in synthetic seawater.

Another issue that must be addressed is the cost to wild fisheries of raising farmed fish. Currently about one-third of the world's wild-caught fish go into the production of fishmeal and fish oils to feed cattle, chickens, and farmed fish. It takes about three pounds of wild-caught fish to raise one pound of salmon.

Clearly, like many new industries, aquaculture holds both great promise and some peril, but in places where wild salmon and salmon fishermen are still viable indicator species for clean oceans, independent livelihoods, and healthy rivers, salmon farming doesn't make a lot of sense.

Nor perhaps does drag trawling, although this fishing method plays a large role in providing seafood for America and the world. About half the world's wild catch comes from bottom-trawling gear for shrimp and fin fish. Some rigs use big-mouthed otter nets pulled along the seabed by chains and held open by steel slabs called otter doors. Scallop and clam dredges are made of chainmail bags and bar spreaders that drag across the bottom like heavy plows.

A number of studies have identified bottom dragging as the major cause of ecological damage to the oceans' complex sea bottoms and the plants and animals that live there. Each year trawl nets scour benthic communities twice the size of the United States. The parts of New England's Georges Bank not shut down because of overfishing are bottom trawled three to four times a year.

Peter Auster of the National Undersea Research Center at the University of Connecticut described putting on diving gear and sitting on the seafloor as a scallop dredge rumbled by. He then swam into the dragged area to see what had happened. He reported, "What was a complex of sponges, shells, and other organisms was smoothed to a cobblestone street."

Until the 1980s extensive bottom areas containing rocks, wrecks, and reefs were inaccessible to bottom trawling. Then came new inventions called rockhoppers and street sweepers: big rubber rollers and brushes that allowed trawl nets to penetrate these last wild refuges of biodiversity without getting their gear hung up. In response the state of Alaska banned bottom trawling in a number of places to protect rocky crab habitat. Fish nurseries off North Carolina are protected from bottom gear, as are Florida's coral reefs and Maine's lobster coves. In California the state is slowly expanding a system of marine protected areas or "no-take zones" that will exclude not only bottom gear but all commercial and recreational fishing in an attempt to rebuild and propagate marine wildlife.

In the summer of 2005, following models already established by the European Union, New Zealand, and other nations, Senator Frank Lautenberg of New Jersey introduced the Bottom Trawl and Coral Habitat Act, which, if passed, will ban trawling gear from parts of the ocean where unique deep-sea coral and sponge communities exist.

The size and extent of bottom trawling as a threat to habitat reflects an even bigger problem facing America's fishing industry—overcapitalization. For the U.S. fishing fleet this simply means there are too many vessels, or vessels that are too large, catching too few fish. If the nation's more than 100,000 commercial fishing vessels were allowed to fish to their full capacity every day next year, there would be no fish left to catch

the following year. Perhaps it might take the giant factory trawlers fishing in the Bering Sea an extra year or two to wipe out the pollack stocks,
or Gulf trawlers some additional time to kill off quick-breeding shrimp,
but no one questions that the technical capacity to exterminate the blue
frontier's wildlife is already tied up to America's docks. It is only through
fishing seasons, closed areas, gear restrictions, licenses, and other regulations that the battered resource survives at all.

Ironically, this overcapacity came about in response to an effort by
Congress to protect America's fishermen from foreign competition. In the
1950s New England's fishermen were astonished by what they ran into
on Georges Bank. "They're fishing out there with ocean liners," they
reported on returning to port. What they encountered were the first foreign fleets of large trawlers equipped with processing lines and freezers
on board, and stern ramps like those on whaling ships—designed to
haul up not single leviathans but massive nets full of smaller fish. These
are known today simply as factory trawlers. These floating catcher-
processor ships quickly began to outfish the smaller American boats,
which had to return to port to have their catch processed. By the 1970s
they were stripping not only Georges Bank but the rest of New England's
offshore waters of most of their fish. American fishers from towns like
Gloucester and New Bedford, Massachusetts, began appealing to the
government for relief.

The fact that a majority of the foreign factory trawlers were from
Russia and Poland (along with Spain, Britain, and West Germany) helped
provide a Cold War rationale for Congress's decision to ban the "spy
trawlers" and declare a 200-mile U.S. fishing zone. The 1976 Fisheries
and Conservation Act, also known as the Magnuson Act after Washington senator Warren G. Magnuson, who sponsored it, was not really
about conservation. It was an assertion of exclusive U.S. fishing rights on
the continental shelf, much as the Truman Proclamation had been for oil.
It also created a powerful precedent for the Reagan administration to follow when it declared America's blue frontier an Exclusive Economic
Zone (EEZ) seven years later.

Among the Magnuson Act's provisions was the creation of eight
regional fishery councils to advise NMFS on how to promote U.S. fisheries, develop new fisheries, and establish maximum sustainable yields
for fisheries. These maximum yields were supposed to represent the number of fish that could be taken without beginning to wipe out the stocks,
although this theoretical number could be exceeded in any year the councils determined that there was an economic or social need to do so.

Because it was believed to be important that the councils include the expertise of professional fishermen, the councils also were exempted from conflict-of-interest laws that apply to every other federal regulatory body in America. What FEMA flood insurance had done for coastal protection, and the Army Corps of Engineers for wetlands, the Magnuson Act now promised to do for America's fish. "It was naive to believe you could get things to work like that," concedes Senator John Kerry, "but it was probably all that could be achieved at the time."

"We got rid of the foreign flag vessels that were raping our fisheries, and then with our Yankee ingenuity figured out how to do it better," is how John Strong-Cevetich, a former Alaskan fisherman, explains it.

In the wake of Magnuson, the federal government created and expanded a range of fishing subsidies. Under the Capital Construction Program, fishermen could defer taxes on their profits if they put the money into new boats. With the Fisheries Obligation Guarantee, or FOG, the United States pledged its full faith and credit against any loan for a vessel or fish processing plant. The government also set up the National Fish and Seafood Promotion Council, which advised consumers to "Eat Fish Twice a Week."

Just as many family farmers were encouraged to buy new combines and expand their acreage in the 1970s, fishermen in the 1980s were encouraged to take out multiple loans to upgrade their boats. Farm Credit Banks were among the major lenders in the Gulf, while in Alaska the Christiana Bank of Norway put $315 million into fleet expansion, including the construction of new American factory trawlers. Fishermen, flush with easy credit, went on a buying spree, purchasing steel-hulled vessels with stronger engines; Navy-developed Loran (a long-range navigation system); and fish-finding sonar, spotter planes, helicopters, and satellite relays that help locate fish congregations by tracking ocean surface temperatures.

Dramatic production booms occurred wherever this new fishing power was brought to bear on the resource, whether on reef fish in the Gulf of Mexico, the historic cod and scallop banks of New England, or the newly opened king crab waters of Alaska. Ports such as Dutch Harbor in the Aleutians soon took on the look of nineteenth-century frontier mining towns with thousand-dollar-a-hand poker games, booze, speed, cocaine, and knife fights. (Fishermen would rather slash each other than risk fist fighting for fear of bruising their hands. If they couldn't haul crab pots, they might lose a $20,000 or $30,000 share on the next trip out.)

But trickle-down economics was about to take some of that money out of their hands anyway. In 1986 the Reagan administration unveiled an investment tax credit that allowed people to take $10,000 off their taxes for every $100,000 they put into a new capital venture. "I was try-ing to go from a 22-foot boat to a 35-foot fiberglass boat, and I wanted to borrow $25,000 and I sent in an application and was denied 'cause I wasn't asking for enough money. You had to want at least $100,000," says Maine fisherman Paul Cohan. "The Reagan idea was, let's give the big guys big investment credit. They gave incentives to all these doctors and lawyers to get into the industry."

"The biggest impact on the fishery was the tax changes Reagan made," agrees Andy Rosenberg, a former top NMFS official who served on the U.S. Commission on Ocean Policy. "As a result you saw the fish-eries grossly overcapitalized."

One of those grossly overcapitalized fisheries was in New England scallops. Yet when NMFS agents seized five pirate scallop boats in Massachusetts, they were directed to sell them back into the fishery.

"When we seize boats we're directed to get the best return for the gov-ernment," Rosenberg explained to me. "Plus some of these boats have loans to pay off, government capital construction or FOG loans."

"I've busted poachers, real bad guys, and then gotten calls from higher-ups in NMFS," an enforcement agent confided. "They've told me, you can't put this guy out of business. He has government loans he has to pay off."

By the 1990s the capital-driven cycle of boom and bust had played out on the blue frontier just as it once did on the western frontier, where the railroads, hide markets, and Sharps repeating rifles allowed commercial buffalo hunting to reach an economy of scale. King crab populations col-lapsed in Alaska; redfish, shark, and grouper in the Gulf; abalone and rockfish in California. In New England, where in 1784 the people of Massachusetts hung a golden cod in their statehouse to celebrate the abundance of their waters, thousands of square miles of Georges Bank had to be closed down to save the last remaining codfish. Many Massachusetts trawlers quickly shifted their fishing power into the already depleted Gulf of Maine, and within four years that fishery had also collapsed. Today it operates under a set of rigid conservation meas-ures known as Amendment 13.

On a gray, rainy day I meet Rod Avila, a fourth-generation Massa-chusetts fisherman and owner of two trawlers, the *Trident* and the *7 Seas,* at the New Bedford Fishermen's Family Assistance Center. He works there as an outreach specialist. The walls of the waiting area are covered with cut-out paper fish with photos pinned to them. They are photos of out-of-work fishermen, young and not so young, who have "graduated" to new careers. Their labels read, "Brian Mayall, master mate (tugboat); Daniel Gray, trucker; Joseph Froias, computerized accounting; James Acmeida, computerized accounting; Derek Ealy, master mate (freighter); Alfredo Silva, truck driver."

"We've had 842 people come through the program," Avila tells me. "My idea is if they see a picture of a friend, they'll figure they can do it too."

On America's fishing docks there's still a lot of bitterness directed at 1980s politicians who, by refusing to put limits on industry capitalization, helped deplete the resource, encouraged corporate consolidation, and put tens of thousands of people out of work. But not all fishing industry overcapacity was generated out of Washington. In south Florida the Colombian drug lords lent a hand.

"I watched fisheries overcapitalized by drug smugglers," says Billy Causey, a one-time tropical fish collector and now manager of the Florida Keys National Marine Sanctuary. "A guy I knew went from one lobster boat to 10,000 lobster traps. Fishermen were getting $100,000 payoffs for one night's work. In the late 1970s and early 1980s these guys were getting rich and putting the money back into the only thing they knew, which was fishing."

During the 1980s, NMFS agent Dan O'Brian worked the Keys and Florida's west coast. "I'd go alone into places like Everglades City and these guys couldn't believe I wanted to inspect their fish," he says, laughing. "I was always looking over my shoulder. The local sheriff [who was later arrested in a major drug raid] used to follow me around when I'd drive through there."

At one point O'Brian's informants told him that a couple of longline fishing boats were going to pick up some Colombian hit men off the Dry Tortugas. They had been sent north to assassinate the U.S. attorney who had put drug boss Carlos Lehder in jail. O'Brian went out with a Navy helicopter, spotted the boats, and helped coordinate the subsequent Coast Guard boarding and arrest of several suspects. "Fishing and smuggling have always gone together," O'Brian says. "I mean, who's going to notice when a fishing boat pulls into port?"

The anger of fishermen who feel their livelihood threatened is not always directed at the real sources of their problem, however. "If you're going to send armed terrorists aboard my boat, they're going to get an answer, 'cause I'm looking at death through defiance before I go out and put up with this foolishness any longer!" shouts Dave Marciano, staring hard at the Coast Guard representative to the New England Fishery Council, which is meeting in the basement of the Sheraton Plymouth. Behind the gold chain–wearing militant are 150 other pissed-off fishermen, some quite large and muscular from hauling nets and dredges. Four uniformed Plymouth cops in the back of the room are trying to look unintimidated, while several more gather outside, talking to NMFS agent Dick Livingston, a former Secret Service agent who really is unfazed, having seen this all before. Reporters and camera crews from the Boston TV stations have come out for the show.

After Dave makes a few more threats, Paul Cohan gets up to play the voice of moderation. Paul has a reddish-gray ZZ Top beard and a white bill cap. "If we can manage to see some motion toward us and a little bit of compassion, that will help, help the fish, help us help the fish by letting us land what we're catching. We can all come out of here having accomplished something today," he promises. "But if the Fisheries Service is going to hold the company line and remain inflexible, what will happen is that every man in this room and everybody that's not here is just going to go fishing, and we're going to bring in what we catch and the hell with the closed areas, the hell with the days at sea, because we can rip up citations just as fast as you can write them, and then you're going to have a political crisis that's unparalleled."

After more than five years of Georges Bank closures, cod are slowly beginning to reestablish themselves in the no-take zones. At the same time, with prices high, there is increased pressure to target the fish, even if they still represent only a tiny fraction of their historic abundance. Similar closures have been established in the Gulf of Maine, where the cod are near all-time lows. At the previous council meeting four months earlier, the fishermen promised not to target cod in the Gulf of Maine if the council would give up on a plan to expand the closed areas. To prevent a targeted fishery, NMFS said fishermen could keep only 400 pounds of cod bycatch a day. Suspecting that the fish were still being targeted, NMFS quickly cut that to 200 pounds and finally to 30 pounds, about the weight of two fish. Any additional bycatch has to be thrown overboard. Which is why these fishermen are outraged.

A number of fishermen get up to testify that there are ten times more cod in the Gulf of Maine than NMFS biologists are claiming. They can hardly catch a flounder without some cod bumping it out of the way to climb into their nets. "The *Albatross* [NMFS research trawler] couldn't catch a fish if they towed in the New England Aquarium," Massachusetts fisherman Paul Terrio declares to hearty applause.

"We're starvin' here," a 30-something fisherman yells out. Later, I spot him climbing into a new extended-cab truck in the parking lot.

The issue of the moment is cod discards, but the real issue is how the fishing industry controls the councils—in 2004, 58 of 71 council seats were occupied by sport and commercial fishermen—and how NMFS acts as industry's codependent partner in a dysfunctional relationship that would embarrass Jerry Springer. Between 1980 and 1993, NMFS overruled council decisions just 0.4 percent of the time. NMFS got slightly more aggressive in the next decade, but many of these later rulings targeted council attempts to improve conservation measures. As it was explained to me by Congressman Jim Saxton of New Jersey, who is one of the cochairs of the House Oceans Caucus: "NMFS is charged with both conservation and promotion of seafood consumption, but NMFS is also located within [the Department of] Commerce, where its commercial function dominates."

The fishermen press their case. "We can't mindlessly discard the very fish that we're trying to save. It serves no purpose. It doesn't do the resource any good, it doesn't do the consumer any good, it certainly doesn't help the harvesters, and it makes you guys look like jackasses," Cohan argues.

"My kids think I'm nuts, but I'm not nuts, you're nuts," another fisherman tells the council.

After more than six hours of abuse, directed mainly at NMFS and its scientists, a couple of fishermen members of the council offer up a motion requesting the secretary of commerce to declare a resource emergency, thus allowing the fishermen to keep at least 700 pounds of cod per day. The council chairman, Joe Brancaleone, an ex-fisherman and now an executive with Burger King, suggests that "we need this type of motion or another closure."

"Or war!" someone shouts, not liking that closure reference.

Joe calls the question. As tension mounts in the room, the vote goes down to the wire: eight for, eight against. Joe casts the tie-breaking vote for the motion. The fishermen are appeased.

"What you saw isn't typical," one of the council members tells me after the near-riotous meeting. "This only happens maybe two or three times a year." Later I talk to a reporter friend who has been covering the New England fisheries crisis for years. "In terms of the story, it might have been more interesting if the vote had gone the other way," I admit.

"But the vote never goes the other way, and that's the real story," she points out.

After the vote, NMFS decides (against the advice of its own biologists) to return the take-home catch to 400 pounds a day. As the availability of the fish has declined, the price has gone up. Cod, which once wholesaled for 50 cents a pound, is now going for $2.50—which means that while licensed to go after other species, fishermen in the Gulf of Maine can now make $1,000 a day catching what's supposed to be a protected species of fish. It's a lose-lose scenario in which the market's increasing prices on diminishing stocks creates a disincentive for conservation, so that the last fish in the sea should be worth a fortune. If this sounds far-fetched, consider that in January 2001 a single bluefin tuna sold in Japan for $170,000.

"There were some of us who should have spoken out yesterday but we were intimidated both physically and emotionally," John Williamson, a retired Maine fisherman, tells me the day after the council vote. He was one of the eight council members against the motion. "The manipulation of the system is outrageous," he says. "I didn't sleep all night thinking we should have spoken out and maybe swayed that one vote. Those guys crying yesterday how they were starving. They had their best year ever last year, and that's a fact."

The New England council remains dominated by commercial fishermen. Other councils, such as the Mid-Atlantic and South Atlantic councils, are more heavily weighted toward recreational fishing. These "rec fishermen" represent another multibillion-dollar user group, increasingly in conflict with the commercial industry over allocation of an increasingly scarce resource. A National Research Council report issued in 2002 concluded that a major reason for this scarcity was the fishery councils' refusal to follow the advice of their science advisory groups.

In any case much of the science on marine wildlife continues to lag behind industry's ability to track and kill fish. In 2002, eight years after the New England cod closures, the Pacific Fishery Council was forced to declare an emergency ban on bottom fishing off the West Coast following the collapse of certain commercially valuable rockfish species. For years scientists had thought these fish lived to be around 20 years old. But new genetic and other techniques found that some of these fish, such as the bocaccio (sold as Pacific red snapper), may be among the longest-lived creatures on Earth, living well over 100 years. One rougheye rockfish was aged at 205 years; it was swimming around when Lewis and Clark reached the Pacific. Research also showed rockfish were slow to mature and breed (some species don't become sexually reproductive till they're 10 to 15 years old) and that their populations had declined 97 percent in the past 40 years. Of course, the commercial fishers on the council might have figured this out by noting that their bocaccio catches had fallen from 11,000 metric tons in the late 1970s to 214 tons in 2001, but denial is a powerful incentive for catching that last fish.

"It's all too political," says Rod Avila, who served as a member of the New England council for three years before quitting. "I saw too much of that self-dealing on the council, too much of people going out to lunch to trade their votes and making backdoor deals. I think it should be all government controlled to do what's best for the resource."

I'm visiting the groundfish trawlers that are giving way to weekend pleasure craft in the scenic coastal town of Bodega Bay, California. This is where Alfred Hitchcock filmed *The Birds,* and the cawing gulls on the roofline of the Eureka Fisheries warehouse are doing their best to maintain a fearsome reputation. The Pacific council trawling ban has yet to go into effect, and so I watch as a trawler pumps thousands of pounds of black cod, orange-colored thornyheads, sole, and various species of sharp-finned rockfish into large plastic crates called totes. The company's weigh master records the fish poundage as the totes are forklifted onto a scale and then onto refrigerator trucks for the two-hour drive south to San Francisco.

Down on the Bodega Bay municipal pier, second-generation fisherman Andy Philips is directing his two-man crew, fixing the net on his trawler, the *Jo Ellen,* before heading back out to sea. A big man, with a gray beard sans mustache, black T-shirt, jeans, and boots, Philips has a swagger from 40 years on the ocean and a voice rough as salmon gravel. "The real problem is the regulations aren't doing the job," he claims. "Back around 1986 you'd just head out, and when the boat was full the trip was over."

"But you agree the fishing's gotten worse?" I ask.

"Of course the fishing's worse. We killed them all. Electronics [fish-finding sonar] killed them all. The fishing grounds are like freeways now, and we're just wiping them out. Places where I used to get 20,000-pound drags I get 100 pounds now. Decimated is the word. If we just stopped fishing for about 20 years the fish'd come back. But that's not practical. I couldn't do any other kind of work myself." With the trawling ban now in effect, the best estimates indicate that it may actually take 50 to 100 years for West Coast rockfish to come back.

"Who hears the fishes when they cry?" wondered poet Henry David Thoreau. Sylvia Earle does, I'd venture. The famed ocean explorer-in-residence at National Geographic and former chief scientist for NOAA (under the first President Bush), labeled a "Hero of the Earth" by *Time* magazine, believes that commercial fishing no longer makes sense.

"It's not a harvest. It's the commercial taking of wildlife, and there's no history of this ever having been done sustainably," she argues. "The idea of continuing to take hundreds of millions of tons of wildlife is inexcusable, and with these bottom trawl nets! I use the analogy of taking squirrels and rabbits out of the forest using a bulldozer. Unfortunately, the Bureau of Commercial Fisheries was reborn as the National Marine Fisheries Service not to serve the fish but the fisheries industry. I think if people knew fish not as fish but as these amazing animals I've gotten to know, things might change."

"Change has to come, provided we can get beyond this bigger-is-better mentality that was with us through much of the twentieth century," agrees Zeke Grader of the Pacific Coast Federation of Fishermen's Associations. PCFFA, along with the Maryland Watermen's Association, the Cape Cod Commercial Hook Fishermen, the Northwest Indian Fisheries Commission, and other community-based fishing groups, believes that sustainable fishing is still possible.

"For food production, smaller units make sense, plus the cultural element is involved," Grader argues. "Instead of indiscriminate trawlers we need new technologies for gear that's more selective, that harvests less but gets more value. Right now sardines are coming back in California, so we have to learn not to repeat our mistakes of the past, learn to fish them sustainably.

"Also what if instead of 40 to 70 boats fishing 50 to 100 tons a night and grinding them up for fish meal, we had 1,000 boats fishing a ton a night and going into the fresh food market? Instead of surimi [factory-trawler blocks of processed pollack], the Velveeta of fish with the nutrients all washed out, what if we provided pollack as a low-priced white fish fillet for the supermarket? That way it wouldn't always be so expensive to buy fish, and lower-income folks could afford it also."

For the past 40 years the PCFFA has been working in coalition with recreational fishermen and environmental groups including the Sierra Club to find innovative approaches to the use and protection of local fish and marine habitat. The groups originally came together to fight water diversions that threatened California's salmon rivers. As a result of their early and ongoing collaborative work, California today has viable commercial stocks of wild salmon. "These groups that are fighting each other elsewhere are missing the big picture," Grader believes.

A practical solution to America's fisheries crisis has to be at the heart of any big-picture approach to America's blue frontier. What's required is a public understanding and commitment to turning things around on our public seas. That could be done using a combination of already available policy tools.

Let's call this solution the BLUE-plate special. BLUE is yet another fisheries acronym, but an easy one to remember. The B is for buybacks, a financial commitment by both government and industry to reduce the size of the fishing fleet to a sustainable level. In 2003 the government announced a $46 million buyout plan to retire up to half of the West Coast trawler fleet—more than 90 boats—following the Pacific council's bottom-fishing closure.

"But why should the taxpayer buy back boats we may already have helped pay for?" I asked Senator Kerry, who replied, "This country has historically helped people hit by sudden dislocation with retraining and other support. Besides which, there's no other way to reduce the fishing pressure. It's an effective approach but only if done in combination with good management and closures."

Which goes along with the L in BLUE. Limited entry means that only so many people can be licensed to work in a given fishery or biological complex of fisheries in order to prevent them from being overcapitalized again. Some people like the idea of privatizing fisheries with individual transferable quotas, or ITQs, in which a fishing license is like an ownership deed to a given share of the fish stock. Others worry that this method will encourage corporate consolidation and the giveaway of a public resource. One coalition of fishermen and environmentalists has proposed limiting share size and making ITQs into seven-year renewable licenses, which would have to demonstrate conservation benefits as a condition of renewal. Rather than get hung up on a single tool, however, it is important to stick with the larger principle of not allowing more people to fish a living resource than its biology and habitat can sustain—hence, limited entry.

The U in BLUE is for undersea reserves, or what are called marine protected areas. (See chapter 11.) Biologists suggest that 20 percent of the blue frontier needs to be set aside as limited or no-take zones in order to restore and propagate new populations of fish, crustaceans, kelp, and other plants and animals. Where undersea reserves already exist, studies are finding them to be highly effective, with healthy populations of marine wildlife slowly expanding beyond their fluid borders. Having had the opportunity to go diving in no-take zones in Florida, California,

Mexico, and Australia, I've been duly impressed by their diversity and abundance of life, some of it quite large and frisky.

Finally, the E in BLUE: an end to conflict of interest. The management of fisheries must be taken away from people with a direct stake in killing the resource. At a hearing in Washington on the billion-dollar-a-year pollack fishery's impact on Steller's sea lions, I heard a one-time NMFS scientist give testimony. He had quit NMFS to help found the Arctic Storm factory-trawler company and was also vice-chairman of the North Pacific Fishery Council. Such a direct conflict of interest is not permitted in other federal regulatory bodies. For example, someone might quit his or her job as an FAA inspector to found an airline company, but once in that position would not be allowed to sit on the National Transportation Safety Board. The flying public would not tolerate it, nor does the law allow it.

In 1996 the Magnuson Act was reformed with the addition of conservation language. There was even a provision that council members should not vote on fishing matters that would give them a "substantially disproportionate benefit" over other fishermen going after the same catch. The law's basic conflict-of-interest exemptions were maintained, however. Rather than ban Jesse James from the railroad commission, the rules merely ensure that the robbers divide the loot evenly. This is why both the Pew and the U.S. Ocean Policy commissions recommended a major reorganization of the councils.

In March 2005, Representative Nick Rahall of West Virginia (whose coal country constituents know something about what happens when industry sets the rules) introduced the Fisheries Science and Management Enhancement Act. This bill would repeal council members' exemptions from conflict-of-interest rules, expand public participation in the councils, and have scientists set the catch limits for marine wildlife, leaving the councils to allocate how that catch is to be divided.

Whether or not this bill becomes law, any plan involving buybacks, limited entry, undersea reserves, and an end to conflict of interest in our fisheries is not likely to be implemented until far more Americans who say they love the ocean decide to take more responsibility for its stewardship. Unfortunately, under our present system of ocean governance there is no real stewardship. Instead of seeing the blue frontier as a living entity, we have encouraged an array of special interests to attach themselves to various calcified bureaucracies, like so many poisonous anemones clinging to hard rock corals. That leaves the majority of concerned citizens to play the role of passing small prey caught in their tentacles, injected with venom, and slowly drowning in red tape.

CHAPTER 10

Drowning in Red Tape

No one knows who's on first, or even if they're playing
baseball.

> —*Kathy Metcalf, Chamber of Shipping of America,*
> *an advocacy group for companies engaged in*
> *oceangoing commerce, on U.S. oceans policy*

I don't think anyone anticipated the breach of the levees.

> —*President George W. Bush to Diane Sawyer*
> *on the flooding of New Orleans*

After going through security at the Department of Commerce, I buy a
$25 ticket and join a line of some 1,000 people wending their way
through one of the building's big marble and granite galleries. It's June
16, 2004, another hot muggy day in our nation's capital, and the big
crowd is on hand for the annual meet-and-greet put on by the National
Oceanographic and Atmospheric Administration (NOAA). We work our
way past neo-Grecian columns and down a set of narrow stairs to where
a man in a "NOAA Fish Fry" apron takes our tickets and admits us into
the building's main cafeteria. The first thing we encounter is a Recreational Fishing Alliance (RFA) table and "Fishing Simulator." This features a white fighting chair, deep-sea rod and reel, and some sort of cali-
brated pulley system that yanks the fishing line of volunteer tournament
contestants who have lined up to take turns battling a giant sailfish leaping out of tropical waters on a big video screen 20 feet away.

RFA is a major battler in its own right, leading the opposition to no-
take marine protected areas (MPAs), which could function as wilderness
parks in the sea while helping restore America's depleted fisheries. But
RFA believes that no part of the sea should be exempted from recreational fishing hooks, even areas off-limits to commercial fishermen. If
RFA gets its way, people who are into sportfishing may well need to practice their virtual fishing skills, as actual fish may be few and far between.

Next in line is a NOAA T-shirt table, followed by the first of several

205

serving tables full of fried and broiled fish, beginning with grouper, an arguably depleted and downsized species. This is followed by your choice of tilapia, whiting, shrimp, flounder, crab legs, and all sorts of other seafood both sustainable and nonsustainable, as well as corn on the cob, potato salad, soda, and beer.

Outside in the big tree-shaded courtyard below Commerce's walls, tent stations have been set up with more and better seafood samples provided by a range of restaurants and fishing industry outlets. The crowd here is mostly in short-sleeved casual office wear but also some suits, dresses, and aloha shirts. The secretary of commerce and Texas oilman Don Evans, wearing a navy blue suit and NOAA bill cap, is wandering around with a few aides, a photographer, and two secret servicemen. He stops by the Maine aquaculture display to try shucking some farm-grown oysters. After attempting to open an already opened half shell, he is given a whole oyster and manages to get the blade in and pry it open, smiling for his photographer. After Evans retires he will be replaced by Carlos Gutierrez, the former CEO of Kellogg. If the ocean were made of cereal this would be a very wise choice. But of course secretaries of commerce don't come to the job to oversee America's publicly owned ocean, which is part of the problem. If you go to the secretary's Web site you'll see his real job description: "the voice of business in government."

I head over to the open-sided Legal Sea Foods tent, which is serving delicious and politically correct wild Alaska sockeye with seaweed garnish and Asian glaze. There are also University of New Hampshire farm-raised halibut from open ocean cages, mussels, catfish, and many other offerings. Someone wanders by with a paper plate full of sushi. Hubbs-SeaWorld Research Institute is offering fish kabobs, and there are Budweiser and wine stations and the National Estuarine Research Reserves' "Taste of the Reserves."

Personally I can't help feeling a bit strange that the big annual social event put on by the nation's leading agency for our endangered seas is a cookout serving more than a ton of marine wildlife. It's as if the Forest Service were to stage an annual bonfire and feed the flames with one of every kind of tree in America.

After eating my fill and talking with a couple of staffers from the conservation group Oceana, several NOAA employees, a scientist I'd met on an expedition, an editor from *Sea Technology* magazine, and an aquaculture industry rep who complains about fishermen and environmentalists, I wander into the National Aquarium section of the building, which is being kept open late for us. Recently renovated, it still looks like a medium-security fish jail. I watch some leopard sharks swimming in circles and wonder if the fish out in the courtyard may not be better off.

In this fish-eat-fish world I'm not opposed to getting some tasty animal protein from the living seas. I just wish we would learn enough restraint not to kill the golden cod, and that the agency mandated to protect our public seas weren't always partying with the folks it is supposed to be regulating.

This is by no means a recent development. Among the sins of Richard Nixon, few historians count more than 35 years of failed U.S. ocean policy. Perhaps they should. On July 9, 1970, the same day he established the Environmental Protection Agency as an independent arm of government, he created and sank another entity, the National Oceanic and Atmospheric Administration, by assigning it to the Department of Commerce, then being run by his campaign fund-raiser and future Watergate bagman Maurice Stans.

"NOAA wasn't quite stillborn, but it was born feeble. Nixon did the minimum he had to," charges Edward Wenk, a former White House secretary of the National Council on Marine Resources under both Nixon and Lyndon Johnson. Representative John Dingell of Michigan blasted the president's action, describing the newly established NOAA as the handmaiden of a Department of Commerce so dominated by industrial interests "as to be incapable of objectivity on issues of the marine environment."

Logically, an agency designed to study the weather and protect the nation's oceans might have found a home in the Department of the Interior, whose job is to manage and protect America's public lands and wilderness. The smart money in the marine community certainly believed that if NOAA was not going to be an independent agency, then the Department of the Interior was where it would find a home. What the smart money failed to realize is how personal spite and vindictiveness can have hugely disproportionate effects on public policy inside the Washington Beltway.

A few months earlier, on April 30, 1970, Nixon had ordered U.S. troops in Vietnam to invade neighboring Cambodia, which set off massive campus protests and National Guard and police killings of four students at Kent State, two at Jackson State, and one at the University of California at Santa Barbara. Deeply disturbed by this turn of events, Secretary of the Interior Walter J. Hickel wrote a personal letter to the president. In it he expressed his growing reservations about Nixon's refusal to listen to the antiwar sentiments of the nation's young people.

Hickel's letter, dated May 6, 1970, read in part, "About 200 years ago there was emerging a great nation in the British Empire, and it found itself with a colony in violent protest by its youth—men such as Patrick Henry, Thomas Jefferson, Madison, and Monroe, to name a few. Their protests fell on deaf ears, and finally led to war. The outcome is history. My point is, if we read history, it clearly shows that youth in its protest must be heard."

Before reaching the White House a copy of the letter (which had been circulated at Interior) was obtained by the Associated Press and published in the *Washington Evening Star*. The president and his aides Bob Haldeman and John Ehrlichman went ballistic. Nixon told Hickel that he now considered him an "adversary." Hickel was blacklisted from White House events and became the target of a well-orchestrated campaign of press smears. Less than two months later NOAA was placed with the ever-loyal Maurice Stans at Commerce. On Thanksgiving eve, Hickel was fired.

Although it went largely unnoticed in the polarizing political heat of the times, this was a rather sad outcome to one of the more hopeful initiatives of the 1960s. For a period in that decade the exploration of oceanic "inner space" was seen to be at least as important as work in outer space, with astronauts and aquanauts (including astronaut-turned-aquanaut Scott Carpenter) competing for national news coverage. Groups of Navy and civilian scientists were living in underwater "habitats," like Sealabs One and Two off San Diego and Textite off St. John in the U.S. Virgin Islands. Major corporations including GM, Union Carbide, Lockheed, Reynolds, and Alcoa competed for what they imagined would be multibillion-dollar contracts if ocean exploration went the way of the space race with the Soviet Union.

Advocates for new ocean spending likewise were not averse to citing the red menace as justification for America's getting wet. In 1959, two years after the Soviets launched *Sputnik*, the first human-constructed satellite, Senator Warren G. Magnuson of Washington declared, "Soviet Russia is winning the struggle for the oceans. Soviet Russia aspires to command the oceans and has mapped a shrewdly conceived plan, using science as a weapon to win her that supremacy." And six years later, in 1965, he wrote, "The prevention of communist domination of the seas is perhaps our most pressing problem today. . . . This is the immediate challenge our marine scientists can and must help us meet."

New submersibles such as the Navy's *Alvin* were launched into the depths, and the popular imagination was fired by salty tales ranging from Arthur Clarke's science-fiction novel *Deep Range* and Cold War potboilers like *Ice Station Zebra* to television programs such as *Flipper* and *Sea Hunt,* the latter starring Lloyd Bridges as underwater diver and investigator Mike Nelson. There were Jacques Cousteau's books, films, and lyrical *Undersea World* TV specials, as well as the pop sounds of the Beach Boys, Jan and Dean, the Ventures, Dick Dale, and many others who redefined the California dream as a surf safari looking for that perfect tubular wave along the golden shore of youth.

Vice President Hubert Humphrey, who as a senator had issued a 1957 report on the importance of oceanographic studies, became a major advocate for new approaches to America's blue frontier. Of course, many of these approaches—techno-optimistic visions conceived in the 1960s—appear strangely anachronistic by today's standards. There was talk of developing a protein concentrate made from whole fish, which could be added to rice, milkshakes, and other products to feed the world's hungry. Senator Claiborne Pell of Rhode Island, in his book *Challenge of the Seven Seas,* imagined that by 1996 there would be nuclear-powered underwater vacation resorts, submarine oil tankers tapping subarctic oil fields, and surgically altered "fish-men" respirating through artificial gills.

In 1964 the White House Office of Science and Technology proposed building nuclear power plants all along the coasts to desalinate seawater for America's thirsty cities, beginning with Key West, Florida. Later came a proposal to build nuclear power plants on a series of artificial islands off the coast of New Jersey. The Rand Corporation, Scripps Institution, and others looked to Antarctica as a source of fresh water. The National Science Foundation even drew up a proposal for a 20-mile-long iceberg convoy to bring frozen water north to California: the lead berg would be equipped with ship engines and propellers. Recently a more modest proposal called for using giant bladders and single-hull tankers to bring fresh water south from British Columbia.

In 1966 Vice President Humphrey took charge of the White House Council on Marine Resources, and helped launch the Stratton Commission, a 15-member blue-ribbon panel convened to consider America's future regarding the sea. The commission was headed by Julius Stratton, chairman of the board of the Ford Foundation.

In 1969 the Stratton Commission issued its report, *Our Nation and the Sea.* Its findings would result in the passage of a number of ocean protection laws including the Coastal Zone Management Act and the Marine Mammal Protection Act. But its key recommendation was for

the nation to create a unified ocean agency responsible for the steward-
ship and exploration of the blue frontier. It should be an independent
agency, the commission proposed, and encompass the Coast Guard, the
Bureau of Commercial Fisheries, and the National Weather Bureau.
Suggested names for the new organization included Sea Exploration
Agency (SEA), National Marine Agency, and National Oceanic and
Atmospheric Agency. The commission envisioned a watery twin to the
starbound NASA (*Science* magazine even christened it "a wet NASA").

In late 1968, even before the commission report came out, Secretary
of Transportation Alan Boyd got wind of the proposed agency. He
became outraged that anyone would suggest removing the Coast Guard
from his two-year-old department, which had just wrested it from
Treasury. Boyd complained to President Johnson, who considered the
Department of Transportation his personal brainchild. Not only was the
idea of moving the Coast Guard deep-sixed, but Johnson refused to meet
with Stratton. Humphrey, who had championed the commission, felt
humiliated by this slight.

Humphrey would go on to lose a close election to Richard Nixon that
November. After his inauguration President Nixon, like his predecessor,
quickly became obsessed with winning the intractable war in Southeast
Asia. When it came to creating and nurturing a new agency for the
oceans, however, he proved more inclined to sink it like some Vietnamese
sampan.

And so NOAA was born into the relative obscurity of the trade-ori-
ented Department of Commerce. Since it had no strong advocate in the
White House or Congress, its first budget of $330 million was $120 million less than requested, and almost all of that was dedicated to NOAA's
"dry side," the Weather Service.

Robert White, the director of the Weather Service, also became
NOAA's first director, a job he held for seven years. "For a while I wondered if the word *NOAA* would even take hold," he recalls. "We were a
collection of all the cats and dogs of the ocean community, all the programs that weren't strongly attached to their parent agencies. So people
still continued to refer to the Weather Service, or the Coast and Geodetic
Survey, or the Bureau of Fisheries. The Navy sent us a three-star admiral
as a liaison, and he was very helpful. The Navy of course wanted to keep
closely associated with anything having to do with the oceans."

In the more than 35 years since its founding, NOAA's various directors,
designated as undersecretaries of commerce, have come from Navy-linked
oceanographic institutes such as the University of Washington and

the University of Rhode Island, unless, like Vice-Admiral Conrad Lautenbacher, they came from the Navy itself. They have supported a strong emphasis on basic research as a means to "advance our knowledge of the oceans." This science orientation has allowed them to avoid making the hard choices often associated with natural resource management.

Science, after all, is about presenting, challenging, and refining hypotheses over long periods of time to better understand how things work. Policy, by contrast, is about taking the best available science and, based on society's shared values, making decisions—decisions that are often controversial and result in winners and losers. By emphasizing the uncertainty of science and the need for more study, NOAA's directors have avoided making policy decisions that might affect corporate interests, which look to the Department of Commerce for support rather than regulation.

For example, take the salmon (which almost everyone has). A salmon migrates up the Columbia and Snake rivers, bringing nutrients 900 miles from the ocean to enrich the granite soils of Idaho. There it spawns and dies in its natal river gravel, or else some furred or feathered predator deposits its bones and skin in the forest. As its young progeny head back downriver and out to sea, they must make it through some three dozen different governmental jurisdictions, all of them influenced by the votes and money salmon lack—by ranchers, loggers, fishermen, hydroelectric dam operators and their beer- and soda-can-producing customers in the aluminum industry, by shoreside developers and the International Association of Shopping Centers—all wanting a piece of that fish or its habitat. Unfortunately, over 35 years of declining Northwest salmon stocks, NOAA managed to ignore and delay any effective response until an environmental lawsuit under the Endangered Species Act forced the creation of a state and federal task force in the late 1990s. That task force concluded that dam removals would be the most effective means to save this living icon of Northwest wilderness, a course of action the Bush administration refuses to consider.

Today, despite calls for reform by two major commissions (the Pew and U.S. Ocean Policy panels), no strong national leadership for our public seas has yet to emerge. Instead, responsibility for our blue frontier remains up for grabs, claimed by more than half the president's cabinet departments, at least 15 federal agencies, 46 committees and subcommittees of Congress, and hundreds of state and local authorities from 22 coastal states, the Commonwealth of Puerto Rico, and various U.S. territories including Guam and American Samoa.

The following is a simplified breakdown of how our oceans are presently managed within the 200-mile American EEZ:

National Oceanographic and Atmospheric Administration (NOAA) oversees national marine sanctuaries.

NOAA, on its wet side, also remains responsible for federal marine science, fisheries management (beyond state waters), and coastal management (through state agencies). The Coastal Barrier Resources Act, however, is overseen by

U.S. Fish and Wildlife Service. The service also protects marine mammals such as walruses, manatees, and sea otters, whereas

NOAA's National Marine Fisheries Service (with input from the federal Marine Mammal Commission) is responsible for seals, dolphins, and whales. NMFS protects sea turtles at sea, though the Fish and Wildlife Service protects them on the beach. If something happens to a turtle in the surf, it becomes a jurisdictional dispute.

Department of Agriculture oversees the care of captive dolphins and promotes aquaculture (as does the U.S. SeaGrant Program).

National Park Service takes care of national seashores and underwater areas adjacent to national parks.

Mineral Management Service (MMS) leases oil, gas, and mining rights on the Continental Shelf (but not in state waters).

Army Corps of Engineers is responsible for protecting coastal wetlands (and handing out permits for their destruction), along with

Environmental Protection Agency (EPA), which runs the National Estuary Research Program, not to be confused with

NOAA's National Estuarine Research Reserves, or the

Department of Agriculture's Natural Resource Conservation Service, which is working to restore wetlands in Louisiana.

In addition,

Army Corps of Engineers is charged with protecting the shore against flooding and sea surge and keeping coastal traffic moving, by constructing seawalls, replenishing beaches, and dredging ports and canals.

EPA regulates the Corps dredge spoils if they're toxic and oversees ocean dumpsites for toxic and nontoxic muds. EPA is also responsible (under the Clean Water Act) for regulating polluted coastal runoff, as is

NOAA (under the Coastal Zone Management Act).

Department of Homeland Security's Federal Emergency Management Agency (FEMA) steps in when the Corps of Engineers fails to prevent hurricane damage, providing more than $760 billion of flood insurance coverage that allows people to rebuild in harm's way.

U.S. Coast Guard, aside from search-and-rescue, law enforcement, and port security, manages ship traffic, controls ship- and harbor-based pollution, and is responsible for oil spill response (under OPA 90) and fisheries enforcement (with NMFS and state or tribal authorities).

Department of Transportation's (DOT) Maritime Administration licenses ships. DOT also builds roads, bridges, highways, and other infrastructure along the coast, often through wetlands and to and from barrier islands.

Department of the Interior oversees the 200-mile EEZs of U.S. protectorates such as Midway and the northern Marianas.

EPA maintains clean-water agreements with former U.S. protectorates including Palau and the Federated States of Micronesia.

State Department negotiates EEZ rules, coral reef protection, and fishery treaties with other nations.

National Science Foundation funds ocean research, as does the U.S. Navy, NOAA, and NASA.

NASA also studies the oceans from space and is recruiting oceanographers to go into space. Similar networks exist within various coastal regions, states, counties, tribes, and municipalities.

Is the big picture clear? Of course not. Furthermore, this murky mess of competing bureaucracies tends to administer marine activities with little or no regard to their natural interaction within the oceans or the watersheds that flow into them. Agencies are frequently criticized for failing to communicate with one another, failing to listen to their own scientists, and failing to solicit input from conservationists, coastal citizens, and communities.

It has been suggested by the U.S. Commission on Ocean Policy, some in Congress, and the White House that NOAA be given greater leadership responsibility for oversight of America's blue frontier. Then again, it's been suggested by some in Congress and the White House that military detention of U.S. citizens is justified by the war on terror. Despite its rapid growth over the last decade, including important work on climate change and an expansion of marine funding, NOAA seems to have lost the trust of too many people working on the blue frontier to maintain its credibility.

And while NOAA officials like to claim that they must be doing something right because they are attacked by both fishermen and environmentalists, neither group, it can be argued, favors political opportunism in lieu of effective management. "NOAA's run by scientists lobbying for funding for their own institutions," says Zeke Grader of the Pacific Coast Federation of Fishermen's Associations, "so it's big on weather and hard science but not so good on resource protection."

"There should be a separate agency for the oceans, or at least not one in constant conflict," argues the former NOAA chief scientist Sylvia Earle. "The leadership has not been strong on biology, but biology is coming back because of this great wake-up call from nature." The Pew Oceans Commission report agreed, calling for "an independent agency outside the Department of Commerce to address the national interest in the oceans and atmosphere." And before his retirement Senator Fritz Hollings of South Carolina, a leading ocean champion on Capitol Hill, called members of the U.S. Commission on Ocean Policy "sissies" for not recommending the establishment of an independent ocean agency.

Unfortunately, the Coast Guard, which might logically form the core of such an agency, is not available. As had happened with the Stratton Commission recommendation 35 years earlier, the Coasties were relocated in 2003—this time from the Department of Transportation to the Department of Homeland Security. And, having created a monster-sized agency in Homeland Security, Congress seems disinclined to make any other big changes. Instead, in April 2005 it began working on a NOAA Organic Act that would give the agency statutory authority to continue its work, which until then was based only on Nixon's executive order. This change, it was claimed, would help the agency better define its missions and purpose. What it will do is ensure that NOAA remains firmly attached to Commerce like a barnacle to a commercial wharf piling.

What the edge city of Silver Spring, Maryland, lacks in charm it makes up for in low-rent office space for second-tier government agencies, like the $3.5 billion National Oceanographic and Atmospheric Administration. NOAA headquarters is a series of three glass, brick, and concrete office towers strung along the East-West Highway (a fourth tower was evacuated years back because of sick building syndrome).

Halfway up the block is a sculpture of a giant hand releasing four bronze seagulls—soaring off, possibly in search of bycatch to feed on. Inside this complex and throughout coastal America, I've had the opportunity to meet dedicated NOAA employees trying to do right by the blue frontier, but I've also found many of them frustrated and demoralized by the institution's misplaced priorities, misplaced plans, and often literally misplaced reports, schedules, and calendars. This institutional drift, along with its frequent internal restructurings, has led to a popular insider acronym for NOAA: No Organization At All.

A survey filled out by more than 120 NOAA scientists in 2005 found that only one-quarter of them would "trust NOAA decision makers to make decisions that will protect marine resources and ecosystems."

Without a strong advocate for the oceans, the blue frontier has tended to be defined as a marine treasure chest available to whoever has the political creativity to pry it open. Witnessing how ocean policy is made can be kind of unsettling, like the first time you watch a feeding frenzy among large groupers.

It's September 20, 2004, the day of the official release to the president and Congress of the U.S. Commission on Ocean Policy report. Uniformed Secret Service officers direct me out of the cab at the concrete barriers surrounding Capitol Hill, and I make my way through an inner ring of security at the Dirksen Senate Office Building, then upstairs to Room 192. The high-ceilinged, wood-paneled hearing room has thick green carpet, green marble trim, and big decorative golden torches on its walls, as if we really want our public servants to think of themselves as Roman senators.

There are some 90 people in the room including the chair of the U.S. Commission on Ocean Policy, Admiral Jim Watkins, a few of his staff, and five of his fellow commissioners. Also just arriving are Senator Hollings of South Carolina, tall and handsome with leathery skin and a shock of white hair like the admiral's, and Senator Ted Stevens of Alaska, slight and wary with thin-frame glasses and slicked-back receding hair, unusually dark for a man of eighty.

Although much of the media coverage occurred when the draft report was released months earlier, this is still a big day for ocean policy on the Hill. (State governors had 90 days to respond to that draft report, and the president has 90 days to respond to this final one. Some in Congress have already begun cherry-picking parts of the report and turning them into legislative proposals.)

Admiral Watkins introduces his commissioners, notes that ocean governance in America is a "Byzantine patchwork" of bureaucracies that has
failed to protect America's living seas, and expresses his hope that
Congress and the president will pursue the major changes recommended
in the report. He then introduces Hollings as "my longtime friend, even
if he did call me a sissy at our last meeting." Hollings has a deep, reso-
nant Southern drawl that reminds me of a popular orator of my youth,
the Warner Brothers cartoon rooster Foghorn Leghorn, voiced by Mel
Blanc.

"We organized NOAA in 1970," he recalls. "Ted Stevens and myself,
we got coastal zone management, got sanctuaries, and fishing, and the
dumping treaty and all these other things over the last 37 years, and now
we've got a bunch of landlubbers in charge of things."

Stevens follows his Democratic counterpart to the podium. "Fritz," he
says. "It's gonna be so bad without you, it'll almost be like you're here."
That gets a laugh. "I think this report and the report of the Pew
Commission will set the parameters of debate for some time to come,
and I believe in this report. We need to implement this report," he says.
"The administration needs to act on it. I think this is the biggest problem
we have when we get rid of the terrorists, the oceans, this is it. More than
half the people in Alaska derive their income from fisheries. That's why
we're so disturbed with the Pew Commission trying to put a new level of
federal control over our [regional fisheries] council."

Actually, both the Pew and the U.S. Ocean Commissions have called
for reforms of the federal fishery council system to eliminate its built-in
conflict of interest, by separating the science from the allocation of fish.
Both recommend using the best available science and the precautionary
principle to set the catch limits, and then letting the fisherman-dominated
councils allocate which fishing groups get what share. In fact, Stevens's
dubious record on fisheries is a prime example of why more careful controls are being sought.

"I'm a mean, miserable SOB," Senator Stevens has bragged in the
past. It's one of the few things many fishermen and environmentalists still
agree on. In 1998 Stevens sponsored the American Fisheries Act.
Originally based on ideas put forward by shore-based Alaskan fishermen, Alaskan fish processors, and the environmental group Greenpeace,
the bill was aimed at eliminating the giant Seattle-based factory trawlers
that were competing with Alaskans for Bering Sea pollack, which now
makes up half the total U.S. fish catch by weight. The largest of the factory trawler companies, American Seafoods, was a subsidiary of

Resources Group International (RGI), a Norwegian multinational that controls 10 percent of the global whitefish market. (In 2002, as a result of a complex recapitalization scheme, the company came under U.S. ownership.) Other factory trawler operations included Trident Seafoods, which is partially owned by the grain giant ConAgra, and Arctic Storm. In 1999 Trident bought out Tyson Foods' seafood division, further consolidating the factory trawler industry.

When the American Fisheries Act was introduced, the largest capacity fishing boat in the world was tied up to a Seattle pier. RGI's *American Monarch* is capable of catching and processing about a million pounds of fish a day, using a net that could easily swallow the Statue of Liberty. This $65 million, 311-foot-long supertrawler was denied permits to fish off Chile, Peru, and the Falkland Islands by governments fearful that it would quickly deplete their waters of fish and then move on. Because the *Monarch* was built in Norway, and under U.S. law at least the hulls of fishing boats have to be domestically built, the *Monarch* was also excluded from the U.S. Bering Sea pollack fishery.

Meanwhile, the introduction of the American Fisheries Act in Congress was drawing lobbyists like dead fish draw cats. Along with lawyers and former congressmen, American Seafood hired Ted Stevens's brother-in-law, Anchorage attorney William Bittner. By the time the bill had gone through a series of closed-door meetings on Capitol Hill with the At-Sea Processors Association and other factory trawler lobbyists, it had been transformed from a bill to abolish factory trawlers into an industry subsidy. Restructured as a $97 million fishing boat buyback program, it allowed the industry to retire nine obsolete ships while consolidating its operations at sea. Shortly after the bill passed into law, Trevor McCabe, the Stevens staffer who oversaw the legislative dealmaking, quit the senator's office to become executive director of the At-Sea Processors Association with a considerable raise in pay.

While some advocates of the law argue that the American Fisheries Act helped reduce America's overcapitalized factory trawler fleet, it is worth noting that RGI and other global fishing companies also maintain pollack operations on the dangerously overfished Russian side of the Bering Sea, targeting the same fish as their U.S. boats. Among these operators is the "Russian" fishing boat *American Monarch*. The same giant factory ship that had been banned from Latin American and U.S. waters is now working the Russian side of the pollack line.

A few years later Senator Stevens was back with a new proposal. Along with a catch quota, or guaranteed share of the crab harvest for fishermen working the dangerous waters of the Bering Sea, he wanted to allocate 90 percent of crab purchase rights to big shore-based processing companies such as Trident Seafoods, most based in Seattle. He attached his proposal as a rider to a major spending bill so it wouldn't have to come before Senator John McCain's Commerce Committee (the Republican from Arizona described Stevens's proposal as "bizarre"). Stevens also ignored a Bush Justice Department opinion that his plan would create a processor monopoly that might violate antitrust laws. And the fact that his son, Ben Stevens, was a lobbyist for the North Pacific Crab Association (largely underwritten by the big Seattle processors) had no influence on his proposal, he insisted. In Alaska, where Frank Murkowski named his daughter to finish his term as U.S. senator after he was elected governor, these kinds of connections are simply known as family values.

Alaskan crab fishermen complained bitterly that their ability to bargain over price would be destroyed once the processors got their purchase quota. Environmentalists fumed when Stevens added a second provision to the rider that would cut spending to protect deep-sea corals and other essential fish habitat in the north Pacific (a conservation measure included in the 1996 Magnuson-Stevens Act, which carried the senator's name). Despite angry fishermen and environmentalists and outraged editorials from the *Washington Post* to the *Honolulu Advertiser,* Stevens got his processor quota passed, after dropping the anticonservation part of the rider. In 2005 he also got to replace Senator McCain as chair of the Commerce Committee, which oversees NOAA and ocean policy.

His successful power play inspired the Pacific Seafood Group, the largest processor on the West Coast, to begin lobbying for across-the-board processor quotas. In 2003 its lobbying firm invited Bill Hogarth, the head of NOAA's National Marine Fisheries Service, on a four-day trip to the Oregon coast. "Probably everywhere I go I get lobbied a little bit. But I don't look at it that way," said Hogarth, denying any impropriety. Still, Frank Dulcich, the president and CEO of Pacific Seafood, felt he got his money's worth out of the junket, calling Hogarth's visit "a clear indication that the Bush administration is listening." To make sure his ode to monopoly was being heard, Dulcich also became a Bush "Pioneer," raising more than $100,000 for the president's reelection campaign.

I'm flying to New Orleans and the Gulf region by way of Ronald Reagan (D.C.) and George Bush (Houston) airports to see how "less government" functions in the face of a coastal catastrophe. Given that it's three weeks since Hurricane Katrina struck, we already know the answer.

There was a complete failure on prevention (of catastrophic impacts due to shortsighted policies), preparation, and response. Okay, not a complete failure. NOAA's National Hurricane Center gave 72 hours' warning that was mostly ignored, and the Coast Guard surged in behind the storm to do more than 6,400 floodwater rescues during four days of helicopter flying. "I was involved in about 140 rescues. A lot of rooftops on the first day, more balconies on the second. It was nonstop. We were just hoisting and fueling. It was surreal," recalls 21-year-old rescue swimmer Keola Marfil.

At the opposite end of the competency scale, executive agency decision-makers at the Department of Homeland Security and FEMA left New Orleans and the Gulf without any other federal support for four days, resulting in unnecessary deaths, hardship, injuries, and looting.

Clearly the Louisiana National Guard was not up to the task of dealing with more than a million environmental refugees and victims in their state. Fifty-seven hundred guardsmen were operating out of a flooded headquarters, while a third of the state's force, 3,200 members, were deployed in Iraq—along with hundreds of their high-water trucks, fuel trucks, and satellite communications gear.

Although plenty of fault can be found at the local and state level, officials with the greatest available resources ought to be held to the highest standards of accountability. Instead, Secretary of Homeland Security Michael Chertoff, in trying to explain why he delayed mobilizing his forces for 36 hours after the hurricane, claimed that no one had ever predicted a disaster of such magnitude—even though FEMA just a year earlier had staged a war game based on the scenario of a major hurricane named "Pam" striking and flooding New Orleans.

A system of political cronyism had become established within FEMA beginning with the appointment as its director of Joe Albaugh, Bush's former Texas chief of staff and campaign director. Albaugh brought his former college buddy Michael Brown into the agency after Brown was put out to pasture as a long-time commissioner with the International Arabian Horse Association. Like Brown, five of the eight top officials at FEMA had no previous disaster-management experience, though they were well connected politically. After punching his ticket for two years, Albaugh resigned to become a lobbyist for high-end clients including Halliburton and the Shaw Group, major post-Katrina government contractors. Mike Brown became the new head of FEMA, assuring that there would be someone left behind to sign the contracts. Later, after FEMA's well-documented failure to mobilize a timely federal response to Katrina (partly because Brown's boss, Chertoff, didn't authorize it), "Brownie," as President Bush affectionately nicknamed him, was forced to resign, staying on for a time as a $148,000-a-year consultant to FEMA.

Still, not all U.S. marine policy is being made by stealthy politicians, their cronies, or bureaucracies beholden to saltwater special interests. In California people have a sense of entitlement when it comes to the ocean. Unlike much of New England, where people think the water belongs to the fishermen and the beaches to the townships, or Louisiana, where they know it all belongs to big oil, Californians believe the ocean is their birthright, or becomes so when they acquire residency. As a result they regularly put pressure on elected officials to do right by the blue frontier.

It's 7:30 on a September morning, but already hundreds of surfers have gathered on the sand in Ocean Beach, San Diego, stretching, grinning, and downing orange juice and Pop-Tarts. TV trucks with microwave masts raised for live morning-news feeds and traffic cops in patrol cars and on mountain bikes jam the foot of Newport Avenue, the palm-lined main street leading to the beach.

It's Clean Water Day, and time for the annual "paddle out" organized by Surfrider Foundation, the ocean-protection group. In the middle of it all are Donna and Skip Frye. Donna is slim with straight, dark blond hair, aquiline features, and a calm blue gaze that belies a hyperkinetic activism.

Surfers, male and female, keep coming up to hug her or say hi. Skip, a stocky, sun-reddened, curly-haired grandfather, has his wetsuit top unzipped and hanging at his waist, his signature egg-shaped longboard under one arm. He places a lei made of braided green ti leaves (a traditional Hawaiian good-luck symbol) around his wife's neck, which just lights her up. He and some 500 other surfers then paddle out into the water, forming a sinuous broken line around the quarter-mile-long pier. I'm torn between my camera bag and my bodyboard, between taking pictures and joining the sea-besotted throng here in my old but little-changed neighborhood

Donna, an occasional surfer herself, stays on the beach to talk clean-water politics with various wonkish types. The surfers are observed from the pier by scores of anglers, mostly Hispanic and Vietnamese, here to fish for mackerel, bass, and queenfish. Gulls and pelicans perch on the scarred wooden rails, waiting for a handout or fumbled fish. The sky is quilting over with clouds; the air tastes of salt and iodine. This is the ocean at its finest, and if you were to ask the diverse crowd enjoying it who best represents its cause, many would answer "Donna Frye."

San Diego has a reputation as a conservative Navy town with great weather. But 30 years of rapid growth have changed the dynamics. The Southern white migrants who came for defense jobs during and after World War II have been joined by more liberal Northern snowbirds and Hispanic workers drawn by new jobs in high-tech industries, education, and tourism. San Diego also has a strong environmental ethic, going back to the early 1900s when the city was divided between "Smoke-stacks" and "Geraniums": those who favored rapid industrialization, and those who wanted to preserve the city's Mediterranean charms.

Today San Diego's remaining charms mask troubling environmental problems. Since the 1970s, the EPA has filed numerous complaints about the city's scandalously lax sewage treatment. San Diego is the last major coastal city in the country still dumping minimally treated human waste into the ocean. In addition, numerous breaks in its 3,000 miles of sewer lines have resulted in fines, beach closures, and sick surfers.

Enter Donna and Skip. Her family moved here from Pennsylvania in 1957 when she was six. Her father was a Navy civilian employee, her mom a nurse. She had few ambitions growing up: "I just wanted to be an adult, maybe a dancer, a ballerina. I never thought of growing up to be a politician," she says, breaking into a throaty barking laugh, like a sea lion, or the smoker that she is. She graduated early from high school, worked as a maid, a cook, and a heavy-equipment renter. She married young and moved to Sacramento, where she drank too much and took too much physical abuse. Divorced and back in San Diego in 1980, she walked into Pancho Villa's bar in Pacific Beach and won a bet on an LA Rams game with Skip.

"Did you know who he was?"

She looks at me as if I were a complete hodad. "Of course!" Skip was part of the Windansea surf crew of the early 1960s made famous (even to nonsurfers) by Tom Wolfe in *The Pump House Gang*. A one-time top competitor, Skip is also a renowned surfboard shaper, using a sander and a keen sense of flow to turn polyurethane blanks into high-value fiber-glassed boards that are hugely popular on the international surfing scene.

For years, Donna and Skip ran Harry's Surf Shop in Pacific Beach, just up the coast from Ocean Beach. On the low bluff outside Harry's, I watched sunbathers and surfers scattered across the sand and water

beyond a bilingual sign reading "CAUTION: Storm drain water may pose
an increased risk of illness. Avoid contact near outlet." This warning, as
well as many like it up and down the state, is a direct result of Donna's
efforts.

"Around 1994 I got very active because I was dealing with a lot of
sick surfers, Skip being one of them," she recalls. "It didn't make sense.
These healthy, athletic people were getting sick from pollution. What was
doubly insulting is that [the former Republican representative] Brian
Bilbray was running for Congress against [Democrat] Lynne Schenk, saying, 'Vote for me 'cause Schenk don't surf'—the implication being that
Schenk didn't care about the ocean. Bilbray used the surf community to
promote his own political agenda, which included working with Newt
Gingrich to try to gut the Clean Water Act."

Gingrich's (ultimately failed) 1995 "reform" was written by lawyers
for the oil and chemical industries with help from the U.S. Chamber of
Commerce. Among much else, it would have suspended programs to
control storm-drain runoff and waived secondary sewage treatment to
eliminate fecal bacteria if the waste were discharged directly into the
deep ocean. Bilbray explained his support as purely financial: "to save a
billion dollars" in sewer upgrades for San Diego.

As a result of his vote, Bilbray became a target for Donna, who
formed STOP: Surfers Tired of Pollution. STOP printed bumper stickers
reading, "Another Surfer against Bilbray & for Clean Waters." They
began showing up on cars at all the area surf spots. Bilbray's pals
responded with stickers reading "STOD: Surfers Tired of Donna—Truth
Was Her First Victim."

Meanwhile Donna helped write and pass a 1997 state law requiring
weekly testing of recreational beaches that also ordered warning signs
and hotlines to inform the public if their coastal waters were polluted.

In 2000 Bilbray, although now supporting a similar federal act, lost
his bid for reelection. In 2001 a city council seat opened up in Donna's
district, and she decided to go for it, becoming one of ten candidates in a
special election. In addition to the surfer/beach communities, Donna won
the backing of organized labor, affordable-housing advocates, gay civil-
rights leaders, and many others. She won the race by a small margin and
quickly became known as the maverick council member who did her
homework, paid attention to public testimony, and asked tough questions, especially on environmental and development issues. This often led
to her being on the short end of council votes. Nevertheless, when the
2002 election rolled around and her colleagues redrew her district to

exclude most of the beach communities, she still won reelection with more than 65 percent of the vote.

Donna advocated a living-wage initiative and solar power and condemned Mayor Dick Murphy's "culture of secrecy" on financial issues. Her citywide credibility soared when she cast the sole vote against a plan to increase city employee benefits while underfinancing their pension accounts, a move that resulted in a $2 billion pension deficit and investigations by the FBI and Securities and Exchange Commission of a possible attempt to mislead creditors.

Murphy, a moderate Republican, nevertheless ran for reelection to the nonpartisan mayor's post in 2004 against a more right-wing Republican. Donna considered entering the primary, but decided against it. But as the campaign progressed, more and more people began encouraging her to launch a write-in campaign—which she finally did, five weeks before the election. The odds seemed daunting, but her entry electrified what had been a somnambulant race and drew national and global media attention to her "surfer-girl candidacy."

Donna won the election. Or so it appeared. After many weeks and many lawsuits, the final tally stood at 162,364 write-in votes for Donna, 156,852 votes for the mayor, and 141,399 for the other candidate. But the registrar of voters refused to count 5,551 of Donna's votes, cases in which people wrote in her name but failed to fill in the oval bubble for the optical-scan voting machines, and Murphy was declared the winner. In the midst of the electoral debacle, the *San Diego Union-Tribune* ran dual headlines across its front page: "Court Voids Ukraine Election, Orders New Vote" and "Mayoral Vote Stays in Limbo."

In April 2005, as the city's financial scandal deepened, Mayor Murphy resigned and Donna got to run again in a special election that July, coming in first among 11 candidates with 43 percent of the vote. She would go on to lose the November runoff to a former police chief who had the backing of the city's business community. He too would insist that he was a clean-water advocate.

When Governor Gray Davis was fighting the recall campaign to replace him and elect Arnold Schwarzenegger in 2003, one of the first things he did was to call a press conference by the golden shore to brag about his coastal protection efforts. After becoming governor, Schwarzenegger showed his respect for the ocean constituency by signing eight marine conservation bills, including one establishing a state cabinet–level Ocean Protection Council—a key recommendation of the Pew Oceans Commission.

Taking the lead in coastal conservation is nothing new for the state. More than a generation earlier, Californians created a model resource agency in the California Coastal Commission. Still earlier, the world's first coastal management agency, the San Francisco Bay Conservation and Development Commission (BCDC), was founded in 1965 as a consequence of an Army Corps of Engineers plan to fill in San Francisco Bay. Even accounting for the can-do spirit of the times, it's hard to look at the 1959 Corps map of the proposed landfill and not shudder. Richardson Bay in Sausalito, where I lived for seven years, is a sparkling arm of the larger bay blessed with houseboats, sailboats, great blue herons, and occasional barking sea lions chasing herring. It would have become an industrial flatland.

By 1959 San Francisco Bay was already one-third smaller than it had been during the gold rush days. In most places less than 18 feet deep, the bay was too easy to fill. The lower bay was diked off for salt ponds; flying into San Francisco today you can still see the big evaporation ponds, colored red, orange, brown, and purple by different algae—though these are soon to be restored as wetlands. The north bay was reclaimed for agriculture and later by duck hunting clubs. Much of what is now downtown San Francisco was also built out from the shore. During the gold rush, sailors jumped ship to mine the foothills of the Sierras. Their abandoned sailing vessels were converted to jails, hotels, and brothels. Eventually the ships and their piers rotted and sank into the bay mud, where they were covered over with rocks and dirt.

Even though the bay's waters held high-value fisheries—author Jack London was both an oyster pirate and a fish patrol agent on the bay— infilling continued well into the twentieth century. But the 1959 Corps of Engineers plan to fill 60 percent of what remained, a plan that would have transformed the bay into a wide spot on the Sacramento River, marked a turning point for how the region's citizens viewed their world-famous estuary.

Three women from Berkeley, including Kathryn Kerr, the wife of the University of California's president Clark Kerr, formed a group called Save San Francisco Bay. It quickly grew in strength, halting the Corps' plans and prompting the state to establish BCDC. By 1969 the state had empowered the new commission to regulate development on and around the bay and its 1,000 miles of convoluted shoreline. Today, along with reclaiming historic wetlands and preventing new fill, BCDC is involved in opening waterfront parks and trails, working on issues of waterborne recreation and commerce, and developing plans for improved and expanded ferry service. "Our weakness is our jurisdiction only extends 100 feet inland, and we're not authorized to deal with issues like non-point pollution or water allocations," says BCDC's executive director, Will Travis. "Still, we became a model for the California Coastal Commission and similar groups in Oregon, Cape Cod, Japan, New Zealand, and elsewhere."

Along with the Corps of Engineers scheme to fill in San Francisco Bay, the 1960s saw plans to expand California's famous Pacific Coast Highway into a multilane freeway, build hundreds of new homes on what is now Point Reyes National Seashore, construct Miami Beach–style high-rises along the state's central and southern coast, drill for oil off Monterey and Big Sur, and install a nuclear power plant on the scenic Bodega Bay headlands north of San Francisco. By 1971 Peter Douglas, a legislative assistant in Sacramento, had drawn up a bill to counter these threats by establishing a statewide coastal commission based on the BCDC model. Its main purpose would be to assure public access to and scenic protection of the entire California coast. The bill had the support of a broad coalition including the League of Women Voters, the Longshoremen's Union, and the Sierra Club.

"My boss got it through the assembly," Douglas recalls, "but the day the senate was to consider it, our key senate vote didn't show. I ran into a lobbyist in the hallway who said the state senator was flying to his ranch to take delivery of a racehorse he'd gotten from another lobbyist who worked both for the Racing Association and several oil companies. I called the press and they sent TV cameras to his ranch. The horse truck approached, and when the driver saw the cameras he did a 180-degree turn."

Frustrated by the corrupt legislative process, Douglas and his friends decided to go the initiative route, putting coastal protection on the 1972 ballot as Proposition 20. Even though the Homebuilders Association and other developers outspent Prop 20 supporters about 100 to 1, they were unable to counter the state's nascent environmental movement or the public's memories of the Santa Barbara oil spill three years earlier.

"We won not with money but press coverage of coastal damage that was taking place at the time," recalls Congressman Sam Farr of Monterey. "We only had a staff of three—Peter, Bill Press, who's now on CNN, and me. I led a bike group from San Francisco to San Diego, and all along the ride we'd stop and explain to people why we needed Prop 20."

On November 8, 1972, the coastal initiative won with 54.5 percent of the vote. To prevent the commission from becoming the tool of any single politician or agency, the initiative's language required that voting membership come from different parts of government, with four commissioners appointed by the speaker of the assembly, four by the senate rules committee, and four by the governor. The commission in turn required every coastal county in California to develop and periodically update a plan to guarantee local protection and access to the coast.

Today the California Coastal Commission occupies the 19th and 20th floors of a downtown San Francisco high-rise. It's here that I meet with Peter Douglas, the now bald, gray-bearded, and avuncular executive director of the commission, a position he has held since 1985.

"There's no doubt our state has the most accessible coastline in the country, because of the public's activist and outspoken concern in terms of protection," he claims. "Without strong coastal commissions and local plans in states like Texas, Maryland, and Florida, you see these coastal seawalls emerge made up of endless miles of waterfront high-rise hotels and condominiums.

"When Vandenberg Air Force Base converted to a space launch center and wanted to bring in a water pipe, we said no," he tells me, citing one example of the commission's work. "We knew that extra water would have a growth-producing impact because it's so dry along the coast there. We required the base to establish a water conservation program so they wouldn't have to bring in new water, and we required they open up several miles of beach to the public [it's a good surf spot], and that they not launch missiles over the Channel Islands during seal pupping season when it might affect the seals, and they agreed to all that."

Later in the 1990s, when the Army decommissioned Monterey Bay's Fort Ord, the California Coastal Commission made sure that its billion-dollar beach west of Highway 1 went into the state park system rather than to private developers. Under rules of the federal Coastal Zone Management Act, the commission also has fought offshore oil, prevented the Navy from scuttling old nuclear submarines off the coast, and blocked the EPA from giving permits to toxic incinerator ships. "Provisions of the act that allow the states to participate in federal decisions impacting their coasts have allowed California to reach out into the EEZ," Douglas says with a somewhat acquisitive grin.

Forces closer to home almost scuttled the commission back in 1996, when the Republican governor Pete Wilson and the Republican-dominated state legislature packed the commission with real-estate developers and property rights activists, and then asked Douglas to hand them his letter of resignation.

"What happened is they came to me and asked me to recommend building 900 units of housing in Bolsa Chica [an Orange County wetland being developed by the Koll Corporation], and when my staff said they wouldn't recommend building homes in a wetland, Pete Wilson's secretary of resources became furious. They also wanted the commission to allow Southern California Edison to escape mitigation requirements they'd already agreed to when they built the San Onofre nuclear power plant."

Douglas's recollection of what set off his attempted ouster is confirmed by reporters from the *Los Angeles Times* who interviewed the key players. Douglas requested a few weeks to consider his resignation, and then asked for a public hearing. By the time the Coastal Commission met in Huntington Beach, there had been an outpouring of public support for the executive director and his staff. Letters supporting Douglas came from public officials and county governments up and down the coast. Thousands of letters and phone calls of protest also flooded Sacramento, demanding that the Coastal Commission get back to its job of protecting the coast. Angry editorials appeared in every major newspaper in the state. "An Endangered Coast," warned the *San Francisco Chronicle*. "Do you want the coast to be spoiled? Apparently Pete Wilson's administration does," railed the *San Jose Mercury News*. The *Sacramento Bee* labeled Douglas "the coast's best friend," while the *Los Angeles Times* cautioned Wilson that "California's irreplaceable coast is not a political pawn." Editorial cartoonists tended to portray the state's political leadership as either pirates or sharks.

Hundreds of Douglas's supporters (including Alexandra Paul, one of the stars of the TV show *Baywatch*) packed the Huntington Beach meeting on a warm Friday evening in July, calling the pro-development commissioners "cowards" and big-money "shills" until Douglas had to stand up and plead for calm. Amidst boos and catcalls the commission voted to postpone its decision on firing him. "You haven't got the guts to do this in front of everybody here," yelled the liberal holdover commissioner Sara Wan of Malibu at commission chairman Louis Calcagno, a Wilson appointee. Calcagno responded by suggesting that a simple management personnel issue had been "turned into a circus by some in the media and by vocal special interest groups."

In the wake of that meeting, Sara Wan helped organize Vote the Coast, a political action coalition that targeted ten races in that fall's election, supporting winners in eight of them. This effort proved pivotal in putting Democrats back in control of the state assembly. Coastal protection became an even larger issue in the 1998 election, when Vote the

Coast candidates won all their races and Democrat Gray Davis made coastal protection a top issue in his successful run for the governorship—as would his replacement, Arnold Schwarzenegger, who, although a die-hard Republican, shrewdly distanced himself from the more rapacious environmental policies of the Bush administration.

"California is a place where you can still get elected running against offshore oil and for protection of the coast," explains Congressman Sam Farr, who has done it himself.

Today, Sara Wan remains an influential member of the Coastal Commission, and the Bolsa Chica wetlands, through a cooperative agreement between the developer, local environmental activists, and a statewide land trust, have been sold to the state as a coastal wildlife reserve.

"Wilson tried to drive us off a cliff, and it backfired, and now we probably have a stronger commission than we've had since the 1970s," says an unabashedly pleased Peter Douglas. He would go on to overcome a strong judicial challenge to the commission in 2003, and a grave personal challenge as he was confronted by and overcame a deadly cancer in 2004.

Peter Douglas's determination, resolve, and commitment to protecting Californians' precious coastal and marine heritage illustrate the possibility that, despite unresponsive bureaucracies and unending red tape, people can still make a difference by taking on a greater stewardship responsibility for our living seas.

Even after President Bush failed to follow up on key recommendations of the U.S. Commission on Ocean Policy, which he had appointed, new marine conservation measures were soon initiated in several states including California, Massachusetts, and Rhode Island. Notably, all three have Republican governors but also have strong ocean constituencies.

The challenge is to take the effective, solution-oriented work now being carried out in these local and state jurisdictions and scale it up to the national and global level. President Teddy Roosevelt demonstrated the critical role for good the federal government can play when he created or vastly expanded a system of national forests, wildlife reserves, and national parks. Today much of America's glory can still be found in its wildlands, from Alaska to Yellowstone to the Everglades. Creating a similar system of large underwater reserves and wilderness parks is a challenge worthy of a great nation in a new century. Luckily, despite the ensnaring tangle of red tape, this process is also under way.

CHAPTER 11

Sanctuaries in the Sea

There is, one knows not what sweet mystery about this sea,
whose gently awful stirrings seem to speak of some hidden
soul beneath.

— *Herman Melville*

To heal the ocean, we must heal ourselves.

— *Dr. Rod Fujita, marine ecologist and author*

In its early years Yellowstone National Park counted among its more popular activities trophy hunting for elk and bison. Today, America's national marine sanctuaries are in their early years and inspire in some the same "take what you can while you can get it" frontier mentality.

Florida Marine Patrol (FMP) officer Greg Stanley pulls up to the dock in a sleek Olympia. When the FMP seized this former drug-running muscle boat, it was registered as a 13-foot canoe. In fact, the 31-footer with twin 225-horsepower outboards can do better than 55 miles per hour on the water, faster than almost anything out there except newer drug runners and Mark V Navy SEAL boats.

Tall, with a blond buzz cut, an angular clean-cut face, dark glasses, shorts, and a Kevlar vest under his short-sleeved uniform shirt, Greg wears dual shoulder patches—for the FMP and the Florida Keys National Marine Sanctuary, for which he's been cross-deputized.

Today is the opening of the sanctuary's two-day lobster miniseason, which precedes the sanctuary's commercial lobster season and draws tens of thousands of lobster-hungry hobbyists from throughout Florida and the South. Every boat on the water is permitted six lobsters per person. Unlike California, where you have to work for your lobsters by catching them by hand—a requirement that has left me humiliated by fast-moving crustaceans on more than one occasion—here you can use tickle sticks, nets, nooses, everything but dynamite to make sure you get the limit. It reminds me of the meat fishery for hatchery salmon in Homer, Alaska, except that no one is restocking these animals.

Greg and I leave the Boca Chica Basin north of Key West, jigging and jagging through the mangroves, the wind and engines screaming as Greg leans the go-fast boat over in tight G-pulling turns. We head out into a 9.5-mile SPA (special protected area) and find little activity. Fishers and pirates are learning to stay out of the no-take zones, which cover less than 4 percent of the sanctuary. In 1990, when the Florida Keys National Marine Sanctuary was established, biologists suggested that 20 percent be declared a no-take zone to protect the living resources of the reef. There was a tremendous backlash from charter boat operators, treasure hunters, salvagers, and collectors of tropical fish and live coral. The sanctuary manager Billy Causey was hanged in effigy at a series of angry rallies backed by the late treasure hunter Mel Fisher and his attorney. The feds retreated. More than fifteen years later a solid majority of local residents now support increased protection.

Greg tells me that tropical fish poaching is a problem in the no-take areas because the aquarium trade pays such high prices for the jewel-like little fish. On this patrol, however, he's looking for undersized or over-the-limit "bugs" (lobsters). There's a $210 fine for the first five undersized lobsters, an amount that jumps to $315 from six to a dozen. "The guys I really want are the big poachers with 125 lobster tails on board, but they all came out last week. They know today will be heavily patrolled."

His first inspection is of a little green boat that looks like a refugee from a carnival ride. A father and his young daughter are on board. The only problem Greg sees is one of safety. The man has two adult lifejackets, neither of which will fit his 75-pound little girl. "Square it away," Greg advises, declining to issue a ticket.

We next stop by the *Filet & Release,* an open dive boat with two guys in the water and a woman waiting on board with fresh beer and lobsters on ice, ready for a good day. We then check out a family of eight, with three kids and 14 lobsters, four Navy guys and a gal with 16 lobsters, six people with a cooler full of lobsters and three speared hogfish—all easy kills, they tell us.

Off Snipes Point, Greg stops a poorly maintained 25-foot Boston Whaler with a Bimini shade top. On board are two boys, a teenage girl in too-tight jeans and a halter top, an older woman, and an unshaven gray-haired man with a large beer gut, an orange T-shirt, and greasy jeans. There are also two divers in the water. Greg begins spotting undersized lobsters and throwing them onto his boat.

"Those shorts, Daddy?" the nearest scuba diver calls from the water. He's also gray-eyed and gray-haired, a construction worker from Key West. Greg calls him over by our boat and asks to see his capture bag. He swims up alongside. The bottom of the net bag is open. Only one lobster is left clinging to its side.

"How'd your bag get open?" Greg asks.

"I don't know."

Greg takes his measuring gauge and finds that the lobster stuck to the side is legal, if just barely.

"You have to measure from between the eyes?" the diver asks unconvincingly.

Greg begins writing them up for five undersized lobsters.

Then Dad tosses his cigarette in the water.

Greg just stares for a second or two. "Don't put that in water. That's littering, sir. Did it have a filter?" Dad shakes his head vaguely. "A filter will never dissolve," Greg explains before taking Polaroids of the confiscated bugs, writing our GPS position on the back of the photos, and then tossing the lobsters into the water where I watch them skitter away into the eelgrass. Maybe they heard what he had to say about the filter.

"That guy had a bagful he dumped. Nothing I could do about it," Greg says as we speed off.

The next boat he stops is a cabin cruiser carrying four adults, four kids, and an unbelievable amount of toys—coolers and a barbecue, snorkel and dive gear with eight air tanks, an expensive underwater scooter, two rafts, six legal lobsters, and five undersized ones. Greg has to shake several loose from his glove, dropping them hard onto his boat.

The boat's owner, a musician, is about six feet tall, fleshy, with a T-shirt reading "The older I get the better I was." He seems offended to be getting ticketed. We drop the lobsters back into the water. I watch one fall, then right itself and take off like a rocket.

"I shouldn't treat the lobsters so rough," Greg worries as we pull away. "It doesn't hurt them, they're tough critters, but it makes it look like I just want to give tickets and don't care about the environment, which I do."

A few dolphins glide past us in the translucent aquamarine water. Greg pulls up next to a big sportfishing boat named *E-Fish-N-Sea*. A second boat and raft are tied off behind it. There are nine on board the main craft, including an infant.

"You count for six [lobsters]," the baby's aunt coos, holding her up for our inspection. There are 37 lobsters in one boat, 17 in the other, and they want to know if they can catch more tomorrow since they're staying onboard overnight. "Only if you leave these ones on land," Greg explains the rules.

Looking across the crowded coral flats, it's easy to believe there are 17 million recreational boats plying America's waters. Half the fleet seems to be in the Keys today hunting lobster. Nearby a motorboat is towing a pontoon boat towing a Jetski.

Greg talks to three people with 19 lobsters instead of 18 and judges the extra one an honest mistake. "You should count and recount again," he reminds them before tossing one lucky lobster back into the sea.

He pulls up to a pair of tanned, short-haired, 16-year-old boys having engine problems. They also have 21 lobsters and some undersized fish on the bottom of their blue skiff. He takes all but 12 lobsters and tells them he's writing them juvenile citations. "You'll end up doing community work hours. You won't get a criminal record, but in a few years you could end up with a record over something as stupid as lobster if you keep doing this," Greg warns. One of the boys calls his dad on a cell phone, tells him they've been stopped and are being cited. He listens, then says, "Some are on his boat. We still have twelve."

"Most Keys residents don't like miniseason. It teaches people how to rip off and abuse the reef," says Dave McDaniel, another sanctuary patrol officer I ride with.

A couple of miniseasons later I'm back in the Keys, snorkeling with Craig Quirolo of the marine protection group Reef Relief, checking for regrowth of elkhorn coral in the Eastern Dry Rock area off Key West. Most of the corals here are either dead or dying. He points to numerous marine snails that are eating the still-living corals. "Normally those snails are eaten by lobsters," he explains as we climb back on the boat, "but between miniseason and the commercial traps the lobsters are having a hard time getting in or out of here."

While there may be local opposition, it's up to the State Fisheries Commission to determine whether the annual meat fest will continue, be folded into the commercial season, or be phased out. Unlike most national parks, America's 13 national marine sanctuaries share jurisdictions with states where their waters overlap. Two-thirds of the 220-mile-long Keys Sanctuary is in state waters. The sanctuaries also allow a range of commercial activities within their boundaries, including commercial fishing, cable-laying, and oil transport.

The National Marine Sanctuary Program was created in 1972, 100 years after Yellowstone was dedicated by Congress as the first national park. In contrast to the establishment of Yellowstone, which involved a high-profile campaign to open up the wonders of the interior West to railroad tourism, the legislation enabling the creation of marine sanctuaries was passed as a rider to an ocean-dumping bill, one of a number of environmental acts passed by Congress in the early 1970s. According to the act's original language, sanctuaries are supposed to protect the "conservation, recreational, ecological, historical, research, educational or aesthetic qualities" of America's blue frontier, allow for multiple use of the marine environment, and protect the long-term integrity of its natural resources. Beyond excluding oil and gas drilling, mineral mining, and ocean dumping, how marine sanctuaries might achieve these often-contradictory aims remains an open question.

The push to create marine sanctuaries was in large measure a response to public anger and frustration over the disastrous Santa Barbara oil spill of 1969 and reported dumping of military nerve gas and nuclear waste off the East Coast. The oil and gas industry opposed the establishment of the sanctuary program, as did the Departments of Defense and Commerce (even though NOAA would be given charge of them). While appearing to stand firm against the pressure, Congress nonetheless failed to provide the new program with any funding during its first seven years of existence.

In 1975 the first marine sanctuary was established 16 miles off Cape Hatteras, North Carolina. It was a one-square-mile box reaching down 230 feet, to where a Duke University research vessel had discovered the overturned wreck of the USS *Monitor*. The ironclad warship had been built in the Brooklyn Navy Yard, then towed to Hampton Roads, Virginia. It arrived on March 6, 1862, in time to stop the CSS *Virginia* from finishing off the wooden ships of the port's federal blockading force. After a historic, deafening, but indecisive battle on March 10, both steam-powered ironclads withdrew from the scene. The *Virginia* was scuttled when the Confederates abandoned Norfolk, and months later, on the last day of the year, the *Monitor* sank in a storm while under tow to Charleston. Sixteen of its crew drowned. It apparently was involved in one more engagement, however: during World War II it was depth-charged by a surface ship mistaking its sonar signal for that of a Nazi submarine. A few years ago salvage divers and scientists from NOAA and the Navy recovered the ship's coral-encrusted turret for display at the Mariner's Museum in the former Confederate port town of Newport News, Virginia.

At the end of 1975 a second national marine sanctuary was established to protect a fragile coral reef habitat at Key Largo, Florida, a site that had been under a presidential protection order since 1960. Both of these original sanctuaries were financed by monies diverted from other NOAA programs.

Beginning in 1977, President Jimmy Carter accelerated the designation process, leading to the establishment of four new sanctuaries off Florida, Georgia, and California, including the 1,658-square-mile Channel Islands Sanctuary off Santa Barbara, whose waters are frequented by some 22 species of whales and dolphins, at least 20 species of shark, and some 150,000 sea lions.

During the eight years of the Reagan administration, however, only one new minisanctuary was established, at the 162-acre Fagatele Bay in American Samoa. Political appointees within NOAA who oversaw the sanctuary program made it clear they were not going to impede the plans of Secretaries of the Interior James Watt and Don Hodel to open up a billion acres of the Outer Continental Shelf to oil and gas development. These plans included expanding the number of drilling platforms off the coast of California from 20 to 1,100 and opening up New England's historic fishing grounds and Florida's coral reefs to drilling for the first time. What Congress, the administration, and NOAA's political appointees failed to count on was an explosion of grassroots outrage over the proposed leases. In Central California, antidrilling groups such as Save Our Shores linked up with commercial fishermen, local governments, farmers, and the tourist industry to lobby for permanent protection of the coastline.

"I'd never seen such a broad coalition form so quickly in my life. It was a real groundswell," says Leon Panetta. Panetta, who was Monterey's congressman at the time (and would later become White House chief of staff under Bill Clinton and chairman of the Pew Oceans Commission), added a rider to the Hurricane Andrew Relief Act of 1992 that would create a new sanctuary of uncertain size off the coast of Monterey. The sanctuary's proponents drew up maps for a small-, medium-, or large-sized reserve. The largest would cover more than 350 miles of coastline and extend as far as 53 miles out to sea.

"Leon said, let's compromise on the middle one, but the people just went nuts at all these public hearings and insisted on the biggest deal," Representative Sam Farr of Monterey recalls. "Luckily '92 was an election year and we reminded George [H. W.] Bush that in '88 he'd run a TV ad in California showing the Big Sur coastline, saying he was going to be the environmental president—so he went for the biggest boundary." (Bush would still lose California to Clinton in the election.)

On the weekend of September 19–20, 1992, the Monterey Bay National Marine Sanctuary was dedicated. Monterey's Shoreline Plaza was crowded with visitors checking out the more than 50 booths and exhibits at the sanctuary celebration. At 10:30 AM a parade of boats arrived, led by the 145-foot *Californian*, a replica of an 1849 revenue cutter. Behind the tall ship were modern-day Coast Guard cutters and patrol boats, an oceanographic research vessel, a fishing trawler flying Old Glory, sailboats, kayaks, and Zodiacs. The Monterey Symphony struck up Copeland's "Fanfare for the Common Man" as the *Californian* fired a loud, smoky volley from its guns. The gunfire did not seem to deter dozens of curious sea lions that were leaping and nosing their way among the somewhat nervous kayakers. The woman next to me turned to her husband. "How'd they get them to do that?" she wondered.

Years have passed, but my own wonder remains. It's an overcast winter day on the waters of Monterey Bay as I gear up with NOAA Corps Lieutenant Mark Pickett; Ed Cooper, the diver representative to the Sanctuary Advisory Committee; and Carrie Wilson from California Fish and Game. We're all in full wetsuits with hoods and booties, except for the boat's captain in the partially enclosed cabin, who is wearing jeans and a hooded sweatshirt and looking distracted as he backs off the anchor chain. Suddenly there's a splash, and we all turn to see a large smooth footprint on the surface. It's right next to our 28-foot boat and about the same size.

"Did you see it?" I ask. "No." "No." "How about you?" come the replies. None of the five of us has seen whatever it is that just left this watery mark, whose rippling edge is now lapping up against our hull. We all look toward the kelp bed to our seaward side, no one making any motion toward the dive platform. Nor is anyone saying what we're all thinking. Monterey is the southern point of California's infamous Red Triangle, which extends north past Stinson Beach and out to the Farallones Marine Sanctuary. It's the world center for human–white shark "encounters," and California's white shark population is, according to experts, "robust"—which is supposed to be a good sign, the presence of top predators being an indicator of a healthy ecosystem. Just as our silence begins to get uncomfortable, a juvenile gray whale surfaces snout first on the other side of the kelp and gives a loud steamy blow of air. We grin and point, checking out the huge young animal, then checking out our masks and regulators and stepping off the dive platform into the bracing 55-degree water, flipping over and heading down along the anchor chain.

Below the surface a large shoal of bluefish hangs suspended amidst yellow green stalks of 65-foot-tall giant kelp rising up from their holdfasts on the bottom. Pinnacles of rock also rise from a bottom littered with orange starfish, faster-moving sunflower stars, and purple black sea urchins. We swim along rock walls carpeted with pink strawberry anemones, where bulbous-faced lingcod and other species of rockfish shoot from crevices; where decorator crabs, covered in red seaweed and green algae, camouflage themselves among the red-plated mollusks, white anemones, and purple ring-top snails. Frisky sea lions dart through the surrounding waters, inspecting the awkward bubble-blowing humans. The sun breaks through the surface cloud cover and suddenly the water is infused with cathedral light, giving the sea lions the spotlight attention they deserve.

The majestic giant kelp stalks (*Macrocystis pyrifera*) have been called the redwoods of the ocean, although they remind me more of Jack's beanstalk, growing up to two feet a day. Giant kelp not only creates a forestlike alternative to tropical reefs that justifies (if barely) cold-water diving but also adds inestimable zest to our daily lives. Harvested by giant lawnmower-like ships, the kelp's algin is used as a binder in some 70 household products, ranging from lipstick to ice cream. It is even used to give beer a longer-lasting head, a phenomenon we'll evaluate later on at a Pacific Grove pub.

Back by the Coast Guard pier I spot a sea otter grooming itself, diving and resurfacing, swimming on its back, cheerfully tearing the legs off a freshly caught crab with its pointy little teeth. The sea otter is the unofficial symbol of the Monterey Sanctuary and a major income earner for gift shops and gallery owners from Santa Cruz to Carmel. You can buy plush otter dolls, ceramic otter candy dishes, or $2,000 cut glass otters. This may explain why few locals are willing to mention that these terminally cute and cuddly mammals are also voracious predators, eating up to 25 percent of their body weight every day, competing with commercial fishermen for octopus, crab, and urchin. Nor is it often noted that this species of marine weasel is into rough sex. Although effective for grooming their fine pelts or cracking shells against small stones they place on their bellies, the male otter's forelegs are simply too short for getting a good grip on a mate. So the male gets firm purchase by biting down on the nose of the female before going for a little splendor in the kelp. Afterward you can often spot the females hauled up on rocks along the shore, their fur matted and their noses bloody. Breeding females are easily distinguished by the scars on and around their black nose leather. Knowing this, it's hard not to imagine that a female with a heavily scarred nose might get a reputation as an easy otter.

However you might feel about sea otters as role models for America's youth, we still owe these weasels big time. There used to be as many as a million of them corkscrewing through the coastal waters of the Pacific, from the Russian Far East along the Alaska coast, all the way down to Baja. Unlike most marine mammals, sea otters lack a protective layer of blubber and so are dependent on their dense luxuriant fur to keep themselves warm in these chill waters. They must constantly groom themselves to fluff air between their inner and outer layers of fur for extra insulation. For generations California coastal Indian tribes kept warm in otter fur wraps, with no notable impact on the wild animal populations, according to marine archeologists and historians.

Things changed, however, when otter fur became a tradable commodity for Russian and American hunters in the eighteenth and nineteenth centuries. The result was industrial-scale killing and a century-long marine weasel massacre. In California, the sea otter was thought hunted to extinction until 1938, when a raft of up to 300 was discovered living along the rugged coast of Big Sur. With the help of an environmental group called Friends of the Sea Otter and protection under the Endangered Species Act, the species rebounded, and by 1999 almost 2,400 animals were living along the coast.

Beginning in the late 1990s, however, the otter population began an unexplained decline of around 5 percent a year. Suspected causes include the mammals losing out in their competition with commercial fishermen, drowning in fishing traps, or being sickened by an unidentified toxin. Wildlife pathologists and vets carried out necropsies (animal autopsies) of hundreds of dead animals. What they found is that disease killed nearly two-thirds of them, with almost half the dead in their adult breeding prime. Infected otters also were four times as likely to be eaten by sharks because of the animals' confusion, seizures, and other disabilities. Among the emerging diseases that have been identified are *Toxoplasma gondii* and *Sarcocystis neurona,* which are carried by single-celled parasites associated with cat and opossum feces. How are these parasites getting into the water? Although no definitive links have yet been made to sewage facilities, runoff from development, or storm drains, these are likely implicated. Populations of humans, cats, and introduced opossums have boomed along the coast at the same time that California has lost 95 percent of its wetlands, which act as filters of pollution. In addition, sea otters like to dine on crabs, mussels, clams, and abalone—all filter feeders that tend to concentrate bio-toxins from the water.

Although the otter is listed as threatened under the Endangered Species Act, there is presently no organized effort to stem its decline. Representative Sam Farr has proposed spending $25 million on otter recovery. This is the sort of proposal talk-radio hosts love to attack as absurd government waste (while ignoring multibillion-dollar subsidies for agribusiness, highways, and the fossil fuel industry). But the economic payback for keeping these keystone predators in the California marine ecosystem is demonstrably worth far more than $25 million. Sea otters, for example, eat sea urchins, which eat kelp. Left unchecked, urchins would quickly decimate the Monterey kelp forests that draw fish, fishing boats, and enthusiastic fish voyeurs (recreational divers). The kelp forests also prevent damaging storm erosion, which could occur rapidly on the barrens urchins leave behind.

By 2005 America's marine sanctuaries encompassed 18,000 square miles of ocean, or approximately 0.05 percent (one-twentieth of one percent) of our EEZ frontier. California has a third of them, while Alaska has none. Alaska's three-member congressional delegation does not want any more federal presence in their state.

Like our national parks, each of America's marine sanctuaries has its unique history and stories. In Massachusetts, for example, the threat of oil drilling and sand mining on Stellwagen Bank, a rich fish habitat and whale feeding area, inspired a successful campaign to establish a sanctuary. Today a million whale-watchers a year visit Stellwagen. Another sanctuary was established along the wild Olympic coast of Washington with its huge bird rookeries, cobbled beaches, pine-covered sea stacks, and mysterious deep-ocean geothermal vents.

A hundred miles out in the Gulf of Mexico, the Flower Garden Banks Sanctuary is home to endangered loggerhead sea turtles, manta rays, whale sharks, and spotted dolphins. It also hosts an extraordinary phenomenon: every August, at around 9:15 PM on the eighth day after the full moon, star corals start releasing smoky sperm while other parts of the reef seem to explode, releasing millions of tiny gametes—fertilized and unfertilized coral eggs—which mix with the sperm in the warm summer current. As if on signal, other simple creatures including sponges, tube worms, and brittle stars begin spawning in a literal orgy of life. Darting amongst the predator fish feeding on the eggs are coral researchers with nets and bags, anxious to capture and study samples of this earliest stage of endangered coral reef life. At other times of the year, schools of hammerheads swarm the area in large numbers, along with the occasional 12- to-14-foot tiger shark, bringing East Texas charter boats to Flower Garden for shark dives.

The 50- to 70-foot-deep sandstone bottom of Gray's Reef Sanctuary, off the coast of Georgia, also makes for some fine diving with lots of grouper, angelfish, sea bass, big sponges, and jelly-munching turtles. This preserve lies near the only known calving grounds for the northern right whale, the most endangered large whale in the world.

At the Hawaiian Islands Humpback Whale Sanctuary, I have snorkeled with turtles and watched humpbacks breaching, leaping full-bodied out of the water as if their great winglike pectoral fins might actually lift them into that other blue domain. I've also seen them at the other end of their migratory pattern, feeding and breaching off Point Adolphus in southeast Alaska near Glacier Bay National Park. No one really knows why they do this, although theories range from its being a way of removing parasites to "wouldn't you if you could?" Other whales swim so close to the boat that all you can hear is the "humphing" exhalation of their breaths and the snapping of camera shutters. Since the end of commercial whaling, humpbacks by the thousands have followed this migratory pattern, spending their summers feeding in Alaska and their winters making babies in the protected waters of their sanctuary off Hawaii—which certainly convinces me that these animals are highly intelligent.

"Should we be keeping these areas in a natural state? Does the public want to preserve areas as marine wilderness? That's not the way the [sanctuary] statute reads," points out Brad Barr, the longtime manager at the Stellwagen Sanctuary and now the program's senior policy analyst, based out of Woods Hole, Massachusetts. Although he says he left Stellwagen to make way for new blood, knowledgeable people suggest that Barr was kicked upstairs for having pushed too hard for the establishment of no-take zones, in a New England sanctuary where a single bluefin tuna can earn a fisherman $20,000.

"Look at the response of the public to drilling for oil in the Arctic Wildlife Refuge," he suggests. "We value that. Isn't there a similar value in the marine environment? It's important for the public to weigh in. Do you want that [as] wilderness or not? Because every area can be exploited now. There's deep-water corals in the Gulf of Maine being destroyed by

fishing gear—unique unstudied ecosystems, where now you have fishermen prospecting for new fisheries."

Another reserve visited by whales is the Farallones Marine Sanctuary off
San Francisco. Orcas, grays, sei, fin, sperm, humpbacks, and up to 80 blue
whales—the largest creatures on earth—have been observed here. The
three small craggy islands, sometimes visible from the Golden Gate Bridge
just 28 miles away, are also a major nesting site for several hundred thousand seabirds, including storm petrels, common murres, and clownlike
puffins, which is why they're known as "California's Galápagos."

On the rocky trails above its steep cliffs, South Island is littered with
squawking, nesting birds. Its few small beaches are jammed with snort-
ing elephant seals and barking sea lions that are using their larger cousins
as sofas. But 100 yards offshore, as I float face down in the cold salt
water, all is deathly still. Visibility in the Farallones' gray green waters is
not very good because of nutrient upwellings from the deep ocean below.
A strange sense of timelessness encompasses me as I stare at the fading
shafts of surface light—when suddenly there's a rushing snout like a sea-
launched missile, a flat black eye rolling back in its socket, a gaping jaw,
and rows of razor sharp teeth that—*bang!* The video turns to electronic
confetti as the camera is struck a stunning blow by a 17-foot, 3,000-
pound predator. Even reviewing the videotape, it's not reassuring. As a
diver, kayaker, and body surfer, I wonder what drew the shark to the
video camera attached to the bottom of a small floating surfboard when
there was no bait or chum in the water. Shape recognition is the likely
answer; surfboards look a lot like seals on the surface to certain blurry-
visioned sharks.

Surfer Rob Williams was in the lineup off the north jetty in Humboldt
Bay when he was misidentified. "I saw a set forming outside and began
paddling toward it when the back end of my board pushed up," he
recalls. "I looked back and just had a quick impression of a shark's
mouth open and all these teeth, and it got a grip on me and the board
and took us under. I was sort of sideways in its mouth. I felt it let up a little and then bite down again to get a better grip on my legs, and then it
just started shaking me like a dog shakes the hell out of a toy. It must've
lasted maybe ten seconds. I thought I was dead. I was hitting it without
effect and then I saw its eyeball rolled back and ran my hand up its nose
and just jammed my thumb into its eyeball and held it. Then it spit me
out and shook its head like it was irritated and took off fast—just
boom—shot down into the darkness and I was there underwater alone.

I popped up to the surface and climbed back onto my board. I thought I was okay but then looked back and saw this huge gaping wound in my thigh surrounded by bits of flesh and all this blood in the water, and I started yelling and guys came and got me to shore."

After losing about a third of his blood on the way to the hospital, Williams was rushed into surgery, where he was operated on for three hours. He survived his ordeal with 160 stitches, a dinged surfboard, and a nasty scar. Today, he again rides the waves off Humboldt, although a bit more cautiously. "The shark was in its element. I just had the bad luck to get nailed that day," he reflects. "I figure I'm still safer in the water than driving around in my car."

Farallones researcher Ken Goldman, who tricked out the surfboard with the camera, spent more than four years studying white sharks off South Island from a 17-foot Boston Whaler, where he got a close-up feel for his subjects. He's convinced that on the rare occasions when these sharks do attack humans they quickly realize that they have hit the wrong prey, which is why so few attacks off California (about 1 in 40) prove fatal. "I believe most of the time they will check out people in the water and realize they're not prey, and the people will never know the sharks are there below them." He means that to be reassuring.

Not a lot is known about *Carcharodon carcharias,* the great white shark. It can grow to more than 20 feet in length (the size of an average living room), weigh more than three tons, and rip 30-pound slabs of meat off its prey with a single scooping bite. Recent research, including dissection of dead animals, suggests that the sharks pup off Baja and Southern California. They produce litters of six to nine young that emerge from mama shark as formidable, toothsome, and independent-spirited four- to five-footers. Great whites live from 35 to 70 years in the wild, spending their early years darting around the ocean gorging on fish, squid, and smaller sharks. As they grow larger and less flexible, their diet and habits begin to change. At around 10 to 12 feet in length they reach sexual maturity, taking on a hard, rounded shape. Instead of chasing after fast-moving fish, they begin ambushing fat-laden, energy-rich pinnipeds including elephant seals and sea lions. White only on their bellies, the sharks are shaded gray and black above for camouflage as they cruise rocky coastal bottoms stalking their prey from below.

Possibly the greatest concentration of white sharks in the world occurs every fall off the Farallon Islands during elephant seal breeding season, when as many as 40 sharks gather in an area about the size of Central Park.

"I get a call a month from people asking, 'Can I go out and dive with great whites?' I say I won't allow my people to do it, but *can* you? Yes, you can," Ed Ueber once told me with a weary shrug. Tanned and nearly bald with a gray corona of hair and warm brown eyes etched with crow's feet, wearing tan chinos and a checked flannel shirt, Ueber worked out of a converted red-roofed Coast Guard station on the waterfront in San Francisco's Presidio. He and Billy Causey in Florida were the sanctuary program's old salts, until Ed retired in 2004.

Ed served on Navy submarines, in the merchant marine, as a ship-wright on the *Morgan*—a tall ship in Connecticut's Mystic Seaport—and as a commercial fisherman on a dragger and lobster boat before join-ing the sanctuary program. In the years I followed his career, he roamed the sanctuary from the top of the old Coast Guard lighthouse on South Island to 14,000 feet below the surface, where he traveled in a sub-mersible trying to determine the fate of 50,000 barrels of nuclear and toxic waste the Navy dumped there during the Cold War.

"The majority of the barrels are around 5,000 feet down. In 1998 we had the British out there, with a towed wire that detects radiation. It got some readings about three times normal background, but nothing dra-matic," he reports.

His other concerns have included ship traffic in and out of San Francisco Bay, oil spills, including three in the late 1990s that killed more than 10,000 birds and tarred coastal beaches and estuaries, and people getting too close to the islands.

When sealers first arrived on the Farallones in the early 1800s they wiped out the northern fur seal, elephant seal, and sea lion populations. During the 1840s "eggers" wiped out seabird colonies by taking their eggs to feed the booming gold rush population of San Francisco. In 1909 Teddy Roosevelt established the islands as a refuge, and since 1969 human visitation has been restricted mainly to a handful of biologists (no more than eight) studying the rebounding wildlife. I was privileged to visit there while shooting a PBS documentary on offshore oil in 1987 and found it so densely packed with critters that my cameraman had to retreat in the face of a pissed-off elephant seal.

In February 2005 the House Resources Committee chairman, Representative Dick Pombo (R-CA), cosponsored a bill to open the islands to public visitation by, among others, ham radio operators who like to broadcast from remote locations. Pombo has also championed the cause of snowmobilers in Yellowstone National Park.

But in the face of overwhelming opposition from scientists, editorial writers, and citizens organized by the volunteer Marine Sanctuary Association, he dropped his support for the bill two months later. For now the Farallones remain a highly valued Bay Area property and home site for a wide variety of species other than our own.

I'm back in the Florida Keys, riding the fast ferry *Yankee Freedom* to the Dry Tortugas, 70 miles west of Key West, with a group of people celebrating the establishment of a new marine wilderness there. At 197 square nautical miles, Dry Tortugas is the largest no-take marine protected area (MPA) in the United States. (Still, it constitutes less than 4 percent of the Florida Keys Sanctuary. By contrast, one-third of Australia's Great Barrier Reef has been set aside as fully protected ocean wilderness.) Within the MPA, fishing, dumping, drilling, treasure hunting, and anchor dragging are no longer allowed. Nor is any other activity that threatens the natural wonder of the place. You can come to snorkel, sail, or dive. But take only pictures and leave only bubbles.

Overhead, chevron-tailed frigate birds sail gracefully on cloud-stacked thermals. Before reaching Fort Jefferson, a stark pre–Civil War brick redoubt on a sandy spit of an island, we stop briefly to release five rehabilitated hawksbill sea turtles. A small female shoots away from the boat like a torpedo, while a young male loiters around before paddling off. "The female seems more directed. The male seems confused," I say to the scientist standing next to me. "And that surprises you?" she grins mischievously.

Once we're docked I scoot into the warm water, snorkeling around the pilings of the old coal pier at the side of the fort. Here I swim through shimmering shoals of baitfish, schools of blue- and yellow-striped grunts, and aloof-seeming angelfish the size of saucepans. I spot a five-foot nurse shark, hold my breath to listen to big aqua green, red, and purple parrotfish munching contentedly on coral.

If all goes well, Dry Tortugas may be only the first of a string of underwater wilderness parks. There are projects afoot to establish fully protected ocean zones in the Gulf of Maine, off Washington state, in Puerto Rico, and elsewhere. But the most promising efforts—and the most contentious battles—are taking place in California, where ocean activists are trying to win enough popular support to create what could become the nation's most complete network of saltwater wilderness parks, including the 175-square-mile Channel Islands marine wilderness, established in 2002.

Yes, wilderness. "I am glad I shall never be young without wild country to be young in," Aldo Leopold once wrote. "Of what avail are forty freedoms without a blank spot on the map?"

As terrestrial beings, we tend to forget that most of our planet's hidden surface remains a blank spot in the Earth's known geography. We have mapped less than 10 percent of the oceans with the accuracy we have achieved in mapping 100 percent of the moon. Back in 2000, a National Academy of Sciences report called for wilderness protection of one-fifth of America's coastal waters in order to sustain dwindling fisheries and wildlife populations. President Clinton then issued an executive order establishing the framework for a national system of protected marine areas. He also created the Northwestern Hawaiian Islands Ecosystem Reserve.

In 2004 I attended a gathering of marine scientists at Scripps in San Diego at which former secretary of the interior Bruce Babbitt offered insight into the political reality of how conservation initiatives like these often get started.

"It was at the end of his [Clinton's second] term," Babbitt recalled, "and he was establishing a lot of protected areas through executive orders, but he hadn't paid much attention to this vast marine area we'd been telling him about. So there was this White House reception, and while waiting on the receiving line I took a piece of paper and folded it in half. On one side I wrote 'Teddy Roosevelt' and under that all the acreage Roosevelt had protected, and on the other side I wrote 'William Jefferson Clinton' and under that all the acreage he'd protected to date. And then I added in Northwest Hawaii, to show that if he did this one thing he'd have protected more wilderness than Teddy Roosevelt.

"We went through the reception line and I handed him the folded-up piece of paper, and we shook hands and I moved on. I looked back and he was about to put it in his pocket, and then he stared at it for a minute and opened it up. And I knew what he'd been staring at were the two words I'd written on the outside: 'Your Legacy.'"

Two-thirds of the Hawaiian Islands chain is made up of reefs and coral atolls that are a largely unknown ocean wilderness. The reserve, stretching nearly 1,500 miles from Kauai to Midway Island, contains some of the healthiest and least disturbed coral reefs on the planet. It is also one of the last predator-dominated coral reef ecosystems on Earth: lots of sharks and other bad boys. The reserve's waters are home to more than 7,000 marine species, one-quarter of which are unique to the Hawaiian archipelago. This uninhabited area contains critical habitat for many endangered and threatened species, including the Hawaiian monk seal and the green sea turtle. Because the waters here are at the lower end of the temperature range for tropical coral reefs, this ecosystem also has the best chance of surviving coral bleaching linked to fossil-fuel-driven climate change.

Unlike some of Clinton's other environmental initiatives, his action in creating the reserve has survived the subsequent administration; the U.S. government is in the process of declaring the Northwestern Hawaiian Islands Ecosystem Reserve the fourteenth national marine sanctuary. At 131,000 square miles it will be seven times larger than the other 13 combined—the largest marine reserve in the world after Australia's Great Barrier Reef and the most critical protection of a unique natural treasure that our nation has carried out since Yellowstone was established in 1872. The designation process has been a contentious but productive one involving native Hawaiians, environmentalists, fishermen, university researchers, and the state and federal governments, including the U.S. Fish and Wildlife Service and, of course, NOAA.

Not all our important marine ecosystems are anywhere close to full protection, however. Given competing saltwater special interests, protecting ocean wilderness is proving even more challenging than protecting terrestrial wilds. "If we get reserves at the levels environmentalists want, you'll devastate opportunities for recreational fisheries and anglers," predicts Bob Fletcher, the tall, trim, gray-eyed president of the Sportfishing Association of California. "You have to balance the interests of the environmentalists with our right to make a living." We're at a sportfishing landing on San Diego Bay, and the docks behind us are lined with dozens of big party boats emblazoned with names like *Top Gun, Prowler,* and *Conquest.* Fletcher has been a fierce opponent of the Channel Islands Reserve, even though it was inspired by the late Jim Donlon. Donlon was a recreational fisherman who, beginning in the 1940s, saw the islands' once abundant fish populations plummet despite the establishment of Channel Islands National Park and National Marine Sanctuary.

But Fletcher believes that traditional fisheries management can and will restore the sea's living resources. "I think reserves will decrease rather than increase yields," he tells me. "There will be more fish or whatever in the reserve, but for fisheries you lose more yield by taking habitat away [through protection]. Let's not alienate everyone," he continues. "Let's start small, move them away from the coast, and document them over five to ten years."

I suggest that if environmentalists aren't satisfied with this kind of plan they may sue, and if Fletcher's group isn't happy, he may sue, the result being years of additional delay as the promise of reserves gets tied up in court.

"I don't see that as such a bad thing," he grins. "I'm not against inaction."

"There's always been this 'out of sight, out of mind' thinking about the seas," says Dr. Gary Davis, the senior scientist at Channel Islands National Park and a leader of the National Park Service's marine programs. "Now we're beginning to understand how people can have devastating effects on marine productivity." I'm interviewing the sun-burnished researcher at the park's gray wooden headquarters building by the seawall in Ventura harbor. Davis, stout, casual, and authoritative, reminds me of the skipper on *Gilligan's Island.*

"We're fragmenting marine habitats to where they're not viable," he tells me. "We're losing species like abalone and rockfish. The predators and large grazers are being fished out. Then when you have El Niño storms that take out the kelp, you discover that it's only in the reserves that the [kelp] forests consistently recover, because the red urchins and lobsters and big sheephead and abalones are still there, keeping the system in balance."

As I talk with Davis I'm distracted by the view out his office window across the Santa Barbara Channel to the islands, where wind-whipped six-foot waves mean there's no way I'm going to be able to scuba dive the reserve. Still I've gotten to dive a few of California's smaller cold-water reserves such as Point Lobos, south of Monterey. Davis talks of an "edge" or "spillover" effect from these kinds of reserves, with large fish and other creatures spreading beyond the boundaries to areas under traditional fisheries management.

I see what he means a few days later at La Jolla Cove Reserve, some 200 miles to the south. Just past the yellow buoys that mark the edge of the reserve, beyond the surfers, divers, cold-water swimmers, kayakers, and joggers enjoying the sparkling waters, the sea surface is thick with marker floats for lobster traps. Clearly these fishermen have noticed that the catch is good right by the protected area.

There's plenty of evidence to back them up. The first large-scale study of marine ecological reserves, released at the 2001 annual meeting of the American Association for the Advancement of Science, found higher densities of fish, larger fish, and greater biodiversity in no-take zones. In Florida, world-record catches of three species of sport fish occur more frequently near Cape Canaveral—off-limits since 1962 for national security reasons—than in all the rest of the state combined.

Interestingly, California's commercial fishing industry hasn't been as vocal in opposing reserves as the state's recreational fishing industry. One reason may be that commercial fishermen are effectively the top predators in the marine ecosystem. When the prey disappear, they feel it. "Some of our members say, 'Don't agree to anything,'" says Zeke Grader of the Pacific Coast Federation of Fishermen's Associations. "But I tell them that if we do right by the resource, we do right by our industry. If you get fishermen involved, they'll be the ones promoting new reserves and feeling that the scientists and others are working for them."

The recreational industry, on the other hand, is less interested in the makeup of the fishery than in selling the fishing "experience" to its clients, many of whom lack the long-term perspective of a sportfisherman like the late Jim Donlon. Today, California's $2.5 billion recreational industry lists mackerel among its daily catches. When I moved to San Diego in the 1970s, mackerel was used as bait to catch the big fish that are no longer around.

MPAs have become a bugaboo for a number of recreational fishing groups. The Recreational Fishing Alliance (RFA), for example, is expending tremendous energy trying to pass Freedom to Fish acts in Congress and various statehouses. If passed, these laws would prevent the establishment of any designated marine wilderness areas. Given such polarization, it will take more than enthusiastic scientists and conservationists to promote the cause.

One logical constituency for underwater wilderness parks is the more than 15 million Americans who are certified scuba divers and the tens of millions more who enjoy snorkeling in clean waters full of life. On a cool December evening in 2002, I attend a meeting of San Diego's Council of Divers. Some three dozen recreational divers, men and women in denim, wool, and fleece, have gathered to hear a talk on marine reserves by Scripps Institution of Oceanography scientist Paul Dayton. When Dayton shows a slide of a juvenile abalone hiding under a red urchin, the crowd "Awwws" its appreciation. Only divers could find a baby ab cute, I think.

Dayton calls the kelp forests of today "ghost forests," because so many of their inhabitants are missing—giant black sea bass, big lobsters, moray eels, billfish. He has slides from a few decades ago showing lobsters the size of bulldogs and black sea bass larger than the men who caught them.

"I just don't see why there is such opposition to these reserves," Dayton tells the divers. "In Western Australia, [lobster] fishermen are demanding larger reserves because they're making so much money off the spillover." A woman diver speaks of having grown up in Cardiff (in north county San Diego), where the beaches were covered in shells when she was a child, but are no longer. Another diver wonders whether he will ever be able to collect abs again in his lifetime. "In your lifetime, probably not. I think it will be over 50 years before we see their recovery," Dayton admits.

After the presentation the president of the group (the only one wearing a sport jacket) encourages his members, who represent some 1,500 local divers, to get involved in the MPA designation process. I like this group in part because they know what you're saying when you talk about marine wilderness.

In Washington, D.C., I attend a meeting of the U.S. Coral Reef Task Force. Established in 1998 under President Clinton, it is supposed to find ways to protect and enhance America's coral reefs, but has made little or no progress during the Bush years. During a break in the proceedings a fishing industry representative chats with Rod Fujita, a senior scientist with Environmental Defense, a market-oriented conservation group.

"If you can prove to me that this spillover effect will generate a gross fisheries catch outside the reserves greater than if you didn't establish them, then maybe I'll get interested in the MPA idea," he tells Fujita. Standing there listening, my immediate take is to imagine someone saying, "If you can prove that this spillover effect means elk hunting outside Yellowstone will improve, then maybe I'll get interested in this national parks idea of yours."

I don't see why it's such a hard concept for people to get, that saving wilderness, whole and undivided, is also about saving ourselves. Just as generations of writers and poets have given voice to trees, rivers, and mountains, we need a new generation of artists and explorers to write the hymn of our ocean wilds. Some time ago Henry David Thoreau wrote in *Walden*, "Heaven is under our feet as well as over our heads. . . . We need the tonic of wilderness." I'd just amend that to say, heaven is also under our flippers.

Some people are getting it, though. Aside from fishermen, divers, surfers, sailors, lifeguards, and others whose work or primary recreation is on the sea, there are countless people whose souls just cannot find peace away from the shore. From San Diego to Seattle, Laguna Beach to Cape Cod, people struggle to maintain their connections to the sea, often for reasons they cannot easily explain, reasons as deep as the ocean itself. This may be why, despite the conflicts that surround them, our national marine sanctuaries have something going for them that better-funded government programs lack.

Marine sanctuaries, national seashores, public beaches, and marine protected areas are increasingly acting as social magnets, attracting the support of citizen groups and coastal communities committed to the long-term conservation, restoration, and preservation of these special places. That commitment, organized at the grassroots—or seaweed—level, may yet save our last frontier from being pacified, tamed, or degraded.

CHAPTER 12

The Seaweed Rebellion

We can't wait another five or ten years to make changes,
or it will be too late.

— Retired Admiral James Watkins, chair,
U.S. Commission on Ocean Policy

If you like to eat seafood or swim in the ocean, it's time to
get involved.

— Julie Evans-Brumm,
Friends of Long Island Sound

In the wake of Katrina, New Orleans has lost both its color—it literally looks sepia-toned, all mud brown, russet, and gray—and its people, the hurricane having created a million environmental refugees from the city and the coast. The smell I often encounter is not of dead bodies but of a dead city: like dried cow pies and mildew with a strong chemical aftertaste. I try not to breathe too deeply or get my feet wet where oily stagnant waters and dark wet mud have pooled.

It's three weeks after the storm and flooding, but the city is still closed to its residents. Passing through a police roadblock near Interstate 10, I find myself in Lakeview, one of the communities that sat underwater for two weeks. Driving for hours and days through the debris-strewn streets, I'm forced into my own frame of reference. Young soldiers talk about it being like a sci-fi or zombie movie. Older residents of the Gulf compare Katrina's impact to Hurricane Camille in '69 (and agree this was worse). I'm reminded of wars I've covered, scenes of destruction after heavy street battles with trees and power poles down, electric lines hanging, metal sheets, smashed cars, and torn-open houses—only on a far grander scale and with more regional incongruities (shrimp boats on levees, barges on highways, houses blown into bayou swamps).

Without its people, New Orleans has become a Woodstock for first

250

responders, occupied by some 30,000 troops, cops, reporters, relief workers, and contractors from every part of the country and the world. There are New York firemen, Detroit cops, Japanese TV crews, Oklahoma national guardsmen, Salvation Army volunteers, Customs agents from San Diego, and sheriffs from Kentucky. Driving around listening to the United Radio Broadcasters of New Orleans—a consortium of local stations now acting as the city's 24/7 town meeting and bulletin board—I share empty streets with abandoned cars and boats, big Army trucks, Humvees, and SUVs (aside from my rental, one of the few compacts I encounter belongs to an animal rescue group). Overhead, Army Blackhawks, Chinooks, and big C-130 transport planes fly about while contract helicopters drop 3,000- and 7,000-pound sandbags on the industrial Canal break that reflooded the Ninth Ward following Hurricane Rita.

Thousands of acres and tens of thousands of homes, neighborhood malls, schools, banks, and churches in the city will have to be bulldozed. I take pictures of the brown waterline that indicates how high they were flooded and the orange spray paint markings with dates, zeroes, and numbers indicating if any bodies were found inside. At the time, more than 1,000 deaths from Katrina have been confirmed, along with 100 more due to Hurricane Rita, which passes through while I am here— most of those deaths from evacuation accidents rather than direct impacts.

I also travel through the geographically varied forms of devastation Hurricane Katrina wrought throughout the region, often as a result of human greed and folly, such as replacing wetlands with floating casino barges. I visit Plaquemines Parish on the west bank of the Mississippi; Waveland, Ocean Springs, and Biloxi, Mississippi; and Dauphin Island, Alabama, where I'd previously spent time at the Sea Lab.

From these travels and from talking to survivors, rescue workers, sheriffs, military people, and of course fishermen, local activists, and marine scientists, I'm able to piece together some of the costs not only of this natural catastrophe but of the reckless policies that helped multiply its impacts. I'm reminded of the old Irish saying about the great Potato Famine: God brought the blight, but the British brought the famine.

Even three to four weeks after the storm, hundreds of thousands of people still haven't gotten to see what's left of their homes, or are just beginning to dig through the debris. One official estimates that the rubble from Katrina could cover 28 football fields to the height of the Empire State Building. Whole Mississippi neighborhoods look like they were flattened by a tornado (except that tornado winds don't come with 35-foot waves). Brick buildings and reinforced concrete buildings seem to have fared better than FEMA-compliant stilt homes and wooden buildings with storm shutters (though the storm shutters look pretty intact amidst the rubble). However, even bunkerlike concrete condominiums aren't going to last long if you build them on barrier islands like Dauphin Island.

Miles of beaches and standing trees are festooned with strips of plastic that look like Tibetan prayer flags (if monks prayed over the deaths of seabirds and turtles). There are oil spills and loose barrels of unknown origin that I encounter in the bayou while driving with a sheriff's deputy, who becomes nervous when I take a picture of a Shell refinery. The good news is that many of the live oak, hackberry, and cypress that look dead are starting to re-bud, meaning that winds had sucked the moisture out of them rather than their having been soaked by salt water for so long that it killed them. Some 25-foot trees survived, along with roads and seagrass meadows, because the storm waves were so high above them that they weren't scoured away.

America's demographics have also changed as whole populations were scoured away. In the fall of 2005 Baton Rouge has become the largest city in Louisiana, with major traffic jams, and arenas and hotels packed with evacuees. New Orleans' service industries are relocating there and elsewhere. Like the dustbowl of the 1930s, the Storm Bowl of '05 could result in a new wave of homelessness. My friend Buck Bagot, a leading homeless housing organizer, says there's a kindly attitude toward the new "deserving" homeless versus the "undeserving" old kind, but predicts that this tolerance may be gone in six months. I hang out with a group of Cajuns spending their days and nights in a carport under a damaged three-story office building where they sleep every night. There are black and white folks camped out in tents, campers, and RVs under a damaged bridge in Mississippi; there are refugees in marine lab dorms and KOAs and a Mormon tent colony by a lake, or in the homes and yards of friends and family, or in motels, or, as a last resort, at evacuee centers. I'm skeptical whether the tens of billions of federal recovery money heading south will ever reach many of them.

During my visit it was too early to talk about the environmental impacts on the coast and ocean with any authority. The oil companies lost at least 50 rigs in the Gulf, with more than 110 others damaged. The Coast Guard estimated that 9.1 million gallons of oil were spilled (three-fourths of an *Exxon Valdez*), but even a month after the storm that figure kept rising. Nancy Rabalais at the Louisiana Universities Marine Consortium (LUMCON) lab in Cocodrie told me the lab's roof was lost during Katrina, and then Rita flooded its ground storage area and lab vehicles. On a cruise she conducted to see how the storms had affected the Gulf's nutrient-fed dead zone, she encountered a seven-foot alligator that had been washed 15 miles out to sea. I also visited the Gulf Coast Research Lab in Ocean Springs, Mississippi, which took a big hit: major buildings lost and flooded and its education center in Biloxi totaled. Director Bill Hawkins thought the pollutants in the New Orleans floodwaters that were pumped back into Lake Pontchartrain would likely flow through the wetlands to affect the Gulf of Mississippi sometime in 2006.

Most vessels of the region's shrimp and commercial fishing fleet were sunk or thrown up onto land. The possibility that federal fisheries managers might use this as a chance to buy out part of the destroyed fleet in order to reduce fishing pressure was the source of much speculation and little certainty in the wake of Katrina.

The Chandelier Islands, east of Louisiana, are mostly gone. Whether these important barrier islands and their bird colonies will reemerge from the sea along with floating wetlands and other lost lands is unclear. Best guesstimates were that Louisiana lost another 30 square miles of marshy wetlands to Katrina and Rita (on top of the average annual land loss of as much as 30 square miles). Louisiana 2050—the state and federal plan to restore coastal wetlands at a cost of $14 billion over 50 years—seemed to be back on the table. I talked to Mark Davis of the group Restore Coastal Louisiana, who once told me that if they couldn't win political support for this plan, "a hurricane will make the case."

"It sure sucks to be right," he says now.

Still, despite the losses, the spirit of many survivors I interview is surprisingly hopeful and/or philosophic, given the hit almost everyone and every creature down here has taken.

While traveling the region I saw opportunity as vast as the devastation. Things can be done right in terms of building wisely by the shore, creating social and environmental equity, and addressing big issues like wetlands protection, federal subsidies for destructive development, and the role of fossil-fuel-fired climate change in extreme weather events such as Katrina and Rita (the latter also reached category 5 status in the Gulf's overheated waters). Yet even in the wake of the worst hurricane season to date, too many are anxious to make money and generate jobs recreating the same patterns as before. The only reform we know for sure will come out of this disaster is that Mississippi will allow land-based gambling, since the gaming industry can no longer get insurance for giant casino barges that got tossed around like bathtub toys.

If we want to bring about major changes in the way our nation relates to its coasts and oceans, we are going to have to support and work with our fellow activists in the Gulf to build a credible constituency for our public seas, our battered shores, and the blue frontier beyond. Meanwhile, small but touching examples of how we can restore the ocean continue to offer me hope and some measure of amusement.

I'm thigh deep in clear tropical water, one of 16 people moving Sheri and Florence around in a circle. Sheri is five feet and Florence is five feet three inches; they're both a little disoriented after a long day's flight from Chicago and the drive down from Miami—followed, like any celebrities, by cameras and reporters. This small cove near Captain Slate's Atlantis Dive Center has been enclosed with orange plastic fencing and iron rebar so the girls can spend a safe night getting used to the warm, 82-degree salt water. They've spent the last 18 hours in aerated, water-filled giant coolers.

Sheri and Florence, if you haven't yet guessed, are nurse sharks. Captured as little nippers, they grew up at the Seashell Pet Shop in Chicago, where they eventually grew too large for their pool. That's when Wendy Rhodes, a pale, blonde animal-rights activist from Los Angeles, found them and decided to launch a rescue mission. She made a call to Rick Trout, an ex-Navy dolphin trainer who now lives in an old Keys cottage surrounded by cats, coconut palms, and bougainvillea, works as a commercial diver, and helps coordinate marine mammal rescues. Rick organized the planned shark release from this end and is now pushing Florence in my direction. She seems to be losing a little of her jet-lag lethargy. Her skin, as I guide her through the water, feels more like raw silk than sandpaper, and I can feel her muscles beginning to work beneath it. She tries to turn away from the circle, but I firmly direct her back along the line.

Shark wrangling could seem macho, except for the fact that Sky, a seven-year-old blond pixie in a blue wetsuit, is now hugging Sheri. "No hugging the shark, you have to pass her along," her mother gently chides. There are five kids aged 7 to 12 carefully dispersed in the circle, including two preteen brothers, Brady and Brandon. "Hey, have you heard of fish and chips?" Brady asks one of the sharks he's pushing along, trying to get a response from his brother, who ignores him. Wading around the edge of the circle is a video crew from Miami's Channel 7, including a young Latina reporter who keeps trying to get control of her hair in the evening breeze. Their lead news tease tonight will be "Sharks gone wild in south Florida."

Soon the sharks are swimming on their own, and we quickly leave them to their adjustment. Back on shore I talk to Clifford Glade, a medical doctor and veterinarian who is here with his young daughter, Nikki. A day earlier he had set the broken legs of two rare cranes who had flown into newly constructed electrical towers. I mention that this release may be a net gain of only one shark for the reef: earlier in the day, while on patrol with sanctuary cop Dave McDaniel, we'd spotted a cabin cruiser named *Sea E Oh* with three guys cheering on a woman companion who was hauling in a large nurse shark on rod and reel.

"You have to start somewhere," Dr. Glade says. "I'm 48. Nikki is ten. I want her to grow up where there are still sharks and wild birds and a coral reef she can enjoy."

The next morning the sharks are riding in black tubs on the fantail of the 42-foot *Coral Princess* as we head out to Elbow Reefs. Here lies the wreck of the USS *City of Washington,* a nineteenth-century navy ship that returned the bodies of the battleship *Maine*'s dead from Havana harbor at the beginning of the Spanish-American war. The *Coral Princess*'s captain, Spencer Slate, a fair-sized, mustachioed good ole boy and a newlywed (he just married Sky's mom), suggested this release site. He brings scuba divers there every week, which may give the sharks some level of protection from fishermen.

The young woman reporter from Channel 7 is back with her crew, interviewing Rick. "Hopefully, this will show people that this is where sharks belong, and that keeping them as pets is just a bad habit they should get over," he says.

We arrive at the reef and prepare for the sharks' send-off. Spencer and Rick have stapled small ribbon tags onto them for future identification— the sharks did not seem to mind, although Wendy went a shade paler than normal. Some of us are going down to observe the sharks in the water, and Spencer tells us about a barracuda on the reef known as Lightning and an eel named Perry. On his dives Slate holds a fish in his mouth for the barracuda to grab; so far Lightning has been able to distinguish the fish from Spencer's masked nose.

We dive down to the shallow wreck lying in 25 feet of water. There are some nice fan corals growing on its iron ribs, and we see wrasses, sergeant majors, parrotfish, and lobsters in the wreck's rusted-out holes and rock crevices nearby. After everyone is settled on the bottom, Rick and Captain Slate swim the two sharks down. Slate tries to feed pieces of squid to them, but they spit it back out. Suddenly a six-foot green moray eel—it's Perry—swims out from under the wreck and slides over Slate's shoulder to grab some of the squid, catching him by surprise.

This is a long way from the Seashell Pet Shop, and the two nurse sharks don't look too happy, lying on the bottom together, one with its pectoral fin over the other as if to comfort it. I imagine them thinking, "Where the heck are we? Where are the goldfish, hamsters, and parakeets?" There are now 17 divers and two sharks on the bottom, plus a small local nurse shark who's willing to be fed if Sheri and Florence aren't. Half a dozen water-sealed cameras are recording the event in a kind of media feeding frenzy, which will replay on Miami's TV stations this evening.

Of course, it is going to take more than a few news stories to educate the public about marine wildlife. A few days after the nurse shark release, a tourist from St. Petersburg boating off Key Colony Beach spots a bunch of fins in the water. Deciding that he's going to swim with wild dolphins, he jumps into the middle of a school of aggressive seven-foot bull sharks, one of which bites him in the foot.

I call Rick six months later to see how the nurse sharks are doing. They're now feeding themselves, he tells me. And they moved off the wreck to Finger Reef, where they've been seen in 50 feet of water. Meanwhile, Wendy has located and shipped three more nurse sharks from a Pizza A Go Go in San Jose, California.

If restoring sharks to the wild is not your thing, you're probably not going to sign up for underwater ordnance removal, either. That's Jim Barton's occupation and the name of his company, whose scuba divers remove old bombs and artillery shells that threaten the health of coral reefs, using innovative sleds and winches of his own design. You might also be skeptical about following conservationist David Guggenheim as he pilots a single-person submersible to inspect deep-sea corals, sponges, grouper holes, and other habitats he is fighting to protect from drag trawl fishing gear. Luckily, you have many other options.

All across coastal America people who care about the sea are beginning to act on their beliefs. The number of blue groups is growing, along with public awareness about the state of our oceans. I recently edited an *Ocean and Coastal Conservation Guide,* which lists some 2,000 blue groups. Major activist organizations include the 150,000-member Ocean Conservancy, which sponsors the annual National Beach Cleanup Day and is headed by a former Coast Guard admiral. Surfrider Foundation is a chapter-based group made up of 45,000 surfers and other watermen and -women who got fed up with oil and waste spoiling their ocean stoke with water-borne infections. There is Oceana, founded by the Pew Charitable Trusts, which is targeting "dirty" fishing practices and threatening to sue the barnacles off polluting ocean liners. Another outfit, Seaweb, has spawned work on sustainable seafood, aquaculture, and aquarium education. Jacques Cousteau's grandson Philippe runs Earth Echo, a group working on coral restoration and alternative energy sources derived from the oceans, while the *Titanic* discoverer Bob Ballard is bringing the ocean into thousands of classrooms through his JASON project, using remote-sensing underwater cameras.

Then there is the increasingly salty Water Keepers Alliance. Starting out as River Keepers, they followed the flow so that now they're also bay, inlet, and coast keepers, operating from the frigid waters of Cook Inlet, Alaska, to the warm but not-so-pristine waters of Puerto Rico. To be a keeper requires three things: a boat, a boat captain, and a willingness to sue polluters. "The future of the environment is in God's hands. I just want to be able to tell my children that I did all I could do," explains Robert F. Kennedy Jr., the group's president.

Across the nation, coalitions of blue groups such as the Marine Fish Conservation Network, Restore America's Estuaries, Clean-Water Network, and others are working on a range of issues from fisheries management reform to the establishment of marine protected areas.

More regionally oriented groups include the New Jersey–based American Littoral Society, Gulf Restoration Network, and REEF (Reef Environmental Education Foundation), which every June cosponsors the "Great American Fish Count," during which scuba divers help scientists census local fish populations. The influential Chesapeake Bay Foundation in Maryland is fighting to restore America's largest estuary to at least 76 percent of its precolonial natural state. (Presently it rates the estuary at 26 percent of that goal.) Among many others are the venerable Save San Francisco Bay, the North Carolina Coastal Federation, and People for Puget Sound.

A number of groups focus on specific marine wildlife. These include the Pelagic Shark Foundation, Protect Our Wild Salmon, the Sea Otter Project, the Sea Turtle Restoration Project, and Save the Manatee Club, cochaired by singer-songwriter Jimmy Buffett, who notes that "each species is the spoke in a magic wheel: to lose one is to diminish the whole."

Hundreds of local organizations are also making their presence felt through constructive engagement with fellow citizens. In Santa Cruz, California, for example, Save Our Shores (SOS), a group that was founded to protest offshore oil drilling, has evolved into a citizen watchdog and resource for the Monterey Bay National Marine Sanctuary. I gave a talk for SOS aboard the *Princess of Whales,* a commercial whale-watching vessel out of Moss Landing, California, addressing a crowd of hundreds that day, if you count sea lions, pelicans, and humpback whales. Like many other businesses on the bay, its operators support the local seaweed rebels, recognizing that protecting our public oceans also provides expanded economic opportunities ashore.

In Key West, Reef Relief continues to expand, recently opening a new education center on Key West's sister island of Green Turtle Key, Bahamas. Today Reef Relief has some 5,000 members working to protect and restore coral, with a larger number turning out every year for its Cayo Caribbean Music festival by the town's old fort

"For years we worked mainly on a grassroots level," Craig Quirolo tells members at the annual Reef Awareness Week dinner. Craig founded the group with his wife, DeeVon. "After working here in the Keys we decided to go to D.C. and lobby for a sanctuary, which we got. We figured the government would get involved and save the reef, only it hasn't. Then we thought science would save the reef, only there's all this disagreement among the scientists. So now we're back to saying it's up to us to save it. We can't expect the government or the scientists to save our reef for us. We're going to have to do it ourselves, by educating young people and reaching out to people in other parts of the nation, and the world, and telling them about this living treasure we've got down here."

Concern over the impact of coastal development isn't limited to Florida, however. On New York's Staten Island the Crescent Beach Civic Association, organized by housewife-activist Eileen Monreale, is fighting to prevent developers from putting hundreds of upscale condos on top of a popular recreational beach where working families swim, fish, and kayak. More recently Eileen helped start a campaign to restore the borough's blighted north shore. In ports and fishing towns from San Pedro, California, to Cape May, New Jersey; in low-income communities of color from Molokai, Hawaii, to Sapelo Island, Georgia; and in laid-back surfer towns like San Diego's Ocean Beach, where I lost a decade one endless summer, people are struggling to maintain their traditional connections to the sea.

Dauphin Island, Alabama, reminds me of what Key West was like when I was a kid: a relaxed island without a lot of commercial distractions from the magic of its open sky and rainbow-streaked waters. I'm here with Dr. George Crozier, the director of the Dauphin Island Sea Lab. George is a tough old salt with blond hair turning white, a craggy, sun-reddened face, and a fun-loving hyperkinetic style not often found among the more staid northern breed of scientist. "Our lab started in 1971 on a mosquito-, bug-infested peninsula," he tells me. "Now we're on a mosquito-, bug-infested barrier island."

Fourteen miles by 1.5 miles at its thickest, with some 2,000 winter residents and as many as 15,000 summer visitors, Dauphin Island has been repeatedly hit and reshaped by tropical hurricanes, including Frederick in 1979, Danny and George in 1997 and 1998, Ivan in 2004, and Dennis, Katrina, and Wilma in 2005. From the water the island's narrow west end looks like a forest of wooden stilts atop which several hundred houses have been temporarily secured. You could fish off the decks or out the bathroom windows of many of them where the storm-eroded sand has retreated under their pilings. After Hurricane George, FEMA spent millions of tax dollars to protect the single road out here, but without requiring any additional public access to what's left of the beach.

"I'll be damned if public money should be spent for these owners to be making more money than they already do with their summer rentals, and with no benefit to the public," Crozier declares as we rock in a windy chop 100 yards offshore in one of the lab's 26-foot research vessels. After my visit, in 2004, Hurricane Ivan delivered a glancing blow to Dauphin, destroying 50 west end homes and badly damaging another hundred, leaving a rubble of wooden debris, grounded boats, and two new ocean channels in its wake. Yet again FEMA returned to help the vacation-rental developers rebuild in harm's way.

On my next visit, a few weeks after Katrina, there are 200 homes destroyed on the west end and a new visitor to the area: the massive oil rig *Ocean Warwick,* grounded in the surf. George and I pass through a police roadblock and hike down the beach amidst an apocalyptic scene of broken and vanished stilt houses, downed power lines, flooded roads, buried cars, and shallow quicksand. A $1.1 million protective sand berm built by FEMA after last year's hurricane has also washed out to sea. Meanwhile, we're getting sand-blasted and drenched by 25-knot winds and rain squalls that mark the outer bands of Hurricane Rita, which was then threatening to do to Houston what Katrina did to New Orleans.

"The rush to rebuild is understandable. It's basic human sympathy," George says, pausing to examine a fuel drum lying in the sand. "But we have to build in a different way. The fact is, we're in a new situation. What we saw in the summer of '04 in Florida and the summer of '05 in Louisiana is no longer the exception. It's the new rule. My position from a policy point of view is to condemn it [the west end]—just don't allow any more building out here."

Along with George Crozier, other marine scientists—including Oregon State University's Jane Lubchenco (a marine ecologist and the president of the International Council for Science), Louisiana's Nancy Rabalais (who discovered the Gulf of Mexico's Dead Zone), Scripps's Jeremy Jackson and Nancy Knowlton (the cofounders of the Center for Marine Biodiversity and Conservation), and Canada's Ransom Myers (one of the world's leading fisheries biologists)—have begun to speak out on threats to our living seas. Much of their work is publicized through COMPASS, the Communication Partnership for Science and the Sea.

Groups concerned with human health and the oceans also are becoming active on the blue frontier. One is Harvard's Center for Health and the Global Environment; another is the San Diego Environmental Health Coalition, which has challenged the home porting of Navy nuclear aircraft carriers and the bay dredging it entails. The coalition recently joined with the San Diego Bay Keeper, the Sierra Club, and other groups to form the Bay Council, which coordinates local marine protection efforts. Among their champions is Donna Frye. Mainstream green groups like the Natural Resources Defense Council, the Nature Conservancy, Conservation International, and Environmental Defense have also begun to take on a bluer tinge.

The practice of labeling sustainable seafood has become increasingly popular. Pocket guides, cookbooks, and certification programs promoting sustainable seafood are now being produced and embraced by various aquariums, leading restaurant chefs, and activists including the Seafood Choices Alliance, whose list also notes which fish may pose a human health risk (because of chemical contamination). Overfishing, explains Julie Packard, the director of the Monterey Bay Aquarium, is "an environmental problem whose solution is in people's hands every time they buy seafood."

"Where diverse opinions have been sought out, programs like the Monterey Aquarium's have a lot of credibility," adds Pietro Parravano, a commercial fisherman from Half Moon Bay, California, who was also a member of the Pew Oceans Commission.

In 2000 this labeling effort expanded under the sponsorship of the Marine Stewardship Council, set up by the World Wildlife Fund and the

Dutch-based multinational Unilever, one of the world's largest commercial buyers of fish. Among the first human prey items to win the Council's "Fish Forever" seal (certified sustainable by independent experts) were West Australian rock lobster and Alaskan wild salmon. More controversial was its decision in 2004 to certify Alaskan pollack—a decision challenged by the Alaska Oceans Program and other blue groups concerned that America's largest fishery may be in decline. The activists claim that too little is known about the impact of Russian fishing on pollack, the relationship of the pollack fishery to other species such as sea lions and seabirds, and the changing state of the Bering Sea habitat to certify the catch as sustainable.

Among the first U.S. companies to use the Fish Forever seal is the Boston-based Legal Sea Foods restaurant chain, which buys some 20 tons of fish and shellfish every day. "We've been in the fish business for fifty years, and I'm interested in being in the business another fifty years," explains Legal Sea Food's CEO, Roger Berkowitz, a buff, gregarious guy who does his own TV ads. "The only way we can do this [stay in business] is to participate in some kind of conservation effort. What I like about this program is that it's a positive approach that can help motivate people. It's a way we can help educate our consumers and also encourage fisheries to sustain themselves."

Roger gives me a tour of his new plant on Boston Harbor, just across the water from Logan Airport. It contains state-of-the-art equipment from Iceland, including machines that sort live lobsters and laser-guided filleting machines that cut exact servings for his 30-plus restaurants. "I want to increase efficiency in how we process the product and reduce efficiency in how it's acquired," he explains—meaning that we can't keep using technological overkill to empty the seas faster than the fish can reproduce.

"I believe all the ocean issues will get dealt with when people demand we take action," says Curt Weldon, the Republican representative from Pennsylvania. "My district's not on the ocean but my people go to the ocean to enjoy themselves," he says. "I like to boat and fish, and I see the ocean as a glue that can bring people together."

Thirty-five million people a year now visit the Jersey Shore. An equal number go to New York's Jones Beach. Even after a huge decline due to concerns over water quality, the beaches of Los Angeles still attract some 20 million visitors annually. There are 20 million annual visitors to our national seashores, and even more to our marine sanctuaries.

We are eating more seafood than ever before and moving to the beach in record numbers. We love the ocean, we use the ocean, but we don't think enough about the ocean. We've mapped less than 10 percent of the seas at the detailed resolution with which we have mapped 100 percent of the moon. If you're into lifeless places, you should visit the moon or check out Washington, D.C. If you want to see life on its own phantasmagorical terms, go to sea. If today we are loving our oceans to death through ignorance and short-term greed, we can stop doing that. After all, the hope of any frontier is that we do not have to repeat the mistakes of our past.

Of course, the ocean itself is monumentally indifferent to all of our human hopes and desires. But it can also provide solace, give you a sense of being a part of something larger, even when large parts of your own soul have torn away.

In 1978, while I was still living on that cliff in San Diego, my dad died. He'd had a heart attack and stroke three years earlier and never recovered. To overcome my grief I went off to cover wars in Central America for five years, with my photographer friend John Hoagland. Between reporting on combat, civilian massacres, and death squads, we'd go to the beach in El Salvador to recharge. John, a recidivist surfer, liked the left break at La Libertad. After a dozen people I knew and respected were killed—including John and photographer Richard Cross, another friend who was like a brother—I returned to the beach in San Diego. Burned out on reporting and needing a break, I got my private investigator's license.

Then I moved to the San Francisco Bay Area, got scuba certified, and met Nancy. She was my adventure mate and life's love. We ended up in a Sausalito duplex above Richardson Bay. She did computer graphics and photography; I did TV documentaries on a range of topics from Navy nukes to the AIDS epidemic and an investigative book on the antienvironmental backlash. We dove California, Australia, Mexico, and the Caribbean; went to Hawaii every year; hiked Point Reyes National Seashore every other weekend. We were shipwrecked during a storm in Mexico. She got jealous once when I rode a whale shark that she didn't know was a vegetarian. "It's lucky he didn't mistake you for a veggie burger," she groused.

After ten years we broke up, but not cleanly. I moved to Washington, D.C., away from Nancy and my other love, the sea—figuring if I was going to traumatize myself I might as well go all the way, using work as an excuse. Right after I started the oceans book I'd always wanted to write, she found a lump in her breast. I traveled back west to be with her through the chemo, which was awful but seemed to work. I finished the first edition of this book in 2001 and was on the Deep East expedition 100 miles off Nantucket (see chapter 1) when Al Qaeda hit the twin towers. When I returned to land, Nancy told me that her cancer was back. I was with her for the last few months, in the hospital and the home hospice, where we could watch the waters of Richardson Bay change with the tides, life ebbing and flowing.

After she died at 43 we had a memorial service on one of her favorite beaches. It was a gusty day, feisty like the gal, with the winds whipping the sand and frothing the cold translucent waves. She used to say I never looked happier than when I was coming out of the water after getting beat up by the waves.

I moved back to Washington with our cat, not sure what to do next, tired of freelancing and of life. I soon found I had three options. I could move back to California and do PI work for Scott Fielder, my lawyer friend and diving buddy, but I'd already done that. I could return to war reporting, as President Bush was clearly planning a preemptive war on Iraq, and that had some appeal. But I also started meeting with Ralph Nader, who had read the oceans book and, out of the blue, given me a call to say how much he liked it. He encouraged me to organize the marine grassroots community that I'd dubbed the Seaweed Rebellion.

Nader offered me some support to work on mobilizing this blue movement, including free office space in D.C. amidst a rabbit warren of public interest start-ups in a building near Dupont Circle. After a lot of reflection I decided that, while we'll probably always have wars like that in Iraq, we may not always have wild fish, living reefs, or healthy coastal wetlands. Plus, if I went to war I wouldn't know what to do with the cat.

Having committed myself to the other 71 percent of our planet, my next step was to ask some of the people I'd been reporting on (or had asked for book blurbs) if they would now join me in starting yet another fish-hugger organization. Among those willing to join my boards of directors and advisors were Bobby Kennedy Jr., biologist Paul Ehrlich, Legal Sea Foods CEO Roger Berkowitz, San Diego city councilwoman Donna Frye, *Sherman's Lagoon* cartoonist Jim Toomey, and leaders of various blue groups including Surfrider Foundation, The Ocean Conservancy, the New England Aquarium, the California Coastal Commission, Clean Ocean Action, Reef Relief, and the Pacific Coast Federation of

Fishermen's Associations. Assured that I wasn't stepping on anyone's flippers, I incorporated as a nonprofit in December 2002, ordering Blue Frontier Campaign letterhead in early 2003. I wrote up a ten-point plan of action and printed a brochure. I figured I had the vision thing down: to strengthen the ocean constituency through building unity, providing tools, and enhancing public awareness. What I hadn't counted on was the administrative and fund-raising stuff.

I found my first interns through a professor friend at Georgetown. They in turn helped me research nonprofit business requirements and potential funding sources. I hired an accountant and counted pennies. Luckily it didn't cost much to talk to and share ideas with other groups such as Pacific Environment in California, the Assateague Coastal Trust in Maryland, or the Metropolitan Waterfront Alliance in New York.

I spoke at aquariums, government agencies, journalism conferences (pushing the need for a "blue beat"), and to the Pew Oceans Commission and the U.S. Commission on Ocean Policy, two prestigious panels whose very dissimilar personnel reached very similar conclusions: that our oceans are in deep trouble and need ecosystem-based solutions. I also spent a lot of those early months sitting at my desk, chewing on gummy sharks, missing the ocean, and trying to figure out what to do next.

I was at an Oceans Week (actually two-day) event on Capitol Hill that June when my lunch companion, a real-estate lawyer and surfer from Sacramento, mentioned that he had just read my book. I mentioned that I'd just started a nonprofit, and he wrote me a check for $500—my first new funding, wow! Later, when Stuart Smits began working as the campaign's West Coast director, I asked him why he had signed on. "I called 2002 my year of being angry," he said. "I was so pissed off at what Bush was doing, I just had to get active in something I believed in, something positive."

I then approached my old Bay Area buddy Buck Bagot. Buck is the best low-income-housing organizer in America and has gotten more than a billion dollars out of a Republican Congress by beating up on politicians in their home districts. As a reporter I'd already figured out that, while a lot of advocacy groups spend time in Washington trying to educate policy-makers, most politicians—like sharks and stingrays—are simple predators, hard-wired to two things: money and votes. Buck knew how to mobilize votes. So I flew out to San Francisco and sat down with Stuart and Buck; we designated Buck the campaign's political guru (he would later help plan our first congressional visits). We then went out to

8 both1111

celebrate at the waterfront bistro Pier 21 with 25 seaweed activists including a fisherman, a surfer, and the head of the California Coastal Commission, picking their brains about what they might want from a seaweed movement.

In November 2003 we held our inaugural "Celebration of the Sea" dinner at the historic Carnegie Institution, during a torrential Washington downpour. At 6 PM, when it was supposed to start, we had a dozen soaking people. An hour later we had 120 happy activist, government, and media types drinking fine California wines, sniffing exotic Hawaiian flowers, and eating delicious and sustainable wild Alaska salmon with seaweed garnish (donated by Legal Sea Foods). Also in attendance were Representatives Sam Farr (D-CA), George Miller (D-CA), and Wayne Gilchrest (R-MD). Farr spoke on behalf of the bipartisan House Oceans Caucus.

"You're going to create the seaweed revolution," he told us. "It's got a better name. It's called the Blue Frontier Campaign. Essentially it's about a grassroots ability to get people all on the same message, to get them to go research who their legislators are. . . . The point is, we have to get to every single member of Congress. If we fail, we've missed an incredible political opportunity, and it won't come back as it is right now. The table is set, the time is here—let's begin the revolution."

The timing he referred to was the release of the Pew and U.S. Commission on Ocean Policy reports (in 2003 and 2004, respectively). Both pointed to the ecological collapse of our seas as a threat to the U.S. economy, environment, and security and proposed democratic, ecosystem-based management organized around marine watersheds as the best way to protect and restore our public oceans.

Blue Frontier's response was to organize a Blue Vision Conference in July 2004 to show that there was (and is) a growing constituency for action.

By now we had a growing network of volunteers including Jean Logan, a patent attorney who used to work reinventing government with Al Gore (and would become our program director); Diane Williams, a Long Island mother of three and marine studies major; and Jon Christensen, my old sailing buddy from San Diego. We also expanded our board with the addition of Phil Renaud, a recently retired Navy captain who'd commanded the service's oceanographic fleet, and Philippe Cousteau, the activist grandson of the famed ocean explorer. We set up a conference steering committee and worked with a number of groups, getting them to sign on (and contribute financially) as cosponsors. We made calls, sent e-mails, designed and mailed brochures, and made more calls. We met with hotels and caterers, hired a conference coordinator, did more fund-raising, and made more calls. As the spring blended into summer, almost no one registered early. And the more I didn't get to the beach or into the water, the more pissed off I got. I'd be damned if I was going to save the seas from a concrete-covered swamp.

Still, my gut instinct proved right as 250 people representing 170 organizations from 25 states and Puerto Rico ultimately showed up for the three-day conference in the fry-heat of a Washington summer.

The keynote speaker, marine conservationist and *Jaws* author Peter Benchley, contrasted his youth on Nantucket Island, when you couldn't haul in a swordfish without a shark taking a chunk out of it, with today's rapid decline of large predators. He recalled a dive off Costa Rica where he found the bottom littered with dead sharks killed for their fins to be used in shark-fin soup.

A number of conference panels focused on local and regional solutions that work, from a watershed restoration effort that's saving salmon and uniting communities in Northern California to a pollution reduction program in Narragansett Bay, Rhode Island. Local solutions aren't enough, however, where impacts can be felt not only across bays and bights, but across ocean basins. That's why Blue Frontier will keep working to connect and mobilize groups around their congressional districts so they can put political muscle behind policy changes at the national level. A panel on expanding this blue constituency included representatives from marine recreation, tribal nations, religion, and public health. Other panel participants and speakers included members from the two ocean commissions, the media, and representatives from the Bush and Kerry presidential campaigns.

At one session we presented the first annual Blue Frontier Awards for Excellence in Marine Science, Media, and Policy, and a special Hero of the Seas award. The latter went to Dery Bennett of New Jersey (see chapter 7), the kind of bottom-up organizer and mentor who reminds us that we all come from salt water. Along with a certificate, each winner received a "Kissing Dolphins" sculpture donated by the marine artist Wyland.

On the final day of the three-day conference some 50 attendees visited Capitol Hill, where they were greeted by the cochairs of the House Oceans Caucus and met with three senators, 12 House members, and dozens of their staffers. They encouraged their representatives to work with or join the House Oceans Caucus and support a range of marine legislation including fisheries reform, cruise ship cleanup, and deep-sea coral protection.

Between visits we encountered a live buffalo on the Capitol grounds. The animal, named Harvey Wallbanger, was being used to promote the reintroduction of the Buffalo nickel. Once there were 60 million bison running wild across the American plains, and none had cute names or a paid handler. It brought home why we were there: to protect sharks and tuna and marlin from becoming the next bison—and to fight for our last great public trust from sea to shining sea.

The consensus of the Blue Vision conference was that we really need a comprehensive Ocean Protection Act, on the scale of the Clean Air and Clean Water Acts of the last century—something that can fire the public's imagination and become a central organizing focus for the seaweed rebellion. Unfortunately, after George Bush's reelection the White House in December 2004 put out an Ocean Action Plan that, like the industry-friendly "Clear Skies" and "Healthy Forests" policies, could just as easily be labeled "Happy Oceans." "Building on previous successes," it calls for privatizing America's fisheries, endorses the Law of the Seas treaty (which Bush's anti-UN supporters continued to block from Senate ratification), and rejects a $4 billion ocean trust fund proposed by Bush's own Ocean Policy Commission. At the same time, the administration cut hundreds of millions of dollars of Clean Water funds to the states and promoted energy "surveys" and liquid natural gas transfer stations in coastal waters where oil and gas drilling are banned.

Some lawmakers are trying to do better. In June 2005 Senator Barbara Boxer (D-CA) introduced a comprehensive National Oceans Protection Act in the Senate. Shortly thereafter the bipartisan House Oceans Caucus introduced a complementary act on its side of the Hill. On 48 hours' notice the Blue Frontier Campaign was able to get 25 marine and coastal conservation groups to endorse the Boxer bill. These included organizations from Texas, Florida, California, Alabama, Louisiana, Maine, Massachusetts, Maryland, and New York. Still, we realized that to win passage we would need the votes of at least 51 senators and 214 House members. And to win their support, we would also need much more bottom-up seaweed power.

In April 2005 Blue Frontier held its first regional conference at the Baltimore Aquarium for some 50 mid-Atlantic activists from 30 blue groups working between New York and North Carolina. "Blue Frontier is a new model for us," said Glenn Page, the aquarium's director of conservation. He went on to suggest that "the kind of blue vision we're looking at involves outreach and engagement with the public and groups like yours so that we [aquariums and zoos] don't just become displays of what habitat used to look like."

Participants talked about local solutions they were involved in. In North Carolina a string of community-based oyster hatcheries and sanctuaries are bringing people together around coastal stewardship. In New York and New Jersey a coalition of environmental, fishing, and community groups on the New York Bight put together a Clean Ocean Zone proposal, which was endorsed by the governor of New Jersey. The afternoon ended on a light note with a contest between teams of attendees named Dolphins and Seals, who competed to answer a series of ocean-policy *Survivor* questions about how we win change in Congress.

At the end of the conference participants expressed strong support for continued regional network building and their commitment to working in both their home districts and Washington for comprehensive ocean conservation measures.

In summer 2005 we began planning a Blue Vision–Gulf of Mexico conference for that fall in New Orleans, but it would be preempted by the Katrina disaster. Plans go forward, though, for a second national Blue Vision conference in 2006, aiming to raise the blue banner and organize blue votes before the midterm elections. We also produced several new books and other media work aimed at expanding the blue movement and the public's awareness of how they can help restore our common seas.

What we have begun with this campaign may be the first ripple in a rising tide of citizen action that will protect, restore, and revive our blue frontier. Given the cascading disasters our seas confront, and the political powers that seem to favor the rapid liquidation of public resources, it's hard to say for sure. I can't know if we will be able to organize ourselves and educate and mobilize the public in time to keep this crucible of life on our blue planet from becoming a dead sea. All I do know for sure is that if we don't try, we lose.

I've been lucky in my explorations: I have survived near-drowning in big surf off Oahu's north shore, been humbled by wild waves and salmon in Alaska, found peace in the tranquil waters of the U.S. Virgin Islands, ridden a whale shark, and shipwrecked a sailboat in the Sea of Cortez. I have met unforgettable watermen and -women whenever I've ventured on or near the blue frontier.

Right now I'm standing on a cliff at Point Lobos State Park, just south of Monterey. From here I can look to my left and see several rocky offshore islands covered with hundreds of lazing sea lions; some have wad-

dled up to the highest crags, 50 feet above the water. The surging sea
breaks turquoise and white below them. In front of me is a horseshoe-
shaped cove under wind-sculpted cliffs topped by thick stands of dark
green cypress and pine. On a crescent beach, several gray and black spotted harbor seals have hauled up on the coarse sand. Out on the water a
raft of a half-dozen sea otters loll in the kelp, rolling themselves in the
green translucent plants like so many servings of otter sushi. Pelicans are
making kamikaze dives on a shoal of sardines. Cormorants and gulls are
flying about like busy rush-hour commuters. A great blue heron stands
on a floating piece of plywood, looking down into the water, poised like
the predator that he is. He strikes below the surface with his rapier bill
and tumbles in after it, sinks, and resurfaces, flapping back onto his float
in an undignified ruffle of feathers. The wildlife here is as abundant and
easy to spot as my own species back in town and equally uninterested in
my observing them.

The only place I know with a richer variety of life is below the water's
surface. I lean into the sea wind and recall last night's video feed from the
Monterey Bay Aquarium's deep-diving robot sub. It was 600 feet down
in the cold black canyon's midwater range when a white shark, wide as a
jet fighter's fuel tank and sleek as death, swam through the ROV's spotlight beam. A visceral shot of adrenaline ran through my body, remind-
ing me of Edward Abbey's line, "If there's not something bigger and
meaner than you are out there, it's not really a wilderness." Our waters
remain rich in potential adrenaline jolts and revelations, in waves that
call to be ridden, winds made to snap a sail, shells newly tossed upon the
shore, sunsets not to be believed.

Our oceans remain full of strange wonders and grand experiences
that will thrill generations yet unborn. Despite all the problems and challenges we face in fighting for America's living seas, that is still enough to
give one hope. After all, it is not every great nation, forged by its early
frontier experiences, that gets a second chance.

Notes and References

INTRODUCTION: THRASHED

Page 4, *icy crust of the Jupiter moon Europa:* For an in-depth look at the possibility of life on Europa and the theories that support it, see Jill C. Tarter and Christopher F. Chyba, "Is There Life Elsewhere in the Universe?" *Scientific American,* December 1999.

Page 4, *Among these is* Pyrococcus: For a good telling of the discovery of *Pyrococcus,* see William Broad, *The Universe Below* (New York: Simon & Schuster, 1997), 278–281.

Page 5, *or you can be eaten by great beasts:* Interview with Ken Kelton, reported in "Great White Comeback," *Men's Journal,* June/July 1996, 133.

Page 7, *and other self-conscious stylists:* See Robert Hughes, *American Visions* (New York: Knopf, 1999), 303–316; Benjamin W. Labaree et al., *America and the Sea* (Mystic, Conn.: Mystic Seaport, 1998), 396–397; and various exhibits and prints.

Page 10, *according to the United Nations Food and Agriculture Organization:* United Nations Food and Agriculture Organization (UN FAO), *The State of World Fisheries and Aquaculture* (Rome: UN FAO, 1995), 8.

Page 11, *Exclusive Economic Zone (EEZ):* Presidential Proclamation 5030, March 10, 1983. Only 532 words, the proclamation established the world's largest EEZ, an area of some four billion acres.

Page 11, *which had operated for 107 years:* U.S. Congress, House of Representatives, Committee on Merchant Marine and Fisheries, *Final Report on the Activities of the Merchant Marine and Fisheries Committee* (Washington, D.C.: Government Printing Office, 1995).

Page 12, *pass the Oceans Act:* Information from Representatives Jim Saxton and Sam Farr and Washington congressional, NOAA, and U.S. Navy staffers.

Page 13, *dealt with climate in any depth:* Pew Oceans Commission, *America's Living Oceans: Charting a Course for Sea Change* (Arlington, Va.: Pew Oceans Commission, 2003); U.S. Commission on Ocean Policy, *Report of the U.S. Commission on Ocean Policy* (Washington, D.C.: Government Printing Office, 2004).

Page 14, *may very well be saving ourselves:* As quoted in Douglas Gantenbein, "Making Room for Salmon," *Sierra Magazine,* July/August 1999, 19. The same quotation ran in several other publications.

CHAPTER 1: FOOL'S GOLD

Page 16, *recovering several tons of nodules:* David Helvarg, "Race to Control the Sea Floor," *In These Times,* December 14, 1977.

Page 16, *depths in the mid-Pacific:* Elisabeth Mann Borgese, ed., *Ocean Frontiers* (New York: Abrams, 1992), 9–10.

Page 16, *space exploration was then receiving:* Borgese, *Ocean Frontiers,* 48; and various interviews.

Page 17, *adopted by the United Nations in 1970:* Clyde Sanger, *Ordering the Oceans* (London: Zed Books, 1986), 18–20.

Page 18, *before the 1972 elections:* Sherry Sontag and Christopher Drew, *Blind Man's Bluff* (New York: Public Affairs, 1998), 75–85.

Page 18, *added weight to the charge:* Nathan Miller, *Stealing from America* (New York: Paragon House, 1992), 330.

Page 18, *launched on its "mining" mission:* Clyde W. Burleson, *The Jennifer Project* (College Station: Texas A&M University Press, 1997), 57.

Page 19, *more than a half-billion dollars by 1985:* U.S. Congress, Senate, Committee on Commerce, *The Economic Value of Ocean Resources to the United States,* 93rd Congress, 2nd session, Committee Print (Washington, D.C.: Government Printing Office, 1974), 20–22; and Letter of Transmittal.

Page 20, *one light in the Pacific never went on:* Interview with Michael Molitor, now director of the University of California Climate Change Program, November 5, 1999.

Page 21, *Richardson told me:* Interview with Elliot Richardson, July 1, 1999. Richardson died of a cerebral hemorrhage at age 79 on December 31, 1999.

Page 22, *before the Lord returns:* Quoted in Philip Shabecoff, *A Fierce Green Fire* (New York: Farrar, Straus, 1993), 208.

Page 22, *strategic minerals for future defense:* William J. Broad, *The Universe Below* (New York: Simon & Schuster, 1997), 262.

Page 22, *newly discovered life-forms:* Richard Charter, *A Citizen's Guide to Ocean Stripmining* (San Francisco: Gorda Ridge Project, 1984).

Page 23, *greater vote than anyone else:* Interview with a Senate Foreign Relations staffer who worked for chairman Helms, November 23, 1999.

Page 23, *veto over the treaty:* Various articles and author discussion with House and Senate staffers, May/June 2004.

Page 23, *1990s cover story in Time:* Michael D. Lemonick with Andrea Dorfman, Irene M. Kunii, Alice Park, and Tala Skari, "Mysteries of the Deep," *Time,* August 14, 1995.

Page 24, *according to a number of studies:* The earliest study to raise these concerns was the September 1981 *Environmental Impact Statement on Deep Seabed Mining,* published by NOAA's (since dismantled) Office of Minerals and Energy (Washington, D.C.: Government Printing Office, 1981).

Page 25, *found that out years ago:* Interview with Abraham Piianaia at Hawaii Maritime Center, spring 1990.

Page 26, *with many people in marine science:* Interview with Bill Douros, September 18, 1999.

Page 26, *it was all classified:* Interview with Skip Theberge, April 9, 1999.

Page 27, *as we broke free:* Interviews with Gary Greene in 1996 and on November 23, 1999.

Page 28, *didn't make it back up:* Interviews with Rich Slater in 1996 and 1999.

Page 29, *needed to explore the deep oceans:* Interviews with Don Walsh in 1996 and on December 4, 1999.

Page 29, *report from the National Research Council:* National Research Council, Ocean Studies Board, *Exploration of the Seas: Voyage into the Unknown* (Washington, D.C.: National Academies Press, 2003), ix, 15.

Page 29, *near the top of the oceans:* "The Fate of Industrial Carbon Dioxide," *Science,* July 16, 2004, 5682. Also see "Ocean CO_2 May Harm Marine Life," BBC News online, July 15, 2004.

Page 30, *Grech was chief ROV pilot:* Interview with Chris Grech, December 9, 1996. He has since been promoted to assistant director of marine operations at MBARI. The marine institutes have organized as the Monterey Bay Crescent Ocean Research Consortium.

Page 30, *getting down there intrigued him:* Interview with Julie Packard, 1996.

Page 31, *Tiburon project director Bill Kirkwood:* Interview with Bill Kirkwood, December 9, 1996.

Page 33, *extracted from marine creatures:* Kevin Krajick, "Medicine from the Sea," *Smithsonian,* May 2004, 50–59.

Page 33, *and see what we get:* Interview with David Newman, November 23, 1999.

Page 33, *home to more than 80 percent of the planet's life-forms: Turning to the Sea: America's Ocean Future,* report from the Office of Vice President Al Gore (September 2, 1999), 22. Copies available from the U.S. Department of Commerce/NOAA.

Page 34, *You're a public institution:* Interviews with Zeke Grader, April 14 and September 3, 1999.

Page 34, *that year's presidential and congressional elections:* Figures are from the
Center for Responsive Politics, which breaks down the tidal wave of money
flooding Washington using data from the Federal Election Commission,
Lobbying Disclosure Act of 1995, and other public records. Web site:
www.opensecrets.org.

Page 34, *genetically modified for fast growth:* David Attaway, ed., "Aquacultural
Endocrinology and Molecular Genetics," in *Sea Grant—The Sea's New
Harvest: A Report on Marine Biotechnology in the National Sea Grant
College Program* (Washington, D.C.: NOAA, 1996), 3.

Page 35, *Hudson Canyon off New York:* I was aboard the RV *Atlantis* reporting
for *Marketplace* radio and other outlets September 8–21, 2001, at the invi-
tation of NOAA's Office of Ocean Exploration. Of course, as a journalist I
regretted not being in D.C. when the 9/11 attacks occurred, but my experience until then had been that if I wanted to go to a war zone, I'd have to
leave home.

CHAPTER 2: FROM SEA TO SHINING SEA

Page 41, *America's future oceanic immigrants:* David Sean Paludeine, ed., *Land
of the Free* (New York: Gramercy Books, 1998), 33–34.

Page 42, *and hauling them back up:* For the definitive history of cod, plus some
good recipes, read Mark Kurlansky, *Cod* (New York: Penguin Books,
1997).

Page 42, *in the local timber trade:* Richard Hofstadter and Michael Wallace, eds.,
American Violence (New York: Vintage Books, 1971), 110–111.

Page 43, *in Boston in 1768:* Pauline Maier, *From Resistance to Revolution* (New
York: Vintage Books, 1974), 6–7.

Page 43, *winter of both the poles:* Quoted in Charles A. Beard and Mary R.
Beard, *The Beards' New Basic History of the United States* (New York:
Doubleday, 1960), 51.

Page 46, *hundreds of men were lost:* The author gathered information on whaling while preparing an audio tour for the Hawaii Maritime Center in
1990. Additional information can be found at the New Bedford Whaling
Museum.

Page 46, *including runoff pollution:* From the display Pathfinder of the Seas, U.S.
Navy Museum, Washington Navy Yard, Washington, D.C. See also Naval
Oceanographic Office history page online at www.navo.navy.mil. For a different perspective on civilian versus naval hydrographic history (and the
reef report), visit the NOAA library history page at www.NOAA.gov.

Page 47, *grain bound for northern Europe:* From a display in the San Francisco
Maritime Museum.

Page 48, *arrived as railroad tourists in the 1870s:* According to Shelley Lauzon,
senior news officer (and occasional historian) for the Woods Hole Oceanographic Institution.

Page 48, *cold and treacherous Pacific:* For more on Sutro Baths and Coney Island, see Lena Lencek and Gideon Bosker, *The Beach* (New York: Viking, 1998), 163–171.

Page 49, *America went to war:* For a fuller description of the Navy's growth between the Civil War and World War I, see chapter 7, "Not Merely a Navy for Defense," in Kenneth J. Hagan, *This People's Navy* (New York: Free Press, 1991).

Page 52, *death toll exceeds 25,000:* David McCullough, *The Path between the Seas* (New York, Simon & Schuster, 1977), 610.

Page 52, *24-hour radio watches:* From research the author conducted for the audio tour Titanic: The Exhibition, written with Sally Rudich. Also, author's reporting for "Lessons from the Deep," *George,* December 1997, 38.

Page 53, *between Key West, Florida, and Havana:* Benjamin W. Labaree et al., *America and the Sea* (Mystic, Conn.: Mystic Seaport, 1998), 524–530.

Page 54, *off its elevated rail bridge:* PBS documentary on Flagler (1998) and various history books.

Page 55, *Marine Biological Laboratory already existed:* Elisabeth Mann Borgese, ed., *Ocean Frontiers* (New York: Abrams, 1992), 63–65.

Page 55, *the Great Depression hit hard:* Luc Cuyvers, *Sea Power* (Annapolis: Naval Institute Press, 1993), 233–235; and Donald W. Cox, *Explorers of the Deep* (Maplewood, N.J.: Hammond, 1968), 33–36.

Page 56, *and improved pay:* Richard O. Boyer and Herbert M. Morals, *Labor's Untold Story* (Pittsburgh: United Electrical Radio and Machine Workers of America, 1997), 282–289.

Page 56, *Kennedy pledged:* Labaree et al., *America and the Sea,* 541.

CHAPTER 3: OCEANOGRAPHERS AND ADMIRALS

Page 58, *interviewing a number of veterans:* Interviews conducted for Pearl Harbor tour produced by Antenna Audio in 1991.

Page 62, *came into their own:* Interviews with Walter Munk in 1984 and on October 14, 1999.

Page 62, *research for the Navy:* Judith and Neil Morgan, *Roger* (San Diego, Calif.: Scripps Institution of Oceanography, 1996), 33.

Page 62, *University of Texas at Austin:* National Research Council, *Oceanography in the Next Decade* (Washington, D.C.: National Academy Press, 1992), 32–33; and interviews.

Page 63, *any of the ships decontaminated:* Interview with Roger Revelle for the author's "Three Giants Who Were There," *San Diego,* August 1982.

Page 63, *in February 1949:* John E. Pfeiffer, "The Office of Naval Research," *Scientific American,* February 1949, 11–15.

Page 64, *and later succeeded him:* Interview with Art Maxwell, November 19, 1999.

Page 64, *go out to sea together:* Interviews with Gary Weir, May 10 and 13, 1999; June 4, 2004.

Page 64, *marine science into the 1970s:* Edward Wenk Jr., *The Politics of the Ocean* (Seattle: University of Washington Press, 1972), 13.

Page 65, *the "revolt of the admirals":* The revolt of the admirals is recounted in exhaustive detail in Jeffrey G. Barlow, *The Revolt of the Admirals* (Washington, D.C.: Naval Historical Center, 1994).

Page 65, *advanced guidance systems:* Elisabeth Mann Borgese, ed., *Ocean Frontiers* (New York: Abrams, 1992), 87–92; and Project Nobska files and interviews at Woods Hole Oceanographic Institute.

Page 66, *senior archivist at Scripps:* Interview with Deborah Day, October 14, 1999.

Page 68, *the ship itself:* Laurence Gonzales, "Ballard Surfacing," *National Geographic Adventure,* Spring 1999, 126ff.

Page 68, *next to one of the corrals:* This was part of a tour the author was given of the Space and Naval Warfare Systems Center, San Diego, on October 19, 1999.

Page 69, *as well as in deep waters:* Tony Perry, "Navy Sonar System Draws Activists' Fire," *Los Angeles Times,* October 14, 1999; and interviews with two Navy sources.

Page 69, *deploy the system more widely:* Rick Weiss, "Whales Became Stranded after U.S. Naval Exercises," *Washington Post,* March 22, 2000. Also, "Dead Whales Land in Canaries after Naval Exercises," Reuters News Service, July 23, 2004; Mark Kaufman, "Navy Agrees to Injunction Limiting Sonar Use," *Washington Post,* October 14, 2003; and Kaufman, "Sonar Used before Whales Hit Shore," *Washington Post,* August 31, 2004.

Page 70, *as a Navy technical report:* Stephen Leatherwood et al., *The Whales, Dolphins, and Porpoises of the Eastern North Pacific: A Guide to Their Identification in the Water* (San Diego: Naval Underseas Center TP 282, 1972).

Page 70, *hauled out of the water backward:* David Helvarg, "A Dolphin Disses War," AlterNet.org, April 10, 2003; and other news reports including Kendra Helmer, "Dolphins, Navy Click in Fighting Terrorism," *Stars and Stripes* (European edition), March 1, 2004.

Page 71, *"swimmer nullification":* From a review of Greenwood's testimony; copies were provided to a number of journalists, including Steve Chapple and Robert E. Kesslen, who wrote the story for *Newsday,* April 11, 1976. Also, author's interview with Greenwood from 1985.

Page 72, *talking to each other:* The Ken Woodal interview and other original research referred to in this chapter were for several of the author's articles, including "Marine Mammals Serving the Navy," *Pacific News Service,* June 1985.

Page 72, *for revealing classified information:* Interviews with Rick Trout in 1988, 1999, and 2000; Jane Fritsch, "Company Fires Animal Trainer Who Criticized Navy Program," *Los Angeles Times,* November 3, 1988; and "Dolphin Trainer May Be Prosecuted," Associated Press, reprinted in *San Francisco Chronicle,* November 11, 1988.

Page 72, *to get away from it:* Dianne Dumanoski, "Former Trainer Objects to Military Use of Marine Animals," *Boston Globe,* November 9, 1990; and interview with David Reames, November 1990.

Page 73, *share with our fellow mammals:* U.S. Department of the Navy, *Vision, Presence, Power* (Washington, D.C.: Government Printing Office, 1999), 102.

Page 73, *try and predict them is very difficult:* Interview with Rear Admiral Paul Gaffney, January 6, 2000.

CHAPTER 4: A LITTORAL STATE OF WAR

Page 81, *navigable at any given time,* Interview with Brendan Brewer and other research on the Coast Guard and port security for author's article "Two If by Sea," *Popular Science,* September 2002, 58–67.

Page 82, *for CO_2 reduction:* Interview with Charlie Kennel, October 14, 1999.

Page 82, *than we do today:* Interview with Bob Gagosian, March 8, 2000.

Page 82, *deaths of coral reefs and of cods:* Interview with Deborah Day, 1999.

Page 83, *The same's happening with our fisheries:* Ransom A. Myers and Boris Worm, "Rapid Worldwide Depletion of Predatory Fish Communities," *Nature,* May 15, 2003.

Page 83, *the CIA's short-lived ecocenter:* From the CIA website (www.cia.gov) and interview with Linda Zall, March 8, 2000. Also, author's talk to CIA Public Affairs, August 2, 2004.

Page 84, *how you make your case:* Interview with Representative Curt Weldon, March 30, 2000. The first brief quotation is from his article "Ocean Action 1999: Some — But Still a Long Way to Go!" *Sea Technology,* January 2000, 47–49.

Page 85, *California and Massachusetts:* MEDEA, *Scientific Utility of Naval Environmental Data* (McLean, Va.: MEDEA, 1995); and MEDEA, *Ocean Dumping of Chemical Munitions: Environmental Effects in Arctic Seas* (McLean, Va.: MEDEA, 1997). The author found little federal desire to fund new research on ocean dumps while producing a segment for a syndicated TV show. Rear Admiral Andrew Granuzzo confirmed this lack of interest.

Page 85, *plaque in his honor:* Gordon J. Peterson and David E. Werner, "Under the Sea, at the Top of the World," *Seapower,* July 1999; and Woods Hole Public Relations Office on Al Vine.

Page 85, *environmental data collection:* Jeffrey T. Richelson, "Scientists in Black," *Scientific American,* February 1998. The presidential directive came out in 1993.

Page 86, *to carry out its mission*: Highlights of the Department of the Navy fiscal year 2005 budget. Also, NOAA and U.S. Coast Guard budgets.

Page 86, *banking gently to port*: Visit to the USS *John C. Stennis,* October 15–17, 1999.

Page 87, *Rockefeller Center, and the United Nations*: From "Welcome Aboard" flyer, USS *Stennis,* and presentations by Lieutenant David Oates, public affairs officer.

Page 88, *Navy insists they should be*: U.S. General Accounting Office, *Navy Aircraft Carriers: Cost-Effectiveness of Conventionally and Nuclear-Powered Carriers* (Washington, D.C.: General Accounting Office/NSIAD-98-1, 1998).

Page 88, *in new and exciting ways*: Chief of naval operations address to annual meeting of the Naval Institute, April 21, 1999.

Page 94, *Thirty-second Street Naval Station*: National Oceanographic and Atmospheric Administration, National Status and Trends Program, "Sediment Toxicity in U.S. Coastal Waters," April 1998.

Page 94, *and 50-caliber rounds*: Numerous newsclips, including Terry Rodgers, "Navy Says Ordinance Ends Plan for Sand," *San Diego Union Tribune,* December 16, 1997.

Page 95, *the former bombing range*: Numerous newsclips, including Roberto Suro, "President Intervenes on Vieques," *Washington Post,* November 17, 1999; report, Underwater Ordnance Removal Company and University of Georgia, "Radiological, Chemical, and Environmental Health Assessment of the Marine Resources of the Isla de Vieques . . . ," March 8, 2004. Also, conversations with Jim Barton, 2001–2004.

Page 95, *chemicals in U.S. waters*: Mathew L. Wald, "Royal Caribbean Admits It Dumped Oil and Hazardous Chemicals," *New York Times,* July 22, 1999.

CHAPTER 5: OIL AND WATER

Page 98, *continues to take place here in the Gulf*: Percentages from Mineral Management Service, Public Affairs Office.

Page 98, *back in 1947*: Curtis Rist, "Why We'll Never Run Out of Oil," *Discover,* June 1999.

Page 98, *12 stories above the water*: Visit to Pompano and Skipjack platforms, December 3–4, 1999.

Page 101, *an end to the practice*: Interviews with oil rig personnel, a charter boat operator, a former Louisiana state legislator, and a National Marine Fisheries Service agent.

Page 102, *2,600 feet of water*: "The Genesis Development," *Go Gulf,* July/August 1999.

Page 104, San Jose Mercury News *in 1901*: Cited in Robert Jay Wilder, *Listening to the Sea* (Pittsburgh: University of Pittsburgh Press, 1998), 33.

Page 105, *natural and unproblematic:* Robert Gramling, *Oil on the Edge* (Albany: State University of New York Press, 1996), 40.

Page 106, *to come in there and drill:* Wilder, *Listening to the Sea,* 52.

Page 107, *booms in American history* and *George Bush later recalled:* Quoted from *The Promise and the Reward: 50 Years Offshore,* a 33-minute video produced by the National Ocean Industries Association, 1997.

Page 107, *playing in a Midland movie theater:* Cited in Daniel Yergin, *The Prize* (New York: Simon & Schuster, 1991), 754.

Page 108, *a marvelous business:* Bush interview from the video *The Promise and the Reward.*

Page 108, *competition with customs tariffs:* Interview with Tom Kitsos, deputy director, Mineral Management Service, June 23, 1999; and Mineral Management Service, Public Affairs, District of Columbia and Gulf of Mexico, December 21, 1999.

Page 108, *a bright future for all: Thunder Bay* (1953), Universal Pictures; directed by Anthony Mann and starring James Stewart, Joanne Dru, Gilbert Roland, and Dan Duryea.

Page 109, *skin, eyelids, and hair:* For a good description of Santa Barbara's response to the spill, see Marc Mowrey and Tim Redmon, *Not in Our Backyard* (New York: William Morrow, 1993), 15–19.

Page 110, *tender mercies of OPEC:* Don Hodel's speech taped by author and coproducer Steve Talbot for *Troubled Water,* PBS documentary that aired on California stations, spring 1986.

Page 110, *Prince William Sound:* John McPhee, *Coming into the Country* (New York: Farrar, Straus, 1976), 127.

Page 111, *just not able to let it go:* Two good reports on Prince William Sound ten years later are John Mitchell, "In the Wake of the Spill," *National Geographic,* March 1999; and Charles Siebert, "After the Spill," *Men's Journal,* April 1999.

Page 111, *swamps into sticky asphalt:* For various data in this paragraph, see "Chevron Pipeline Spills Oil on Grand Isle Barrier Island," *Baton Rouge Advocate,* November 25, 1999; radio reports; "Gas Platform Evacuated after Blowout in Gulf," *Times-Morning Advocate,* December 4, 1999; "Pipeline Break Spreads Oil in Gulf of Mexico," Associated Press story, printed in *Washington Post,* January 23, 2000; "Only a Sheen Is Left from Gulf Oil Slick," Associated Press, January 24, 2000. Also, interview with MMS Public Affairs, 2001.

Page 112, *this tough new liability law:* Wilder, *Listening to the Sea,* 168–169.

Page 112, *ask Congress for relief:* Quoted from "OPA 90 Revisited," *Work Boat Magazine,* December 1999, 82.

Page 112, *safeguard the environment:* Joan Biskupic, "High Court Overturns State Law on Oil Tankers," *Washington Post,* March 7, 2000.

Page 114, *hungry sharks to a dead whale:* For more on takings battles and other environmental law conflicts, see the chapter "Up against the Law," in David Helvarg, *The War against the Greens,* revised edition (Boulder, Colo.: Johnson Books, 2004).

Page 114, *keep this federal largess coming:* Center for Responsive Politics (www .opensecrets.org). Also, Aron Pilhofer and Bob Williams, "Big Oil Protects Its Interests" (Center for Public Integrity, July 15 2004). See www.public integrity.org.

Page 114, *they're doing business now:* Interview with Jim Saxton, May 18, 1999.

Page 115, *are all big questions:* Lobbyist disclosure files and various corporate Web sites.

CHAPTER 6: A RISING TIDE

Page 117, *northern winter of 1999:* The author traveled to Antarctica as part of a National Science Foundation program that allows several professional journalists to visit there each year.

Page 121, *60 million years ago:* On March 9, 2000, the Associated Press reported on a new scientific analysis, which found that after a species is extinct it takes 10 million years before anything resembling it reappears. The study "confirms the fears of many scientists, who estimate that half the Earth's species will be wiped out within a century."

Page 124, *by the end of the century:* Office of Naval Research, Naval Ice Center, Oceanographer of the Navy, and the Arctic Research Commission, "Naval Operations in an Ice-Free Arctic," symposium, April 17–18, 2001, final report (unclassified). Also, "Arctic Summer Sea Lanes Open by 2015, Forecasts ONR," *Space Daily,* February 14, 2002.

Page 124, *extinction of polar bears in the wild:* Arctic climate impact assessment (ACIA) report issued at the international scientific symposium on "Climate Change in the Arctic," Reykjavik, Iceland, November 9–12, 2004.

Page 124, *already released into the atmosphere:* See David Helvarg, "Australia, Florida and Fiji: Reefs at Risk," chapter 8 in *Feeling the Heat: Dispatches from the Frontlines of Climate Change,* edited by Jim Motavalli (New York: Routledge, 2004).

Page 125, *impacts of climate change on Pacific islanders:* The PBS documentary *Rising Waters: Global Warming and the Fate of the Pacific Islands* was produced by Andrea Torrice. The tour took place on March 16, 1999.

Page 126, *Chesapeake Bay, Florida, and Louisiana:* Interview with Dr. Vivien Gornitz, May 3, 1999.

Page 127, *works storms in the Atlantic:* The author's visit to the National Hurricane Center took place on July 26, 1999.

Page 129, *from supersaturated graveyards:* Estimates of the number of hogs drowned ranged from the North Carolina State Agriculture Department's low figure of 28,000 to the U.S. Department of Agriculture's estimate of more than 500,000.

Page 129, *like a big Mixmaster:* The highest storm tide mark, 16.9 feet above sea level, was also found on the side of the Burger King World Headquarters, according to NOAA's Natural Disaster Survey Report, *Hurricane Andrew: South Florida and Louisiana, August 23–26, 1999,* 55.

Page 130, *readings of approaching hurricanes:* Interview with Dr. Chris Landsea, July 14, 1999.

Page 130, *$100 billion category:* Steven Leatherman, appearing on the *CBS Evening News,* November 1, 1999.

Page 130, *refused to handle:* According to Federal Emergency Management Agency, Office of Public Affairs, October 14, 2004, based on August 2004 figures.

Page 131, *in 65 years:* Various UN and other news sources including Ross Gelbspan, in the introduction to Motavalli, *Feeling the Heat.*

Page 133, *$80 billion in damages:* Roger A. Pielke Jr. and Christopher W. Landsea, "Normalized Hurricane Damages in the United States: 1925–1995," *Weather and Forecasting,* September 1998, 621–631.

Page 133, *its master plan schematics:* According to interviews with Mike Davis, a deputy assistant secretary of the army (civil works), and Stu Appelbaum, who oversees Corps of Engineers restoration work out of the Jacksonville office.

Page 134, *five days that month:* Interview with Johnny Glover, December 8, 1999.

Page 135, *the next several decades:* A good overview of coastal problems and the "2050" response was written by *Baton Rouge Advocate* reporter Mike Dunne in 1999; reprints of his series available from the *Advocate,* P.O. Box 588, Baton Rouge, LA 70821. The original report, *Coast 2050: Toward a Sustainable Coastal Louisiana,* can be found at www.lacoast.gov/Programs/2050/MainReport.

Page 135, *make the case for us:* Interviews with Mark Davis, November 17 and December 7, 1999.

Page 136, *declines in their marine habitat:* Union of Concerned Scientists and the Ecological Society of America, *Confronting Climate Change in California* (Cambridge, Mass.: Union of Concerned Scientists; Washington, D.C.: Ecological Society of America, 1999), 46. Also, Orna Izakson, "The California Coast: Marine Migrations and the Collapsing Food Chain," chapter 7 in Motavalli, *Feeling the Heat.*

Page 136, *abandoned years ago:* Todd Shields, "Maryland Confronts Receding Shoreline," *Washington Post,* December 22, 1999.

CHAPTER 7: PARADISE WITH AN OCEAN VIEW

Page 138, *the rest of the country:* NOAA National Ocean Service Special Projects Office, "Trends in U.S. Coastal Regions, 1970–1998" (August 1999); Economic Statistics for NOAA, May 2005; U.S. Commission on Ocean Policy, *Report of the U.S. Commission on Ocean Policy,* preliminary report (Washington, D.C.: Government Printing Office, 2004), appendix C.

Page 138, *"fast-tracking" the environmental review process:* "Developer Pleads Guilty to 18 Charges," in Asburypark.net, online version of the *Asbury Park News,* August 18, 2004.

Page 139, *It's called* newjerseyization: Orrin H. Pilkey and Katharine L. Dixon, *The Corps and the Shore* (Washington, D.C.: Island Press, 1996), 42.

Page 140, *an erosion "hot spot":* Michael Grunwald, "Whose Beaches, Whose Burdens?" *Washington Post,* April 20, 1999.

Page 141, *and pumping sand:* Interview with Dery Bennett (and House passage of WRDA), April 29, 1999.

Page 141, *a few big homeowners:* Interview with Representative Jim Saxton, May 18, 1999.

Page 142, *residential beaches westward:* Quoted in Pilkey and Dixon, *The Corps and the Shore,* 230–231.

Page 142, *the nation on coastal policy:* Thomas Maier, part four of the five-part series "Shoreline in Peril," *Newsday,* August 19, 1998.

Page 143, *continues on her way:* Interview with Jim O'Connell, May 5, 1999.

Page 143, *there's American sand available:* Interview with David Schmidt, July 19, 1999.

Page 144, *just over 1,000 feet offshore:* This quick offshore tour was arranged for me by Cry of the Water on July 24, 2004.

Page 145, *Environmental Protection Agency (EPA):* Beth A. Millemann and Cindy Zipf, *Muddy Waters: The Toxic Wasteland below America's Oceans, Rivers, and Lakes* (Washington, D.C.: Coast Alliance, Clean Ocean Action, and American Littoral Society, 1999); and NOAA reports.

Page 145, *the size of Manhattan:* Millemann and Zipf, *Muddy Waters,* 17–18; and newsclips and interviews.

Page 146, *net-loaded break-bulk cargo:* Stewart Taggart, "The 20-Ton Packet," *Wired,* October 1999; and Robert Mottley, "The Early Years," *American Shipper,* May 1996, 26–39.

Page 147, *threaten the whole U.S. economy:* From the author's opinion piece "Ripple Effect of Dockworkers' Strike Could Turn into Tsunami," *Los Angeles Times,* October 8, 2002.

Page 148, *over the past five years:* Lillian Borrone, "Time for Port Alliances?" *Container Management,* August 1999, 49–52.

Page 148, *oversight for marine transport:* U.S. Commission on Ocean Policy, preliminary report, governors' draft (2004), 150–152.

Page 149, *which are also expanding:* Gail Krueger, "Expert Says Ports Are 'Hostages,'" *Savannah Morning News,* November 10, 1999; interview with reporter Krueger; and her ongoing series for the *Morning News.* Also, interview with reporter Krueger and recent reporting (2004) in the paper.

Page 149, *the occasional philosophical possum:* Refers to the comic strip *Pogo,* written and drawn by the late Walt Kelly. His possum character Pogo is often quoted from an Earth Day 1971 strip in which, faced with a heavily polluted Pogofenokee Swamp, he says, "Yep, son. We have met the enemy and he is us!"

Page 150, *including personal watercraft:* NOAA National Ocean Service Special Projects Office, "Trends in U.S. Coastal Regions, 1970–1998" (August 1999), 18–19.

Page 150, *in the United States:* It was called Cabbage Island at the time of the Williams sale. As it was developed for tourism, it was given the more visitor-friendly name Little Tybee Island.

Page 150, *we've got sand gnats:* Interview with Robert DeWitt, November 11, 1999.

Page 152, *a new city on its shore:* The author did extensive research on Playa Vista for an article that appeared in the March 1997 issue of *George* magazine. Among more recent articles are Susan Reines, "Residents, Council Seek to Curb Massive Playa Vista Project," *Santa Monica News,* August 4, 2004.

Page 153, *Missouri, and Mississippi rivers:* Michael Grunwald, "Generals Push Huge Growth for Engineers," *Washington Post,* February 24, 2000; "Army Engineers Reforms Are Set," *Washington Post,* March 30, 2000; "Corps of Engineers Reforms Suspended," *Washington Post,* April 7, 2000; and other articles by Grunwald, including one in *Slate* magazine, summer 2004.

Page 153, *low-lying, hurricane-prone Florida:* FEMA had more than $763 billion in flood insurance coverage as of April 2005, including more than $320 billion in Florida. Source: FEMA Public Affairs office.

Page 154, *fully mortgaged condominiums:* Cornelia Dean, *Against the Tide* (New York: Columbia University Press, 1999), 190.

Page 154, *factored into their rates:* Interview with Steve Ellis, January 3, 2000, and additional conversations, 2004.

Page 154, *his trademark smirk for the camera:* 20/20 segment on federal flood insurance, produced by David Sloan, aired November 26, 1993.

Page 155, *worth less than $250,000:* Nicholas Sparks, "I Will Rebuild," *New York Times,* September 19, 1999.

Page 155, *repetitive loss claims:* U.S. Commission on Ocean Policy, preliminary report (2004), 122.

Page 155, *between 1981 and 1996:* John Riley, part 3 of "Shoreline in Peril" series, *Newsday,* August 18, 1998, for Fire Island figures; Craig Whitlock, part 1 of "Flooded with Generosity," *Raleigh News and Observer,* November 9, 1997, for Topsail figures. Both took their data from FEMA.

Page 156, *Porter Goss of Florida:* According to congressional staffers and copies of the testimony of three representatives before the Subcommittee on Fisheries, Conservation, Wildlife, and Oceans of the House Committee on Resources.

Page 156, *appropriate for you to visit:* Telephone interview with Bob Berry, July 8, 1999; interview with Bob Berry and Tom Hayward, January 5, 2000.

Page 156, *it was a mistake:* Interview with Representative Peter Deutsch, June 30, 1999.

Page 157, *one of our members:* Telephone interview with Bill Hackelton, July 23, 1999.

Page 158, *to assess the damage:* "J.S.R. Seaside Stands Firm as Hurricane Opal Wipes Out Stretches of Florida's Panhandle," *Architectural Record,* November 1995, 15.

Page 159, *and by the water:* Interview with Robert Davis, January 10, 2000.

CHAPTER 8: FLUSHING THE COAST

Page 163, *on a five-minute dive:* The author dove on Aquarius on July 16 and 17, 1999.

Page 164, *between 1960 and 1990:* Peter M. Vitousek et al., "Human Alteration of the Global Nitrogen Cycle: Sources and Consequences," *Issues in Ecology* 7, no. 3 (1997): 737–750; Vaclav Smil, "Global Population and the Nitrogen Cycle," *Scientific American,* July 1997. The 1960–1990 figure is from National Research Council, Ocean Studies Board, *Clean Coastal Waters: Understanding and Reducing the Effects of Nutrient Pollution* (Washington, D.C.: National Academy Press, 2000).

Page 165, *activist group Reef Relief:* PBS series *Green Means,* "Reef Relief," produced by KQED-TV, 1994.

Page 165, *on an ocean planet:* Interviews with Steve Miller, July 15–18, 1999.

Page 167, *another close one:* Interview with Craig Cooper, July 16, 1999.

Page 169, *fertilizer per acre:* Bill Lambrecht, "Fishers Want Farmers to Be More Responsible," *St. Louis Post-Dispatch,* August 24, 1997. Also, "Goals Unlikely to Protect Gulf of Mexico Shrimp Industry," University of Michigan press release, August 4, 2004.

Page 169, *dissolved oxygen in the water:* "Dead Zone May Boost Shark Attacks," BBC News, August 4, 2004.

Page 170, *oxygen levels are lowest:* Betsy Carpenter, "Feeling the Sting," *U.S. News and World Report,* August 16–23, 2004, 68–69.

Page 170, *a conservative think-tank author:* Michael Fumento, "Hypoxia Hysteria," *Forbes,* November 15, 1999, 96–98. Fumento's article "The Myth of Heterosexual AIDS" appeared in *Penthouse* magazine.

Page 170, *but it's going to happen:* Interview with Jonathan Pennock, December 6, 1999.

Page 172, *didn't have any answers for him:* Interview with Nancy Rabalais, December 8, 1999.

Page 172, *he told Newsweek magazine:* Peter Annin, "Down in the Dead Zone," *Newsweek,* October 18, 1999, 60–61.

Page 173, *debilitating neurological disorders:* From Rodney Barker, *And the Waters Turned to Blood* (New York: Simon & Schuster, 1997).

Page 173, *rains out into the water:* Phil Bowie, "No Act of God," *Amicus Journal,* Winter 2000, 16–21.

Page 174, *a 1996 Pulitzer Prize:* The series "Boss Hog," written by Pat Stith and Joby Warrick, ran from February 26 to March 4, 1995, in the *Raleigh News and Observer.*

Page 174, *Perdue sought to play the victim:* From Peter S. Goodman, "Poultry's Price/The Cost to the Bay," *Washington Post,* August 1–3, 1999.

Page 175, *DO levels of one part per liter:* From multiple sources, including Associated Press, "Dead Zone Threatens Carolina," *Marin Independent Journal,* October 9, 1999; and series by James Shiffer including "Forces of Nature and Man," *Raleigh News and Observer,* November 7, 1999.

Page 175, *on the blue frontier:* Woods Hole Oceanographic Institution, *Ecohab: The Ecology and Oceanography of Harmful Algal Blooms, A National Research Agenda* (1995), posted on the Web site of the Woods Hole Oceanographic Institution, www.redtide.whoi.edu/hab/nationplan/ECOHAB /ECOHAB html.html.

Page 175, *along the mid-Atlantic coast:* From *Dallas Morning News,* October 5, 1997; *Washington Post,* September 23, 1997; and *New York Times,* January 10, 2000. Additional stories are listed on the Woods Hole Harmful Algal Blooms Web site (www.whoi.edu/redtide/). Also, "Red Tide Shuts Shellfish Areas in New England," *New York Times,* June 4, 2005.

Page 175, *number of stinging jellyfish:* From interviews at Dauphin Island Sea Lab, December 5–6, 1999; and *CBS Evening News,* "A Stinging Sign?" January 12, 2000.

Page 175, *off their lines and gear:* Cathy Zollo, "Black Water: Fishermen, Scientists Slam State for Slow Reaction to Mystery," *Naples Daily News,* April 7, 2002.

Page 176, *were "too optimistic.":* Various *Washington Post* reports including Anita Huslin, "Ehrlich Eases Liability for Big Chicken Firms," June 14, 2003; and Peter Whoriskey, "Bay Pollution Progress Overstated," July 18, 2004.

Page 176, *end of the century:* Findings presented by the Cornell biogeochemist Robert Howarth at the annual meeting of the American Association for the Advancement of Science, February 20, 2005.

Page 177, *their beach businesses hammered:* "Perspectives," *Newsweek,* September 13, 1999.

Page 177, *for children and adults:* Charles J. Carter, " 'Surf City' Is Riding Wave of Despair," Associated Press, reprinted in *San Diego Union-Tribune,* August 28, 1999; David Reyes and Louise Roug, "Beach Reopened after Needle Cleanup," *Los Angeles Times,* September 18, 1999; and David Helvarg, "Congress Plans an American Clearcut," *The Nation,* December 4, 1995.

Page 178, *those sections of the beach:* Robert W. Haile et al., "An Epidemiological Study of Possible Adverse Effects of Swimming in Santa Monica Bay," Santa Monica Bay Restoration Project (May 7, 1996).

Page 178, *what's going on:* From Judy Wilson's panel talk at the Society of Environmental Journalists Conference, University of California at Los Angeles, September 17, 1999; and interview with Wilson, January 28, 2000.

Page 179, Creature from the Black Lagoon: Nick Madigan, "Los Angeles and Environmental Group Settle on Sewer Repairs," *New York Times,* August 7, 2004.

Page 181, *capable of regeneration for itself:* Interview with Senator John Kerry, January 21, 2000.

CHAPTER 9: THE LAST FISH?

Page 182, *Department of Environmental Conservation (DEC):* Fulton Fish Market visit with National Marine Fisheries Service, May 3, 1999. A friend, the New York high school teacher Mark Ambrosino, came along.

Page 183, *illegally caught fish:* Eric Lipton, "5 Dealers Charged in Sale of Bass from Polluted Waters," *New York Times,* December 9, 1999; and other newsclips.

Page 184, *from Ingold and other fishermen:* Al Guart, "5 Hooked in Toxic-Fish Sales Ring," *New York Post,* December 9, 1999; and Greg Smith, "Bad Fish on Fancy Menus," *New York Daily News,* December 9, 1999.

Page 184, *trade in federal fish:* From a copy of the two-page NOAA general counsel's administrative fine notice dated December 9, 1998, and signed by J. Mitch MacDonald, a NOAA enforcement attorney; and follow-up conversation with NMFS agent James McDonald.

Page 186, *the wall of the dockhouse:* Copies of National Marine Fisheries Service offense investigation reports filed with NOAA legal staff on September 24, 1997, and May 19, 1998.

Page 187, *to support our base:* David Helvarg, *The War against the Greens* (Boulder, Colo.: Johnson Books, 2004), 332–334.

Page 188, *counting hatchery-bred fish as wild salmon:* Helvarg, *War against the Greens.*

Page 188, *the service admits:* NMFS, *Report to Congress: Status of Fisheries of the United States* (Washington, D.C.: Government Printing Office, 1999 and 2004). Also, Josh Eagle, Sarah Newkirk, and Barton H. Thompson Jr., *Taking Stock of the Regional Fishery Management Councils,* Pew Ocean Science Series (Washington, D.C.: Island Press, 2003).

Page 188, *faster than land animals: Conservation Biology,* October 1999; also referenced by Representative Sam Farr in *Sea Technology,* January 2000, 19.

Page 190, *my life by his choice:* The pursuit and interviews took place in early 1997 as the author was preparing an article on National Marine Fisheries Service enforcement agents for *Smithsonian* magazine. Pete Choerny has since retired.

Page 191, *funding for TEDs research:* The author went out on the *Bulldog,* a research shrimper owned by the University of Georgia, on November 11, 1999. For one political history of TEDs, see Center for Marine Conservation, *Delay and Denial* (Washington, D.C.: Center for Marine Conservation, 1995).

Page 191, *in order to protect fish:* Interviews with Zeke Grader, April 14 and September 3, 1999; January 9, 2000; and June 2004.

Page 191, *Louisiana, Idaho, and Appalachia:* National Oceanographic and Atmospheric Administration, *Trends in U.S. Coastal Regions, 1970–1998* (Washington, D.C.: National Ocean Service Special Projects Office, August 1999), 11–12.

Page 192, *to migrate and spawn:* Visit to salmon farm, East Johnson Bay, Maine, July 23, 1998. Also, aquaculture reports from Environmental Defense and the Pew Oceans Commission; reports from SeaGrant and *National Fisherman;* and Juliet Eilperin, "Farmed Salmon Raise Concerns," *Washington Post,* August 11, 2004.

Page 193, a *cobblestone street:* C. J. Chivers, "Scraping Bottom," *Wildlife Conservation,* February 2000.

Page 194, *on returning to port:* From the foreword of William W. Warner, *Distant Water: The Fate of the North Atlantic Fisherman* (New York: Penguin Books, 1997).

Page 195, *how to do it better:* Strong-Cevetich is the founder of SEACOPS (Southeast Alaska Coalition Opposed to the Piracy of Salmon), which fought for the banning of high-seas drift nets in the early 1990s. Quotation is from 1992.

Page 195, *"Eat Fish Twice a Week":* NOAA, *Federal Fisheries Investment Task Force Report to Congress* (July 1999), executive summary, 27.

Page 196, *to get into the industry:* Interview with Paul Cohan, May 26, 1999.

Page 197, *they can do it too:* Interview with Rod Avila, May 4, 1999.

Page 197, *which was fishing:* Interview with Billy Causey, July 19, 1999.

Page 197, *pulls into port:* The author interviewed Dan O'Brian several times while preparing stories on fisheries enforcement. This material is from 1995.

Page 199, *three times a year:* From transcript of New England Fishery Management Council meeting on May 26, 1999, and author's notes. The councilman was Doug Hopkins of Environmental Defense (ED), the only environmentalist on any council. When he left he was replaced by another ED representative; as of 2005 she remained the only enviro on any of the eight councils.

Page 200, *science advisory groups:* As quoted in U.S. Commission on Ocean Policy, *Report of the U.S. Commission on Ocean Policy,* preliminary report (Washington, D.C.: Government Printing Office, 2004), 221.

Page 201, *catching that last fish:* As quoted in U.S. Commission on Ocean Policy, *Report* (2004), 221.

Page 201, *other kind of work myself:* Interview with Andy Philips, September 3, 1996.

Page 201, *rockfish to come back:* "Sea of Anxiety over Rockfish Ban," *San Francisco Chronicle,* June 21, 2002; and other reports. Also interviews with various biologists including Paul Dayton of Scripps.

Page 202, *things might change:* Interview with Sylvia Earle, July 18, 1999.

Page 202, *missing the big picture:* Interview with Zeke Grader, February 8, 2000.

Page 204, *NMFS scientist give testimony:* Dr. Walter Pereyra's testimony at Panel 1, Oversight Hearing on Steller's Sea Lions, House Committee on Resources, May 20, 1999. Pereyra has since retired from the council vice-chairmanship.

Page 204, *divide the loot evenly:* Magnuson-Stevens Fishery Conservation and Management Act, Title 3, Voting Members, and Disclosure of Financial Interest and Recusal, 48; NOAA, *Magnuson-Stevens Fishery Conservation and Management Act,* NOAA Technical Memorandum NMFS-F/SPO-23 (Washington, D.C.: Government Printing Office, 1996), 57.

CHAPTER 10: DROWNING IN RED TAPE

Page 207, *Nixon and Lyndon Johnson:* Interviews with Edward Wenk in 1995 and on November 22, 1999.

Page 207, *of the marine environment:* Quoted in Edward Wenk Jr., *The Politics of the Ocean* (Seattle: University of Washington Press, 1972), 359.

Page 208, *protest must be heard:* Walter J. Hickel, *Who Owns America?* (Englewood Cliffs, N.J.: Prentice-Hall, 1971), 247–249.

Page 208, *win her that supremacy":* Quoted in Wenk, *Politics of the Ocean,* 52.

Page 208, *must help us meet:* Preface by Warren G. Magnuson in E. John Long, *New Worlds of Oceanography* (New York: Pyramid, 1965), 18.

Page 209, *respiring through artificial gills:* Claiborne Pell with Leland Goodwin, *Challenge of the Seven Seas* (New York: Morrow, 1966), 1–24.

Page 210, *a wet NASA:* The Stratton Roundtable; National Ocean Service; NOAA; and Delaware Sea Grant College Program, 1998; and various books and interviews.

Page 210, *the Weather Service:* Wenk, *Politics of the Ocean,* 360.

Page 210, *anything having to do with the oceans:* Interview with Robert White, March 2, 2000.

Page 211, *Bush administration refuses to consider:* Jim Lichatowich, *Salmon without Rivers* (Washington, D.C.: Island Press, 1999); David James Duncan, "Salmon's Second Coming," *Sierra,* March/April 2000; and various news reports.

Page 214, *on resource protection:* Interview with Zeke Grader, February 8, 2000.

Page 214, *wake-up call from nature:* Interview with Sylvia Earle, July 18, 1999.

Page 214, *the oceans and atmosphere*: Pew Oceans Commission, *America's Living Oceans: Charting a Course for Sea Change* (Arlington, Va.: Pew Oceans Commission, 2003), 34.

Page 215, *protect marine resources and ecosystems*: Survey conducted by Public Employees for Environmental Responsibility (PEER) and the Union of Concerned Scientists. Results compiled in May 2005 and released in June 2005. Posted at www.PEER.org.

Page 217, *the factory trawler industry*: Joel Gay, "The Will to Win," *National Fisherman*, December 1999; and David Helvarg, "Full Nets, Empty Seas," *The Progressive*, November 1997.

Page 217, *Anchorage attorney William Bittner*: David Whitney, "Stevens' Factory Ship Bill Sets Off Lobbying Frenzy," *Anchorage Daily News*, March 17, 1998 (from the newspaper's Web site, www.adn.com).

Page 217, *a considerable raise in pay*: From interviews with former Stevens staffers, NOAA officials, Greenpeace and other lobbyists, and At-Sea Processors Association (www.atsea.org).

Page 217, *Russian side of the pollack line*: PA2 Edwin Lyngar, PacArea, "Dicey Icy Rescue," *Coast Guard*, March 1999.

Page 218, *president's reelection campaign*: Numerous articles and editorials such as Hal Bernton, "Crab Group Hires Son of Alaska Senator," *Seattle Times*, October 15, 2003; Charles Pope, "Alaska's 'SOB' Just May Get Crab Bill Passed," *Seattle Post-Intelligencer*, October 29, 2003; and Ben Jacklet, "Seafood Titan Flexes Muscle . . . ," *Portland Tribune*, January 2, 2004.

Page 223, *and then you win*: Most of the material on Donna Frye was incorporated in the author's article "Making Waves" in *Sierra*, May/June 2005; this includes interviews and on-site reporting going back to 1999.

Page 225, *New Zealand, and elsewhere*: Interview with Will Travis, September 10, 1999; and Bay Conservation and Development Commission materials.

Page 225, *did a 180-degree turn*: Interview with Peter Douglas, September 1, 1999.

Page 225, *we needed Prop 20*: Interview with Representative Sam Farr, February 4, 2000. Follow-up interviews 2003, 2004.

Page 227, *interviewed the key players*: "The Coast's Best Friend," *Sacramento Bee*, July 12, 1996; "The Political Game Is On, and Coastline Is the Loser," *Los Angeles Times*, July 8, 1996; and numerous other news and editorial clips.

Page 227, *vocal special interest groups*: Jeffrey I. Rabin and Deborah Schochi, "Coastal Commission Halts Bid to Fire Director," *Los Angeles Times*, July 13, 1996; and Alex Barnum, "Coastal Chief Keeps His Job — For Now," *San Francisco Chronicle*, July 13, 1996.

Page 228, *run for the governorship*: Interview with Sara Wan, September 9, 1999; other interviews; and newsclips.

CHAPTER 11: SANCTUARIES IN THE SEA

Page 230, *restocking these animals:* The author went out on patrol with officer Greg Stanley on July 28, 1999.

Page 232, *towing a Jetski:* Statistics from Department of Transportation brochure, *Our Valuable U.S. Marine Transportation System.*

Page 232, *getting in or out of here:* Interview with Craig Quirolo, July 26, 1999.

Page 233, *remains an open question:* The Marine Protection, Research, and Sanctuaries Act of 1972 established a regulatory framework for ocean dumping in U.S. waters along with the sanctuary program itself.

Page 233, *Newport News, Virginia:* Bruce G. Terrell, *Fathoming Our Past* (Newport News, Va.: Mariners' Museum, NOAA, 1993), 31–32; Labaree et al., *America and the Sea* (Mystic, Conn.: Mystic Seaport, 1998), 353; Sylvia A. Earle and Henry Wolcott, *Wild Oceans* (Washington, D.C.: National Geographic Society, 1999), 194–195; various interviews; and 2003 news reports.

Page 234, *protection of the coastline:* The author did extensive research on the sanctuaries' history for the cover article "Blue Frontiers," *Audubon,* June 1995.

Page 234, *a real groundswell:* Leon Panetta interview in 1995 for author's article "Blue Frontiers."

Page 234, *he went for the biggest boundary:* Interview with Sam Farr, February 4, 2000.

Page 235, *she wondered:* Author's notes from Sunday, September 20, 1992.

Page 235, *from California Fish and Game:* The committee's membership and the NOAA staff at Monterey have since changed.

Page 238, *urchins leave behind:* Sea otter material from Todd Wilkinson, "Marine Mystery," *National Parks,* March/April 2000; Friends of the Sea Otter Web site (www.seaotters.org); and David Helvarg, "Otter Things in California," *Satya,* January–February 2004.

Page 238, *federal presence in their state:* David Helvarg, *The War against the Greens* (Boulder, Colo.: Johnson Books, 2004). Includes the story of how Alaska's Representative Don Young pulled a buck knife on the House floor during a heated debate with a New York representative whose advocacy of wilderness protection Young didn't approve of.

Page 239, *endangered coral reef life:* For a first-person description of spawning coral, see Douglas H. Chadwick, "Blue Refuges," *National Geographic,* March 1998.

Page 239, *animals are highly intelligent:* Observations from the *Gustavus* ferry based out of Auke Bay, north of Juneau, Alaska, August 27, 1998. Also, author's trip to Maui, 1996.

Page 240, *prospecting for new fisheries:* Interview with Brad Barr, May 6, 1999.

Page 241, *sharks are there below them:* Interview with Ken Goldman, 1996; and other shark information from notes for author's article, "Great White Comeback," *Men's Journal,* June/July 1996. Goldman is now at the Virginia Institute of Marine Science.

Page 242, *getting too close to the islands:* Interviews with Ed Ueber in 1991, 1995, 1997, and on September 13, 1999, and various other conversations 1991–2004.

Page 244, *a blank spot on the map:* Aldo Leopold, *A Sand County Almanac* (1949; reissued, New York: Ballantine Books, 1986).

Page 245, *largest marine reserve in the world:* Information provided by the National Marine Sanctuaries office of NOAA on June 2, 2005. They also pointed out that the reserve is about half the size of Texas and about as long as the distance from Los Angeles to Seattle.

Page 248, *talk about marine wilderness:* Trips to Dry Tortuga, Channel Islands Park headquarters, and San Diego were for the author's article "Undiscovered Country," *On Earth,* Spring 2002, 26–29.

Page 248, *national parks idea of yours:* U.S. Coral Reef Task Force meeting, Washington, D.C., February 24, 2004.

CHAPTER 12: THE SEAWEED REBELLION

Page 250, *In the wake of Katrina:* Reporting from author's trip to New Orleans and the Gulf region, September 19–27, 2005.

Page 256, *TV stations this evening:* The sharks' transport and release took place July 21 and 22, 1999, and was widely covered by Chicago and south Florida media, including Miami channels 4 and 7.

Page 256, *bites him in the foot:* Avery Sumner, "Tourist Bit by Bull Shark," *Key West Citizen,* July 28, 1999.

Page 256, *in San Jose, California:* Interview with Rick Trout, February 11, 2000.

Page 257, *the group's president:* Kennedy was speaking at a Toronto restaurant and bar called Bamboos on Saturday, June 21, 2003, during the Waterkeepers annual meeting.

Page 258, *economic opportunities ashore:* The Save Our Shores champagne cruise and book-signing aboard the *Princess of Whales* took place June 9, 2001.

Page 258, *we've got down here:* Craig Quirolo talk given at the Pier House in Key West, July 26, 1999. Other Reef Awareness Week events included a film festival, rope-splicing party, science forums, and sunset cruises.

Page 259, *rebuild in harm's way:* Interview with George Crozier, December 6, 1999. The boat was operated by Dr. John Dindo, also of Dauphin Island Sea Lab. Follow-up discussions with Crozier through 2004. News reports following Hurricane Ivan, 2004.

Page 260, *take on a bluer tinge:* For an extensive list of ocean activist organizations, see David Helvarg, *Ocean and Coastal Conservation Directory, 2005–2006* (Washington, D.C.: Island Press, 2005).

Page 260, *Pew Oceans Commission:* David Helvarg, "Sustainable Seafood: Why Consumers' Choice Matters," *The Green Guide,* June 2003.

Page 261, *Alaskan wild salmon:* Jay Lindsay, "Seafood Seal, New Label Indicates Environmentally Friendly Seafood," Associated Press, March 9, 2000. Also, Fish Forever press kit.

Page 261, *fish can reproduce:* Interview with Roger Berkowitz, March 31, 2000, and visit with Berkowitz at his new plant, February 17, 2004.

Page 261, *bring people together:* Interview with Representative Curt Weldon, March 30, 2000.

Page 261, *our marine sanctuaries:* NOAA National Ocean Service Special Projects Office, *Trends in U.S. Coastal Regions, 1970–1998* (Washington, D.C.: Government Printing Office, 1999), 7; and various other reports and congressional testimony.

Page 262, *100 percent of the moon:* From a speech by Admiral Paul Gaffney, March 8, 2000.

Page 265, *begin the revolution:* Blue Frontier's Celebration of the Sea fundraising dinner took place November 5, 2003.

Page 265, *growing constituency for action:* The Blue Vision Conference took place July 11–13, 2004, in Washington, D.C. Organized by the Blue Frontier Campaign, it was cosponsored by the Coast Alliance, the Ocean Conservancy, the Natural Resources Defense Council, the Khaled Bin Sultan Living Oceans Foundation, the Pew Charitable Trusts, and the Marine Fish Conservation Network, with additional financial and material support from 14 other groups.

Selected Bibliography

Alic, John A., Lewis M. Branscomb, Harvey Brooks, Ashton B. Carter, and Gerald L. Epstein. *Beyond Spinoff: Military and Commercial Technologies in a Changing World*. Boston: Harvard Business School Press, 1992.

Ballard, Robert D., with Will Hively. *The Eternal Darkness*. Princeton, N.J.: Princeton University Press, 2000.

Barker, Rodney. *And the Waters Turned to Blood*. New York: Simon & Schuster, 1997.

Barlow, Jeffrey G. *The Revolt of the Admirals*. Washington, D.C.: Naval Historical Center, 1994.

Bascom, Willard. *The Crest of the Wave*. New York: Harper & Row, 1988.

Benchley, Peter, and Judith Gradwohl. *Ocean Planet*. New York: Abrams, 1995.

Berendt, John. *Midnight in the Garden of Good and Evil*. New York: Random House, 1994.

Berrill, Michael. *The Plundered Seas*. San Francisco: Sierra Club Books, 1997.

Biel, Steven. *Down with the Old Canoe*. New York: Norton, 1996.

Borgese, Elisabeth Mann, ed. *Ocean Frontiers*. New York: Abrams, 1992.

Boyer, Richard O., and Herbert M. Morals. *Labor's Untold Story*. Pittsburgh: United Electrical, Radio and Machine Workers of America, 1997.

Broad, William J. *The Universe Below*. New York: Simon & Schuster, 1997.

Brooke, Steven. *Seaside*. Gretna, La.: Pelican Publishing, 1995.

Brower, Kenneth. *Realms of the Sea*. Washington, D.C.: National Geographic Society, 1991.

Burleson, Clyde W. *The Jennifer Project*. College Station: Texas A&M University Press, 1997.

California Coastal Commission. *California Coastal Resource Guide*. Berkeley and Los Angeles: University of California Press, 1987.

Carey, Richard Adams. *Against the Tide: The Fate of the New England Fisherman*. Boston: Houghton Mifflin, 1999.

Carson, Rachel L. *The Sea around Us*. New York: Oxford University Press, 1951.

Cicin-Sain, Biliana, and Robert W. Knect. *The Future of U.S. Ocean Policy.* Washington, D.C.: Island Press, 2000.

Cicin-Sain, Biliana, Robert W. Knect, and Nancy Foster. *Trends and Future Challenges for U.S. National Ocean and Coastal Policy.* Washington, D.C.: Department of Commerce/National Oceanographic and Atmospheric Administration, 1999.

Clarke, Arthur C. *The Deep Range.* New York: Harcourt, Brace, 1957.

Coastal Zone Management: The Coastal Imperative, Developing a National Perspective for Coastal Decision Making. Proceedings of the 2nd annual Coastal Zone Management Conference, held in Charleston, S.C., March 13–14, 1974. Report prepared for the use of the Senate Committee on Commerce, pursuant to S. Res. 222, National Oceans [i.e., Ocean] Policy Study. Washington, D.C.: Government Printing Office, 1974.

Conrad, David R., Ben McNitt, and Martha Stout. *Higher Ground.* Washington, D.C.: National Wildlife Federation, 1998.

Cousteau, Jacques Yves. *The Living Sea.* New York: Harper & Row, 1963.

————. *The Silent World.* New York: Harper, 1953.

Cousteau, Jean-Michel, and Mose Richards. *Cousteau's Great White Shark.* New York: Abrams, 1992.

Cox, Donald W. *Explorers of the Deep: Pioneers of Oceanography.* Maplewood, N.J.: Hammond, 1968.

Cronin, John, and Robert F. Kennedy Jr. *The Riverkeepers.* New York: Simon & Schuster, 1997.

Cuyvers, Luc. *Sea Power.* Annapolis: Naval Institute Press, 1993.

Davis, Chuck. *California Reefs.* San Francisco: Chronicle Books, 1991.

Davis, Richard A., Jr. *The Evolving Coast.* New York: Scientific American Library, 1997.

DeWitt, John. *Protecting Our National Marine Sanctuaries.* Washington, D.C.: National Academy of Public Administration, 1999.

Dorfman, Mark. *Testing the Waters.* New York: Natural Resources Defense Council, 1999.

Doubilet, David. *Light in the Sea.* Charlottesville, Va.: Thomasson-Grant, 1989.

Duane, Daniel. *Caught Inside: A Surfer's Year on the California Coast.* New York: Farrar, Straus, 1996.

Earle, Sylvia A. *Sea Change.* New York: Putnam, 1995.

Earle, Sylvia A., and Al Giddings. *Exploring the Deep Frontier.* Washington, D.C.: National Geographic Society, 1980.

Earle, Sylvia A., and Henry Wolcott. *Wild Oceans: America's Parks under the Sea.* Washington, D.C.: National Geographic Society, 1999.

Eaton, John P., and Charles A. Haas. *Titanic: Triumph and Tragedy.* New York: Norton, 1995.

Ellis, Richard, and John E. McCosker. *Great White Shark.* Stanford, Calif.: Stanford University Press, 1991.

Environmental Health Center. *Covering Key Environmental Issues.* Washington, D.C.: Radio and Television News Directors Foundation, 1999.

Epstein, Richard A. *Takings: Private Property and the Power of Eminent Domain.* Cambridge, Mass.: Harvard University Press, 1985.

Federal Fisheries Investment Task Force. *Report to Congress.* Washington, D.C.: National Oceanographic and Atmospheric Administration, 1999.

Fisher, David E. *The Scariest Place on Earth: Eye to Eye with Hurricanes.* New York: Random House, 1994.

Fisheries Statistics and Economics Division. *Fisheries of the United States, 1998.* Washington, D.C.: Government Printing Office, 1999.

Fordham, Sonja V. *New England Groundfish: From Glory to Grief.* Washington, D.C.: Center for Marine Conservation, 1996.

Foundation for American Communications. *Reporting on Oceans.* Los Angeles: Foundation for American Communications, 1995.

Friedheim, Robert L. *Negotiating the New Ocean Regime.* Columbia: University of South Carolina Press, 1993.

Fujita, Rod. *Heal the Ocean.* Vancouver, B.C.: New Society, 2003.

Goldburg, Rebecca, and Tracy Triplett. *Murky Waters: Environmental Effects of Aquaculture in the United States.* Washington, D.C.: Environmental Defense Fund Publications, 1997.

Gramling, Robert. *Oil on the Edge.* Albany: State University of New York Press, 1996.

Greenlaw, Linda. *The Hungry Ocean.* New York: Hyperion, 1999.

Greider, William. *Fortress America.* New York: Public Affairs, 1998.

Griffin, M. D., and L. Martin. *Saving the Marin-Sonoma Coast.* Healdsburg, Calif.: Sweetwater Springs Press, 1998.

H. John Heinz Center for Science, Economics, and the Environment. *Designing a Report on the State of the Nation's Ecosystems.* Washington, D.C.: Heinz Center, 1999.

———. *The Hidden Costs of Coastal Hazards.* Washington, D.C.: Island Press, 1999.

Hagan, Kenneth J. *This People's Navy.* New York: Free Press, 1991.

Halberstadt, Hans. *U.S. Navy SEALS.* New York: Barnes & Noble Books, 1999.

Hamilton-Paterson, James. *The Great Deep.* New York: Henry Holt, 1992.

Hansen, Gunnar. *Islands at the Edge of Time.* Washington, D.C.: Island Press, 1993.

Harrigan, Stephen. *Water and Light.* San Francisco: Sierra Club Books, 1992.

Hearn, Chester G. *Tracks in the Sea.* New York: McGraw-Hill, 2002.

Helvarg, David. *Ocean and Coastal Conservation Directory, 2005–2006.* Washington, D.C.: Island Press, 2005.

Hendrickson, Robert. *The Ocean Almanac.* New York: Doubleday, 1984.

Hersey, John. *Key West Tales.* New York: Knopf, 1994.

Hiaasen, Carl. *Sick Puppy.* New York: Knopf, 2000.

———. *Stormy Weather.* New York: Knopf, 1995.

Hickel, Walter J. *Who Owns America?* Englewood Cliffs, N.J.: Prentice-Hall, 1971.

Hofstadter, Richard, and Michael Wallace, eds. *American Violence: A Documentary History.* New York: Vintage Books, 1971.

Holing, Dwight. *Coast Alert*. Washington, D.C.: Island Press, 1990.

Howarth, Stephen. *To Shining Sea*. Norman: University of Oklahoma Press, 1991.

Hughes, Robert. *American Visions: The Epic History of Art in America*. New York: Knopf, 1999.

Idyll, C. P. *The Sea against Hunger*. New York: Thomas Y. Crowell, 1970.

Iudicello, Suzanne, Michael Weber, and Robert Wieland. *Fish, Markets, and Fishermen*. Washington, D.C.: Island Press, 1999.

Jacobs, John. *A Rage for Justice: The Passion and Politics of Phillip Hurton*. Berkeley and Los Angeles: University of California Press, 1995.

Jasny, Michael. *Sounding the Depths*. New York: Natural Resources Defense Council, 1999.

Johnson, Robert Erwin. *Guardians of the Sea: History of the United States Coast Guard*. Annapolis: Naval Institute Press, 1987.

Junger, Sebastian. *The Perfect Storm*. New York: Norton, 1997.

Kleinberg, Howard. *Miami: The Way We Were*. Surfside, Fla.: Surfside Publishing, 1989.

Koplow, Douglas, and Aaron Martin. *Fueling Global Warming*. Washington, D.C.: Greenpeace, 1998.

Kraynak, Joe, and Akim W. Tetrault. *The Complete Idiot's Guide to the Oceans*. New York: Penguin, 2003.

Kunzig, Robert. *The Restless Sea*. New York: Norton, 1999.

Kurlansky, Mark. *Cod*. New York: Penguin Books, 1997.

Labaree, Benjamin W., William M. Fowler Jr., John B. Hattendorf, Jeffrey J. Safford, Edward W. Sloan, and Andrew W. German. *America and the Sea: A Maritime History*. Mystic, Conn.: Mystic Seaport, 1998.

Langewiesche, William. *The Outlaw Sea*. New York: Farrar, Straus and Giroux, 2004.

Larson, Erik. *Isaac's Storm*. New York: Crown, 1999.

Leary, William M. *Under Ice: Waldo Lyon and the Development of the Arctic Submarine*. College Station: Texas A&M University Press, 1999.

Lencek, Lena, and Gideon Bosker. *The Beach: The History of Paradise on Earth*. New York: Viking, 1998.

Lewis, Charles, and the Center for Public Integrity. *The Buying of the President 2000*. New York: Avon Books, 2000.

Lichatowich, Jim. *Salmon without Rivers*. Washington, D.C.: Island Press, 1999.

Lilly, John C. *Man and Dolphin*. New York: Doubleday, 1961.

London, Jack. *Tales of the Fish Patrol*. London: Macmillan, 1905.

Long, E. John. *New Worlds of Oceanography*. New York: Pyramid, 1965.

Maas, Peter. *The Terrible Hours*. New York: Harper Collins, 1999.

Maier, Pauline. *From Resistance to Revolution*. New York: Vintage Books, 1974.

Marine Board National Research Council. *Undersea Vehicles and National Needs*. Washington, D.C.: National Academy Press, 1996.

Marx, Wesley. *The Frail Ocean: A Blueprint for Change in the New Millennium*. Chester, Conn.: Globe Pequot Press, 1999.

Mathews-Amos, Amy, and A. Ewann Borntson. *Turning Up the Heat: How Global Warming Threatens Life in the Sea*. Washington, D.C.: World Wildlife Fund, 1999.

McComb, David G. *Galveston: A History.* Austin: University of Texas Press, 1986.

McCullough, David. *The Path between the Seas.* New York: Simon & Schuster, 1977.

McGinn, Anne Plait. *Safeguarding the Health of Oceans.* Washington, D.C.: Worldwatch Institute, 1999.

McPhee, John. *Coming into the Country.* New York: Farrar, Straus, 1976.

———. *Looking for a Ship.* New York: Farrar, Straus, 1990.

MEDEA. *Ocean Dumping of Chemical Munitions: Environmental Effects in Arctic Seas.* McLean, Va.: MEDEA, 1997.

———. *Scientific Utility of Naval Environmental Data.* McLean, Va.: MEDEA, 1995.

Melville, Herman. *Moby-Dick, or The Whale.* 1851; new edition, New York: Penguin Classics, 1992.

Mileti, Dennis S. *Disasters by Design.* Washington, D.C.: Joseph Henry Press, 1999.

Millemann, Beth, and Cindy Zipf. *Muddy Waters: The Toxic Wasteland below America's Oceans, Rivers, and Lakes.* Washington, D.C.: Coast Alliance, Clean Ocean Action, and American Littoral Society, 1999.

Miller, Nathan. *Stealing from America.* New York: Paragon House, 1992.

Moore, Christopher. *Fluke.* New York: Harper-Collins, 2003.

Morgan, Judith, and Neil Morgan. *Roger.* San Diego: Scripps Institution of Oceanography, 1996.

Motavalli, Jim, ed. *Feeling the Heat: Dispatches from the Frontlines of Climate Change.* New York: Routledge, 2004.

Mowrey, Marc, and Tim Redmond. *Not in Our Backyard.* New York: William Morrow, 1993.

National Marine Fisheries Service. *Report to Congress: Status of Fisheries of the United States.* Washington, D.C.: Government Printing Office, 1999.

National Oceanographic and Atmospheric Administration. *Magnuson-Stevens Fishery Conservation and Management Act.* NOAA Technical Memorandum NMFS-F/SPO-23. Washington, D.C.: Government Printing Office, 1996.

———. *Our Living Oceans.* NOAA Technical Memorandum NMFS-F/SPO 41. Washington, D.C.: Government Printing Office, 1999.

National Research Council. *Oceanography and Naval Special Warfare.* Washington, D.C.: National Academy Press, 1997.

National Research Council. Ocean Studies Board. *Clean Coastal Waters: Understanding and Reducing the Effects of Nutrient Pollution.* Washington, D.C.: National Academy Press, 2000.

———. *Exploration of the Seas: Voyage into the Unknown.* Washington, D.C.: National Academies Press, 2003.

———. *Global Ocean Science.* Washington, D.C.: National Academy Press, 1999.

———. *Oceanography in the Next Decade.* Washington, D.C.: National Academy Press, 1997.

National Weather Service. *Hurricane Andrew, South Florida and Louisiana,*

August 23–26, 1992. Natural Disaster Survey Report. Silver Springs, Md.: National Weather Service, 1993.

Nunn, Kem. *The Dogs of Winter.* New York: Pocket Books, 1997.

Orlean, Susan. *The Orchid Thief.* New York: Ballantine Books, 1998.

Paludeine, David Sean, ed. *Land of the Free.* New York: Gramercy Books, 1998.

Pauly, Daniel, and Jay Maclean, *In a Perfect Ocean.* Washington, D.C.: Island Press, 2003.

Pell, Claiborne, with Harold Leland Goodwin. *Challenge of the Seven Seas.* New York: William Morrow, 1966.

Pew Oceans Commission. *America's Living Oceans — Charting a Course for Sea Change.* Arlington, Va.: Pew Oceans Commission, 2003.

Pilkey, Orrin H., and Katharine L. Dixon. *The Corps and the Shore.* Washington, D.C.: Island Press, 1996.

Preston, Antony. *Navies of World War 3.* New York: Military Press, 1984.

Resources Agency of California. *California's Ocean Resources: An Agenda for the Future.* Sacramento: Resources Agency of California, 1995.

———. *California's State Classification System for Marine Managed Areas.* Sacramento: Resources Agency of California, 1999.

Ricketts, Edward, Jack Calvin, and Joel W. Hedgpeth. *Between Pacific Tides.* 5th edition, revised by David W. Phillips. Stanford, Calif.: Stanford University Press, 1985.

Ridgway, Sam. *The Dolphin Doctor.* New York: Fawcett Crest, 1987.

Safina, Carl. *Song for the Blue Ocean.* New York: Henry Holt, 1997.

Sanger, Clyde. *Ordering the Oceans: The Making of the Law of the Seas.* London: Zed Books, 1986.

Savitz, Jacqueline. *Pointless Pollution.* Washington, D.C.: Coast Alliance, 1999.

Slackman, Michael. *Target: Pearl Harbor.* Honolulu: University of Hawaii Press, 1990.

Sobel, Jack, and Craig Dahlgren. *Marine Reserves — A Guide to Science, Design, and Use.* Washington, D.C.: Island Press, 2004.

Sontag, Sherry, and Christopher Drew. *Blind Man's Bluff.* New York: Public Affairs, 1998.

Steinbeck, John. *Cannery Row.* 1945; new edition, New York: Penguin Books, 1992.

———. *The Log from the Sea of Cortez.* 1941; new edition, New York: Penguin Books, 1986.

Stewart, Frank, ed. *A World between Waves.* Washington, D.C.: Island Press, 1992.

Stone, Robert. *Outerbridge Reach.* New York: Ticknor & Fields, 1992.

Sullivan, Robert *The Meadowlands.* New York: Charles Scribner's Sons, 1998.

Terrell, Bruce G. *Fathoming Our Past: Historical Contexts of the National Marine Sanctuaries.* Newport News, Va.: Mariners' Museum, National Oceanographic and Atmospheric Administration, 1993.

Thorne-Miller, Boyce. *The Living Ocean.* Washington, D.C.: Island Press, 1999.

———. *Ocean.* San Francisco: Collins Publishers, 1993.

Troll, Ray, and Brad Matsen. *Shocking Fish Tales.* Anchorage: Northwest Books, 1991.

U.S. Commission on Ocean Policy. *Report of the U.S. Commission on Ocean Policy.* Washington, D.C.: Government Printing Office, 2004.

U.S. Congress. House of Representatives. Committee on Interior and Insular Affairs. *Alyeska Pipeline Service Company Covert Operation.* 102nd Congress, 2nd session. Committee Print 9. Washington, D.C.: Government Printing Office, 1992.

U.S. Congress. House of Representatives. Committee on Merchant Marine and Fisheries. *National Oceanographic Program: Hearings before the Subcommittee on Oceanography of the Committee on Merchant Marine and Fisheries, House of Representatives.* Parts 1 and 2. 91st Congress, 1st session, 1969.

———. *Final Report on the Activities of the Merchant Marine and Fisheries Committee.* 103rd Congress, 2nd session. H. Rep. 103-887. Washington, D.C.: Government Printing Office, 1995.

U.S. Congress. Senate. Committee on Commerce. *The Economic Value of Ocean Resources to the United States.* 93rd Congress, 2nd session. Committee Print. Report by Robert R. Nathan Associates, Inc., for the use of the Committee on Commerce, pursuant to S. Res. 222, National Ocean Policy Study. Washington, D.C.: Government Printing Office, 1974.

———. *Legislative History of the Coastal Zone Management Act of 1972, as Amended in 1974 and 1976 with a Section-by-Section Index.* 94th Congress, 2nd session. Committee Print. Prepared for the use of the Committee on Commerce and National Ocean Policy Study pursuant to S. Res. 222. Washington, D.C.: Government Printing Office, 1976.

U.S. Coral Reef Task Force. *Coastal Uses Working Group Summary Report.* Washington, D.C.: Government Printing Office, 1999.

U.S. Department of the Navy. *Vision, Presence, Power — A Program Guide to the U.S. Navy.* Washington, D.C.: Government Printing Office, 1999.

U.S. Department of Transportation. *An Assessment of the U.S. Marine Transportation System: A Report to Congress.* Washington, D.C.: Government Printing Office, 1999.

U.S. Federal Agencies with Ocean-Related Programs. *Year of the Ocean Discussion Papers.* Washington, D.C.: Government Printing Office, 1998.

U.S. General Accounting Office. *Navy Aircraft Carriers: Cost-Effectiveness of Conventionally and Nuclear-Powered Carriers.* Washington, D.C.: General Accounting Office, 1998.

U.S. President's Science Advisory Committee. Panel on Oceanography. *Effective Use of the Sea.* Washington, D.C.: Government Printing Office, 1966.

Wallace, Aubrey. *Green Means.* San Francisco: KQED Books, 1994.

Warner, William W. *Beautiful Swimmers.* Boston: Little, Brown, 1976.

———. *Distant Water: The Fate of the North Atlantic Fisherman.* New York: Penguin Books, 1997.

Weber, Michael L., and Judith Gradwhol. *The Wealth of Oceans.* New York: Norton, 1995.

Weems, John Edward. *A Weekend in September.* College Station: Texas A&M University Press, 1980.

Wenk, Edward, Jr. *The Politics of the Ocean.* Seattle: University of Washington Press, 1972.

Wheelwright, Jeff. *Degrees of Disaster.* New York: Simon & Schuster, 1994.

Wilcove, David. *The Condor's Shadow.* New York: W. H. Freeman, 1999.

Wilder, Robert Jay. *Listening to the Sea.* Pittsburgh: University of Pittsburgh Press, 1998.

Williams, Joy. *The Florida Keys.* New York: Random House, 1997.

Wilmot, David, and Jack K. Sterne. *Turning the Tide.* Report to the David and Lucile Packard Foundation, Oak Foundation, Curtis and Edith Munson Foundation. 2003. Posted on the Web site of Ocean Champions, www.ocean champions.org/pdfs/TurningTheTideES.pdf.

Wood, Forrest G. *Marine Mammals and Man.* Washington, D.C.: Robert B. Luce, 1973.

Woodard, Colin. *The Lobster Coast.* New York: Viking, 2004.

———. *Ocean's End.* New York: Basic Books, 2000.

Woods Hole Oceanographic Institution. *Ecohab: The Ecology and Oceanography of Harmful Algal Blooms, A National Research Agenda.* 1995. Posted on the Web site of the Woods Hole Oceanographic Institution, www.redtide.whoi.edu/hab/nationplan/ECOHAB/ECOHABhtml.html.

Yergin, Daniel. *The Prize.* New York: Simon & Schuster, 1991.

About the
Blue Frontier Campaign

The Blue Frontier Campaign is dedicated to the protection, exploration, and restoration of America's living seas.

Today there is desperate need to develop and expand not only our biological knowledge of the seas but also an active and educated political constituency to protect the ocean and its living resources. The Blue Frontier Campaign is working to link seaweed activists and concerned citizens who, getting so much from the sea in the form of recreation, transportation, food, security, livelihood, and spiritual renewal, are ready to give something back.

Recently two major commissions—the independent Pew Oceans Commission and the federal U.S. Commission on Ocean Policy— reported that our marine ecosystems are in crisis. Among the recommendations made by both groups is the passage of an American Oceans Act. Like the Clean Air and Clean Water acts of the twentieth century, this would help ensure the continued life, health, and usefulness of a vital public resource.

Senator Barbara Boxer (D–CA) and the bipartisan House Oceans Caucus have introduced comprehensive ocean protection bills in both the House and the Senate, most recently in 2005. Still, government action at the national scale is unlikely without an upsurge of citizen action to demand change. Blue Frontier works to strengthen the growing ocean constituency by building unity, providing tools, and enhancing public awareness of the problems facing our seas and coastlines as well as solutions being offered by seaweed activists and institutions dedicated to restoring our marine heritage.

Along with regional and national conferences, meetings and events, public speaking, and production of articles and videos, the Blue Frontier Campaign has produced two books. *The Ocean and Coastal Conservation Guide 2005–2006* (Island Press, 2005) is a directory to the blue movement that will be updated every two years. *50 Ways to Save the Ocean* (Inner Ocean, 2006) is a guide to actions individuals can take every day to help our public seas. In addition, the current edition of *Blue Frontier* is an important educational tool for the campaign, which largely grew out of the original edition.

If you consider yourself a water person—someone who loves the ocean and the shore—and wish you could turn that love into productive action, here is your chance to get involved. Contact the Blue Frontier Campaign by email (info@bluefront.org) or check out our Web site at www.bluefront.org. Feel free to use our resources, working with us and thousands of other seaweed activists to make the connections that must be made—from individual hearts to national and global campaigns that protect, explore, and restore our American oceans and our water planet.

Index

About the Author

David Helvarg is founder and president of the Blue Frontier Campaign (www.bluefront.org) and the author of three books including *Blue Frontier*. He is also editor of the *Ocean and Coastal Conservation Guide*, lead organizer of several Blue Vision conferences for ocean activists, and winner of *Coastal Living* magazine's Leadership Award for 2005. An award-winning journalist, Helvarg has worked as a war correspondent in Northern Ireland and Central America, covered a range of issues from military science to the AIDS epidemic, and reported from every continent including Antarctica. His print work has appeared in publications including the *New York Times*, the *Los Angeles Times*, *Smithsonian*, *Popular Science*, *Sierra*, and *The Nation*. He has produced more than 40 broadcast documentaries for PBS, the Discovery Channel, and others, and has done radio work for Marketplace, AP Radio, and Pacifica Broadcasting. He has led workshops for journalists in Poland, Turkey, Tunisia, Slovakia, and Washington, D.C. He is also a licensed private investigator, and his watery avocations include bodysurfing and scuba diving. He currently lives in Washington, D.C.